Snow White
with the Red Hair

SORATA AKIDUKI

The Blue Bird Version

It says that spotting a blue bird will bring us joy.

Oh?

Well, have the servants search for one!

THE END

VOLUME 6

TABLE *of* CONTENTS

THE STORY

Shirayuki was born with beautiful hair as red as apples, but when her rare hair earns her unwanted attention from the notorious prince Raj, she's forced to flee her home. A young man named Zen helps her in the forest of the neighboring kingdom, Clarines, and it turns out he is that kingdom's second prince! Shirayuki decides to accompany Zen back to Wistal, the capital city of Clarines.

Shirayuki has met all manner of people since becoming a court herbalist, and her relationship with Zen continues to grow, as the two have finally made their feelings known to each other.

Shirayuki is currently safe at Prince Raj's palace, but who is the mysterious "pretty boy" hot on her trail...?!

"They say that red is the color of destiny."

SHIRAYUKI

Working as a court herbalist. Has feelings for Zen—feelings that he shares.

PRINCE ZEN

The second prince of the kingdom of Clarines.

PRINCE RAJ

The so-called idiot prince. Hoping to improve his relationship with Shirayuki!

PRINCE IZANA

Zen's older brother and the crown prince of the kingdom. Keeping a close eye on Shirayuki and Zen's relationship...

OBI

Former assassin. Currently Zen's underling and Shirayuki's bodyguard during her stay in Tanbarun.

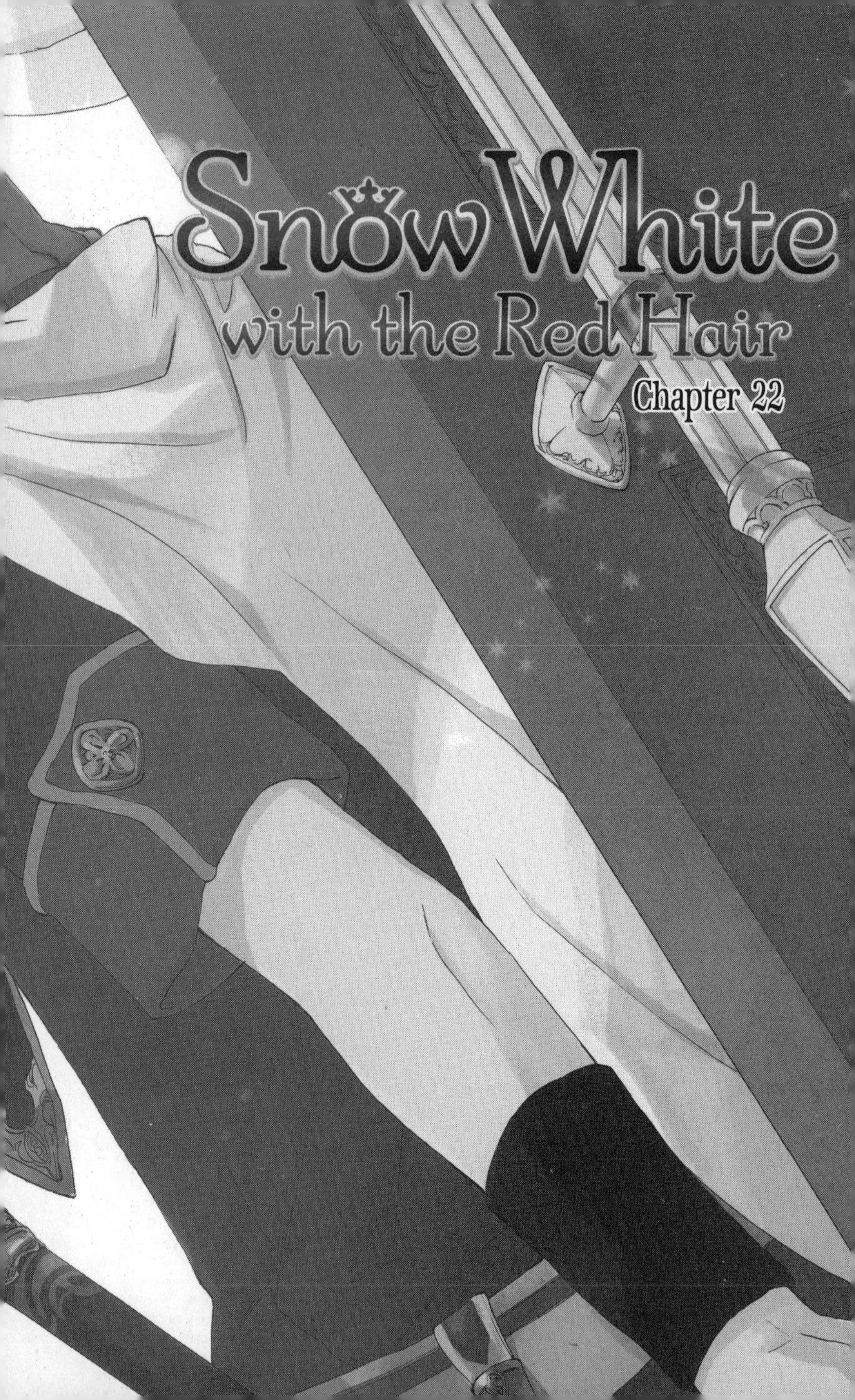
Snow White
with the Red Hair
Chapter 22

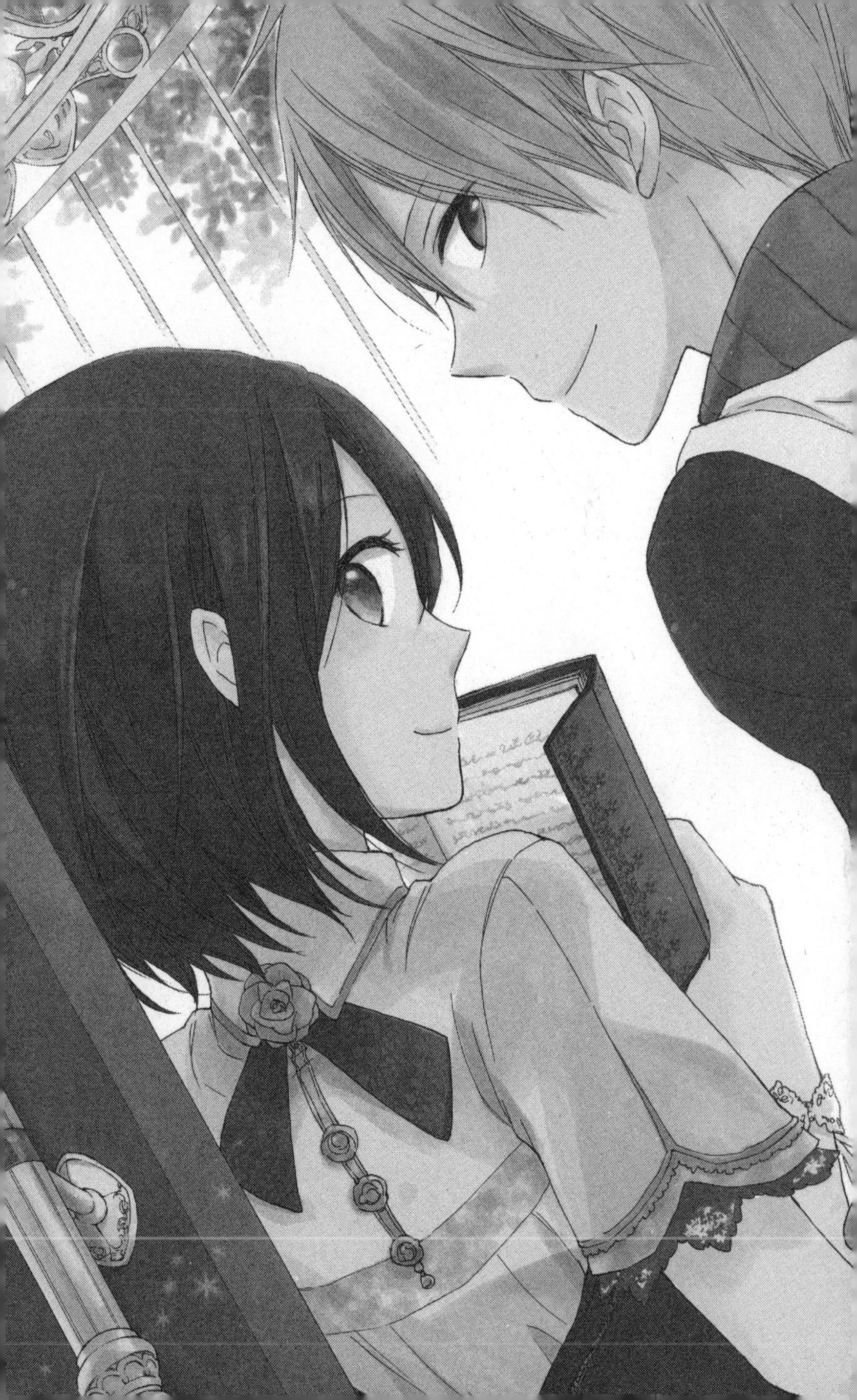

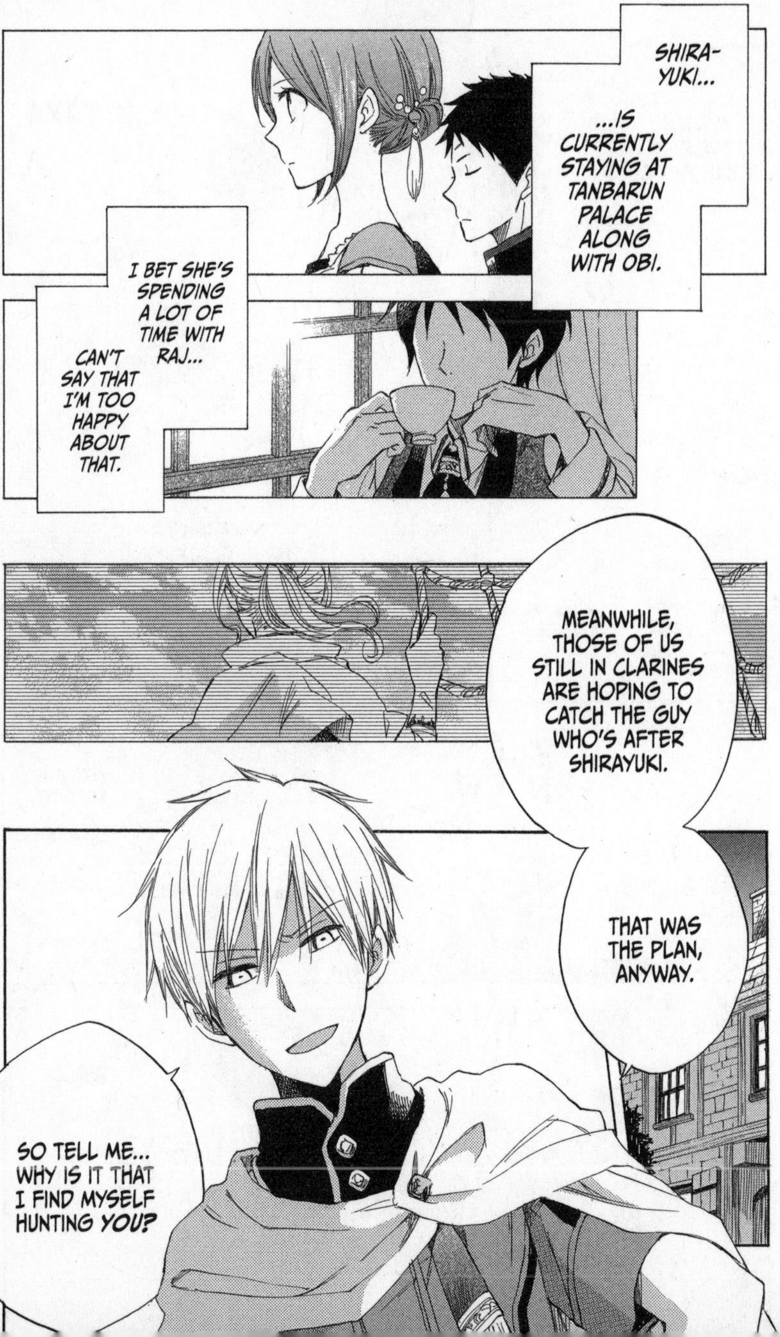
SHIRA-YUKI...
...IS CURRENTLY STAYING AT TANBARUN PALACE ALONG WITH OBI.
I BET SHE'S SPENDING A LOT OF TIME WITH RAJ...
CAN'T SAY THAT I'M TOO HAPPY ABOUT THAT.
MEANWHILE, THOSE OF US STILL IN CLARINES ARE HOPING TO CATCH THE GUY WHO'S AFTER SHIRAYUKI.
THAT WAS THE PLAN, ANYWAY.
SO TELL ME... WHY IS IT THAT I FIND MYSELF HUNTING *YOU*?

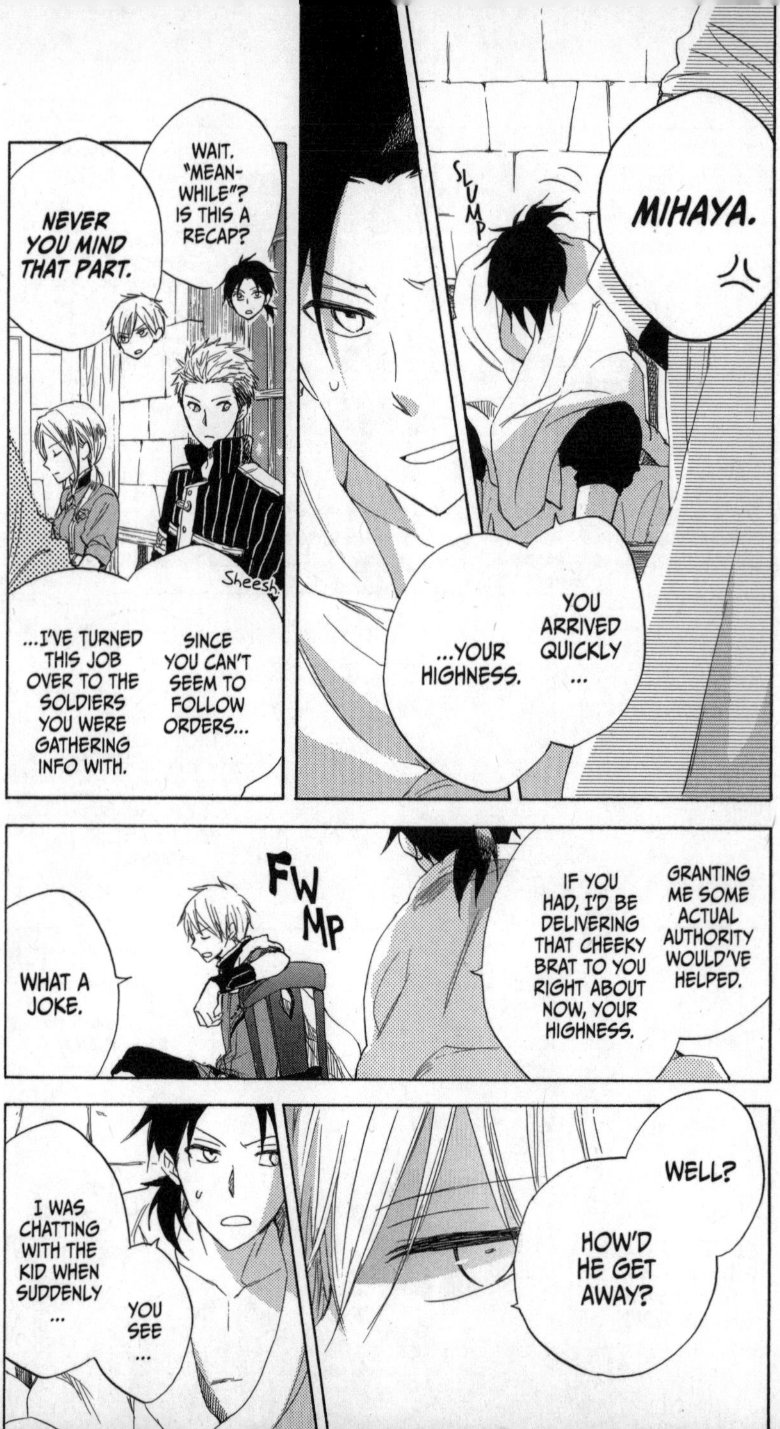
MIHAYA.
SLUMP
YOU ARRIVED QUICKLY ...
...YOUR HIGHNESS.
WAIT. "MEAN-WHILE"? IS THIS A RECAP?
NEVER YOU MIND THAT PART.
Sheesh.
SINCE YOU CAN'T SEEM TO FOLLOW ORDERS...
...I'VE TURNED THIS JOB OVER TO THE SOLDIERS YOU WERE GATHERING INFO WITH.
GRANTING ME SOME ACTUAL AUTHORITY WOULD'VE HELPED.
IF YOU HAD, I'D BE DELIVERING THAT CHEEKY BRAT TO YOU RIGHT ABOUT NOW, YOUR HIGHNESS.
FWMP
WHAT A JOKE.
WELL?
HOW'D HE GET AWAY?
YOU SEE ...
I WAS CHATTING WITH THE KID WHEN SUDDENLY ...

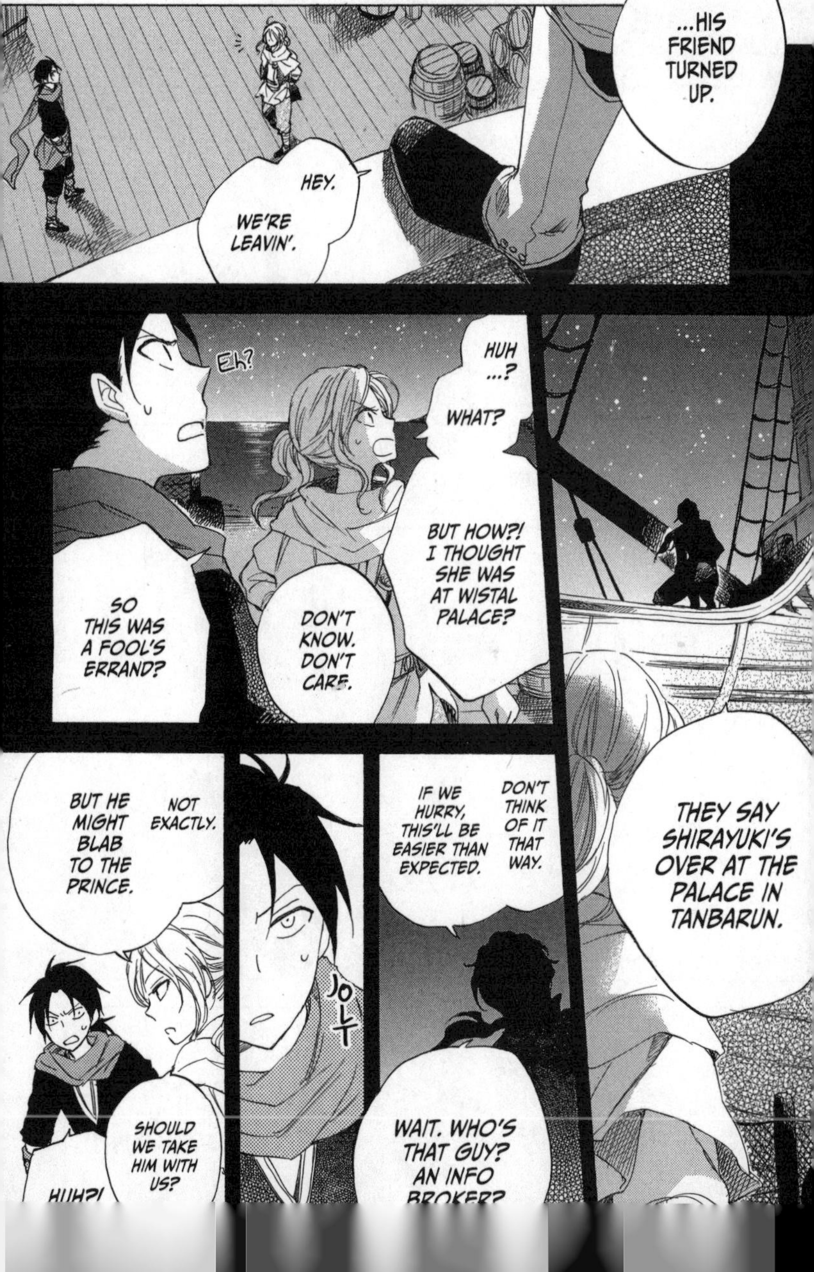
...HIS FRIEND TURNED UP.
HEY.
WE'RE LEAVIN'.
THEY SAY SHIRAYUKI'S OVER AT THE PALACE IN TANBARUN.
Eh?
HUH ...?
WHAT?
BUT HOW?! I THOUGHT SHE WAS AT WISTAL PALACE?
DON'T KNOW. DON'T CARE.
SO THIS WAS A FOOL'S ERRAND?
DON'T THINK OF IT THAT WAY.
IF WE HURRY, THIS'LL BE EASIER THAN EXPECTED.
WAIT. WHO'S THAT GUY? AN INFO BROKER?
JOLT
NOT EXACTLY.
BUT HE MIGHT BLAB TO THE PRINCE.
SHOULD WE TAKE HIM WITH US?
HUH?!

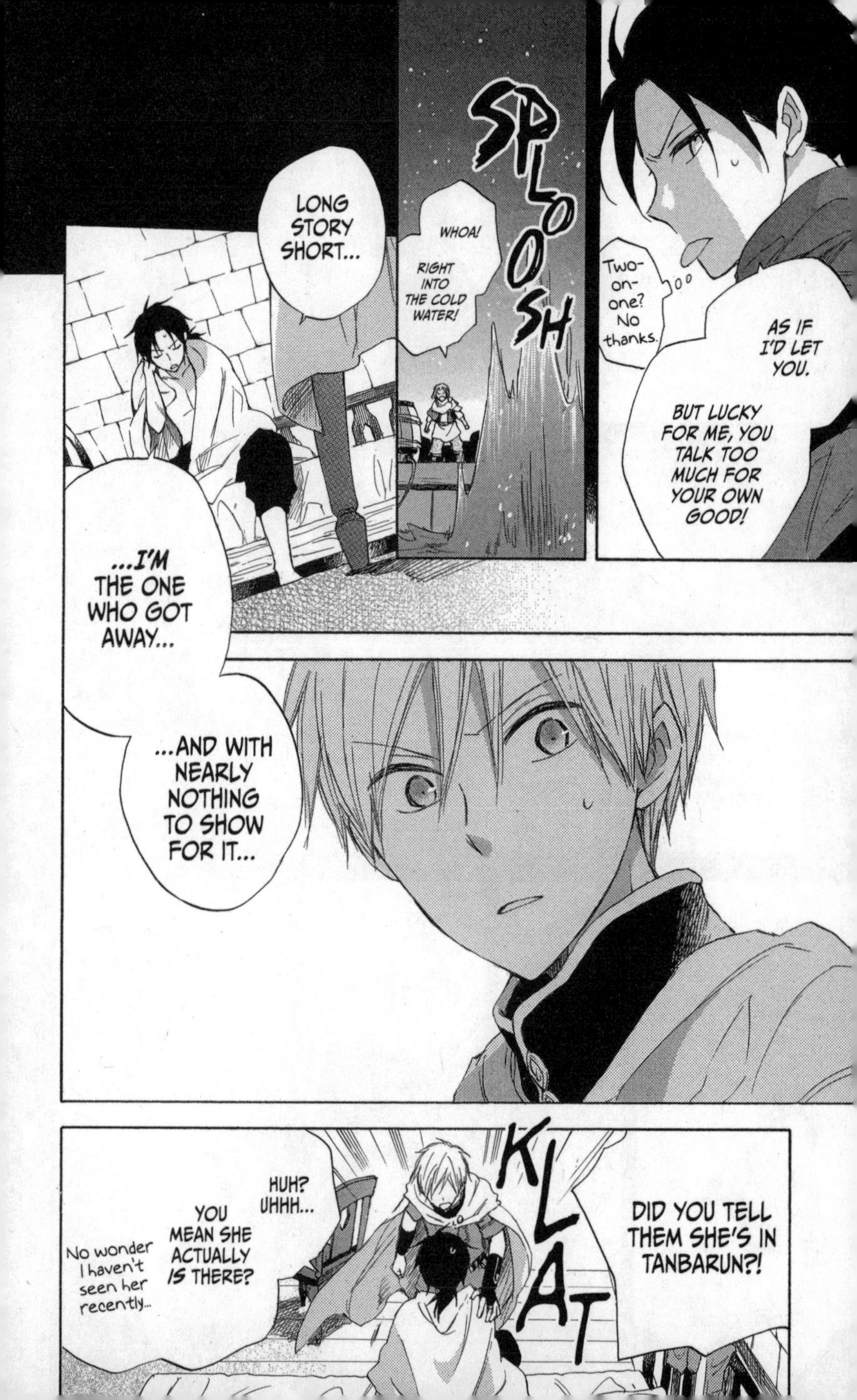
Two-on-one? No thanks.
AS IF I'D LET YOU.
BUT LUCKY FOR ME, YOU TALK TOO MUCH FOR YOUR OWN GOOD!
SPLOOSH
WHOA!
RIGHT INTO THE COLD WATER!
LONG STORY SHORT...
...I'M THE ONE WHO GOT AWAY...
...AND WITH NEARLY NOTHING TO SHOW FOR IT...
DID YOU TELL THEM SHE'S IN TANBARUN?!
KLAT
HUH? UHHH...
YOU MEAN SHE ACTUALLY *IS* THERE?
No wonder I haven't seen her recently...

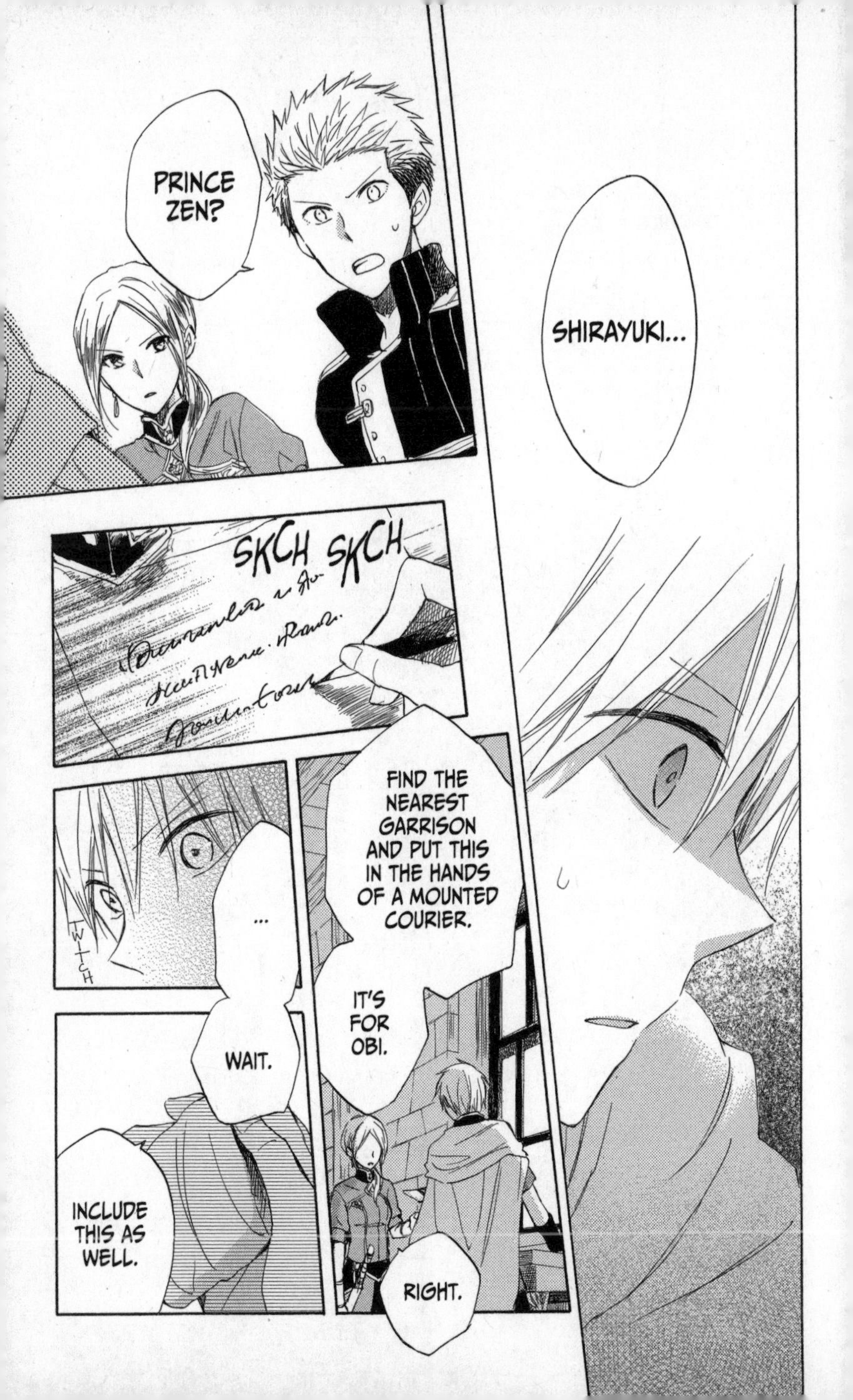
SHIRAYUKI...
PRINCE ZEN?
SKCH SKCH
FIND THE NEAREST GARRISON AND PUT THIS IN THE HANDS OF A MOUNTED COURIER.
IT'S FOR OBI.
RIGHT.
...
TWITCH
WAIT.
INCLUDE THIS AS WELL.

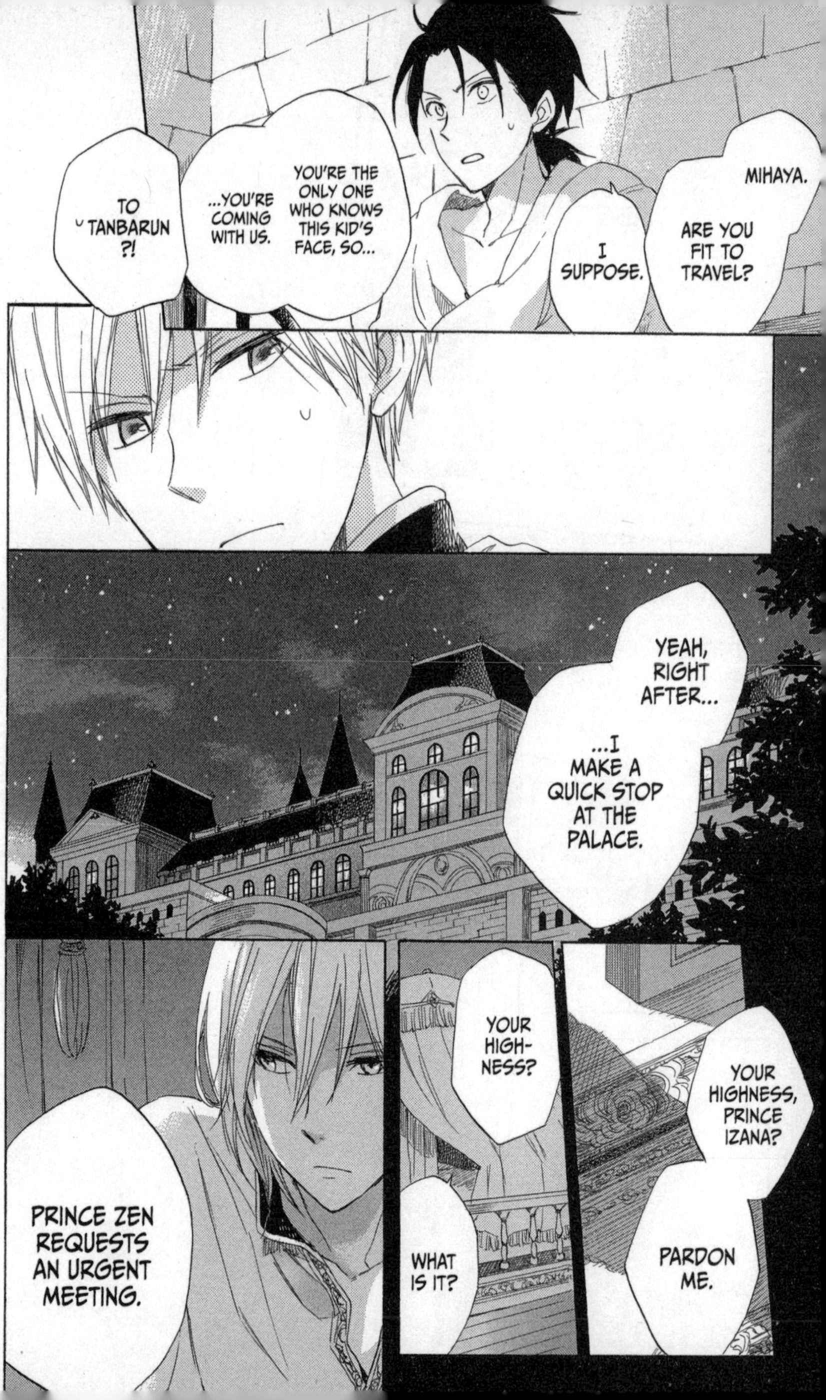
MIHAYA.
ARE YOU FIT TO TRAVEL?
I SUPPOSE.
YOU'RE THE ONLY ONE WHO KNOWS THIS KID'S FACE, SO...
...YOU'RE COMING WITH US.
TO TANBARUN ?!
YEAH, RIGHT AFTER...
...I MAKE A QUICK STOP AT THE PALACE.
YOUR HIGHNESS, PRINCE IZANA?
PARDON ME.
YOUR HIGH-NESS?
WHAT IS IT?
PRINCE ZEN REQUESTS AN URGENT MEETING.

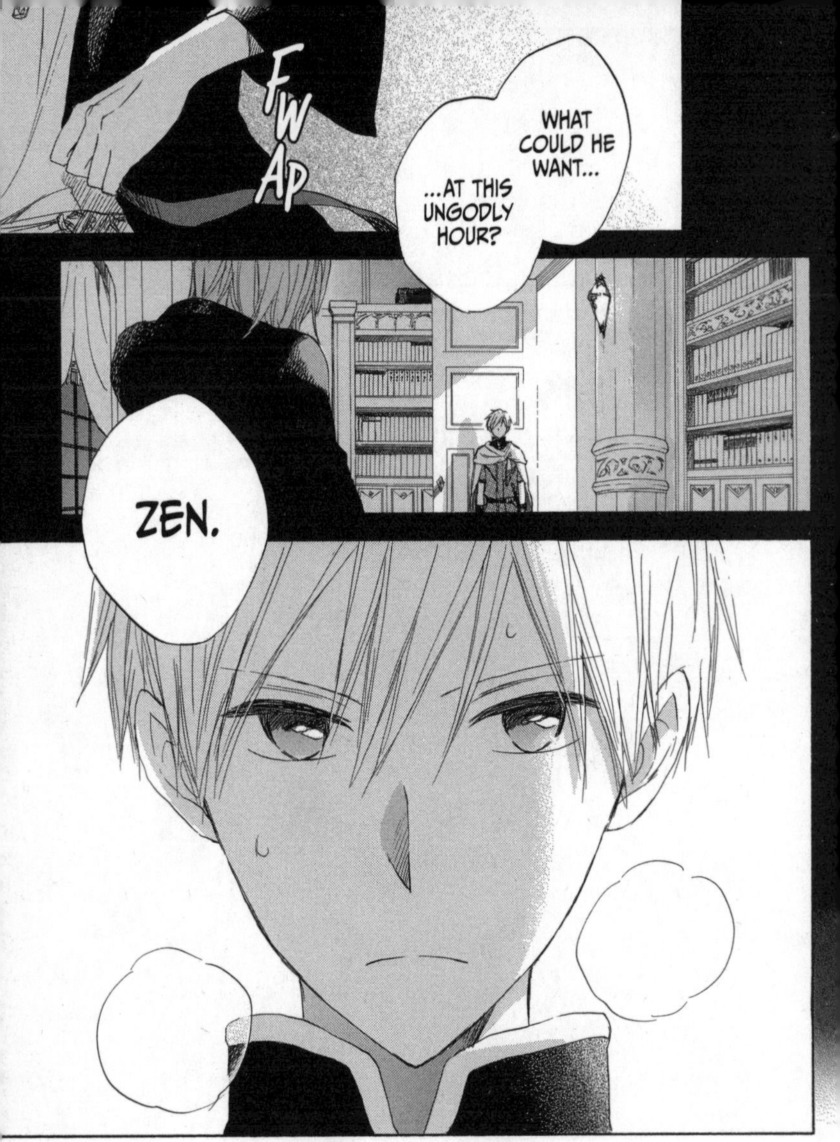
WHAT COULD HE WANT...
...AT THIS UNGODLY HOUR?
FWAP
ZEN.

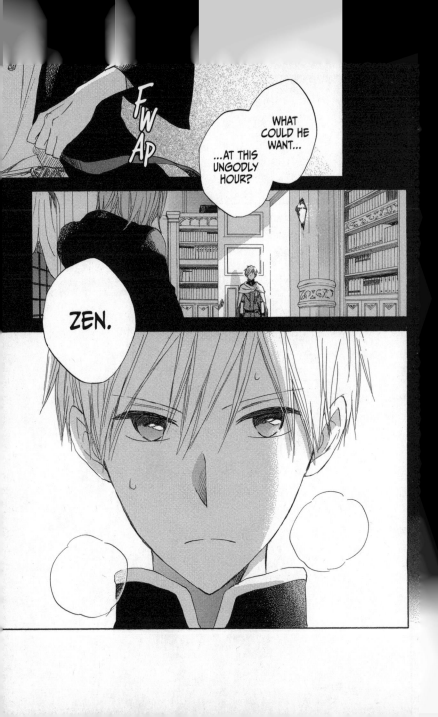

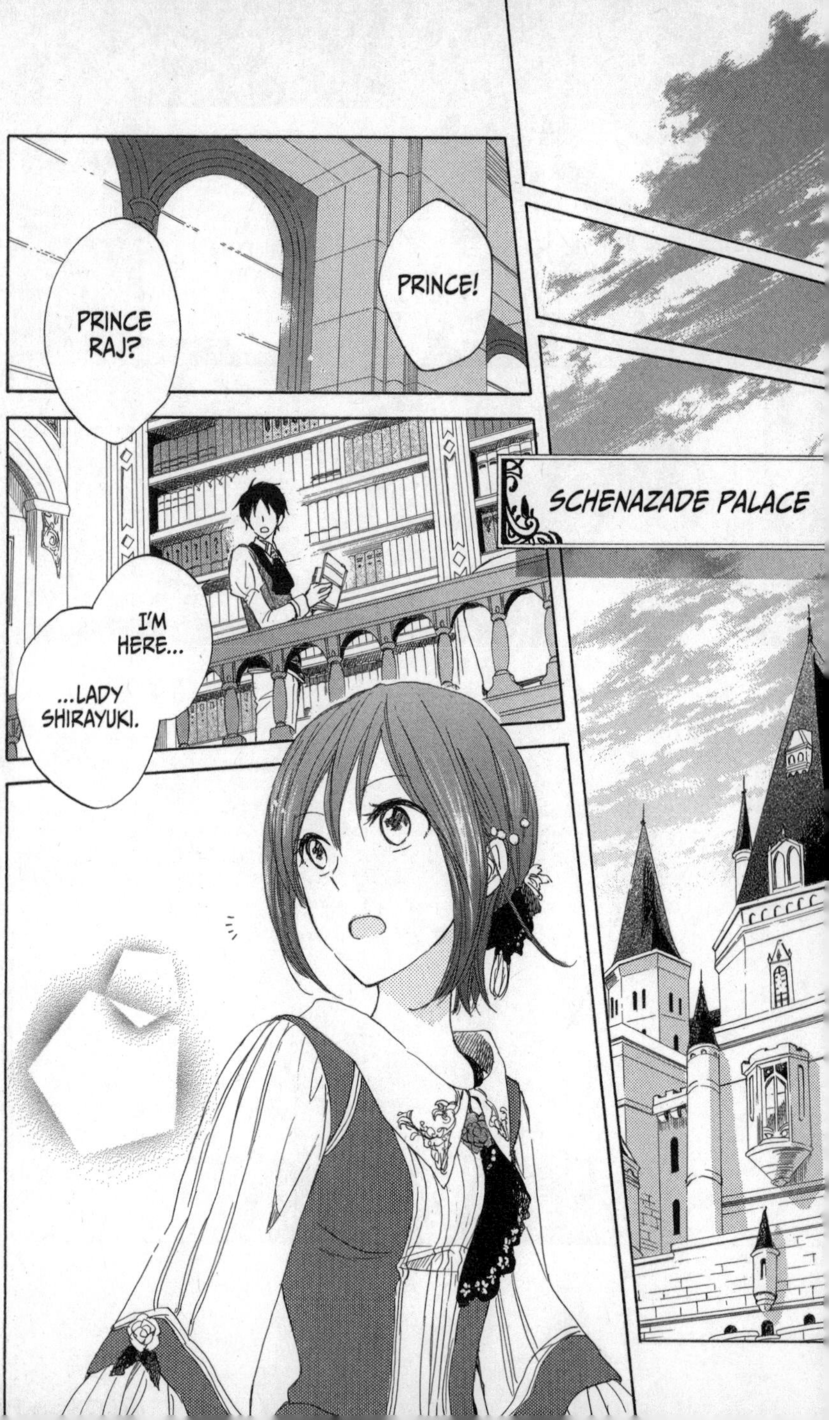
SCHENAZADE PALACE
PRINCE!
PRINCE RAJ?
I'M HERE...
...LADY SHIRAYUKI.

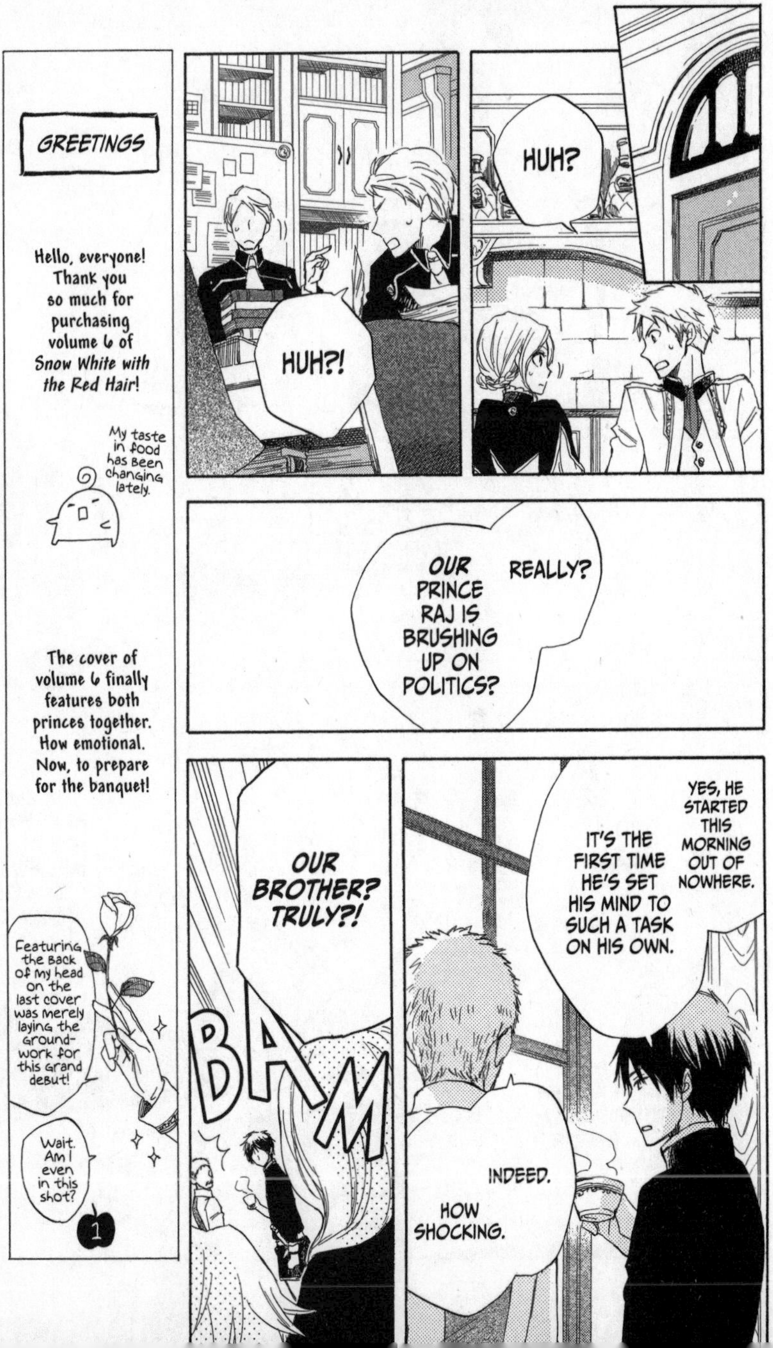
HUH?
HUH?!
REALLY?
OUR PRINCE RAJ IS BRUSHING UP ON POLITICS?
YES, HE STARTED THIS MORNING OUT OF NOWHERE.
IT'S THE FIRST TIME HE'S SET HIS MIND TO SUCH A TASK ON HIS OWN.
INDEED.
HOW SHOCKING.
OUR BROTHER? TRULY?!
BAM
GREETINGS
Hello, everyone! Thank you so much for purchasing volume 6 of Snow White with the Red Hair!
My taste in food has been changing lately.
The cover of volume 6 finally features both princes together. How emotional. Now, to prepare for the banquet!
Featuring the back of my head on the last cover was merely laying the groundwork for this grand debut!
Wait. Am I even in this shot?
1

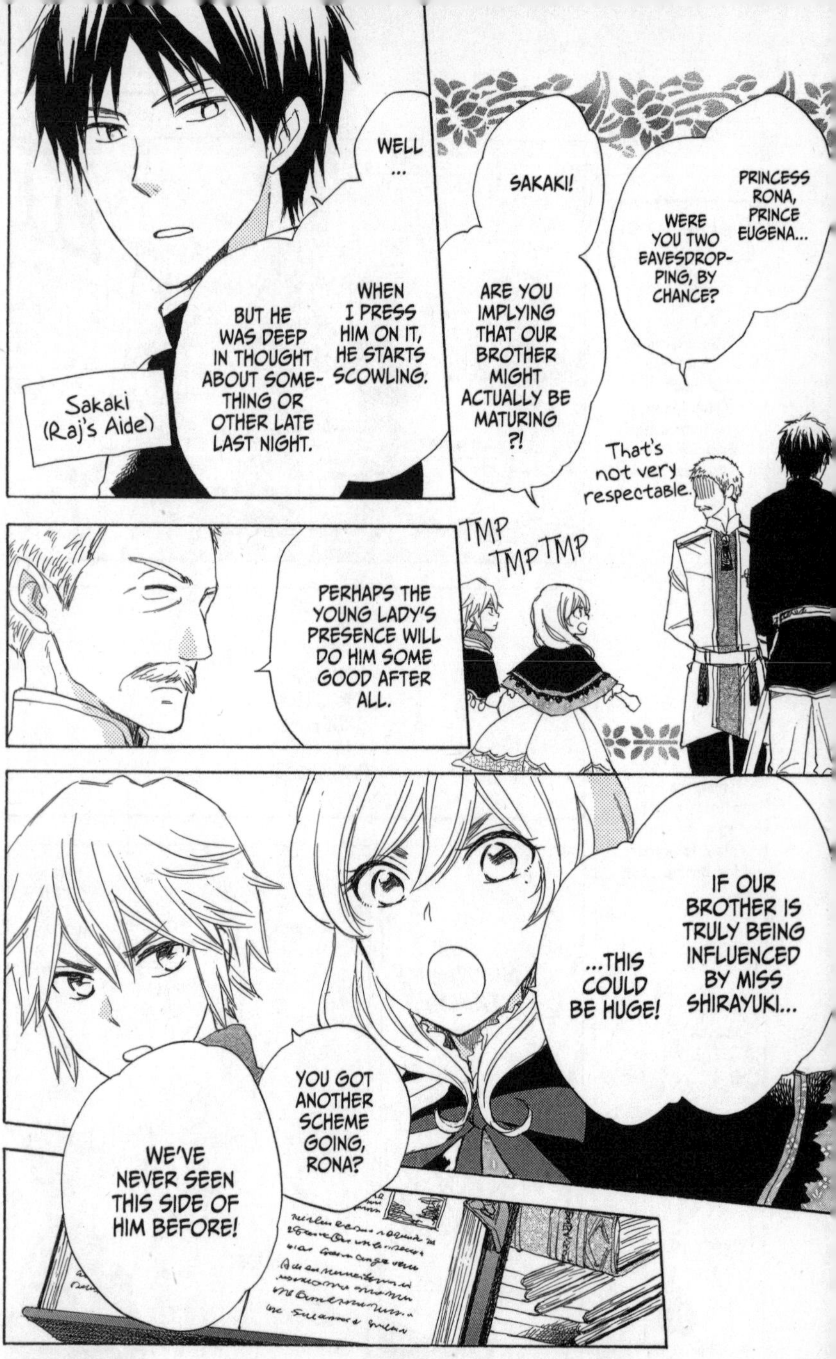
WELL ...
WHEN I PRESS HIM ON IT, HE STARTS SCOWLING.
BUT HE WAS DEEP IN THOUGHT ABOUT SOME-THING OR OTHER LATE LAST NIGHT.
Sakaki (Raj's Aide)
PERHAPS THE YOUNG LADY'S PRESENCE WILL DO HIM SOME GOOD AFTER ALL.
SAKAKI!
ARE YOU IMPLYING THAT OUR BROTHER MIGHT ACTUALLY BE MATURING ?!
TMP TMP TMP
PRINCESS RONA, PRINCE EUGENA...
WERE YOU TWO EAVESDROP-PING, BY CHANCE?
That's not very respectable.
IF OUR BROTHER IS TRULY BEING INFLUENCED BY MISS SHIRAYUKI...
...THIS COULD BE HUGE!
YOU GOT ANOTHER SCHEME GOING, RONA?
WE'VE NEVER SEEN THIS SIDE OF HIM BEFORE!

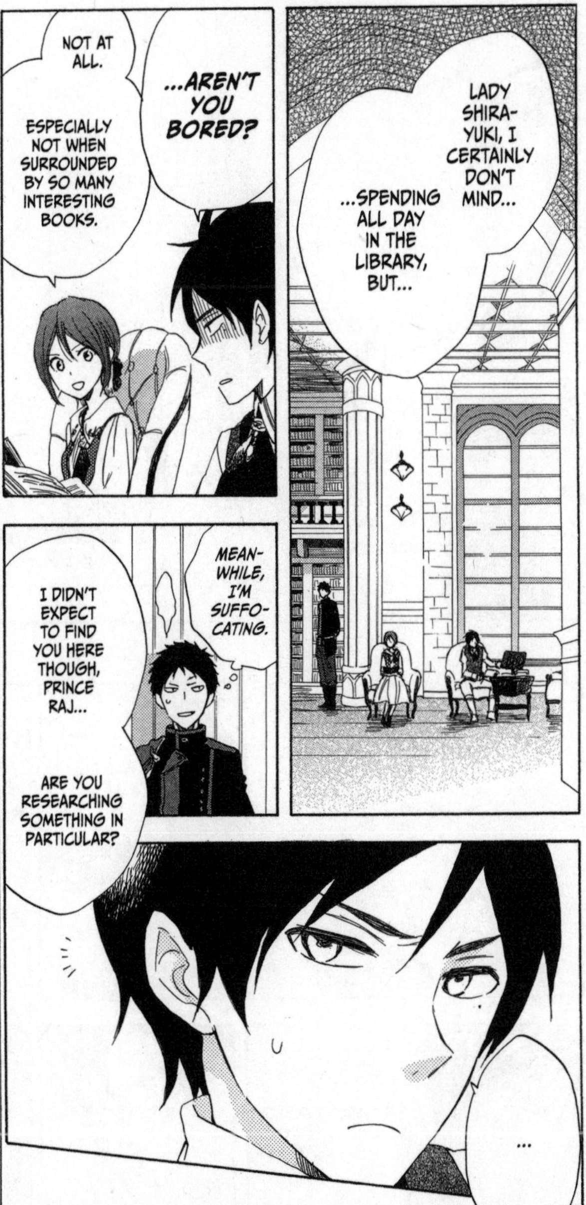
LADY SHIRA-YUKI, I CERTAINLY DON'T MIND...
...SPENDING ALL DAY IN THE LIBRARY, BUT...
...AREN'T YOU BORED?
NOT AT ALL.
ESPECIALLY NOT WHEN SURROUNDED BY SO MANY INTERESTING BOOKS.
MEAN-WHILE, I'M SUFFO-CATING.
I DIDN'T EXPECT TO FIND YOU HERE THOUGH, PRINCE RAJ...
ARE YOU RESEARCHING SOMETHING IN PARTICULAR?
...

Since I have 12 of these sidebars to fill this time around, I thought, "Why not answer some questions from readers?"

One question that I got a lot in the past (and even now) is...

"Are you a man or a woman?"

Oh, Christ.

Even after five whole volumes, I guess I never said anything to indicate one way or the other... Sorry about that.

I'm a woman!

2

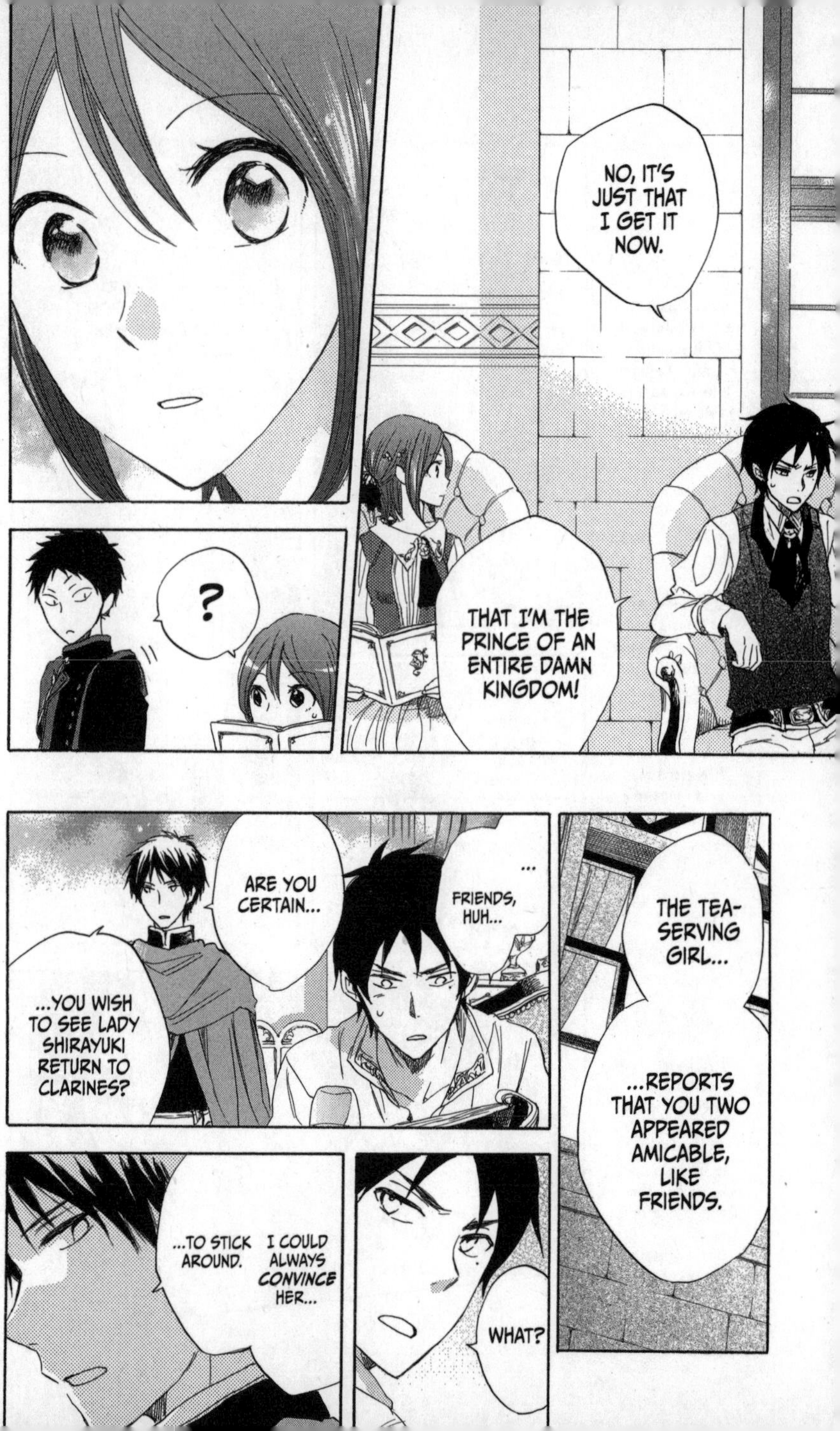
NO, IT'S JUST THAT I GET IT NOW.
THAT I'M THE PRINCE OF AN ENTIRE DAMN KINGDOM!
?
THE TEA-SERVING GIRL...
...REPORTS THAT YOU TWO APPEARED AMICABLE, LIKE FRIENDS.
...
FRIENDS, HUH...
ARE YOU CERTAIN...
...YOU WISH TO SEE LADY SHIRAYUKI RETURN TO CLARINES?
WHAT?
I COULD ALWAYS CONVINCE HER...
...TO STICK AROUND.

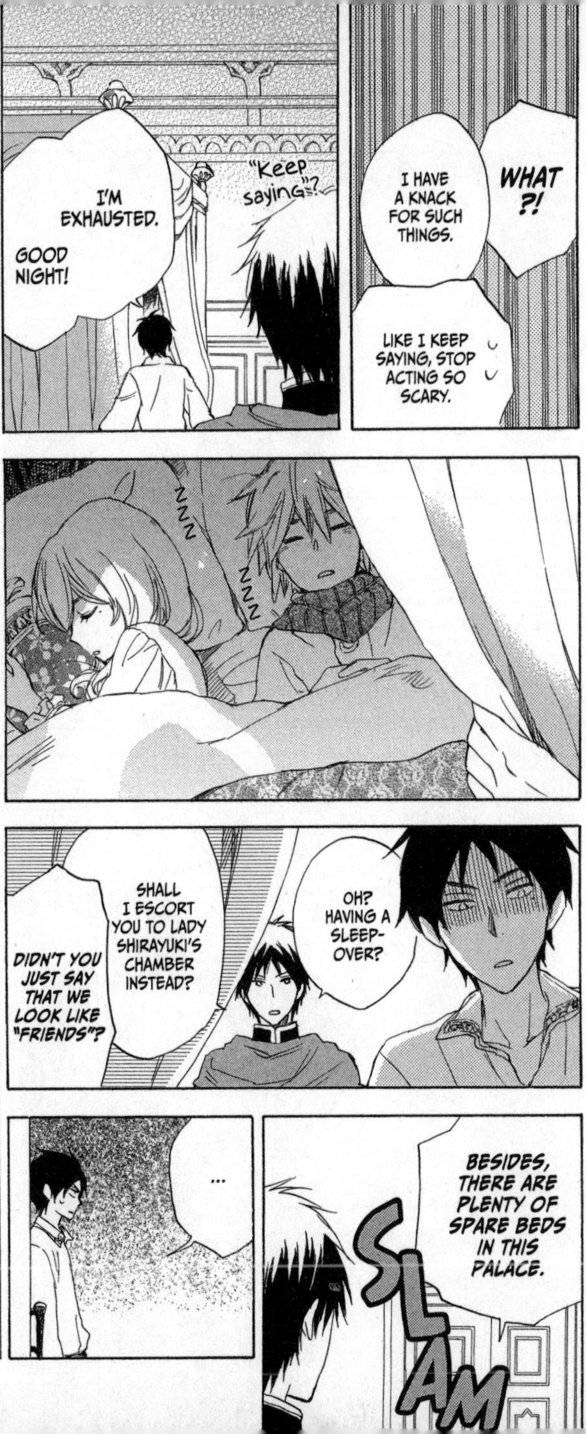
WHAT?!
I HAVE A KNACK FOR SUCH THINGS.
LIKE I KEEP SAYING, STOP ACTING SO SCARY.
"Keep saying"?
I'M EXHAUSTED.
GOOD NIGHT!
ZZZ
ZZZ
OH? HAVING A SLEEP-OVER?
SHALL I ESCORT YOU TO LADY SHIRAYUKI'S CHAMBER INSTEAD?
DIDN'T YOU JUST SAY THAT WE LOOK LIKE "FRIENDS"?
BESIDES, THERE ARE PLENTY OF SPARE BEDS IN THIS PALACE.
SLAM
...

Q: "Who is your favorite character in *Snow White with the Red Hair?*"

pondering

I like whoever I happen to be drawing at the moment...

Each member of the main cast has their ups and downs, so I could never rank them. I love them all equally, and I'm always thinking, "I hope you all find happiness!"

I'm a fan of Mitsuhide's characterization and his role in the story, but he can be a pain to draw... Maybe I should give him the haircut from the flashback of six years prior...

Here's how I would rank the princes, from easiest to hardest to draw:

Izana -> Eugena -> Raj -> Zen

What the ?!

3

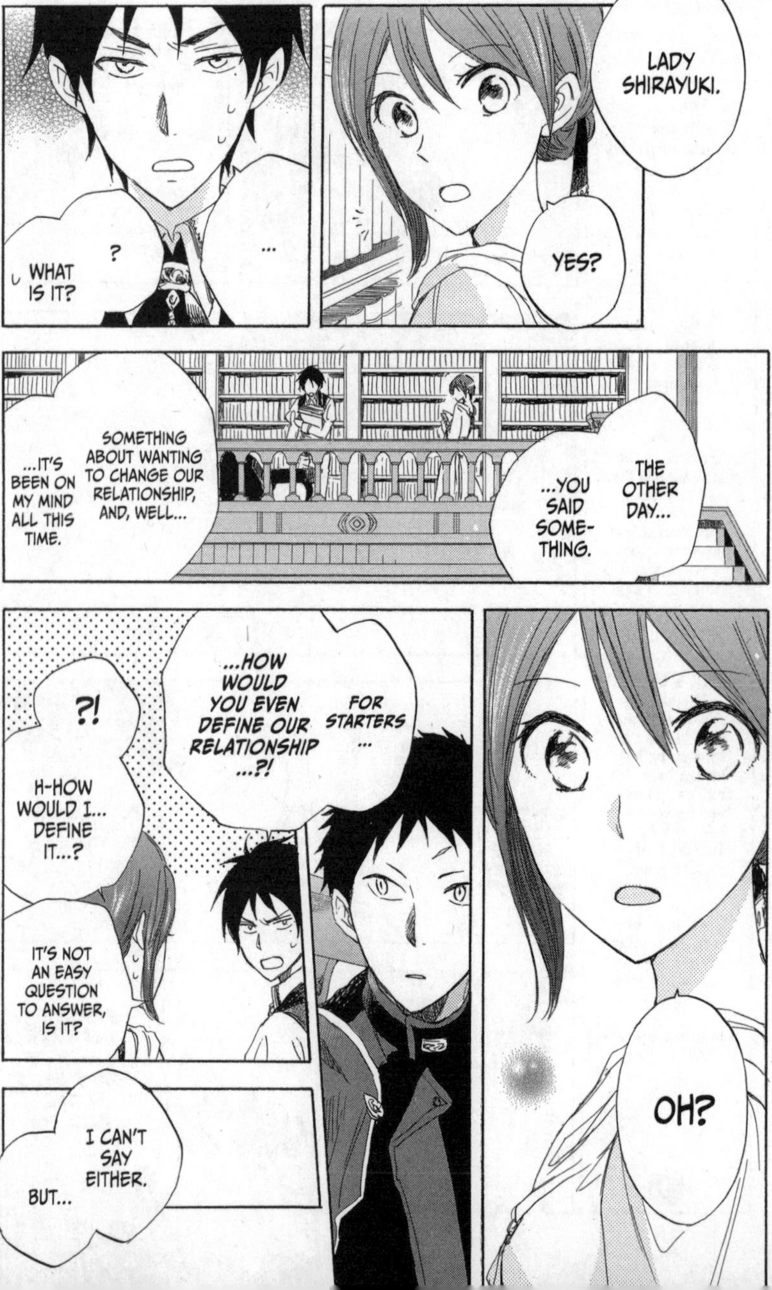
LADY SHIRAYUKI.
YES?
...
?
WHAT IS IT?
THE OTHER DAY...
...YOU SAID SOMETHING.
SOMETHING ABOUT WANTING TO CHANGE OUR RELATIONSHIP, AND, WELL...
...IT'S BEEN ON MY MIND ALL THIS TIME.
OH?
FOR STARTERS...
...HOW WOULD YOU EVEN DEFINE OUR RELATIONSHIP...?!
?!
H-HOW WOULD I... DEFINE IT...?
IT'S NOT AN EASY QUESTION TO ANSWER, IS IT?
I CAN'T SAY EITHER.
BUT...

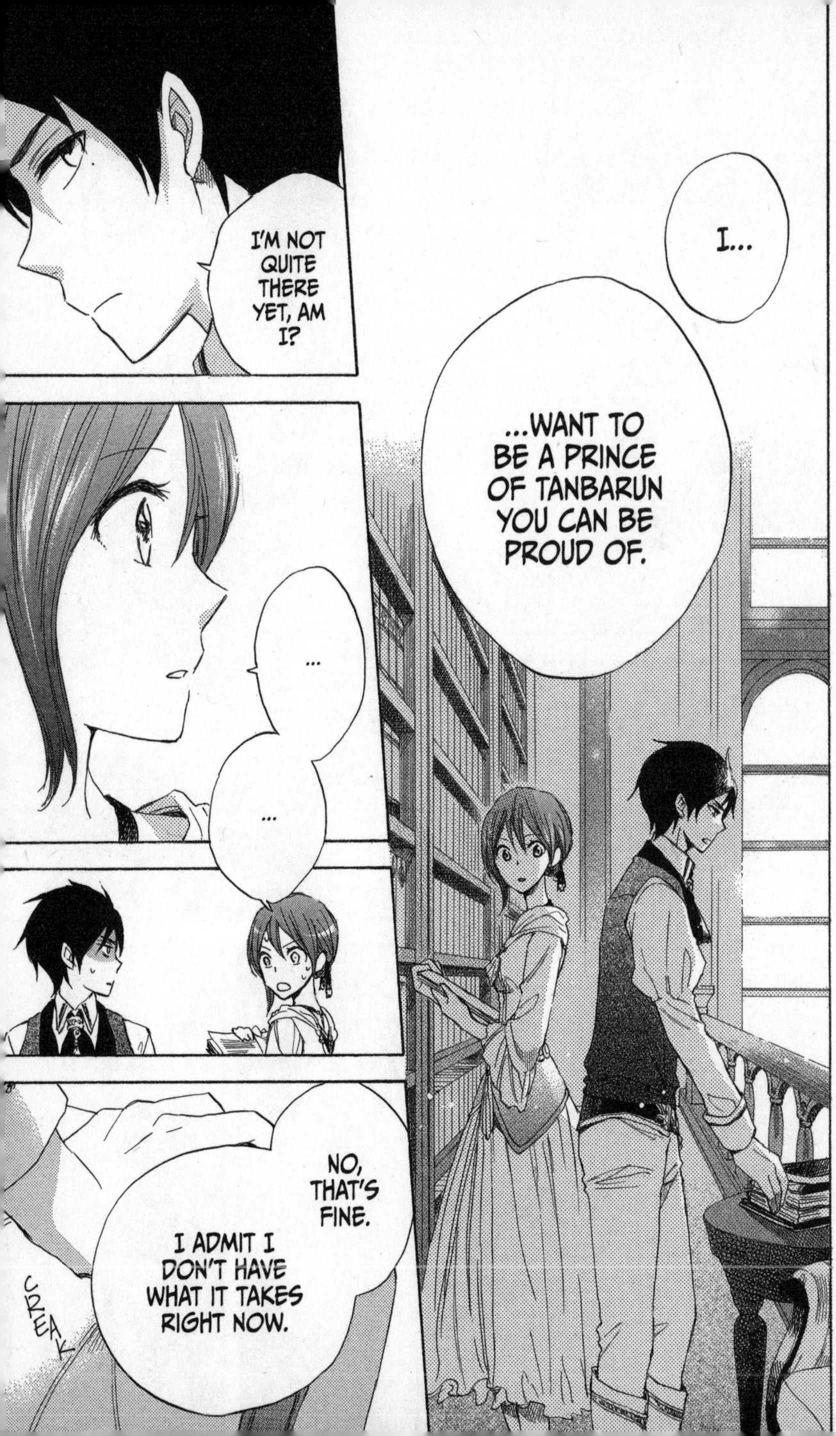
I...
...WANT TO BE A PRINCE OF TANBARUN YOU CAN BE PROUD OF.
I'M NOT QUITE THERE YET, AM I?
...
...
NO, THAT'S FINE.
I ADMIT I DON'T HAVE WHAT IT TAKES RIGHT NOW.
CREAK

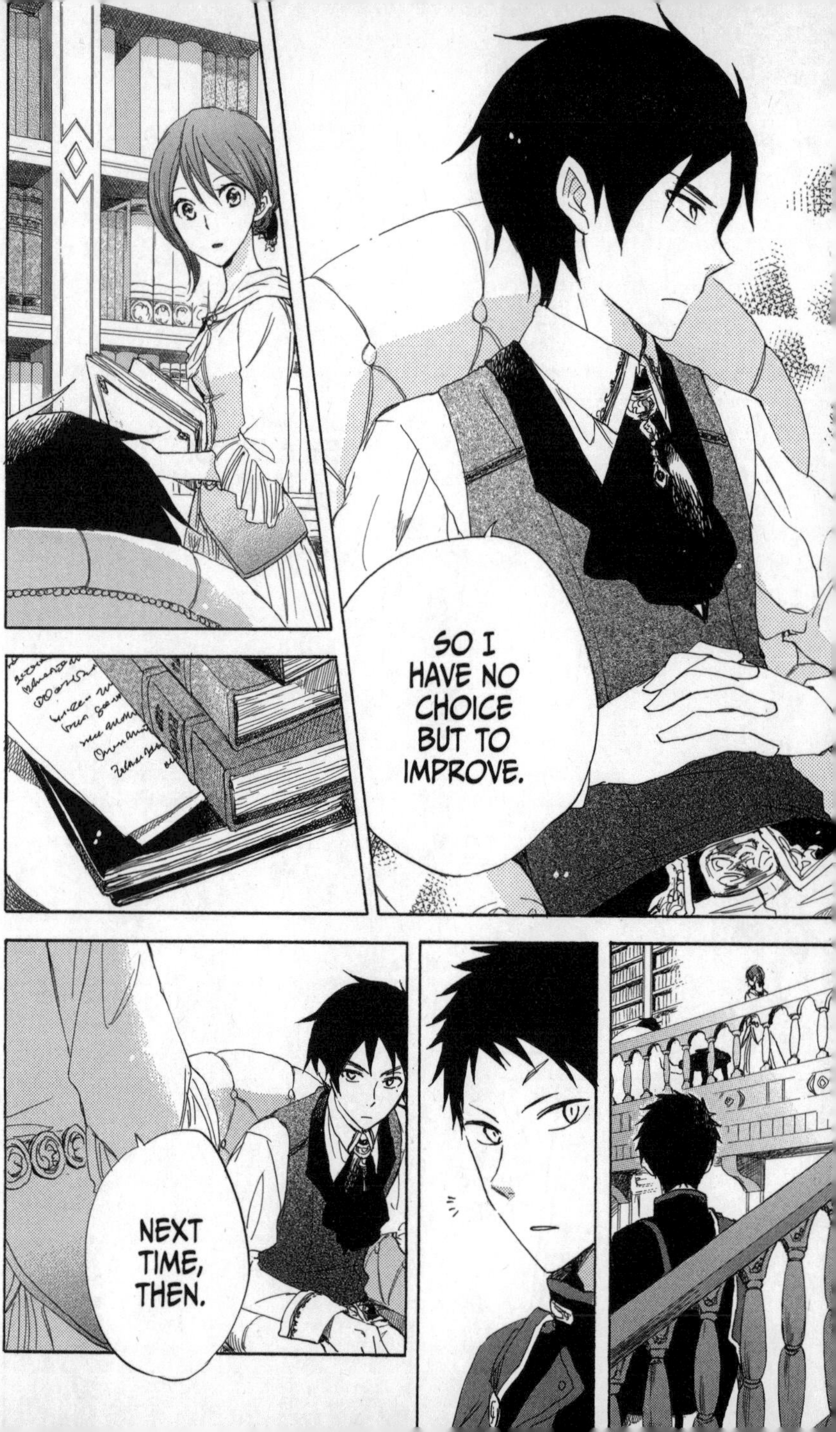
SO I HAVE NO CHOICE BUT TO IMPROVE.
NEXT TIME, THEN.

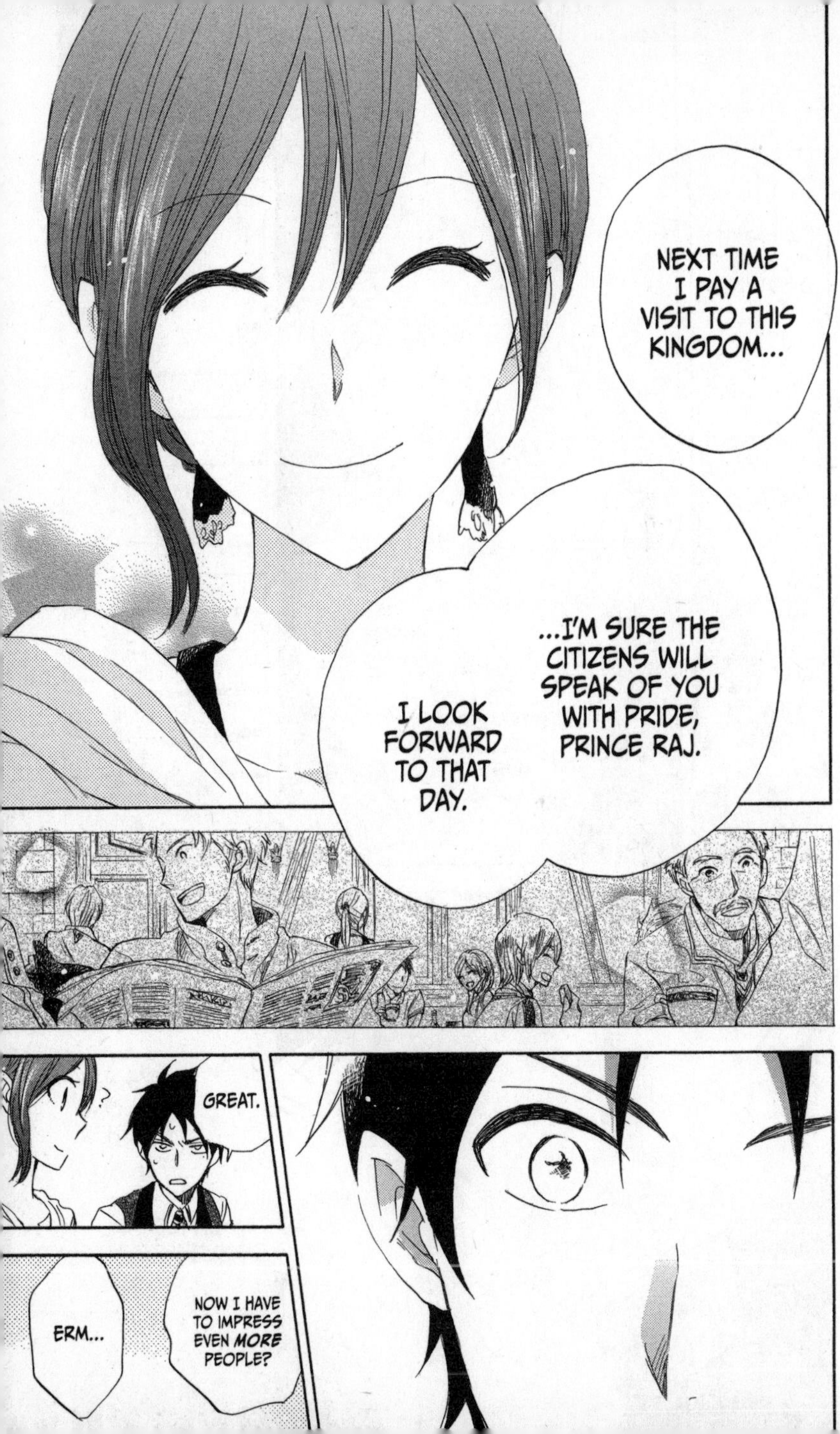
NEXT TIME I PAY A VISIT TO THIS KINGDOM...
...I'M SURE THE CITIZENS WILL SPEAK OF YOU WITH PRIDE, PRINCE RAJ.
I LOOK FORWARD TO THAT DAY.
GREAT.
NOW I HAVE TO IMPRESS EVEN *MORE* PEOPLE?
ERM...

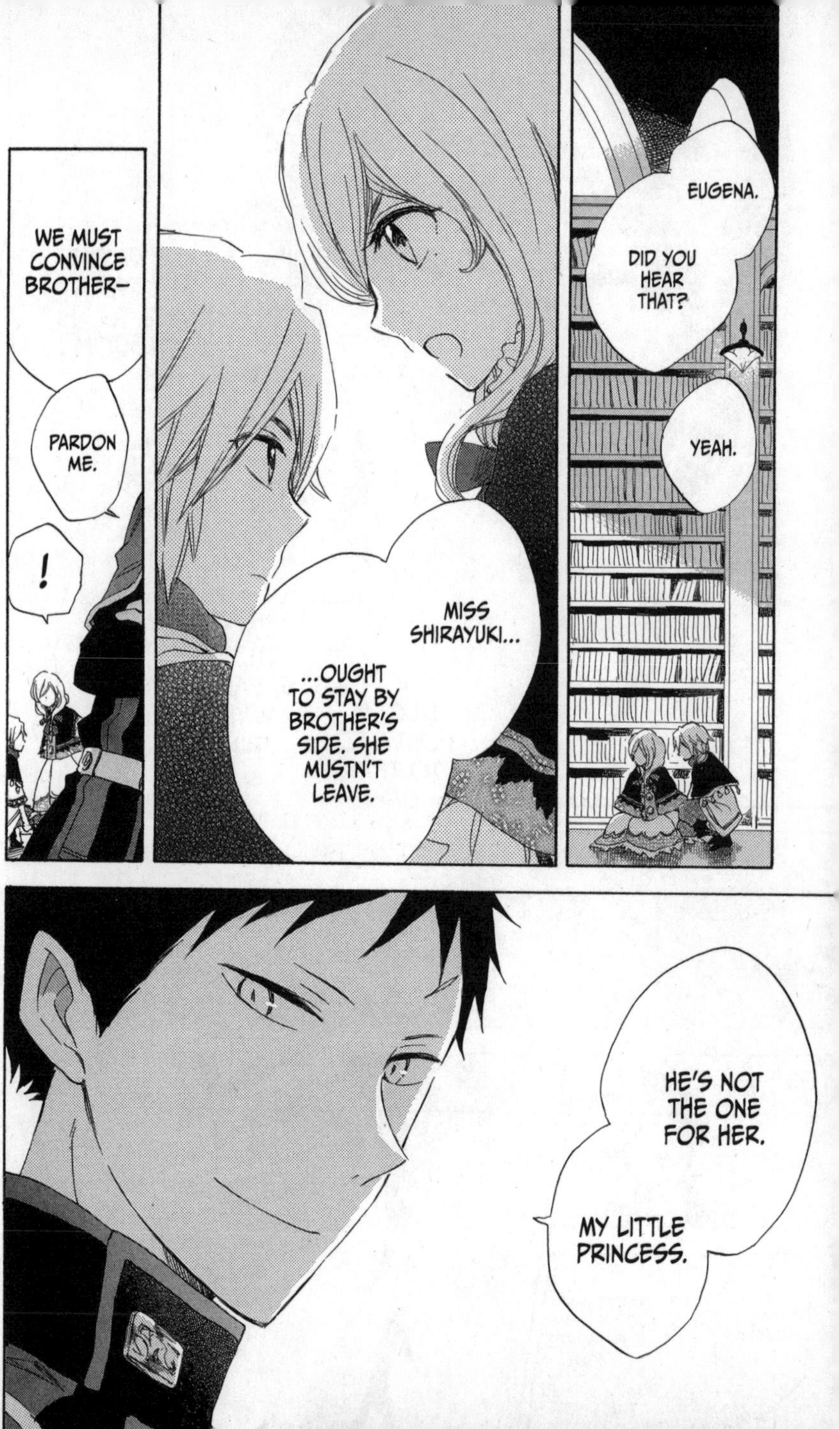
EUGENA.
DID YOU HEAR THAT?
YEAH.
MISS SHIRAYUKI...
...OUGHT TO STAY BY BROTHER'S SIDE. SHE MUSTN'T LEAVE.
WE MUST CONVINCE BROTHER—
PARDON ME.
!
HE'S NOT THE ONE FOR HER.
MY LITTLE PRINCESS.

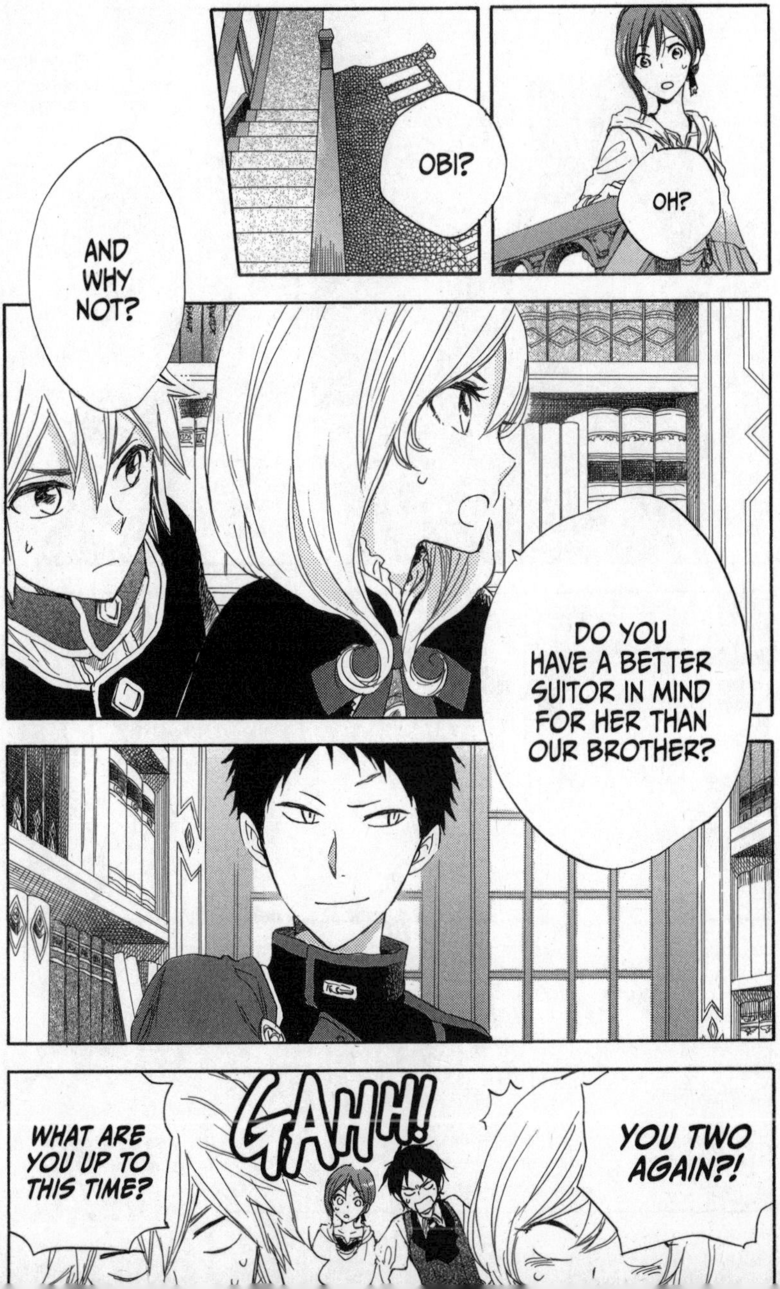
OH?
OBI?
AND WHY NOT?
DO YOU HAVE A BETTER SUITOR IN MIND FOR HER THAN OUR BROTHER?
YOU TWO AGAIN?!
GAHH!
WHAT ARE YOU UP TO THIS TIME?

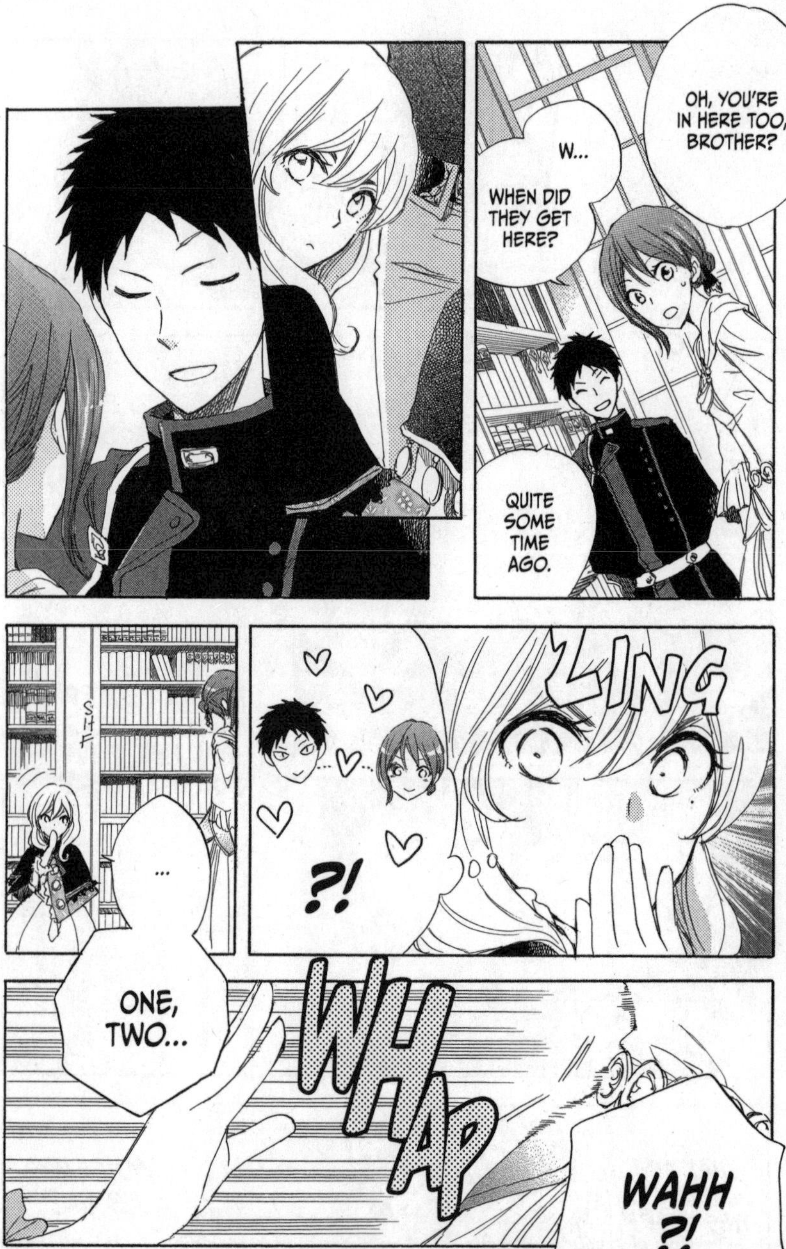
OH, YOU'RE IN HERE TOO, BROTHER?
W...
WHEN DID THEY GET HERE?
QUITE SOME TIME AGO.
LING
?!
...
ONE, TWO...
WHAP
WAHH ?!

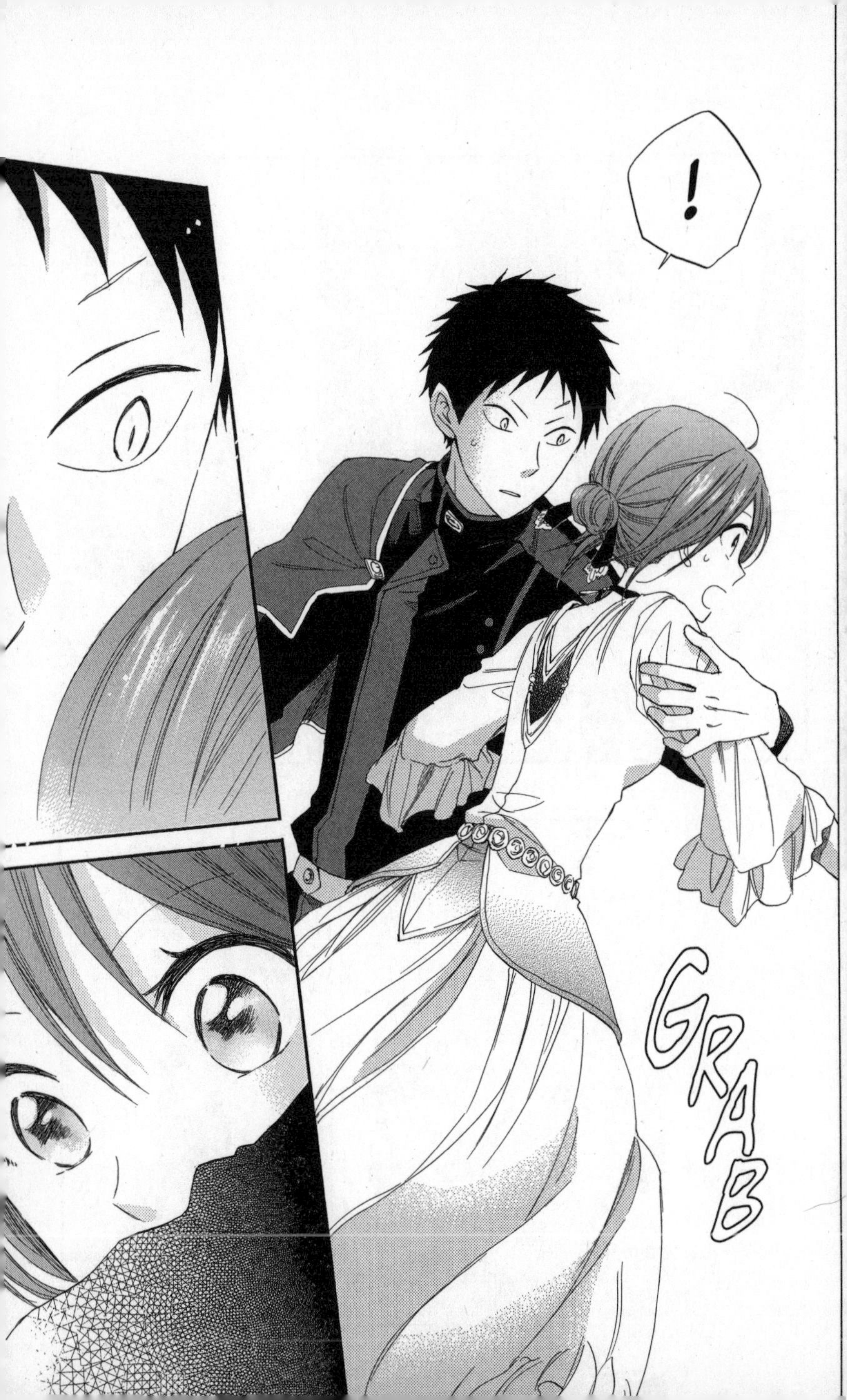
!
GRAB

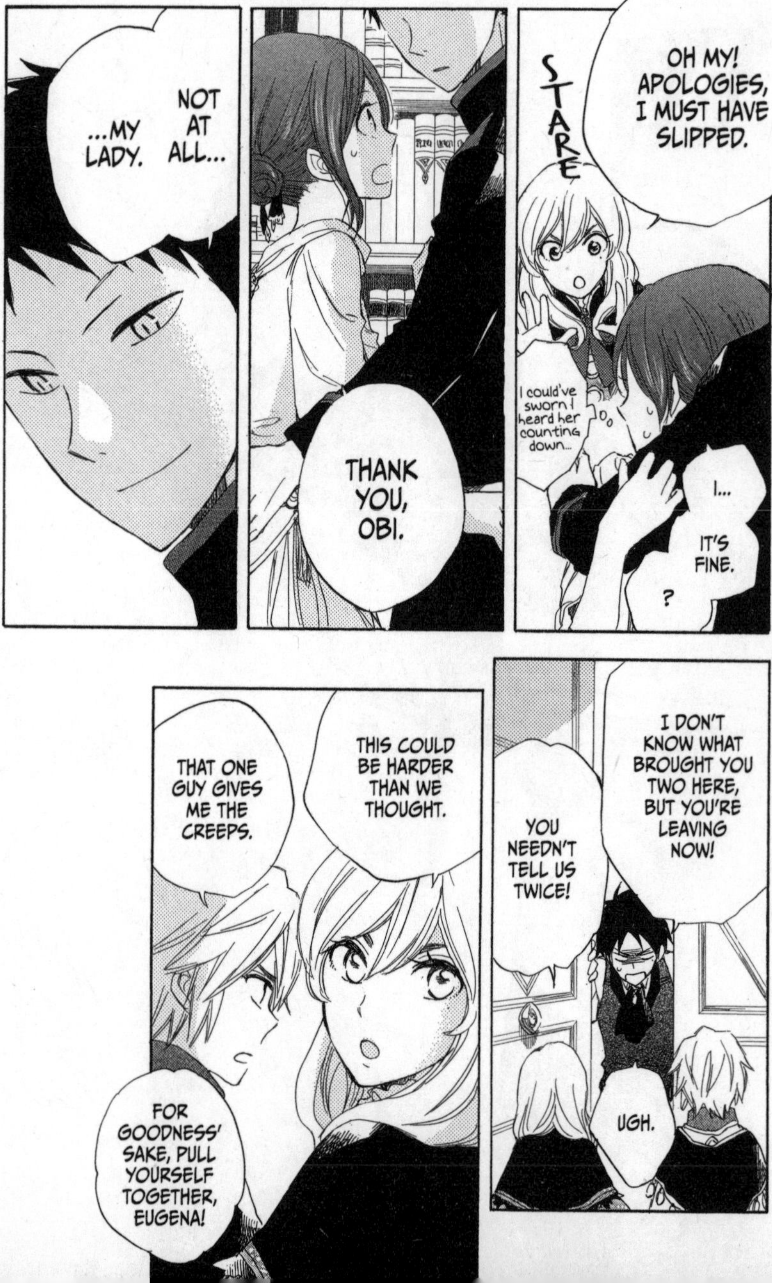
STARE
OH MY! APOLOGIES, I MUST HAVE SLIPPED.
I could've sworn I heard her counting down...
I...
IT'S FINE.
?
THANK YOU, OBI.
NOT AT ALL...
...MY LADY.
I DON'T KNOW WHAT BROUGHT YOU TWO HERE, BUT YOU'RE LEAVING NOW!
YOU NEEDN'T TELL US TWICE!
UGH.
THIS COULD BE HARDER THAN WE THOUGHT.
THAT ONE GUY GIVES ME THE CREEPS.
FOR GOODNESS' SAKE, PULL YOURSELF TOGETHER, EUGENA!

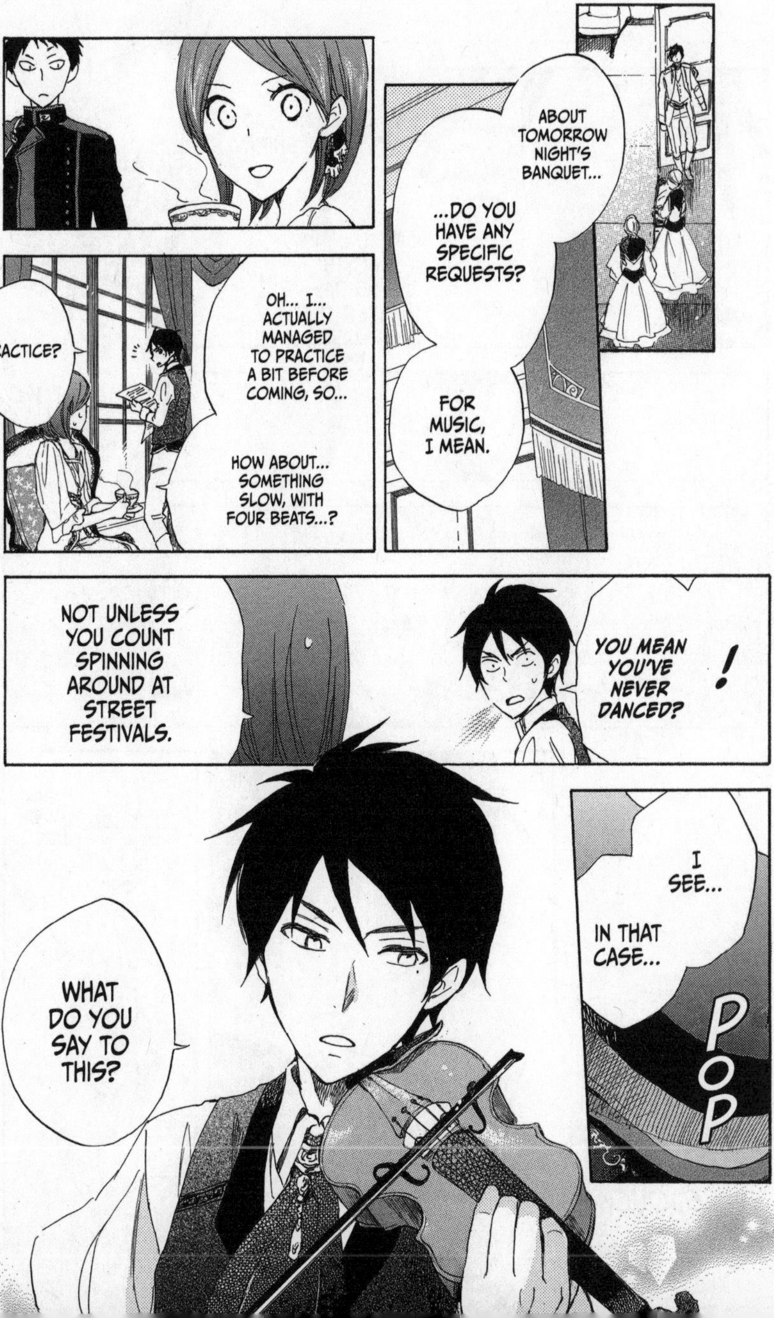
ABOUT TOMORROW NIGHT'S BANQUET...
...DO YOU HAVE ANY SPECIFIC REQUESTS?
FOR MUSIC, I MEAN.
OH... I... ACTUALLY MANAGED TO PRACTICE A BIT BEFORE COMING, SO...
PRACTICE?
HOW ABOUT... SOMETHING SLOW, WITH FOUR BEATS...?
!
YOU MEAN YOU'VE NEVER DANCED?
NOT UNLESS YOU COUNT SPINNING AROUND AT STREET FESTIVALS.
I SEE...
IN THAT CASE...
POP
WHAT DO YOU SAY TO THIS?

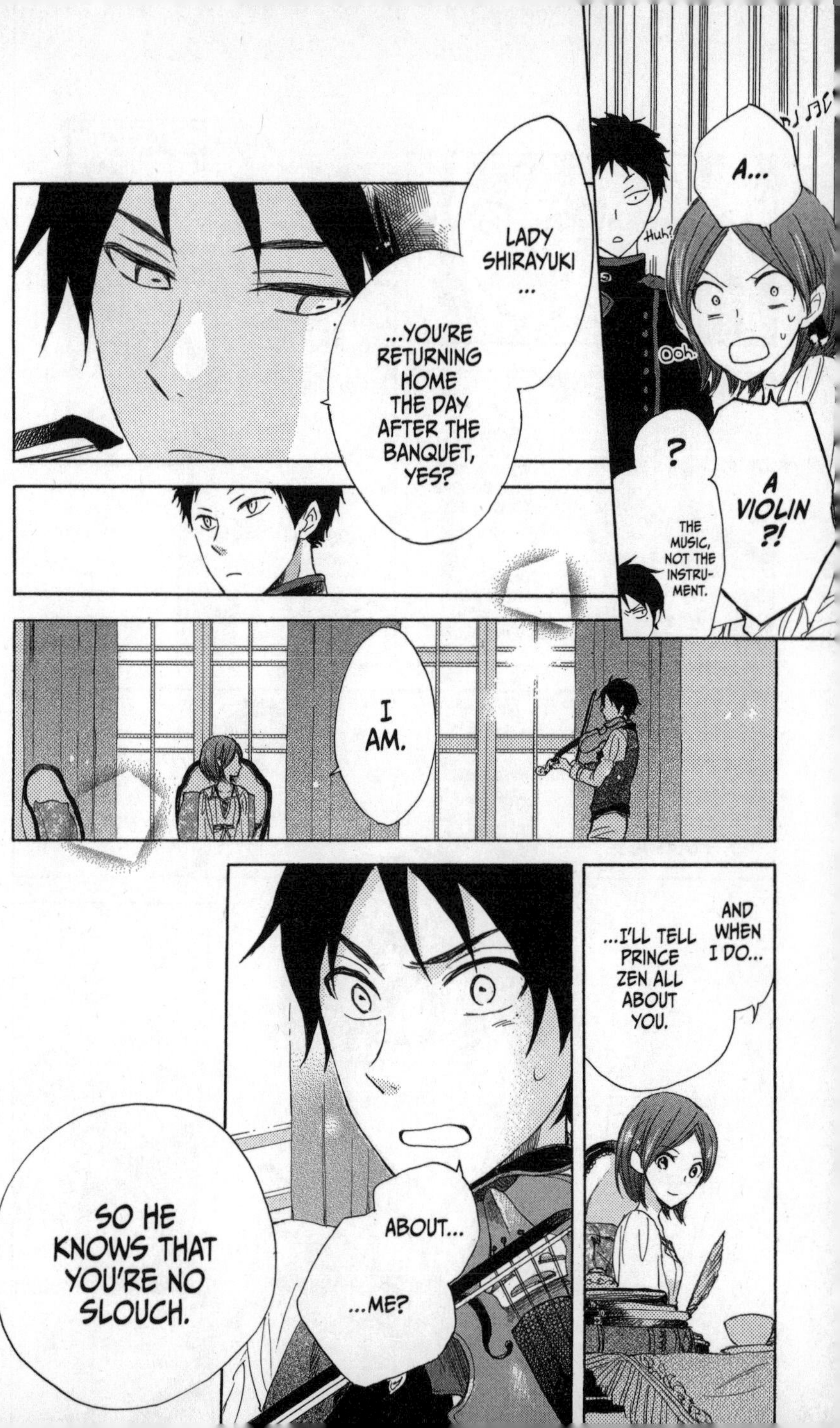
A...
Huh?
Ooh.
A VIOLIN ?!
?
THE MUSIC, NOT THE INSTRU-MENT.
LADY SHIRAYUKI ...
...YOU'RE RETURNING HOME THE DAY AFTER THE BANQUET, YES?
I AM.
AND WHEN I DO...
...I'LL TELL PRINCE ZEN ALL ABOUT YOU.
ABOUT...
...ME?
SO HE KNOWS THAT YOU'RE NO SLOUCH.

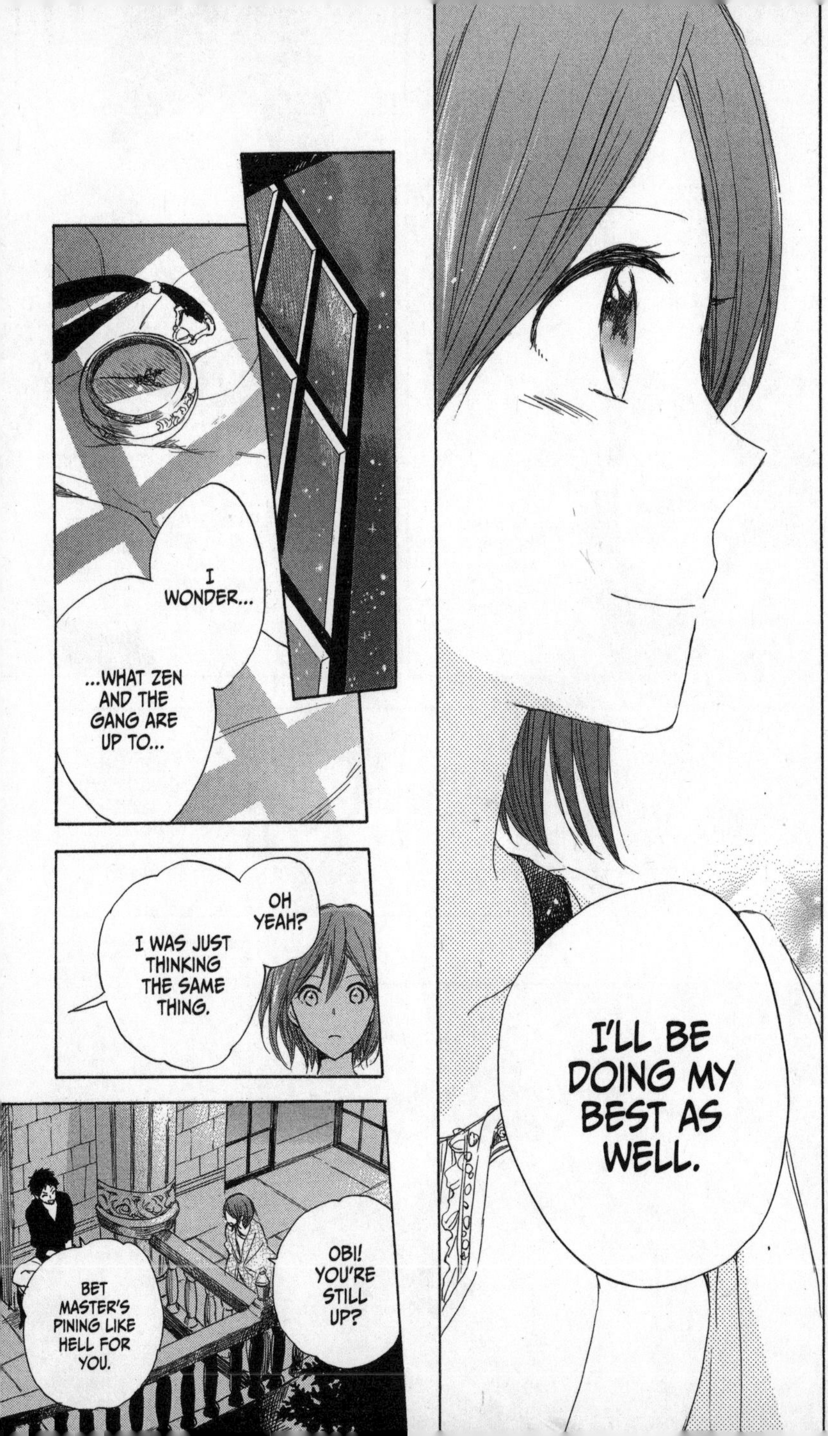
I'LL BE DOING MY BEST AS WELL.
I WONDER...
...WHAT ZEN AND THE GANG ARE UP TO...
OH YEAH?
I WAS JUST THINKING THE SAME THING.
OBI! YOU'RE STILL UP?
BET MASTER'S PINING LIKE HELL FOR YOU.

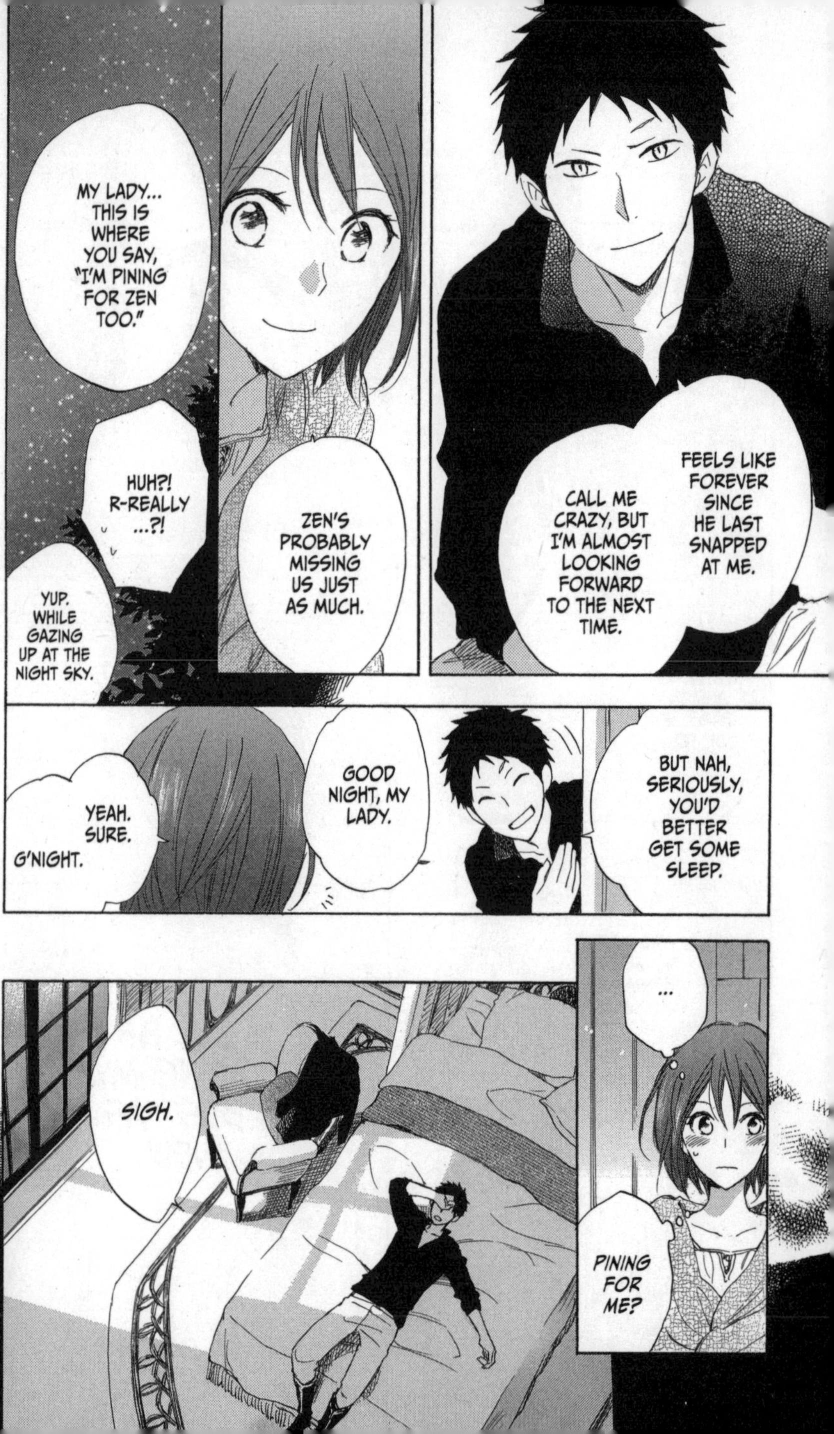
FEELS LIKE FOREVER SINCE HE LAST SNAPPED AT ME.
CALL ME CRAZY, BUT I'M ALMOST LOOKING FORWARD TO THE NEXT TIME.
ZEN'S PROBABLY MISSING US JUST AS MUCH.
MY LADY... THIS IS WHERE YOU SAY, "I'M PINING FOR ZEN TOO."
HUH?! R-REALLY ...?!
YUP. WHILE GAZING UP AT THE NIGHT SKY.
BUT NAH, SERIOUSLY, YOU'D BETTER GET SOME SLEEP.
GOOD NIGHT, MY LADY.
YEAH. SURE. G'NIGHT.
...
PINING FOR ME?
SIGH.

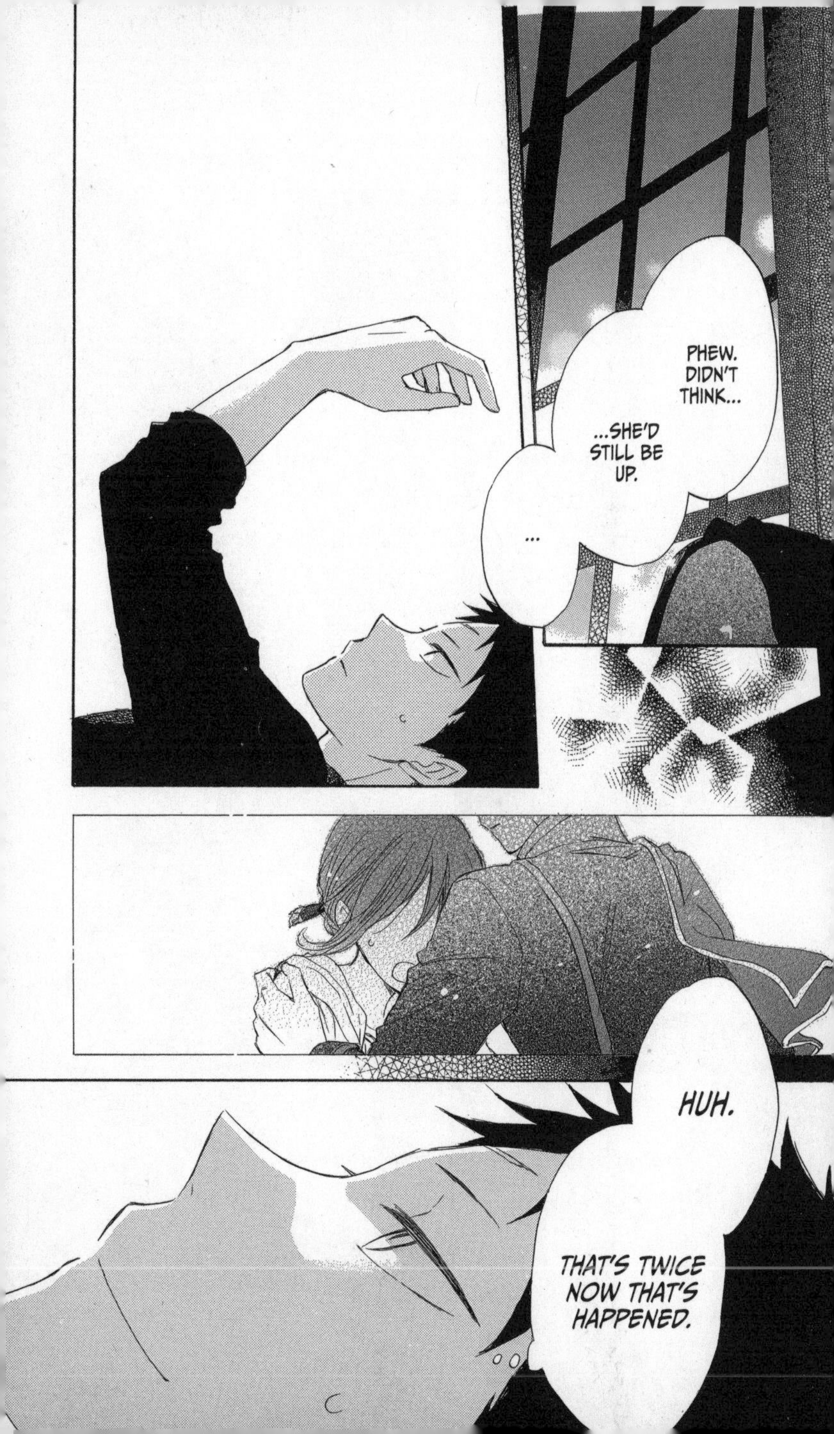
PHEW. DIDN'T THINK...
...SHE'D STILL BE UP.
...
HUH.
THAT'S TWICE NOW THAT'S HAPPENED.

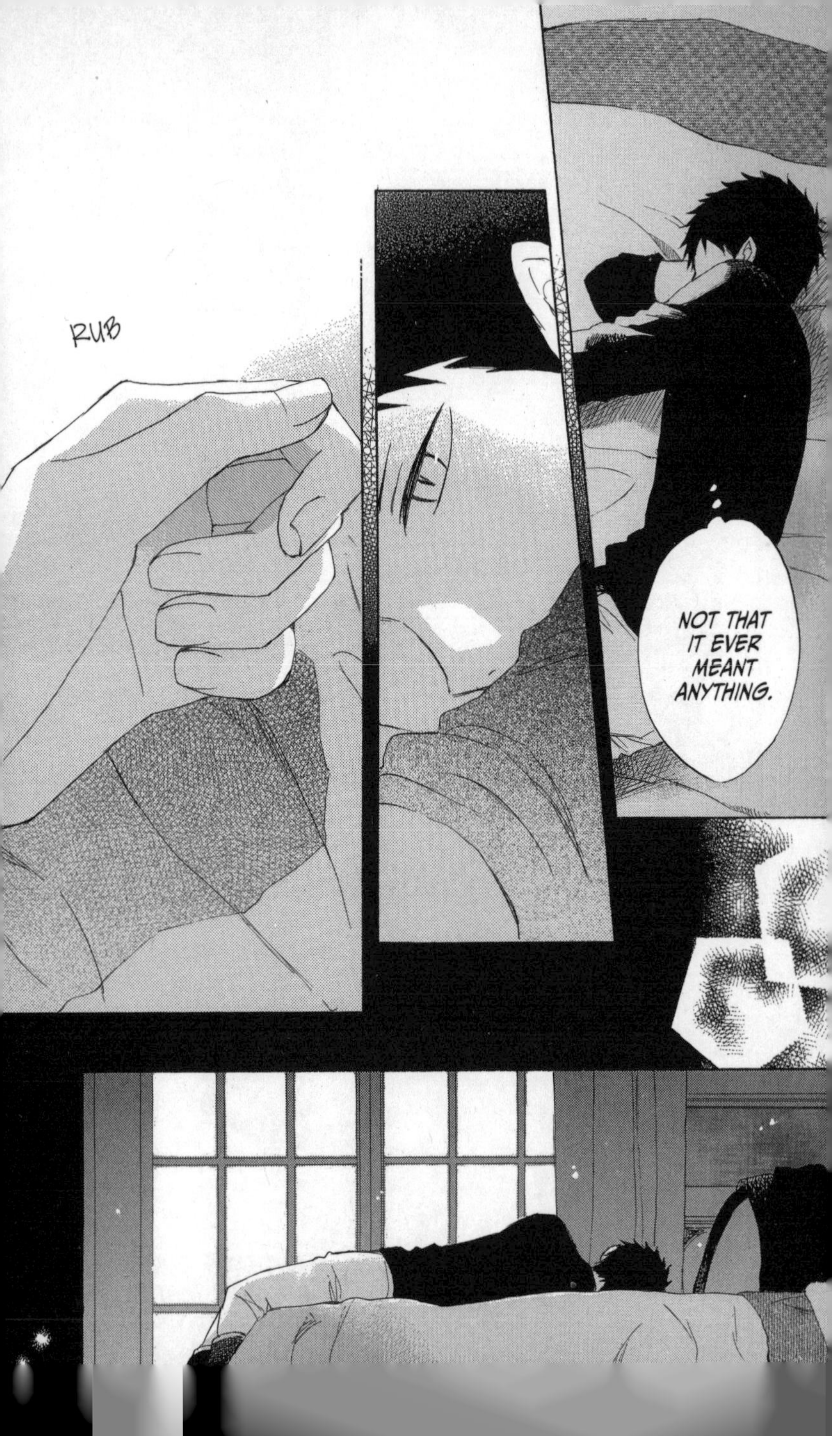
NOT THAT IT EVER MEANT ANYTHING.
RUB

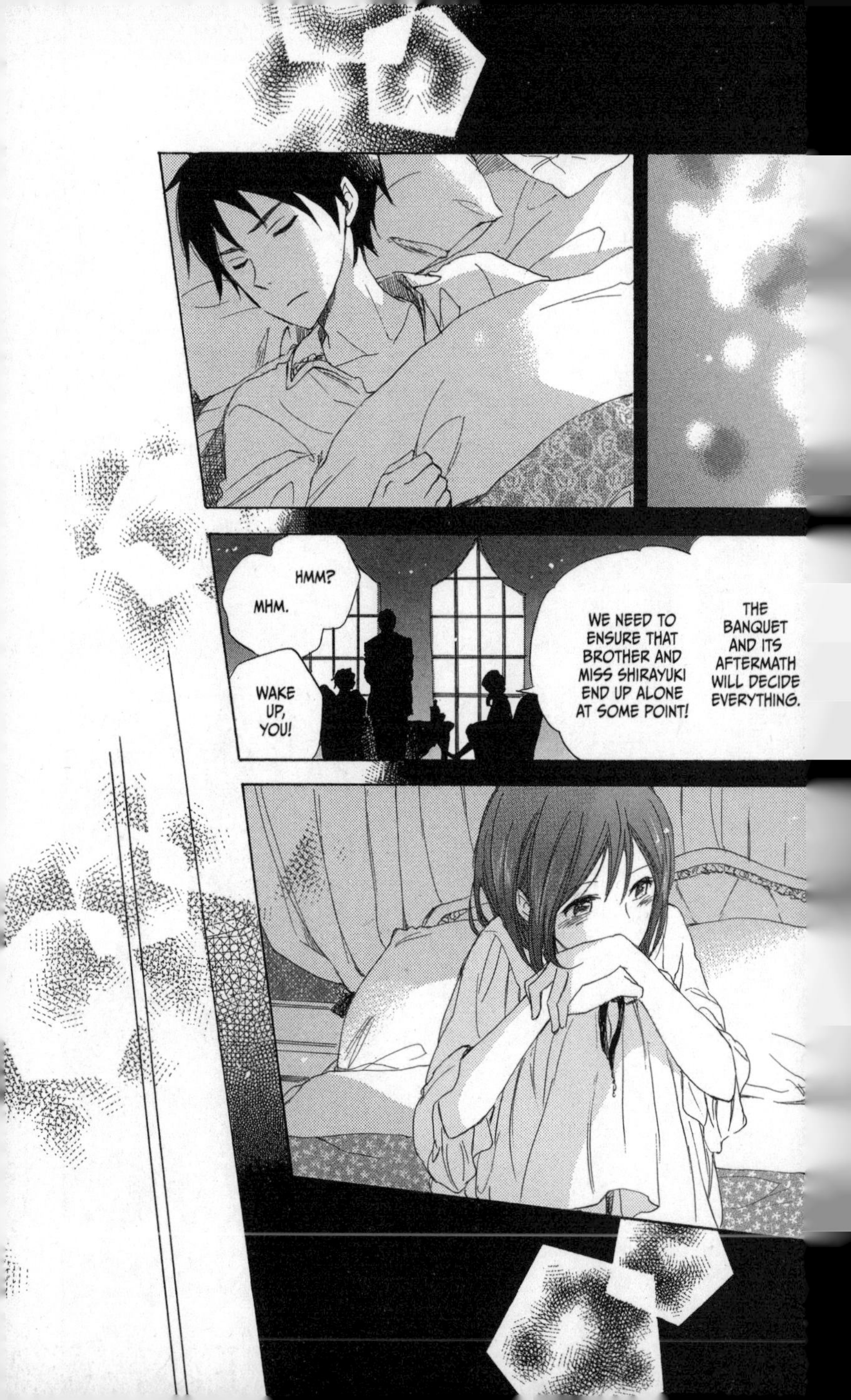
THE BANQUET AND ITS AFTERMATH WILL DECIDE EVERYTHING.
WE NEED TO ENSURE THAT BROTHER AND MISS SHIRAYUKI END UP ALONE AT SOME POINT!
HMM?
MHM.
WAKE UP, YOU!

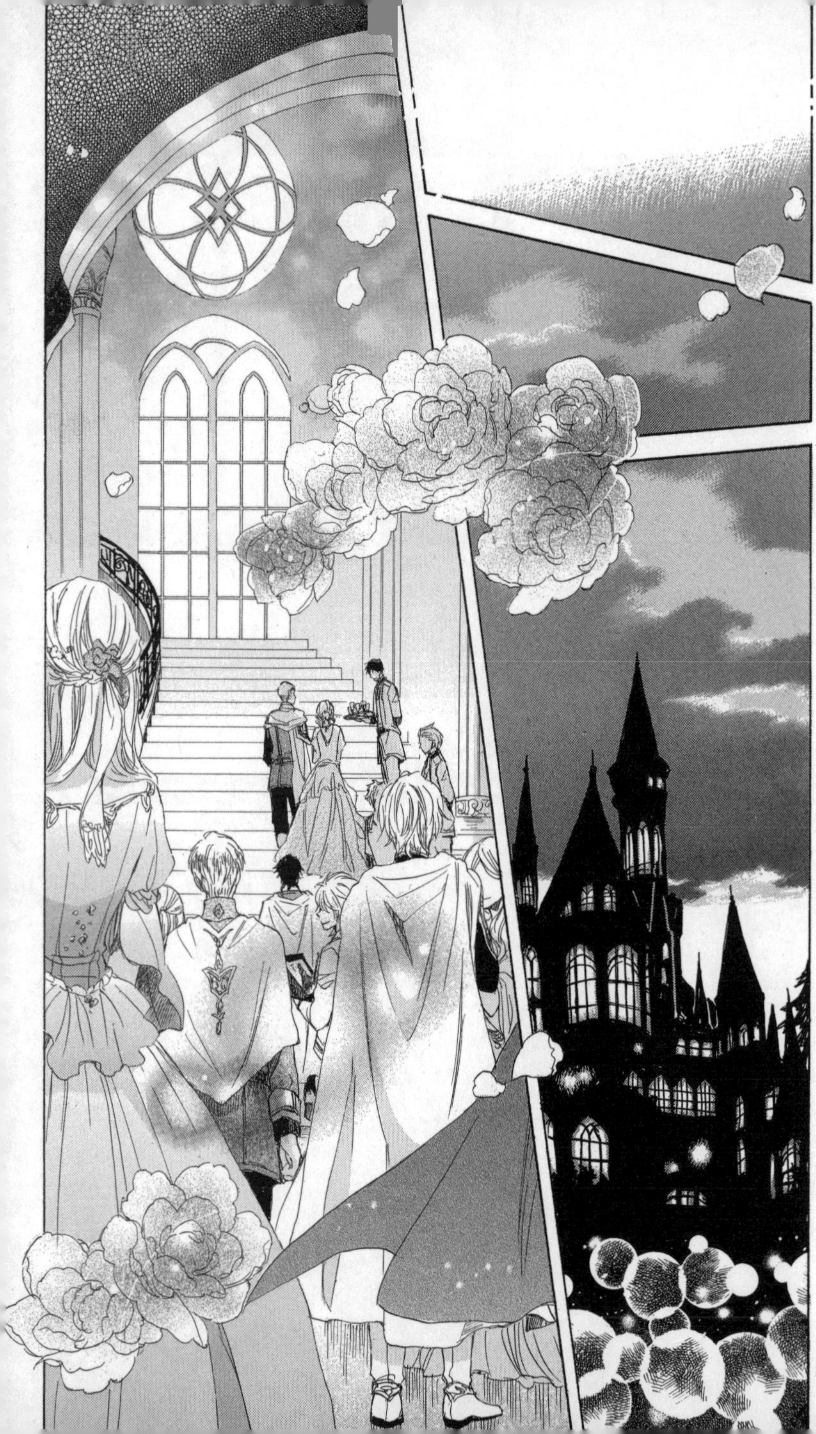

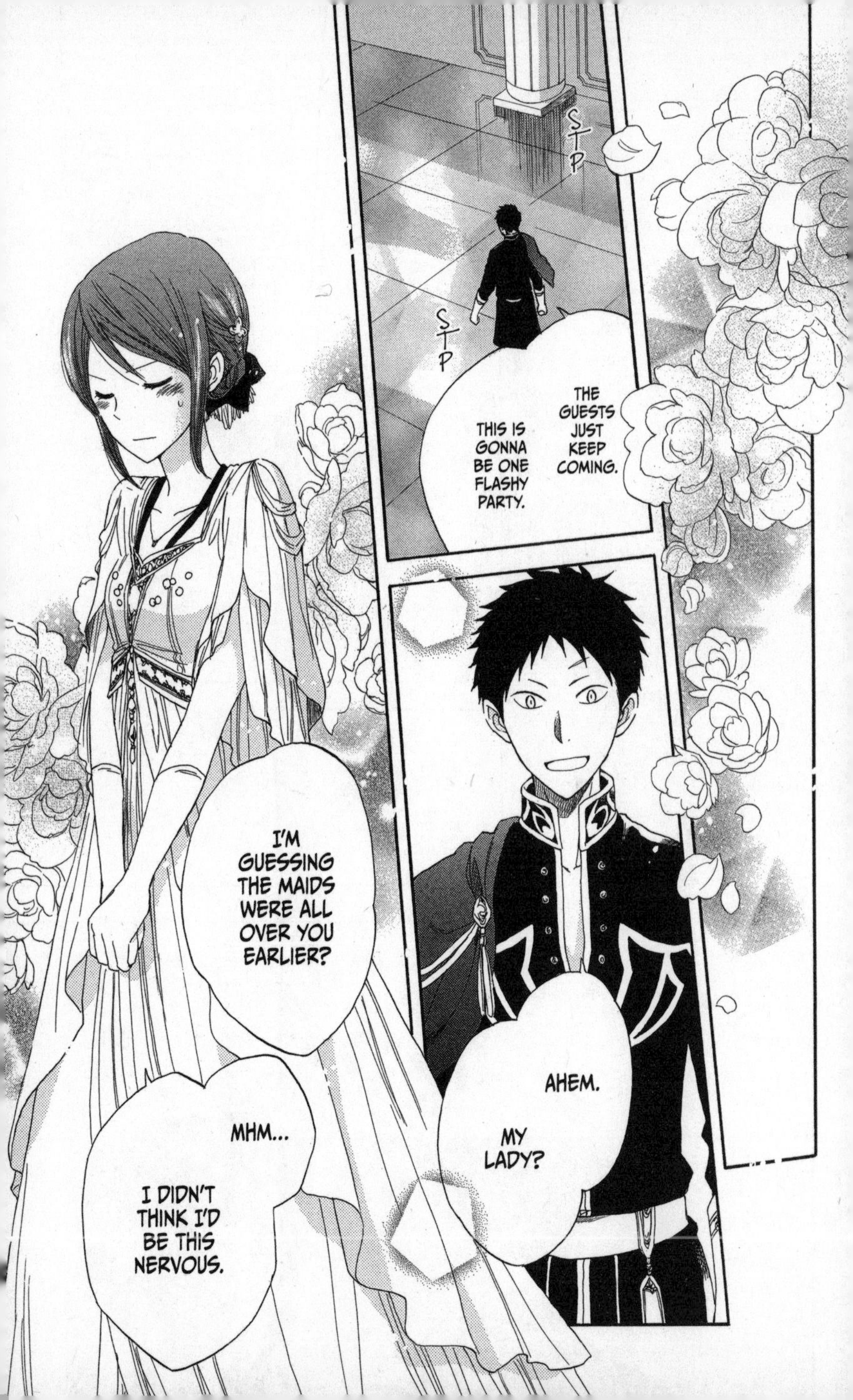
STP
STP
THE GUESTS JUST KEEP COMING.
THIS IS GONNA BE ONE FLASHY PARTY.
AHEM.
MY LADY?
I'M GUESSING THE MAIDS WERE ALL OVER YOU EARLIER?
MHM...
I DIDN'T THINK I'D BE THIS NERVOUS.

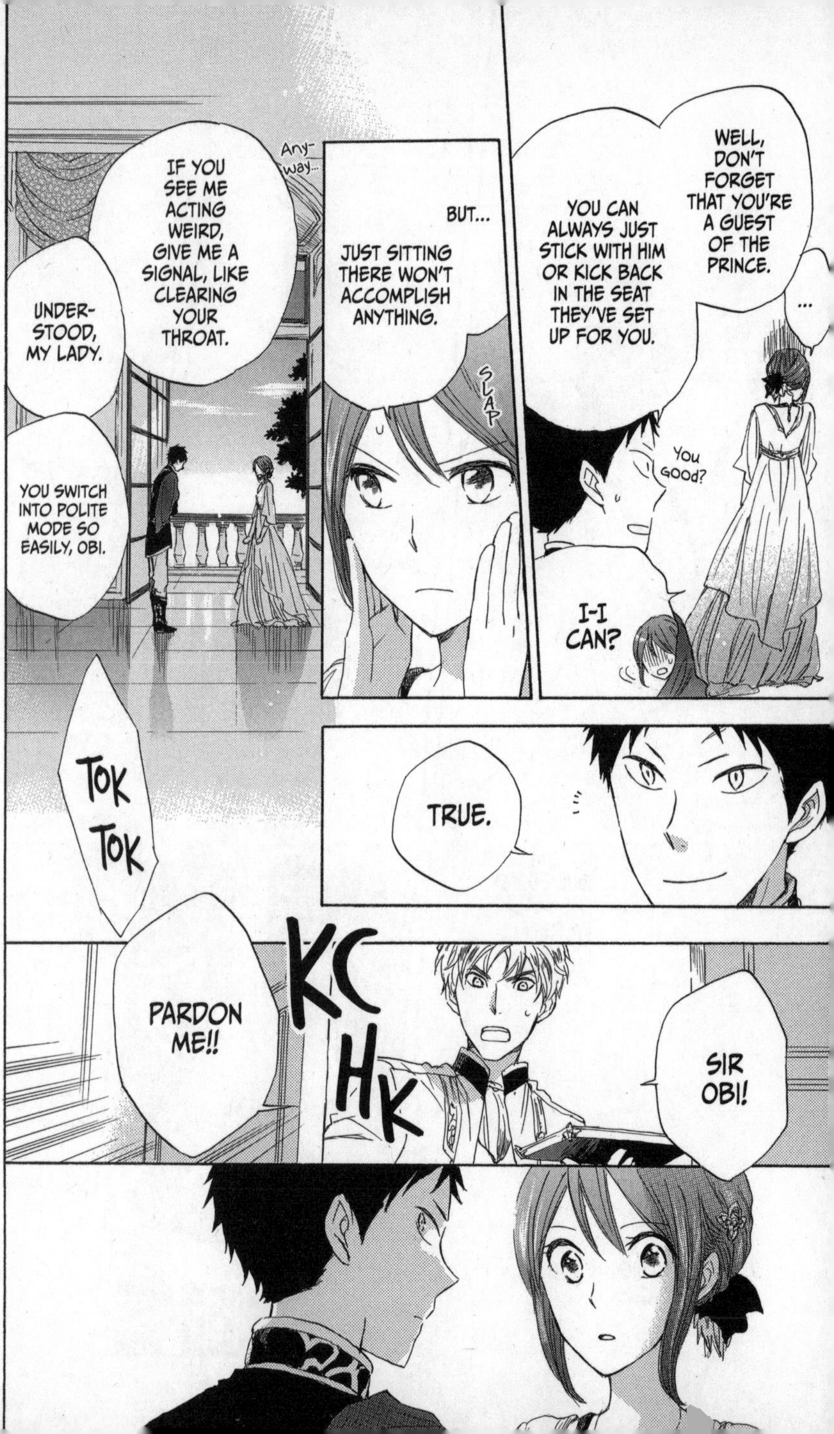
WELL, DON'T FORGET THAT YOU'RE A GUEST OF THE PRINCE.
...
YOU CAN ALWAYS JUST STICK WITH HIM OR KICK BACK IN THE SEAT THEY'VE SET UP FOR YOU.
You good?
I-I CAN?
BUT...
JUST SITTING THERE WON'T ACCOMPLISH ANYTHING.
SLAP
TRUE.
Any-way...
IF YOU SEE ME ACTING WEIRD, GIVE ME A SIGNAL, LIKE CLEARING YOUR THROAT.
UNDER-STOOD, MY LADY.
YOU SWITCH INTO POLITE MODE SO EASILY, OBI.
TOK TOK
SIR OBI!
KCHHK
PARDON ME!!

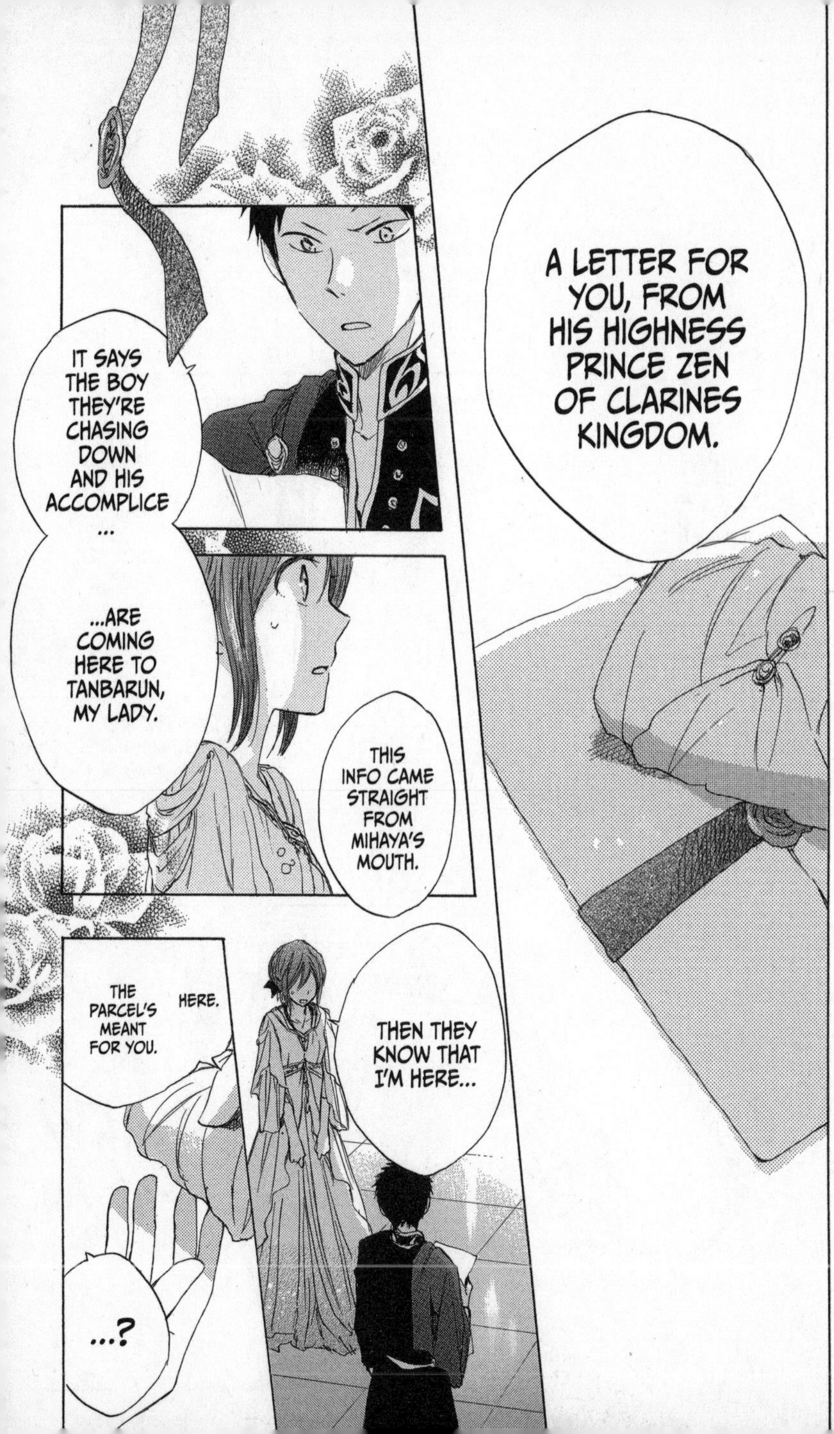
A LETTER FOR YOU, FROM HIS HIGHNESS PRINCE ZEN OF CLARINES KINGDOM.
IT SAYS THE BOY THEY'RE CHASING DOWN AND HIS ACCOMPLICE ...
...ARE COMING HERE TO TANBARUN, MY LADY.
THIS INFO CAME STRAIGHT FROM MIHAYA'S MOUTH.
THEN THEY KNOW THAT I'M HERE...
HERE.
THE PARCEL'S MEANT FOR YOU.
...?

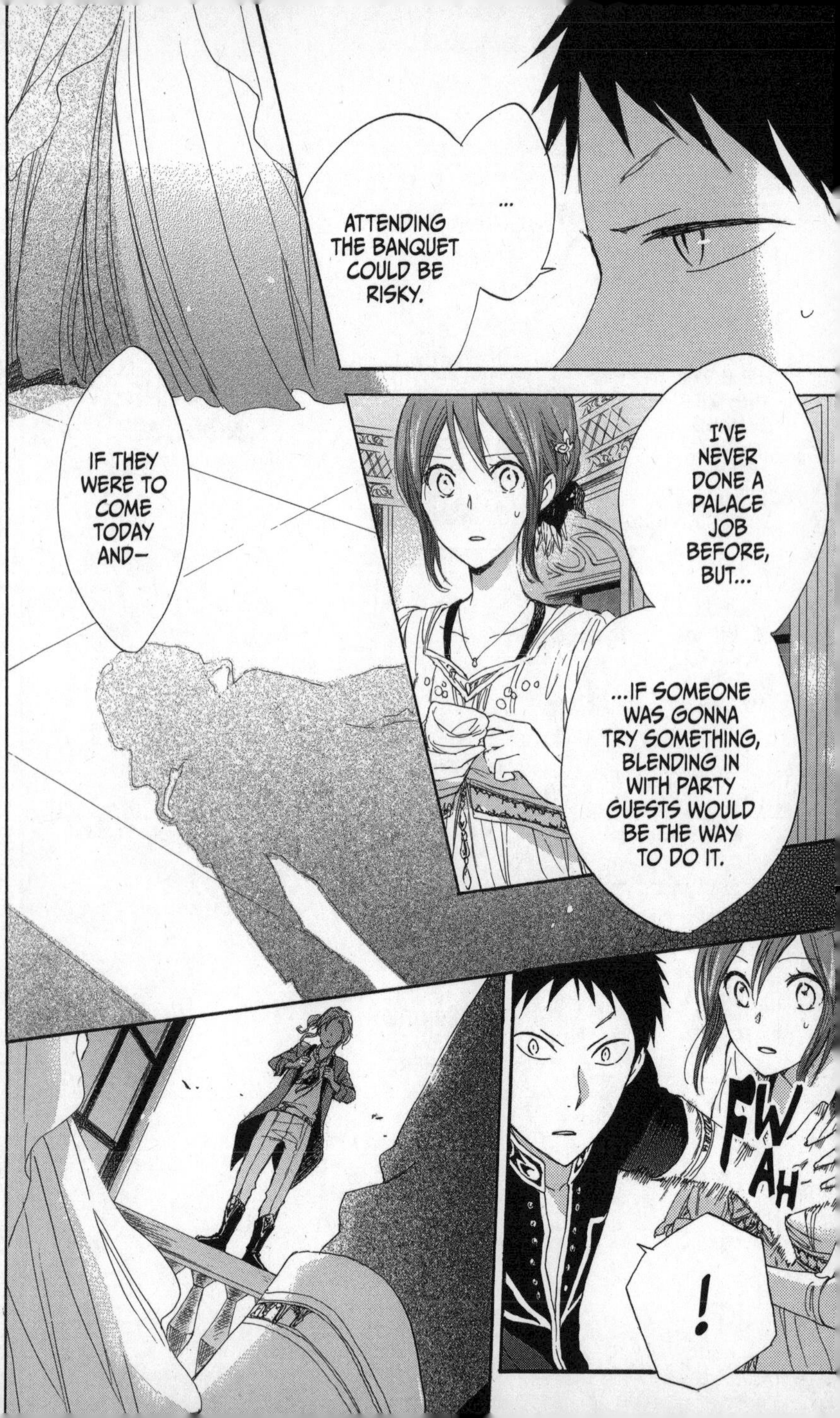
...
ATTENDING THE BANQUET COULD BE RISKY.
IF THEY WERE TO COME TODAY AND—
I'VE NEVER DONE A PALACE JOB BEFORE, BUT...
...IF SOMEONE WAS GONNA TRY SOMETHING, BLENDING IN WITH PARTY GUESTS WOULD BE THE WAY TO DO IT.
FWAH
!

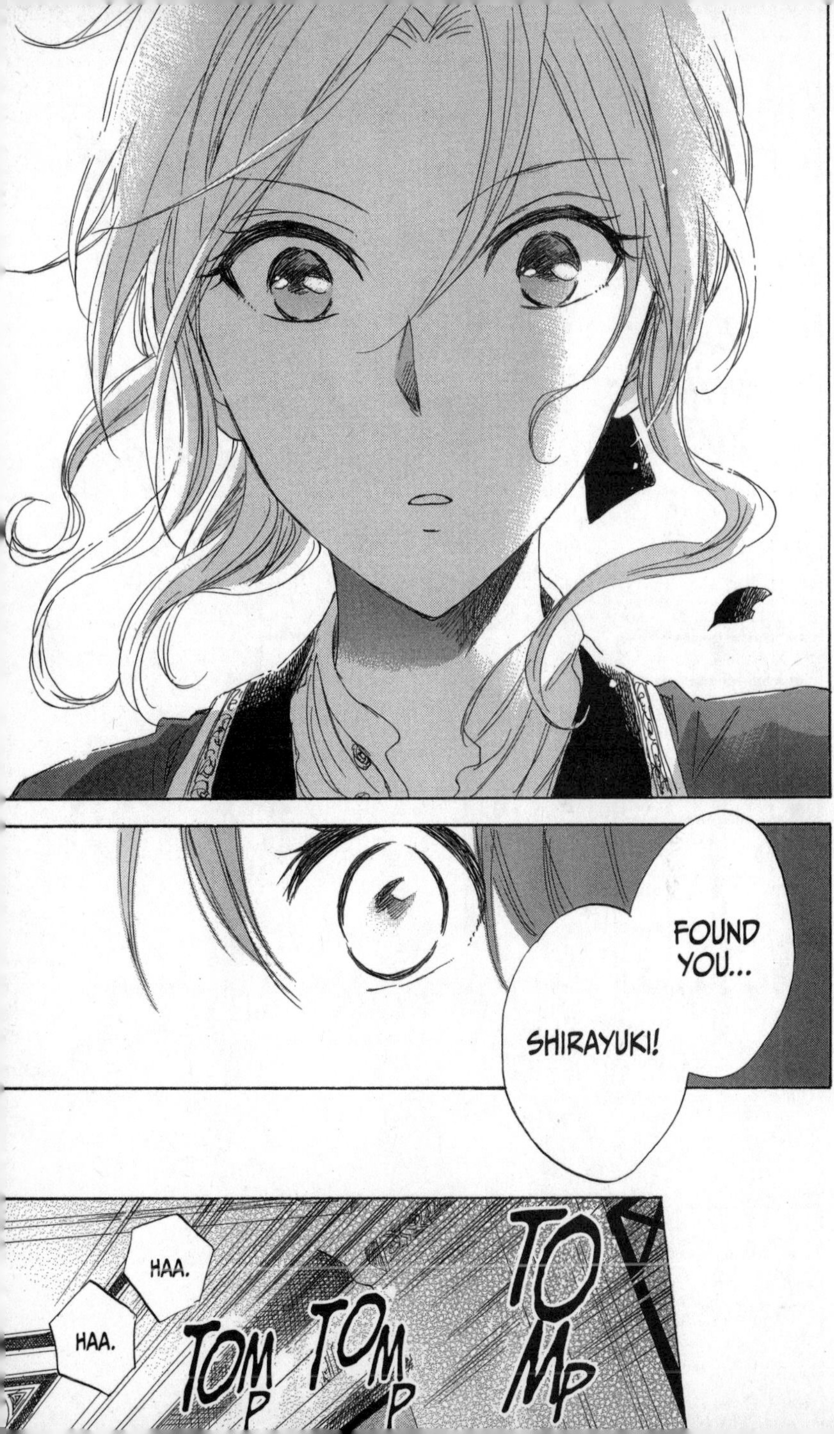
FOUND YOU...
SHIRAYUKI!
TOMP
TOMP
TOMP
HAA.
HAA.

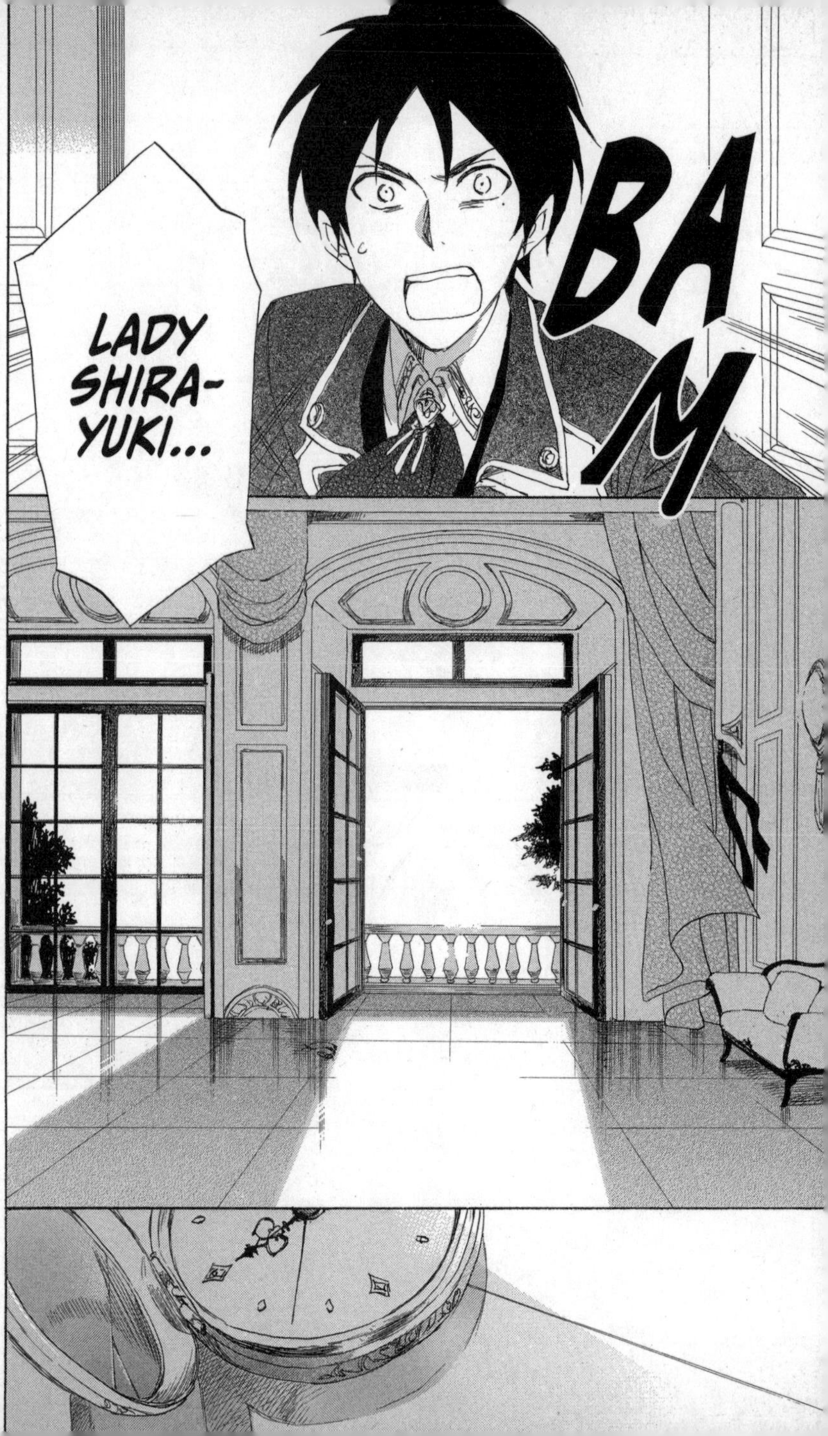
BAM
LADY SHIRA-YUKI...

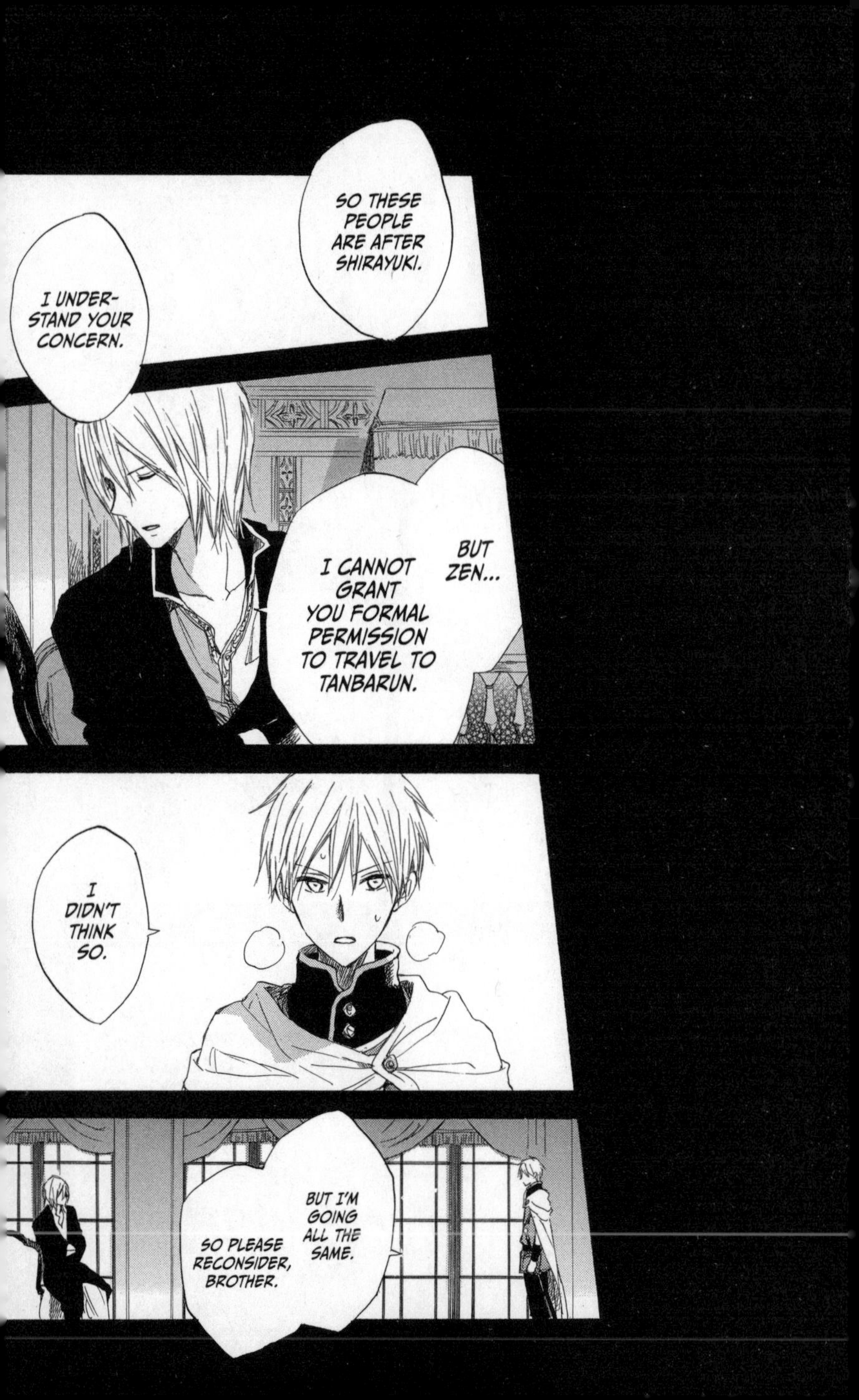
SO THESE PEOPLE ARE AFTER SHIRAYUKI.
I UNDER-STAND YOUR CONCERN.
BUT ZEN...
I CANNOT GRANT YOU FORMAL PERMISSION TO TRAVEL TO TANBARUN.
I DIDN'T THINK SO.
BUT I'M GOING ALL THE SAME.
SO PLEASE RECONSIDER, BROTHER.

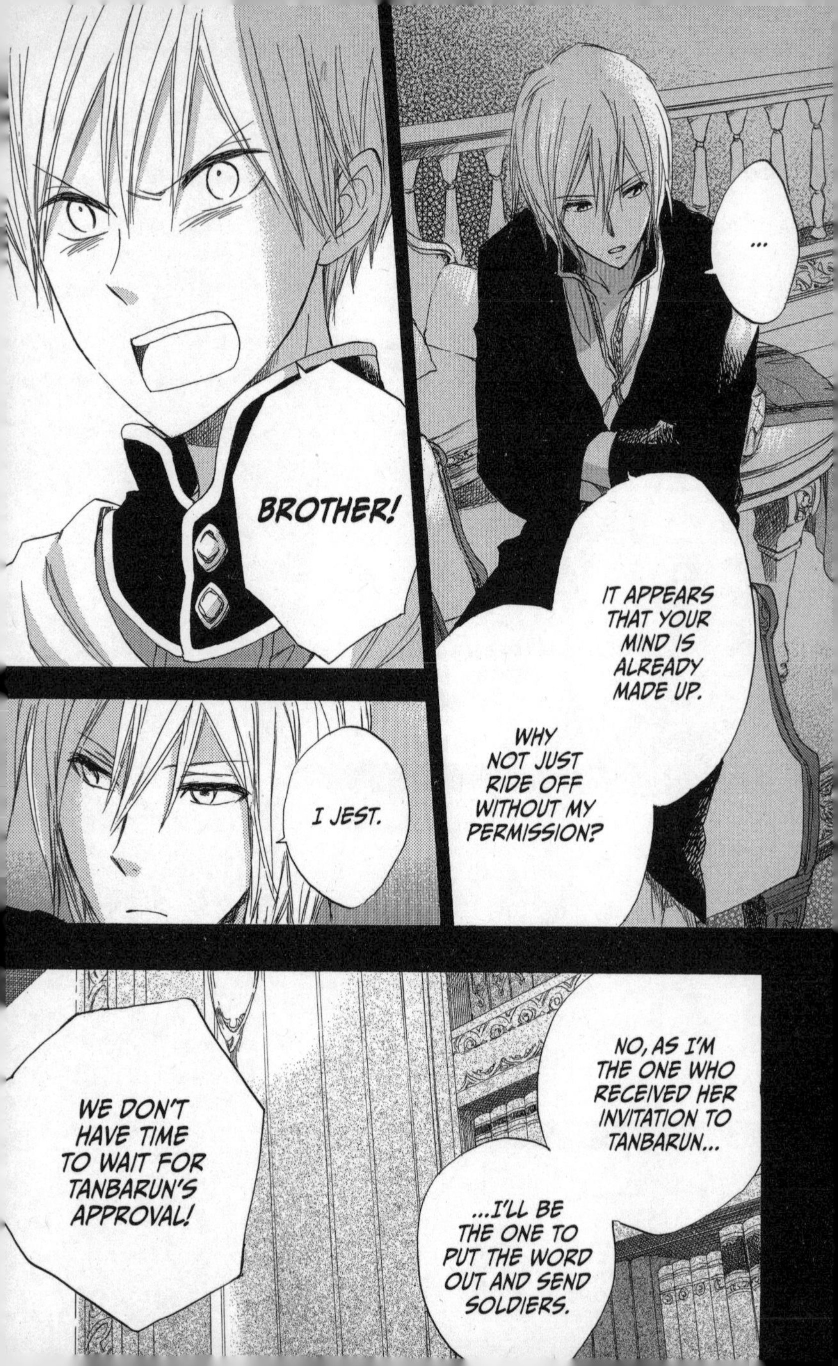
...
IT APPEARS THAT YOUR MIND IS ALREADY MADE UP.
WHY NOT JUST RIDE OFF WITHOUT MY PERMISSION?
BROTHER!
I JEST.
WE DON'T HAVE TIME TO WAIT FOR TANBARUN'S APPROVAL!
NO, AS I'M THE ONE WHO RECEIVED HER INVITATION TO TANBARUN...
...I'LL BE THE ONE TO PUT THE WORD OUT AND SEND SOLDIERS.

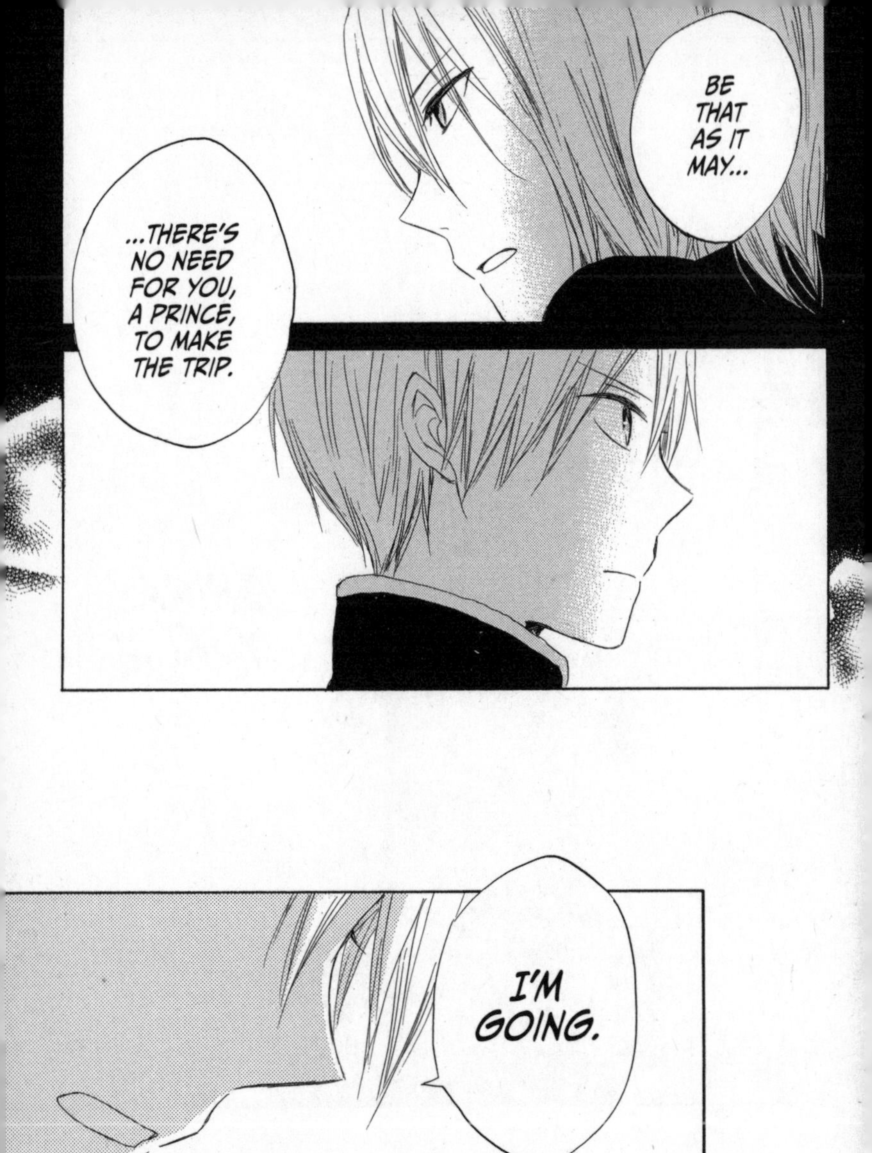
BE THAT AS IT MAY...
...THERE'S NO NEED FOR YOU, A PRINCE, TO MAKE THE TRIP.
I'M GOING.

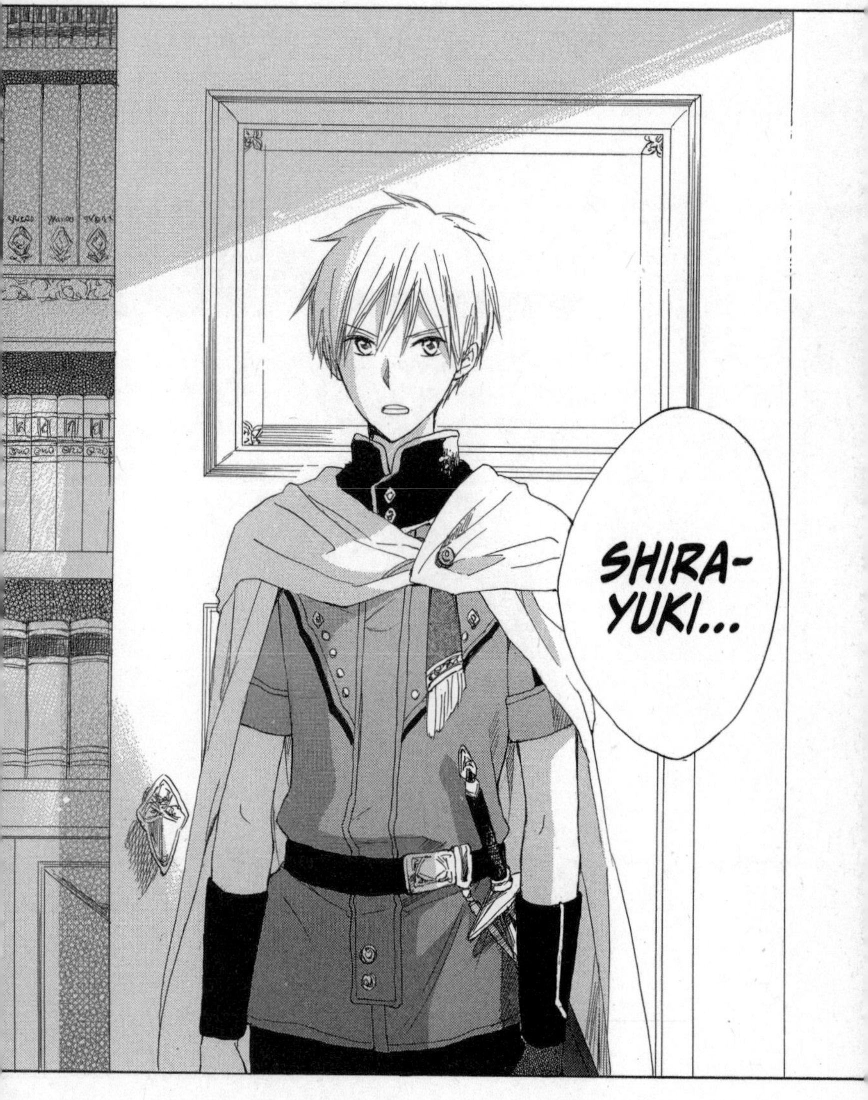
SHIRA-YUKI...

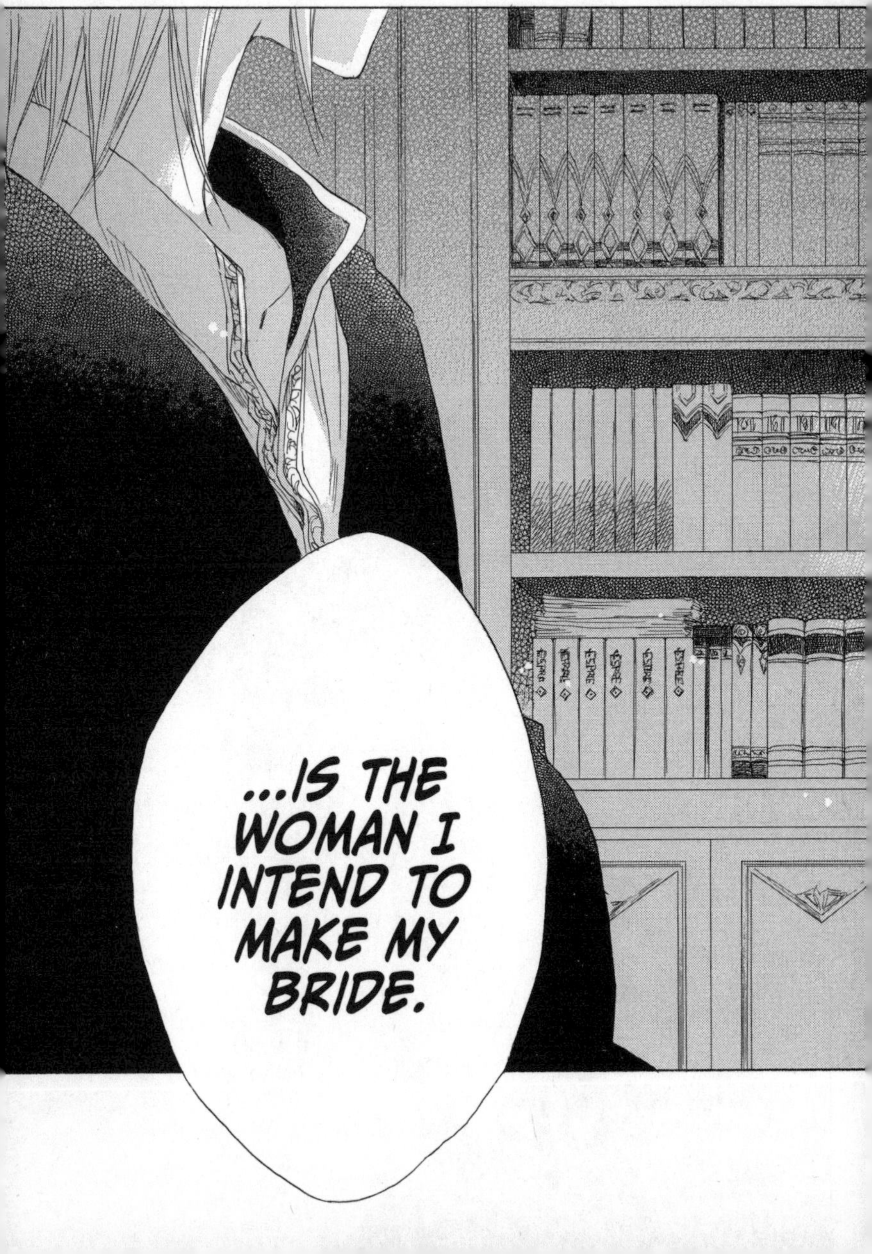
...IS THE WOMAN I INTEND TO MAKE MY BRIDE.

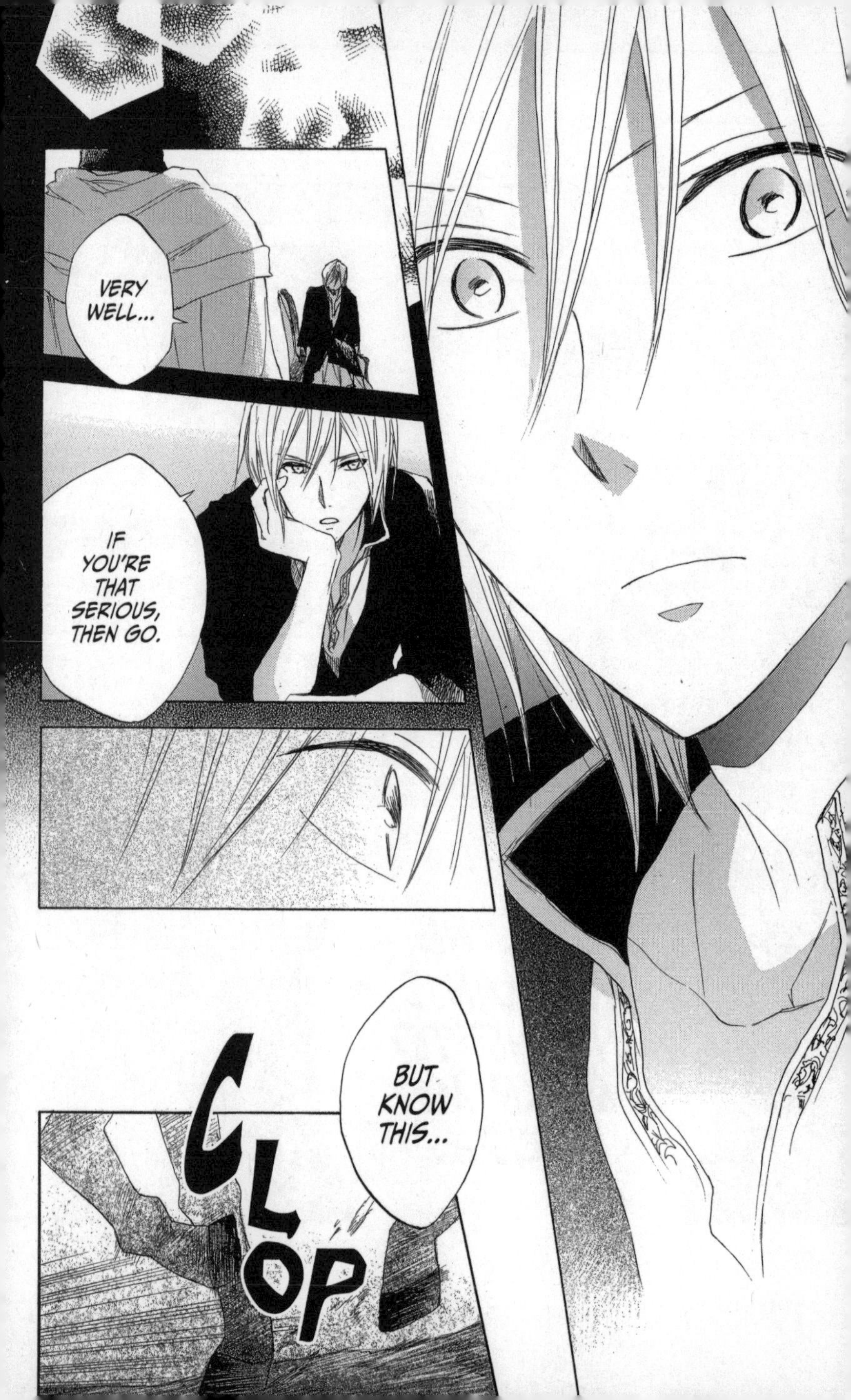
VERY WELL...
IF YOU'RE THAT SERIOUS, THEN GO.
BUT KNOW THIS...
CLOP

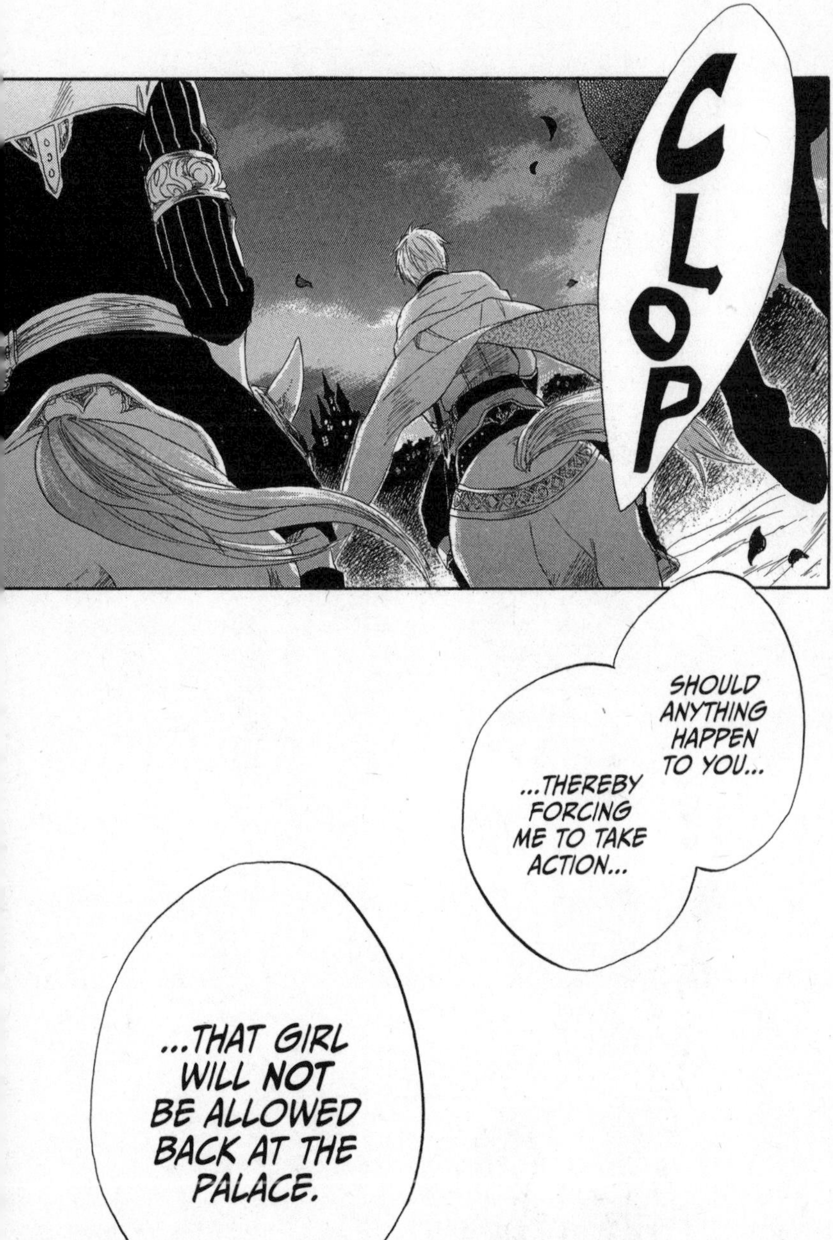
CLOP
SHOULD ANYTHING HAPPEN TO YOU...
...THEREBY FORCING ME TO TAKE ACTION...
...THAT GIRL WILL NOT BE ALLOWED BACK AT THE PALACE.

"Unrelated to the Main Plot" Theater #1

WISTAL PALACE
SPARKL
SPARKL
SPARKL
SPARKL
YOUR FEMALE WAITSTAFF, MASTER...
THEY CERTAINLY AREN'T LACKING IN THE LOOKS DEPARTMENT.
YEAH, I GUESS?
I SEE HOW IT IS...
DON'T YOU DARE IMPLY I'M COLLECTING A HAREM.
Damn you, Obi.
You'd better not bring this up to Shirayuki.
YOU THINK SO TOO, RIGHT, MITSUHIDE ...?
OH. BUT YOU'VE ALSO GOT A BEAUTY BY YOUR SIDE, AND I AIN'T TALKING ABOUT THE MAID.
I DON'T FOLLOW.
Are you listen-ing to me?

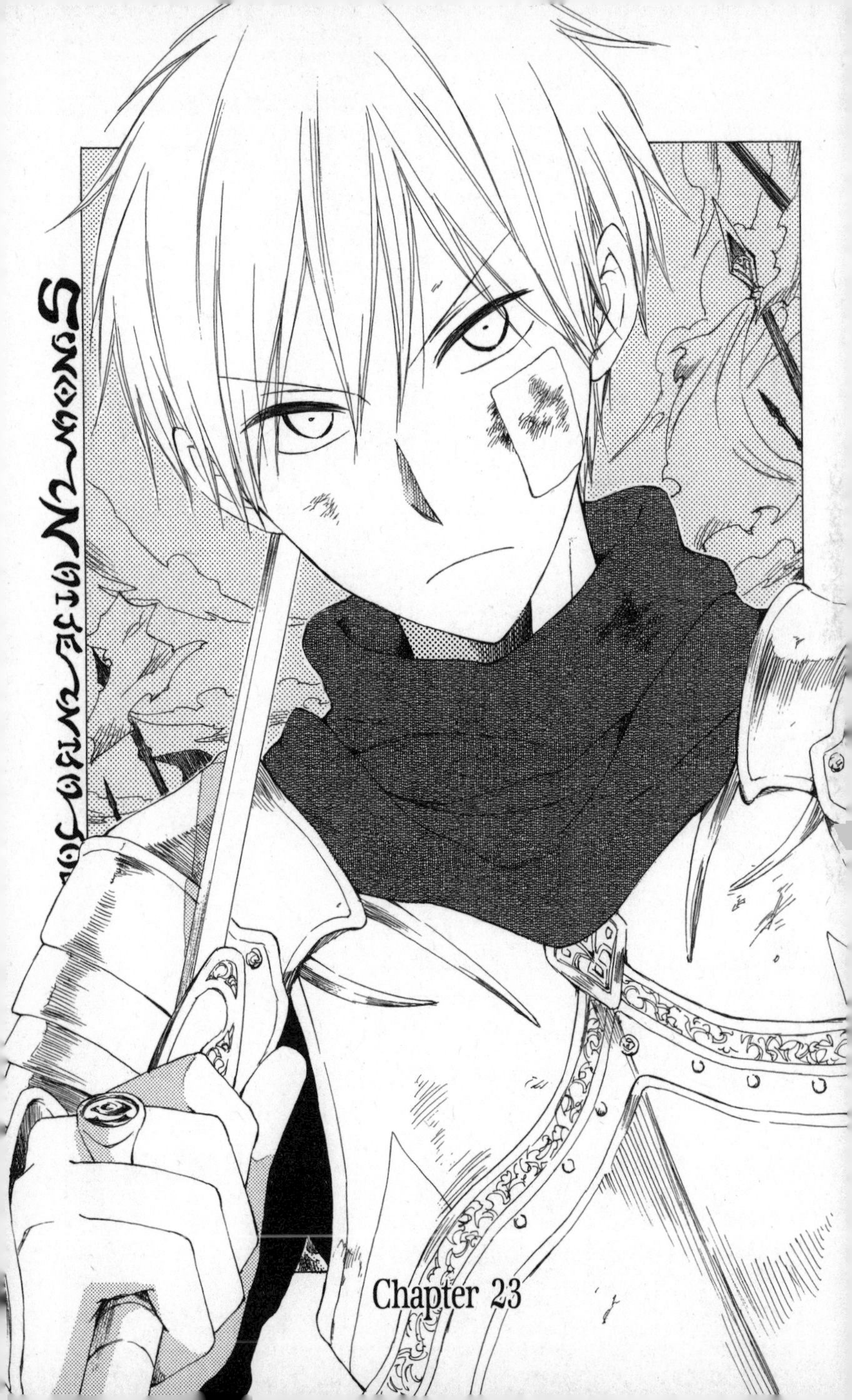
Chapter 23

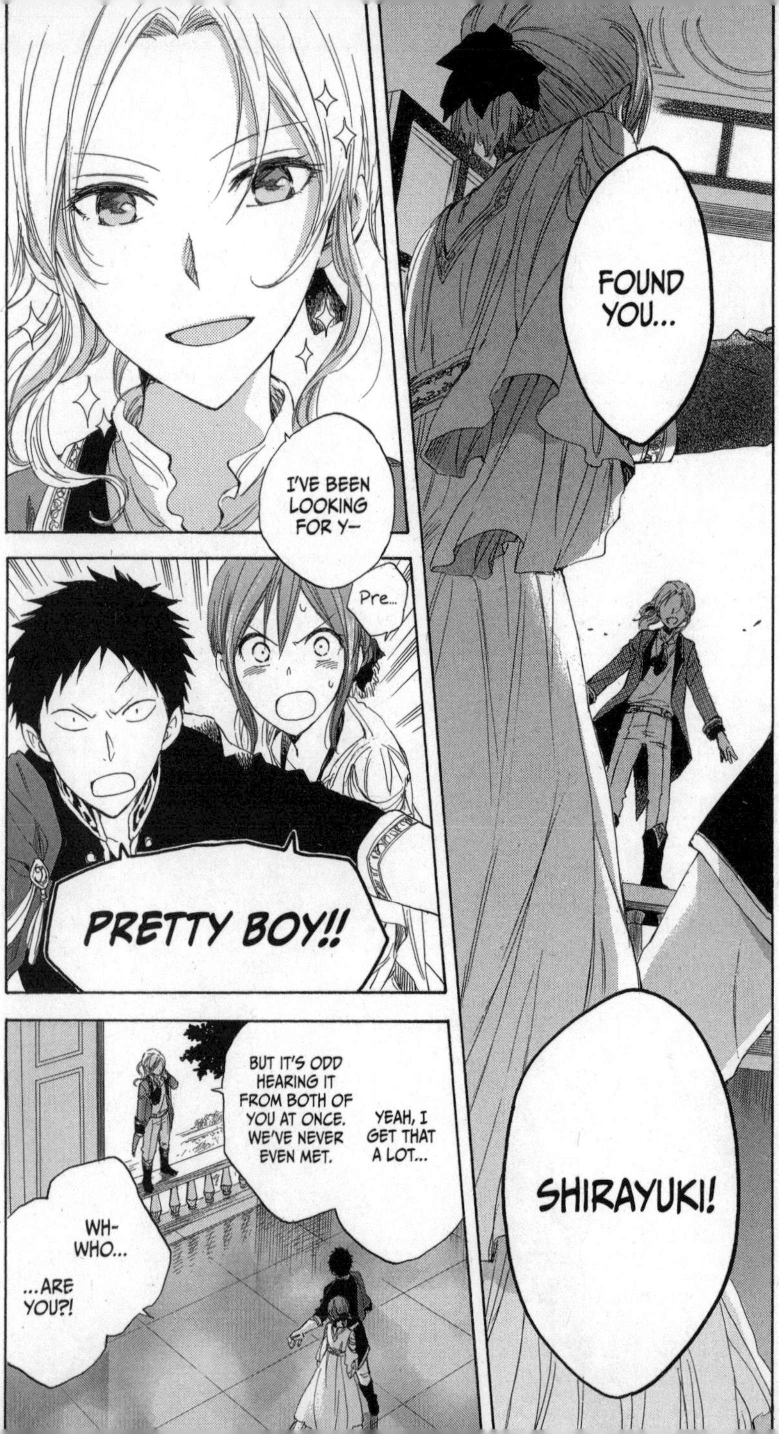
FOUND YOU...
SHIRAYUKI!
I'VE BEEN LOOKING FOR Y—
Pre...
PRETTY BOY!!
YEAH, I GET THAT A LOT...
BUT IT'S ODD HEARING IT FROM BOTH OF YOU AT ONCE. WE'VE NEVER EVEN MET.
WH- WHO...
...ARE YOU?!

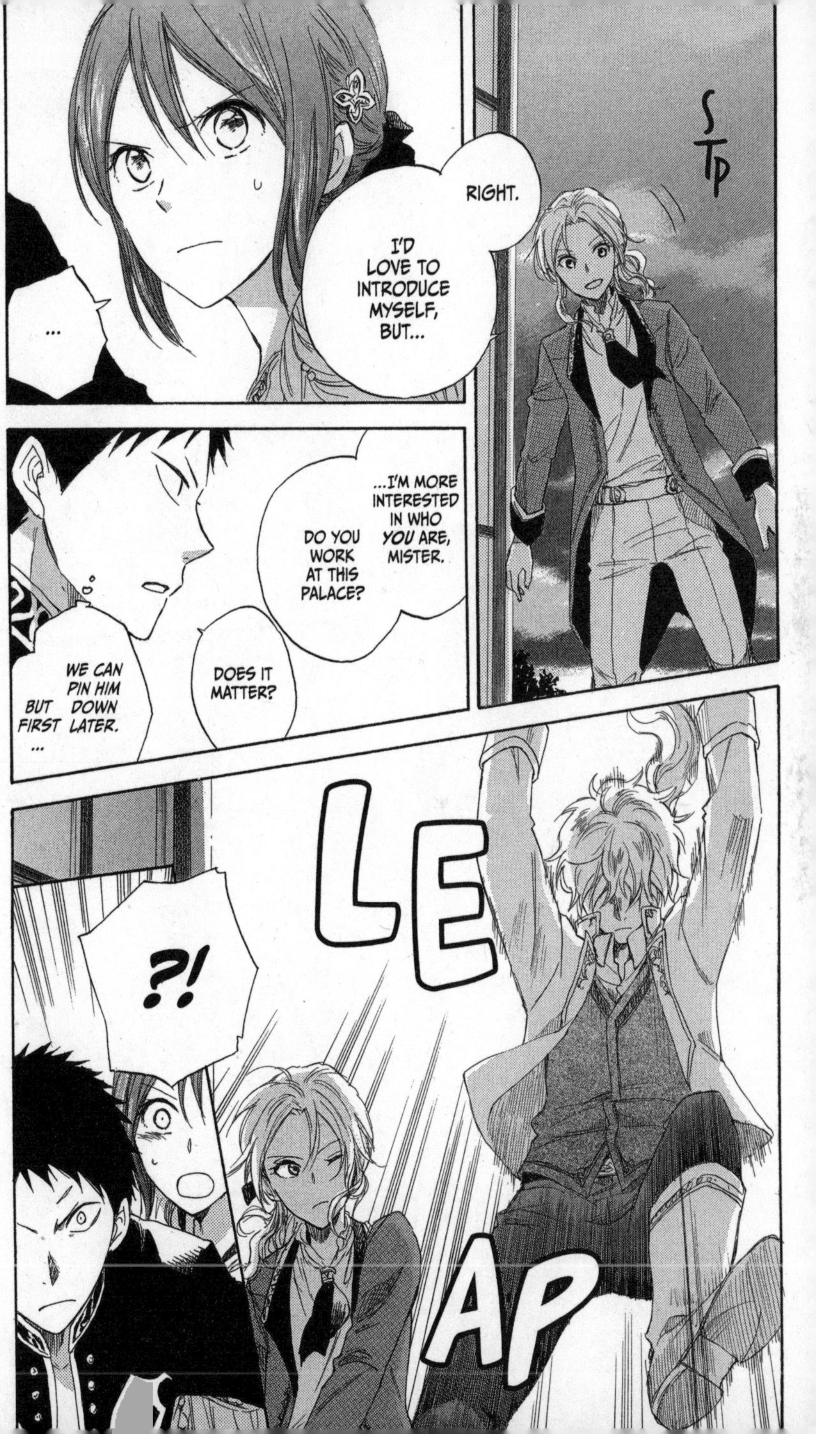
STP
RIGHT.
I'D LOVE TO INTRODUCE MYSELF, BUT...
...
...I'M MORE INTERESTED IN WHO *YOU* ARE, MISTER.
DO YOU WORK AT THIS PALACE?
DOES IT MATTER?
WE CAN PIN HIM DOWN LATER.
BUT FIRST ...
LEAP
?!

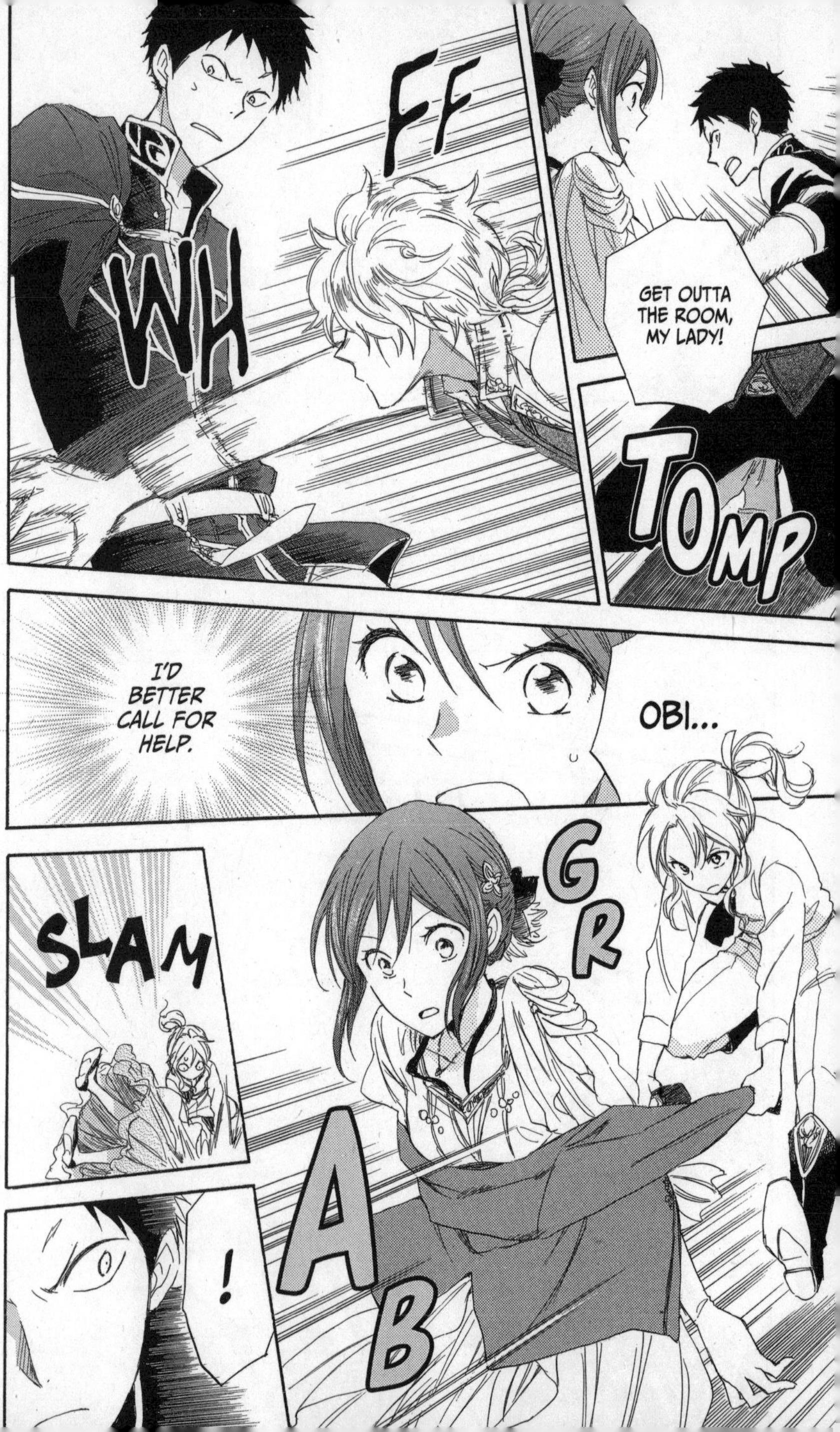
GET OUTTA THE ROOM, MY LADY!
TOMP
WH
FF
OBI...
I'D BETTER CALL FOR HELP.
GR
A
B
SLAM
!

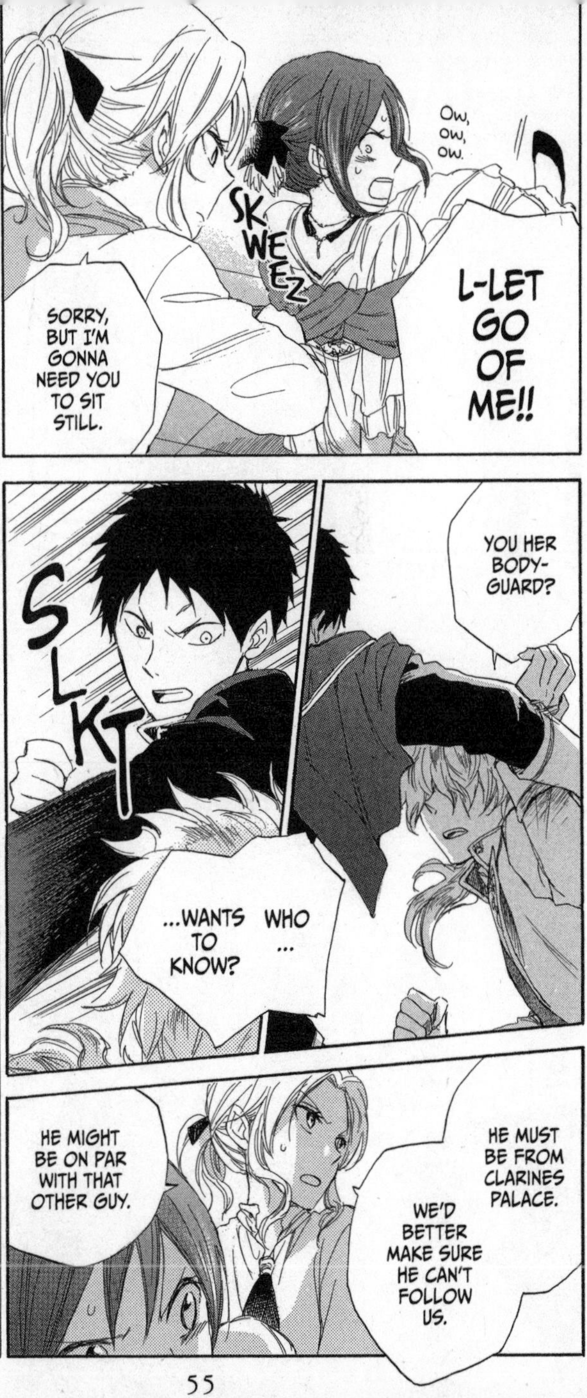
Ow, ow, ow.
L-LET GO OF ME!!
SKWEEZ
SORRY, BUT I'M GONNA NEED YOU TO SIT STILL.
YOU HER BODY-GUARD?
SLKT
WHO ...
...WANTS TO KNOW?
HE MUST BE FROM CLARINES PALACE.
WE'D BETTER MAKE SURE HE CAN'T FOLLOW US.
HE MIGHT BE ON PAR WITH THAT OTHER GUY.

Q: "Does Ryu have a proper room and bed?"

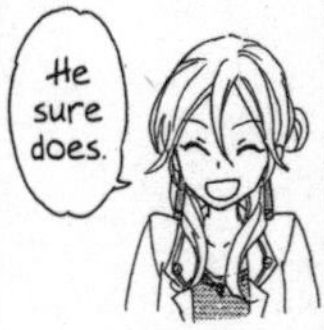
He sure does.

Testimony from his boss

Yes, he does change into pajamas and sleep normally. Though, even in his own room, he often sleeps on the floor.

Since he lives all by his lonesome, Chief Garak stops by to hang out from time to time.

And Shirayuki comes by to greet him in the morning every now and then.

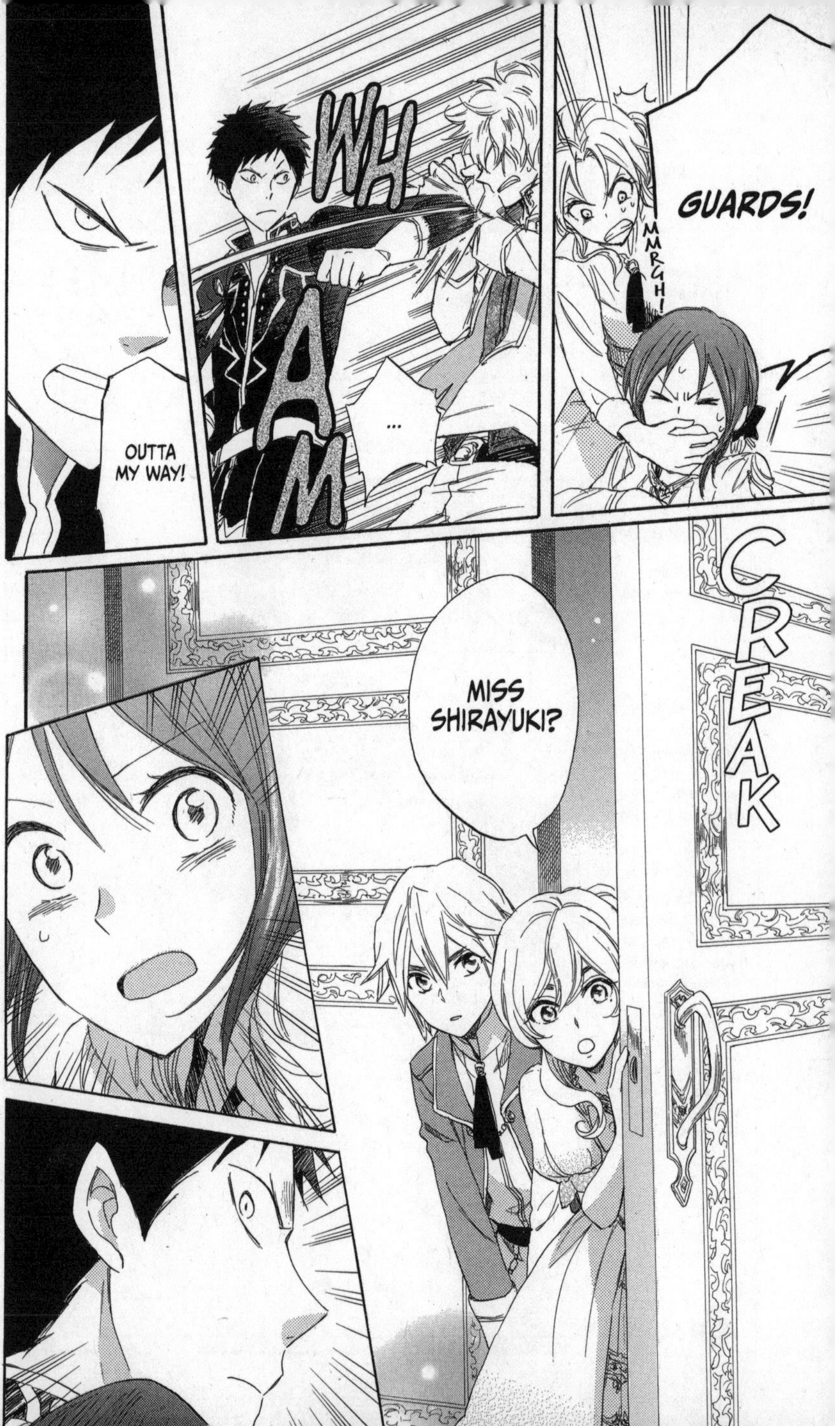
GUARDS!
MMRGH!
WHAM
...
OUTTA MY WAY!
CREAK
MISS SHIRAYUKI?

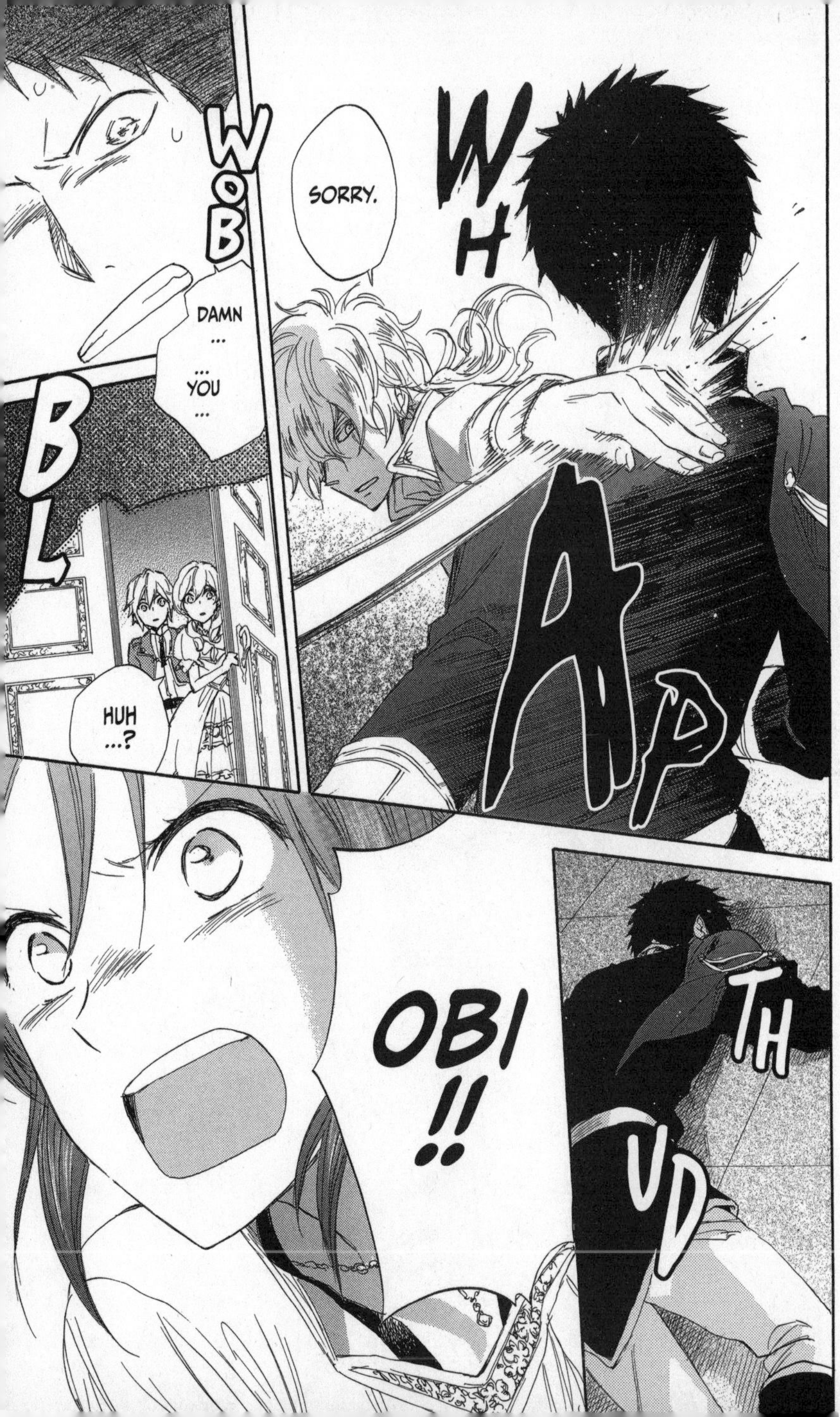
WHAP
SORRY.
WOB
DAMN ... ... YOU ...
BL
HUH ...?
THUD
OBI!!

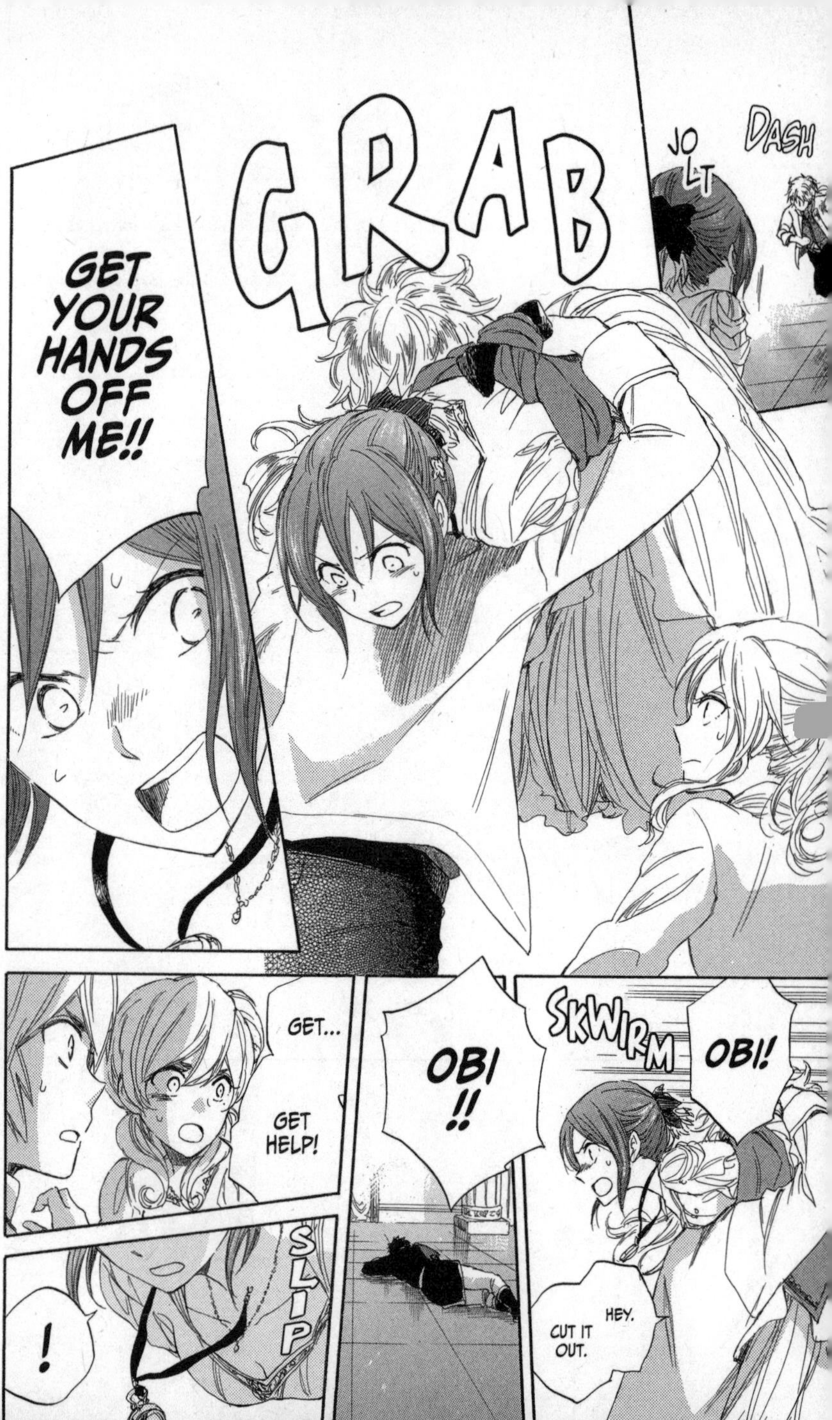
JOLT
DASH
GRAB
GET YOUR HANDS OFF ME!!
SKWIRM
OBI!
HEY. CUT IT OUT.
OBI !!
GET...
GET HELP!
!
SLIP

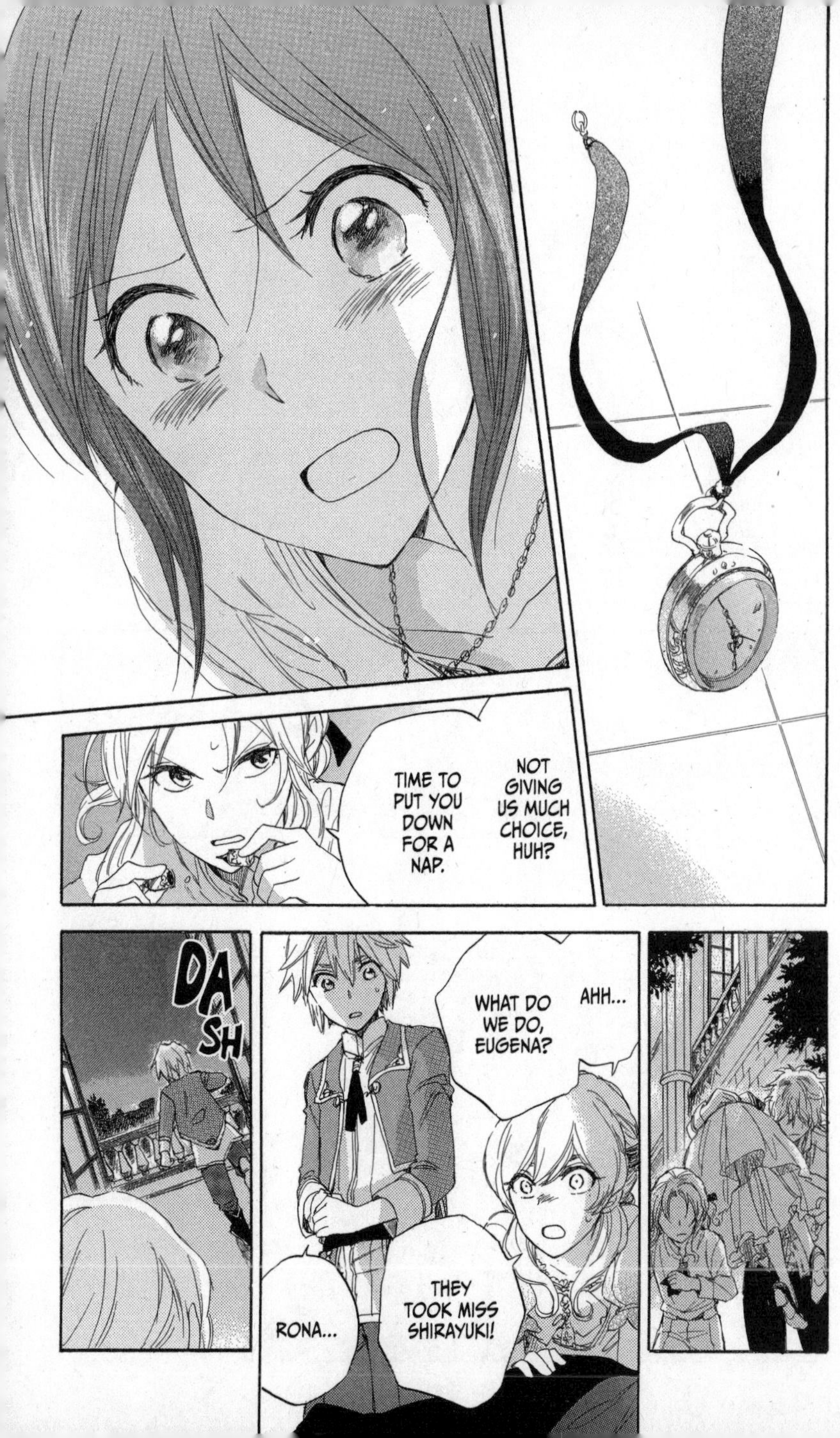
NOT GIVING US MUCH CHOICE, HUH?
TIME TO PUT YOU DOWN FOR A NAP.
AHH...
WHAT DO WE DO, EUGENA?
THEY TOOK MISS SHIRAYUKI!
RONA...
DASH

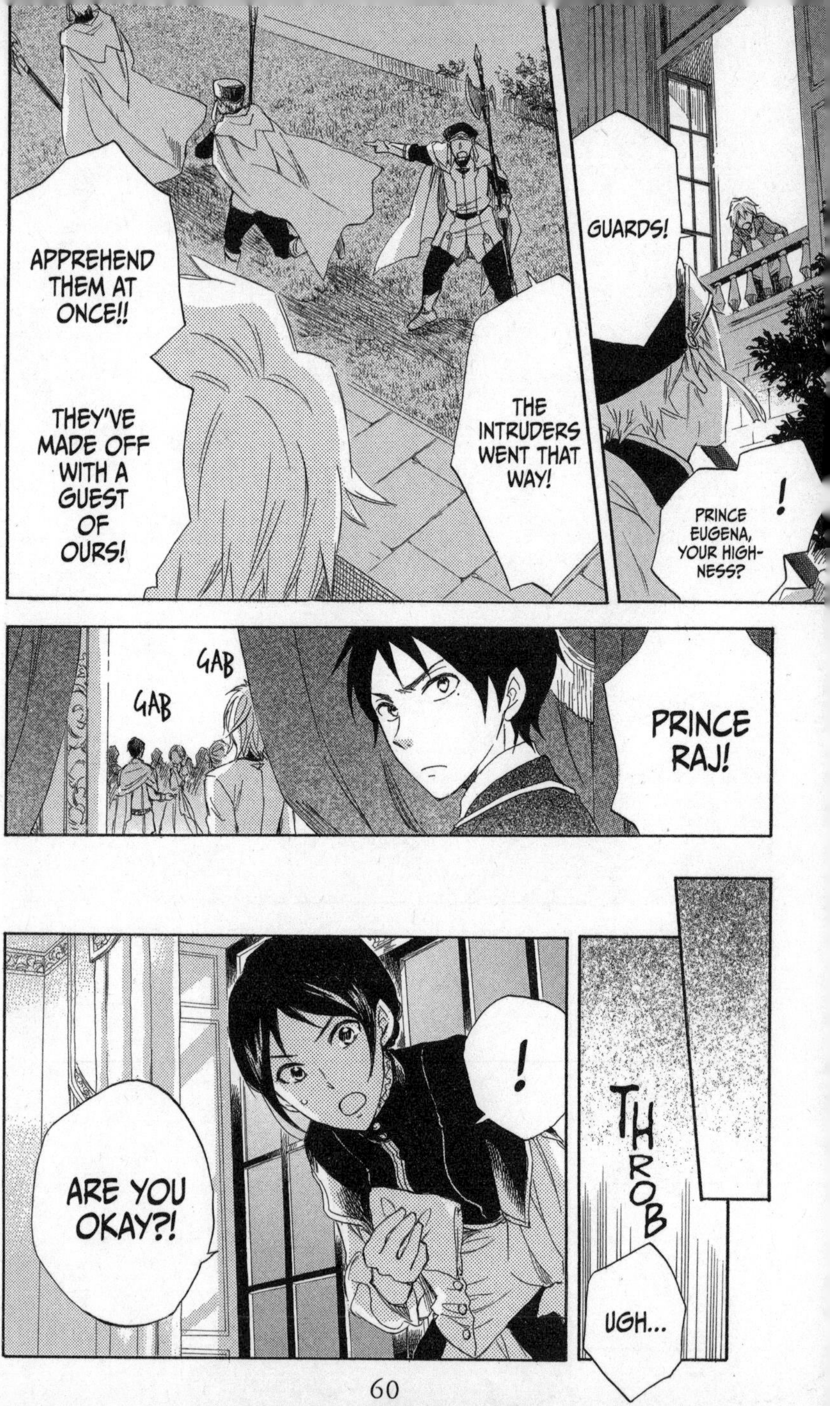
GUARDS!
!
PRINCE EUGENA, YOUR HIGHNESS?
THE INTRUDERS WENT THAT WAY!
APPREHEND THEM AT ONCE!!
THEY'VE MADE OFF WITH A GUEST OF OURS!
PRINCE RAJ!
GAB
GAB
THROB
UGH...
!
ARE YOU OKAY?!

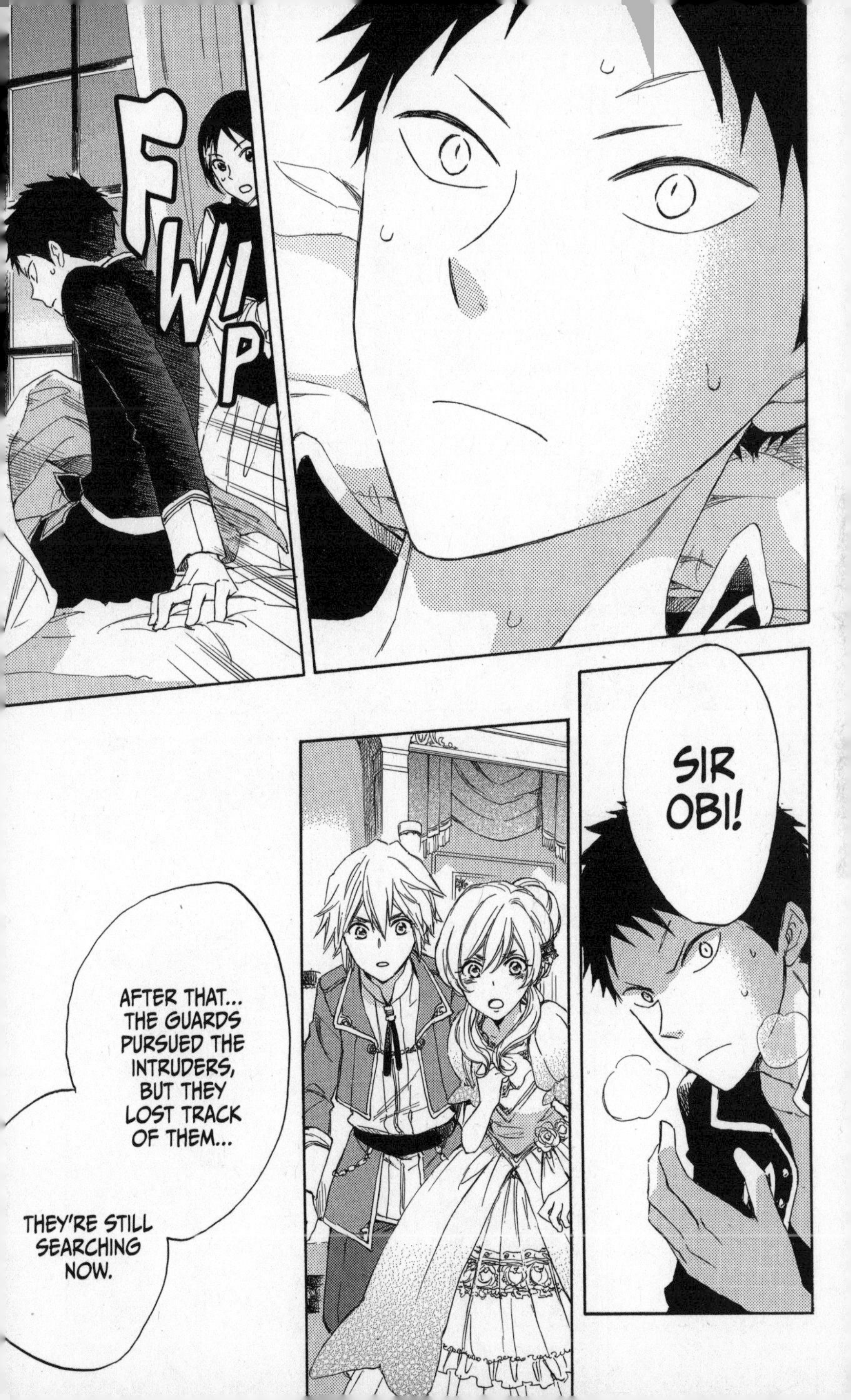
FWIP
SIR OBI!
AFTER THAT... THE GUARDS PURSUED THE INTRUDERS, BUT THEY LOST TRACK OF THEM...
THEY'RE STILL SEARCHING NOW.

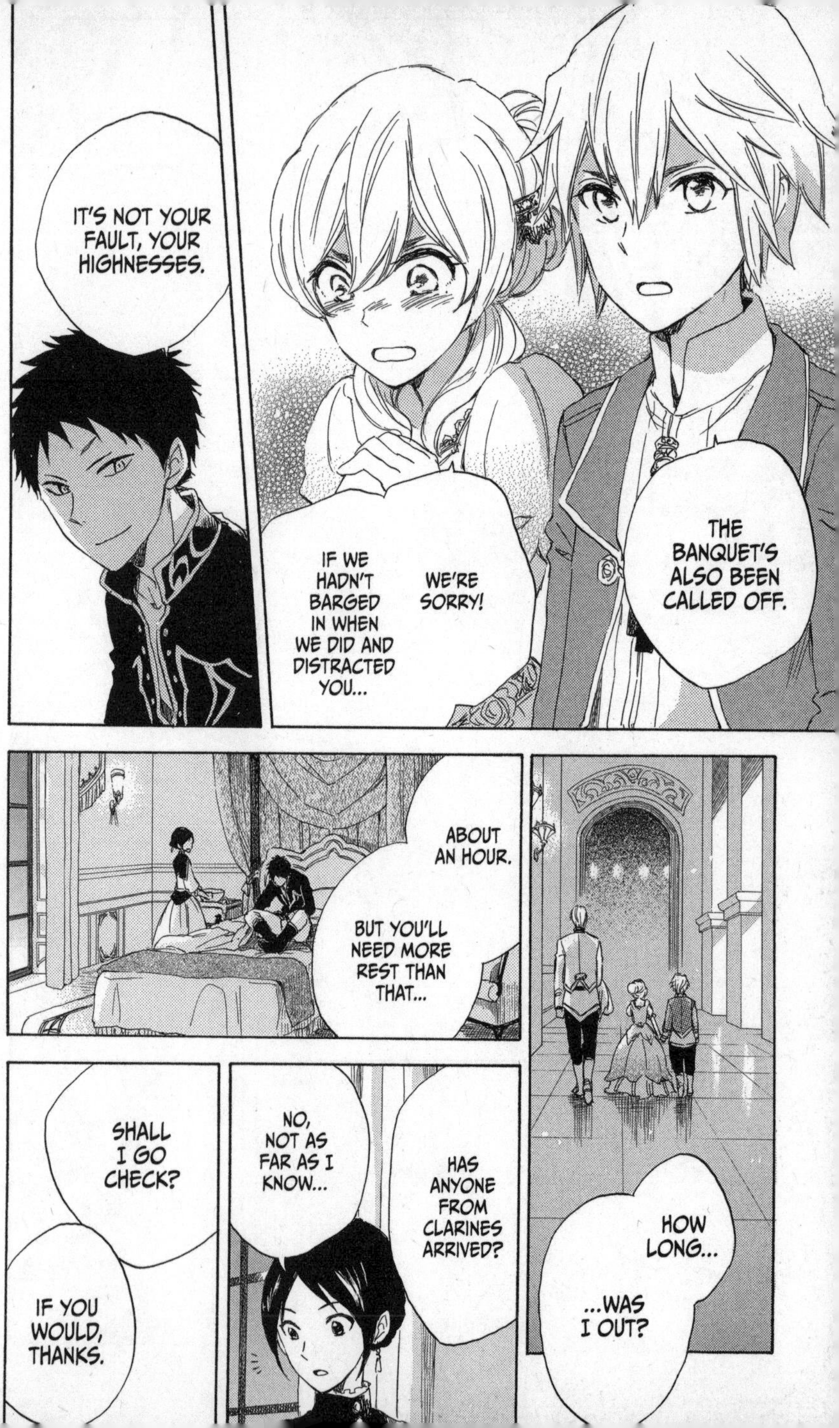
THE BANQUET'S ALSO BEEN CALLED OFF.
WE'RE SORRY!
IF WE HADN'T BARGED IN WHEN WE DID AND DISTRACTED YOU...
IT'S NOT YOUR FAULT, YOUR HIGHNESSES.
HOW LONG...
...WAS I OUT?
ABOUT AN HOUR.
BUT YOU'LL NEED MORE REST THAN THAT...
HAS ANYONE FROM CLARINES ARRIVED?
NO, NOT AS FAR AS I KNOW...
SHALL I GO CHECK?
IF YOU WOULD, THANKS.

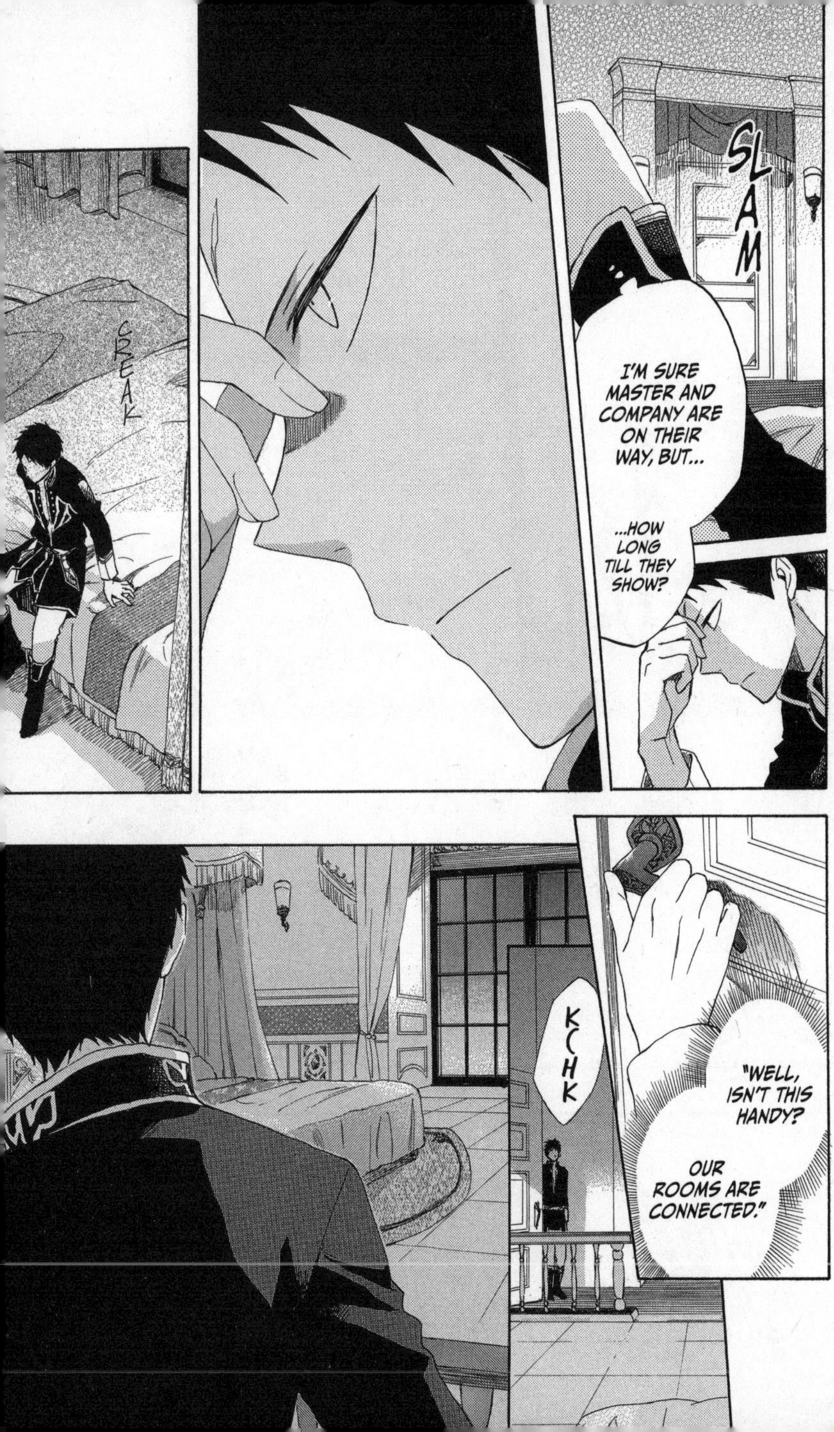

SLAM
I'M SURE MASTER AND COMPANY ARE ON THEIR WAY, BUT...
...HOW LONG TILL THEY SHOW?
CREAK
"WELL, ISN'T THIS HANDY?
OUR ROOMS ARE CONNECTED."
KCHK

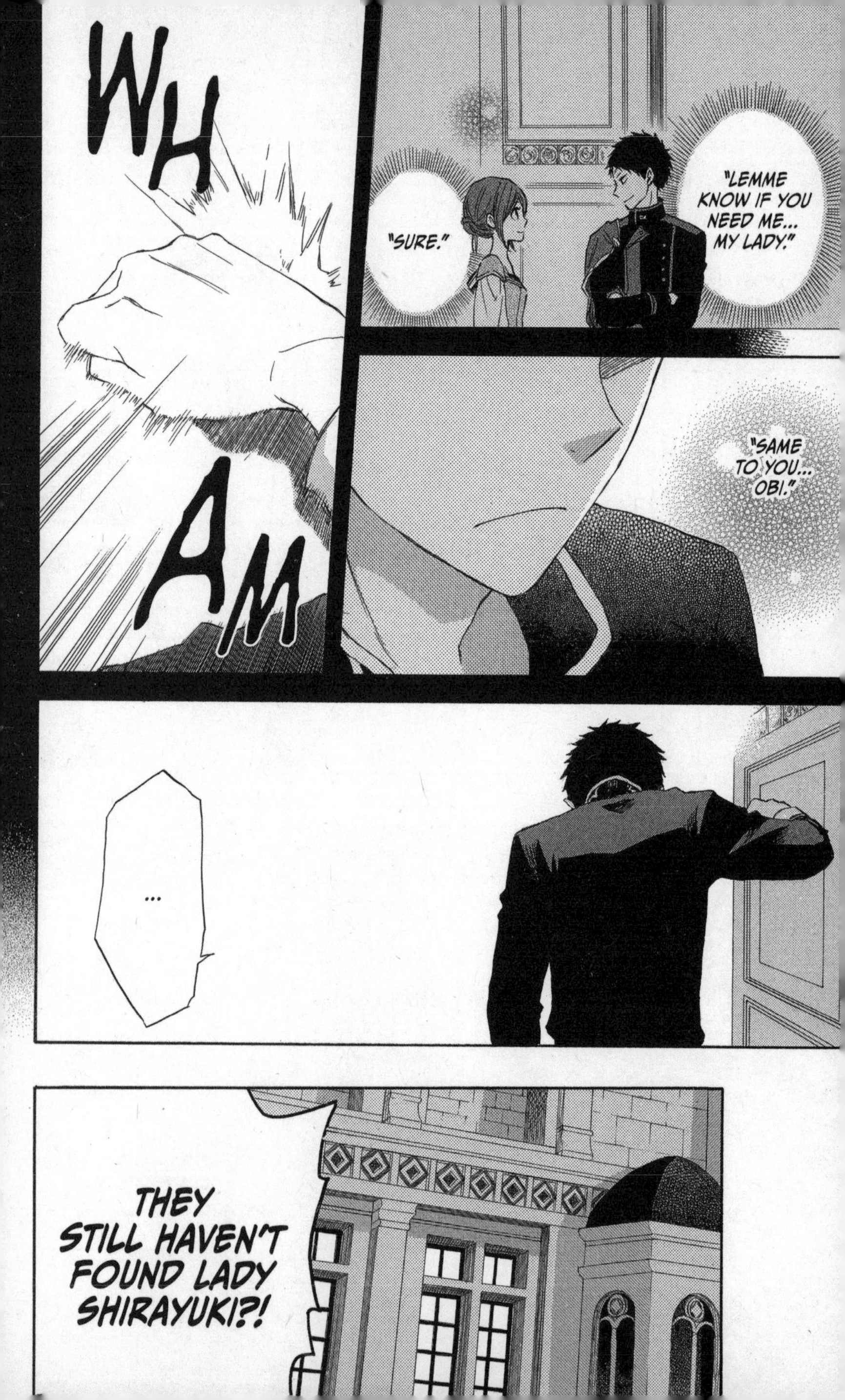
"LEMME KNOW IF YOU NEED ME... MY LADY."
"SURE."
"SAME TO YOU... OBI."
WHAM
...
THEY STILL HAVEN'T FOUND LADY SHIRAYUKI?!

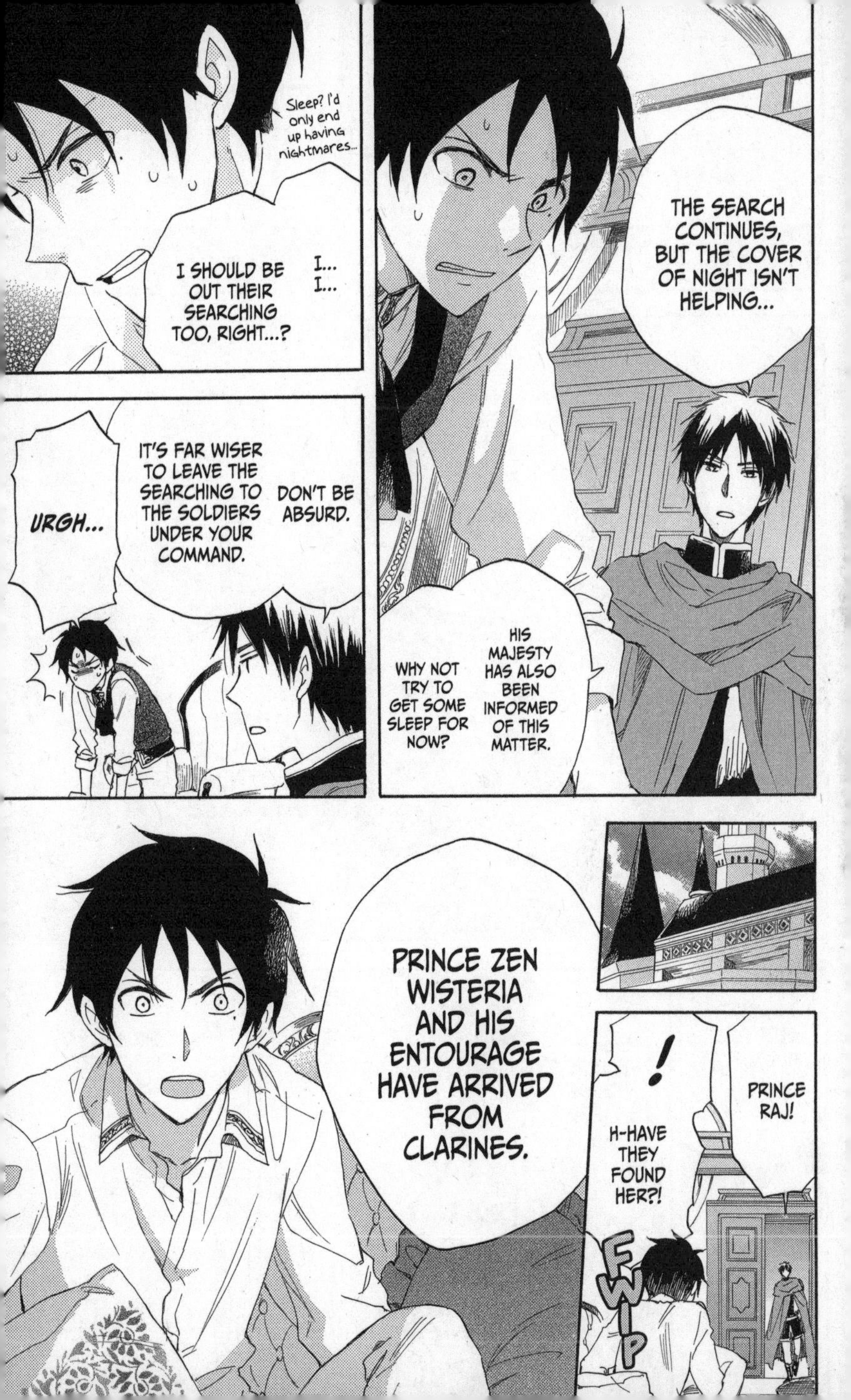
THE SEARCH CONTINUES, BUT THE COVER OF NIGHT ISN'T HELPING...
HIS MAJESTY HAS ALSO BEEN INFORMED OF THIS MATTER.
WHY NOT TRY TO GET SOME SLEEP FOR NOW?
Sleep? I'd only end up having nightmares...
I... I...
I SHOULD BE OUT THEIR SEARCHING TOO, RIGHT...?
DON'T BE ABSURD.
IT'S FAR WISER TO LEAVE THE SEARCHING TO THE SOLDIERS UNDER YOUR COMMAND.
URGH...
PRINCE RAJ!
!
H-HAVE THEY FOUND HER?!
FWIP
PRINCE ZEN WISTERIA AND HIS ENTOURAGE HAVE ARRIVED FROM CLARINES.

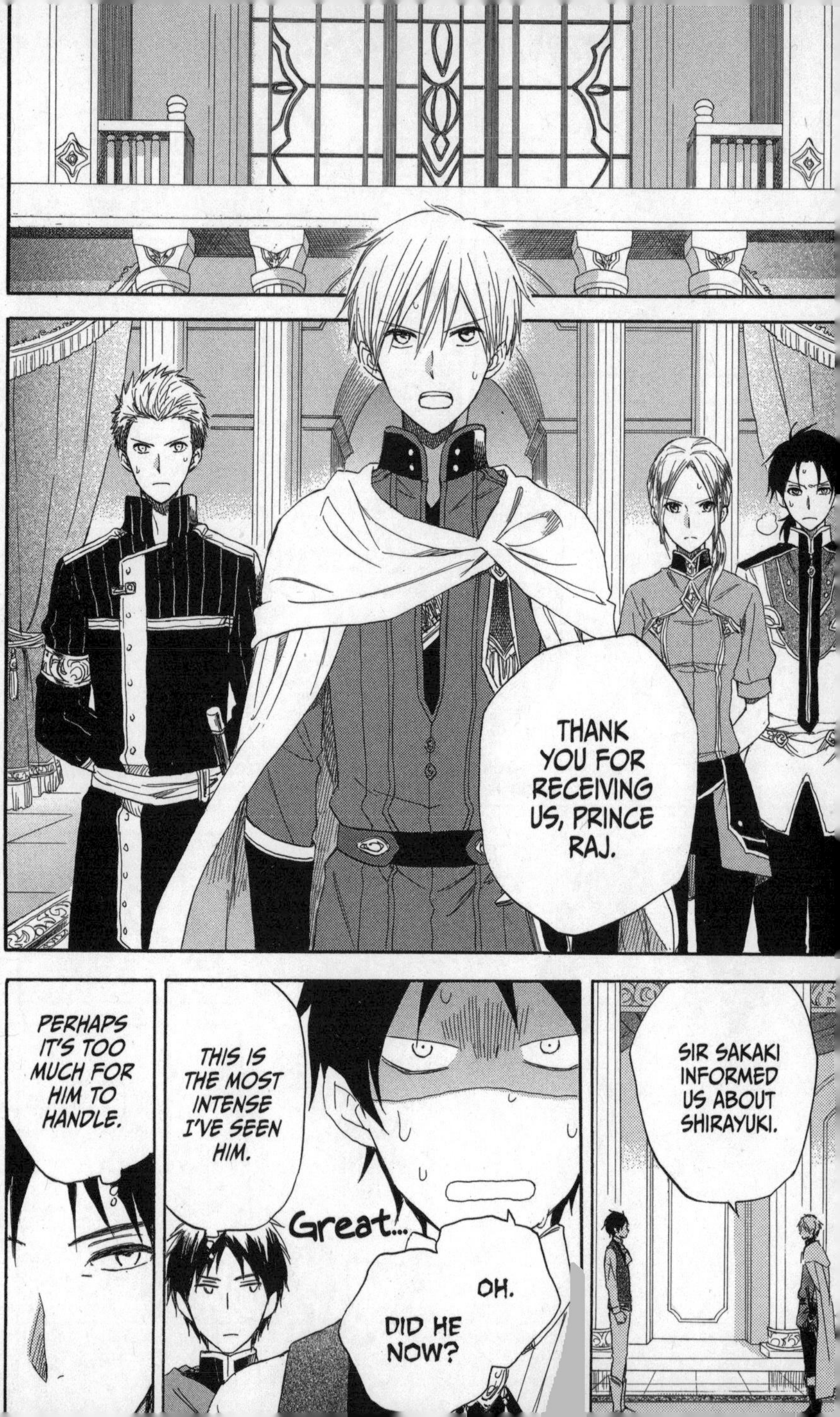
THANK YOU FOR RECEIVING US, PRINCE RAJ.
SIR SAKAKI INFORMED US ABOUT SHIRAYUKI.
OH.
DID HE NOW?
Great...
THIS IS THE MOST INTENSE I'VE SEEN HIM.
PERHAPS IT'S TOO MUCH FOR HIM TO HANDLE.

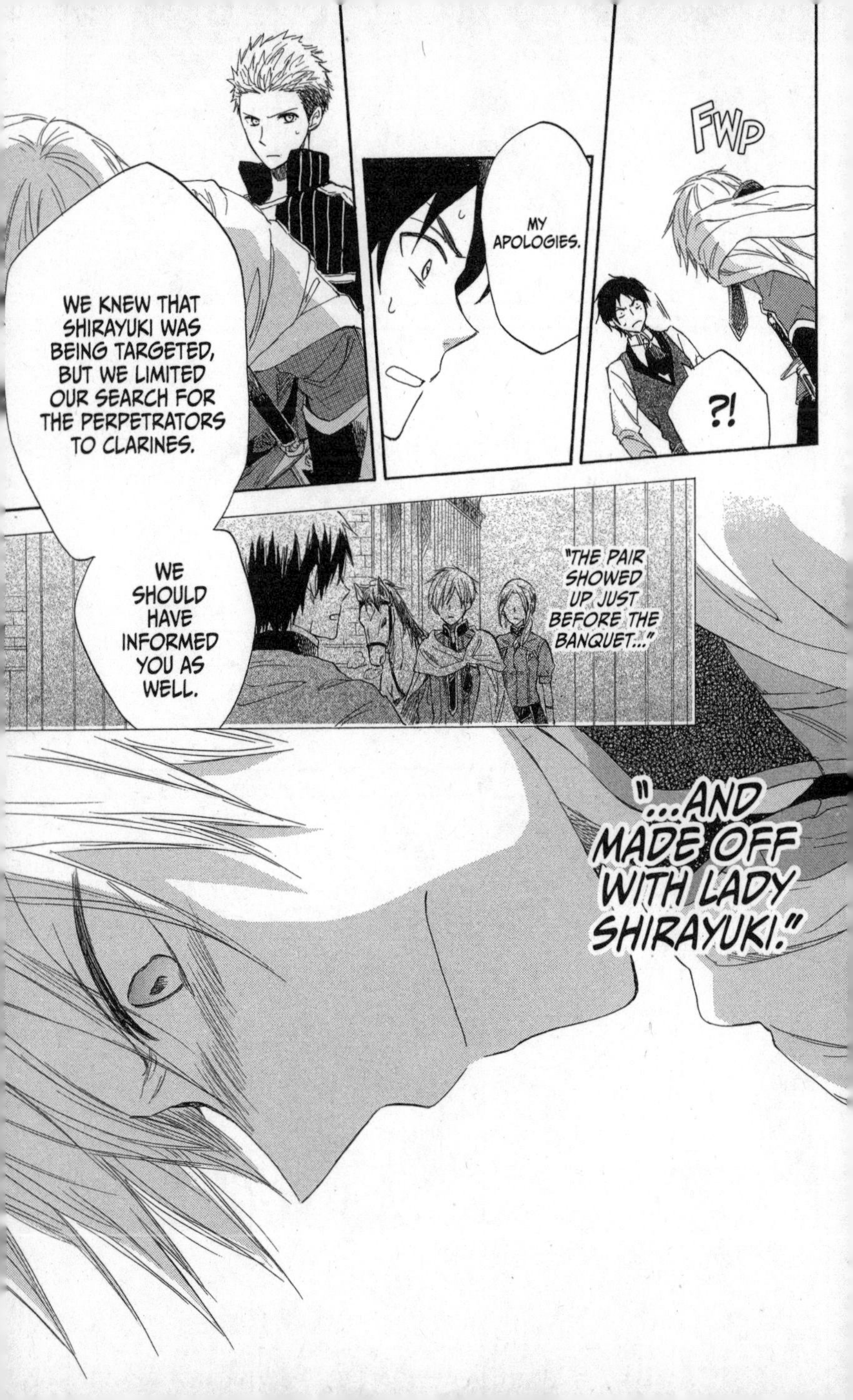
FWP
?!
MY APOLOGIES.
WE KNEW THAT SHIRAYUKI WAS BEING TARGETED, BUT WE LIMITED OUR SEARCH FOR THE PERPETRATORS TO CLARINES.
WE SHOULD HAVE INFORMED YOU AS WELL.
"THE PAIR SHOWED UP JUST BEFORE THE BANQUET..."
"...AND MADE OFF WITH LADY SHIRAYUKI."

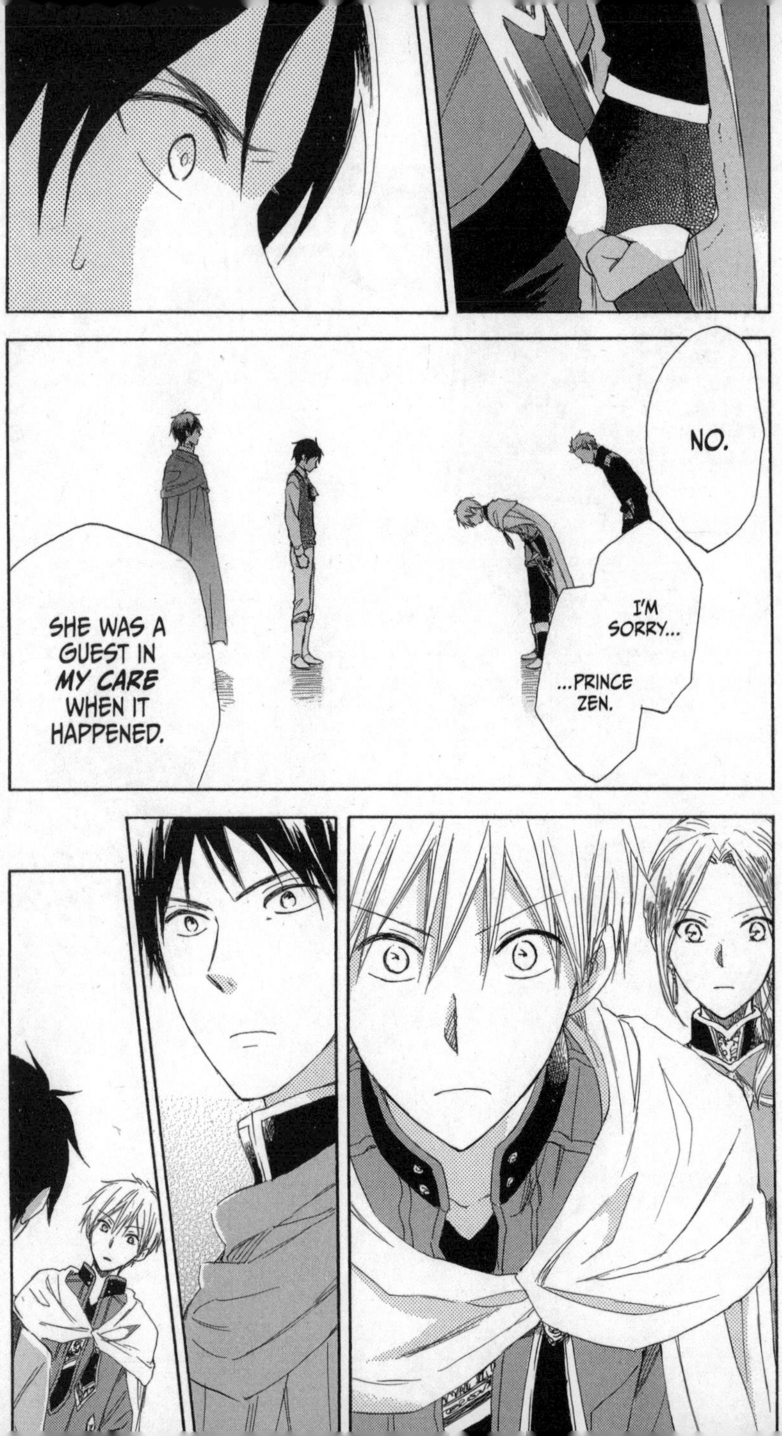
NO.
I'M SORRY...
...PRINCE ZEN.
SHE WAS A GUEST IN *MY CARE* WHEN IT HAPPENED.

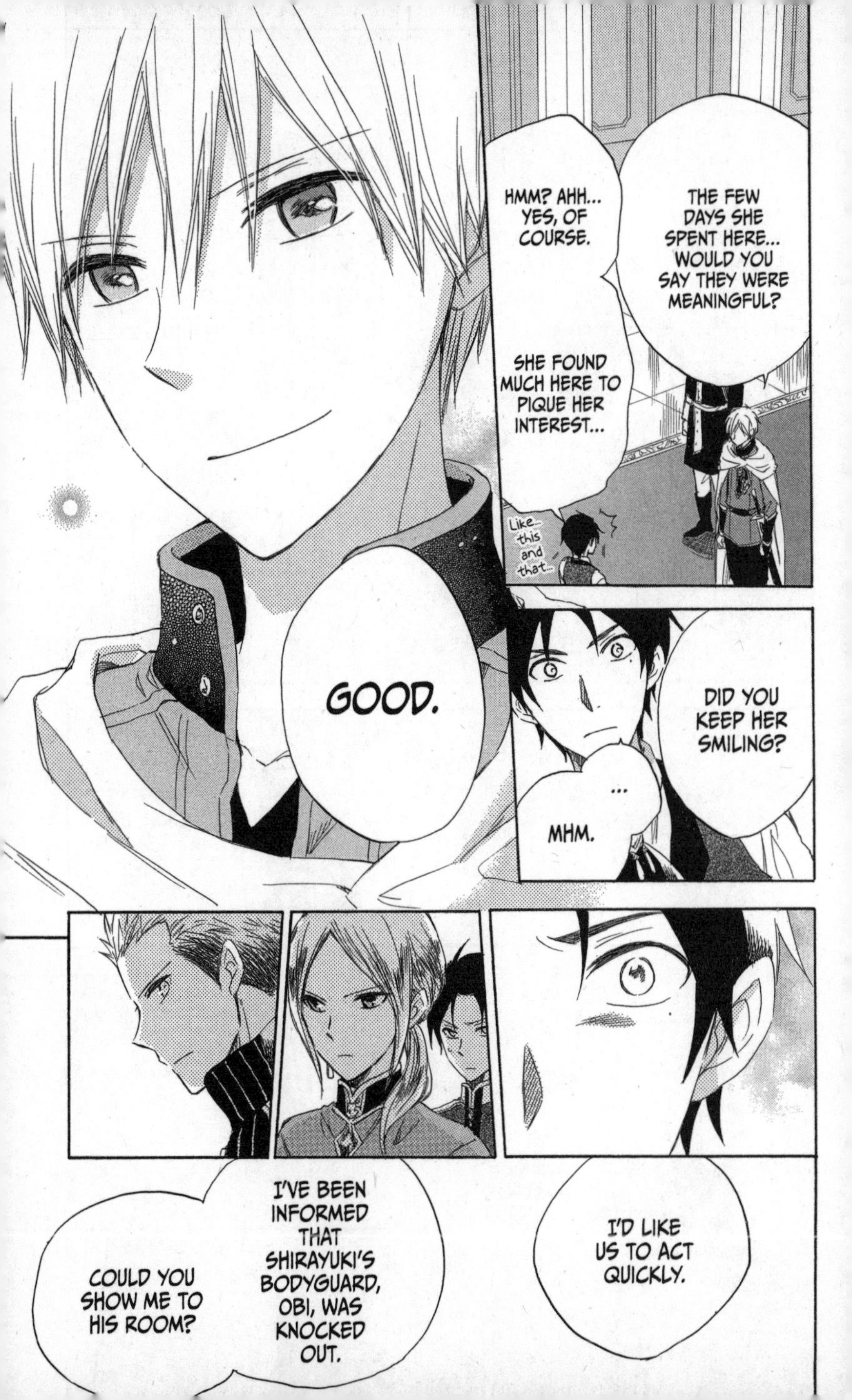
THE FEW DAYS SHE SPENT HERE... WOULD YOU SAY THEY WERE MEANINGFUL?
HMM? AHH... YES, OF COURSE.
SHE FOUND MUCH HERE TO PIQUE HER INTEREST...
Like... this and that...
DID YOU KEEP HER SMILING?
...
MHM.
GOOD.
I'D LIKE US TO ACT QUICKLY.
I'VE BEEN INFORMED THAT SHIRAYUKI'S BODYGUARD, OBI, WAS KNOCKED OUT.
COULD YOU SHOW ME TO HIS ROOM?

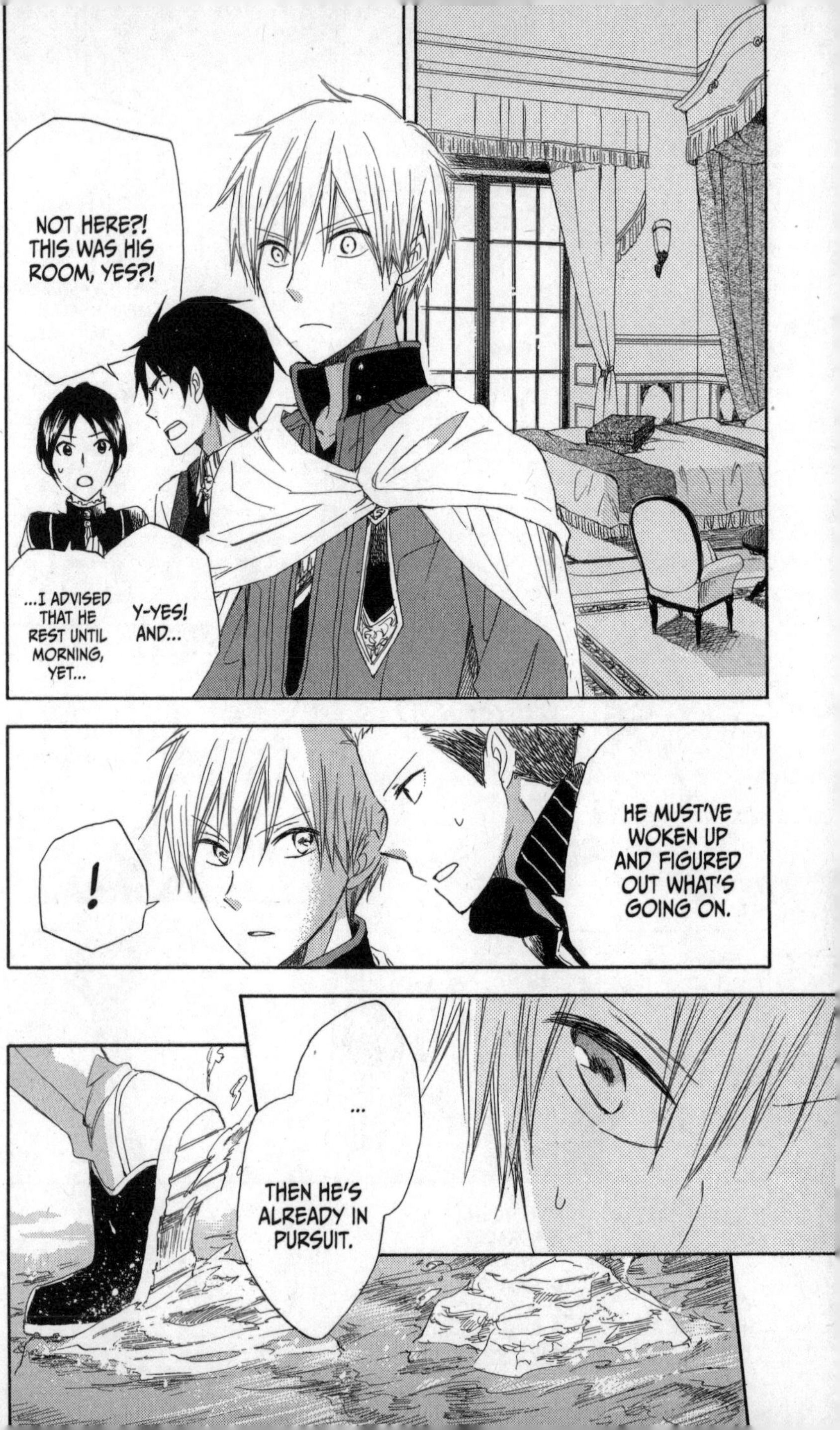
NOT HERE?! THIS WAS HIS ROOM, YES?!
Y-YES! AND...
...I ADVISED THAT HE REST UNTIL MORNING, YET...
HE MUST'VE WOKEN UP AND FIGURED OUT WHAT'S GOING ON.
!
...
THEN HE'S ALREADY IN PURSUIT.

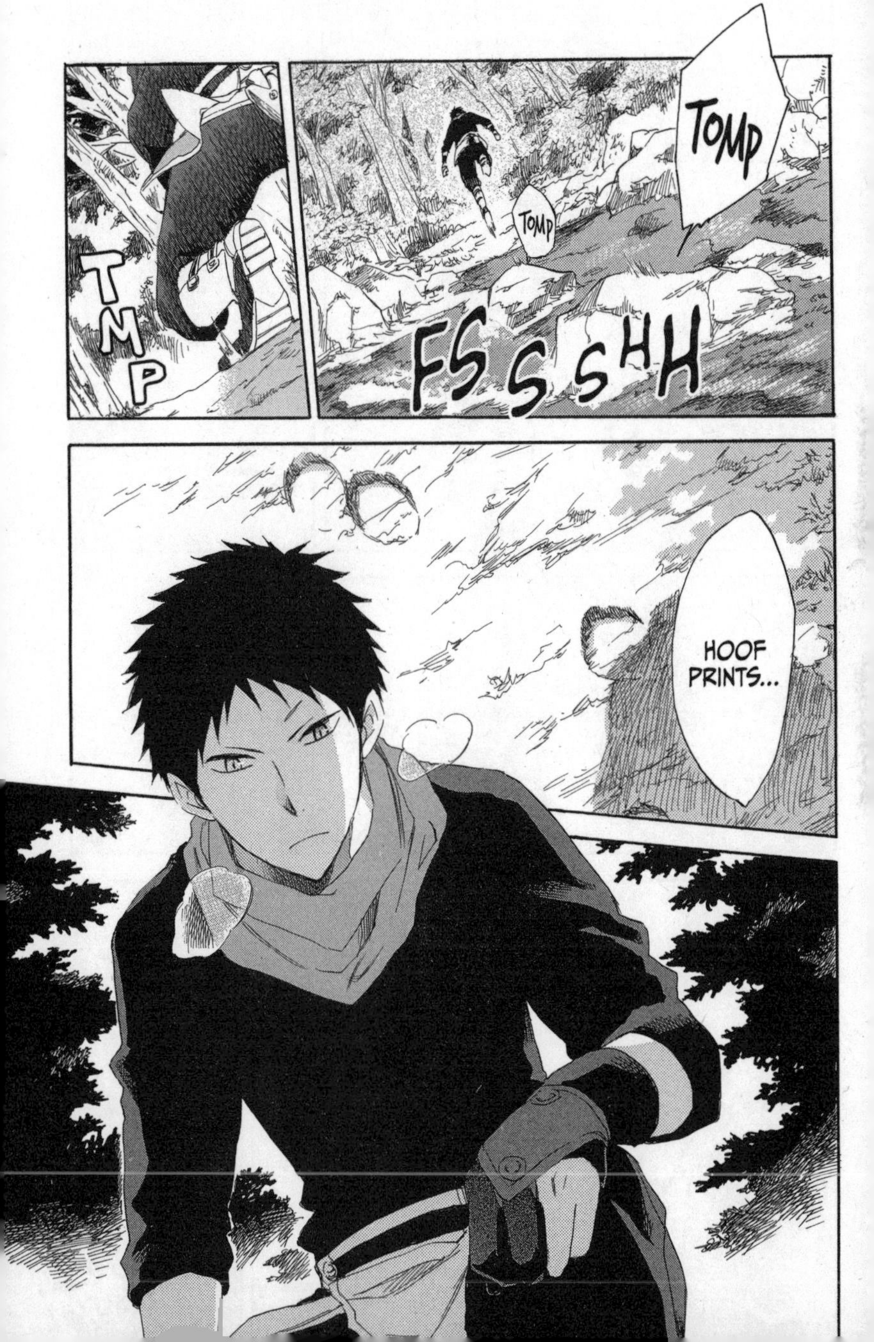
TOMP
TOMP
FSSSHH
TMP
HOOF PRINTS...

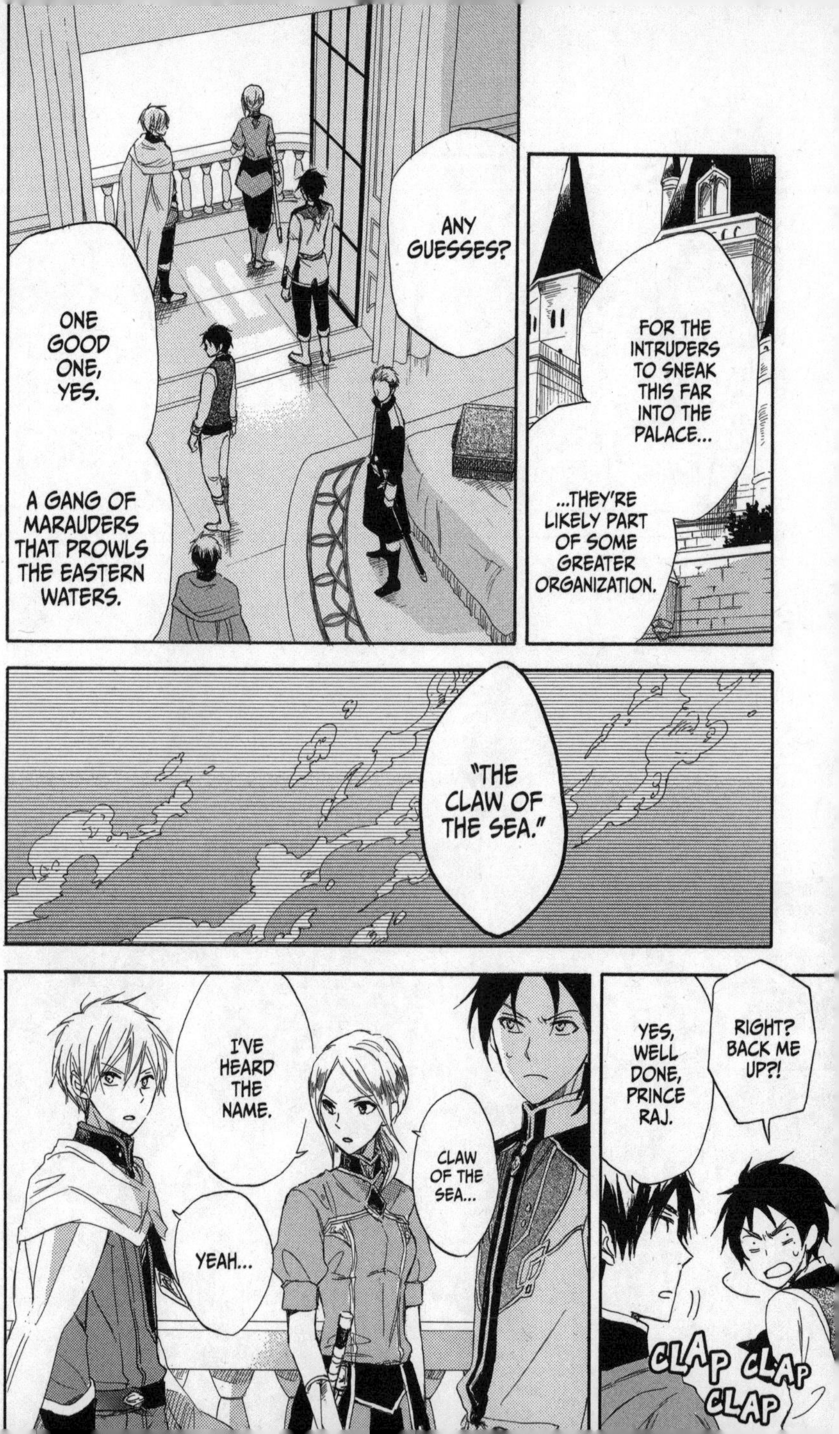
FOR THE INTRUDERS TO SNEAK THIS FAR INTO THE PALACE...
...THEY'RE LIKELY PART OF SOME GREATER ORGANIZATION.
ANY GUESSES?
ONE GOOD ONE, YES.
A GANG OF MARAUDERS THAT PROWLS THE EASTERN WATERS.
"THE CLAW OF THE SEA."
RIGHT? BACK ME UP?!
YES, WELL DONE, PRINCE RAJ.
CLAP CLAP CLAP
CLAW OF THE SEA...
I'VE HEARD THE NAME.
YEAH...

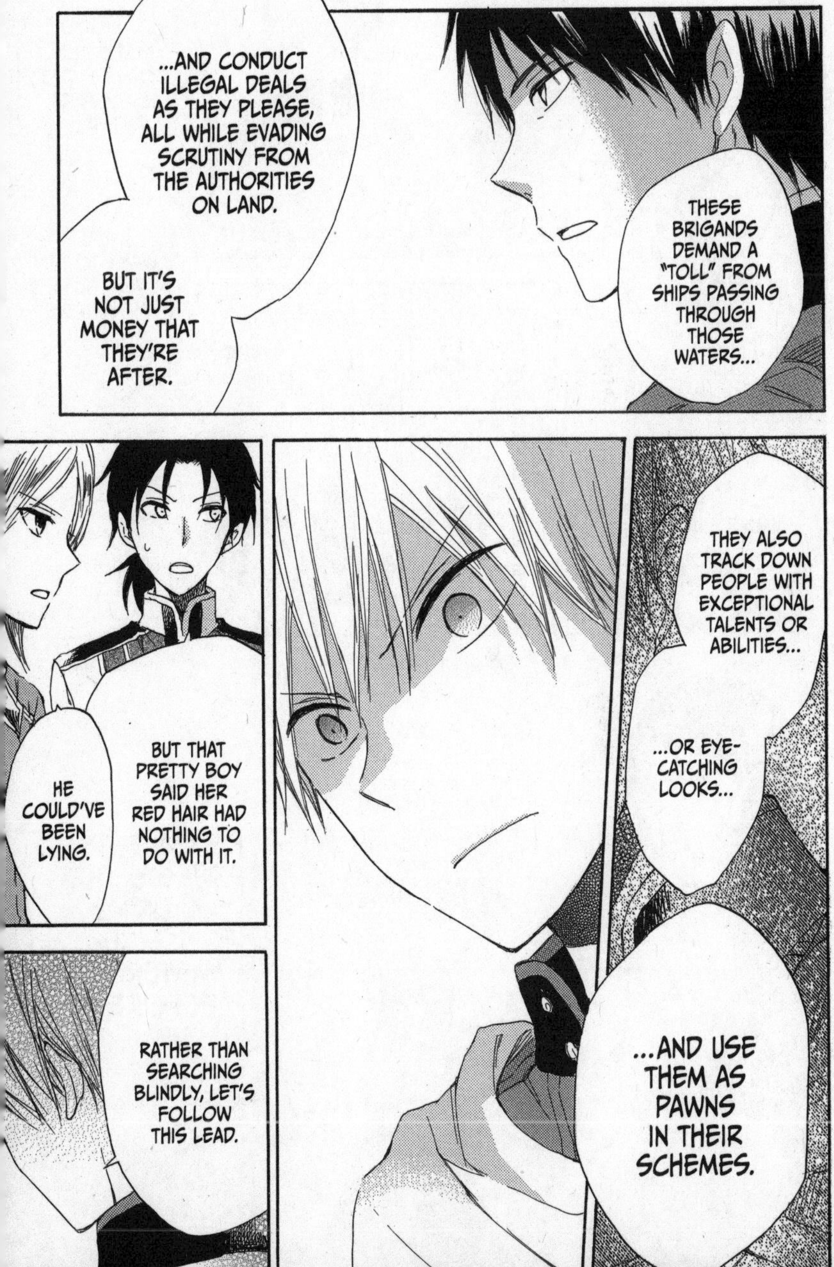
THESE BRIGANDS DEMAND A "TOLL" FROM SHIPS PASSING THROUGH THOSE WATERS...
...AND CONDUCT ILLEGAL DEALS AS THEY PLEASE, ALL WHILE EVADING SCRUTINY FROM THE AUTHORITIES ON LAND.
BUT IT'S NOT JUST MONEY THAT THEY'RE AFTER.
THEY ALSO TRACK DOWN PEOPLE WITH EXCEPTIONAL TALENTS OR ABILITIES...
...OR EYE-CATCHING LOOKS...
...AND USE THEM AS PAWNS IN THEIR SCHEMES.
BUT THAT PRETTY BOY SAID HER RED HAIR HAD NOTHING TO DO WITH IT.
HE COULD'VE BEEN LYING.
RATHER THAN SEARCHING BLINDLY, LET'S FOLLOW THIS LEAD.

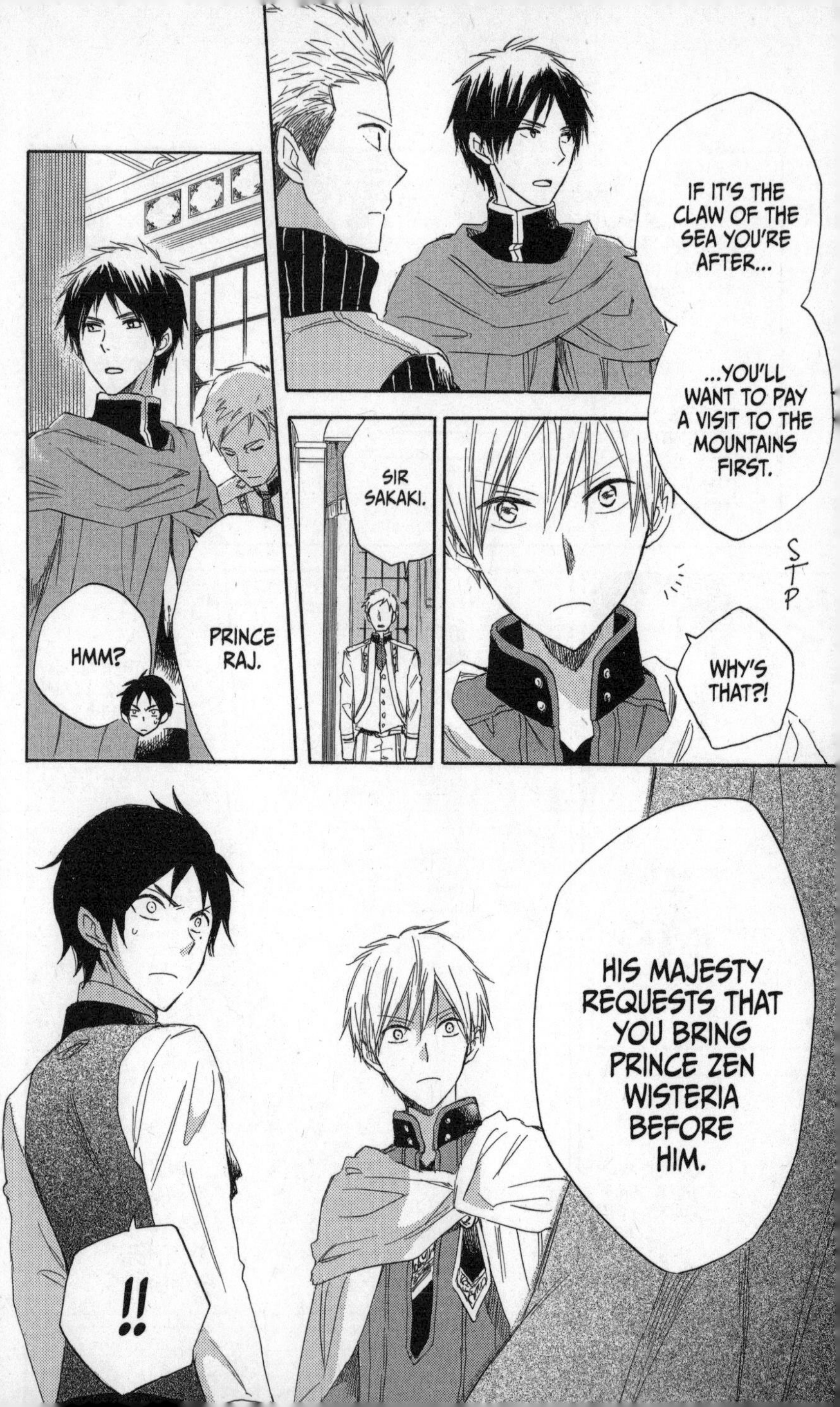
IF IT'S THE CLAW OF THE SEA YOU'RE AFTER...
...YOU'LL WANT TO PAY A VISIT TO THE MOUNTAINS FIRST.
STP
WHY'S THAT?!
SIR SAKAKI.
PRINCE RAJ.
HMM?
HIS MAJESTY REQUESTS THAT YOU BRING PRINCE ZEN WISTERIA BEFORE HIM.
!!

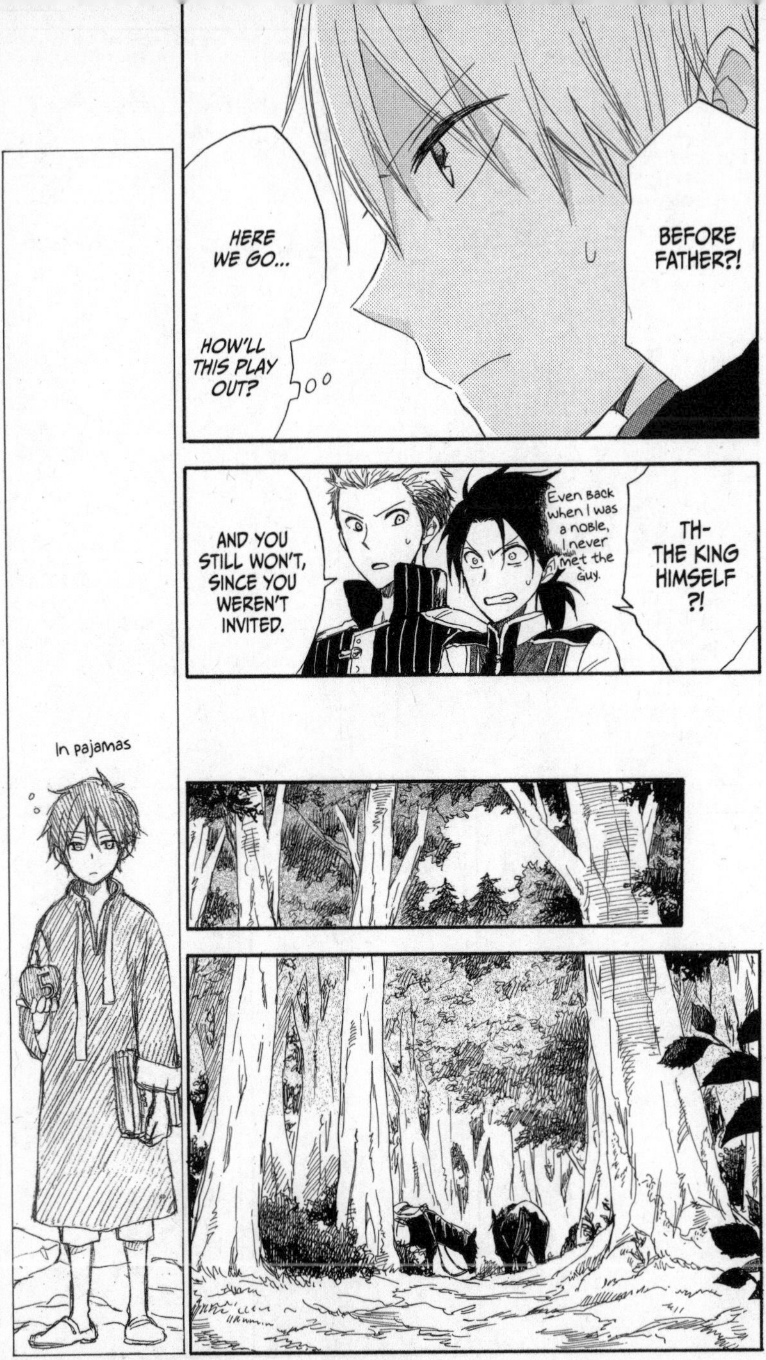
BEFORE FATHER?!
HERE WE GO...
HOW'LL THIS PLAY OUT?
TH- THE KING HIMSELF?!
Even back when I was a noble, I never met the guy.
AND YOU STILL WON'T, SINCE YOU WEREN'T INVITED.
In pajamas

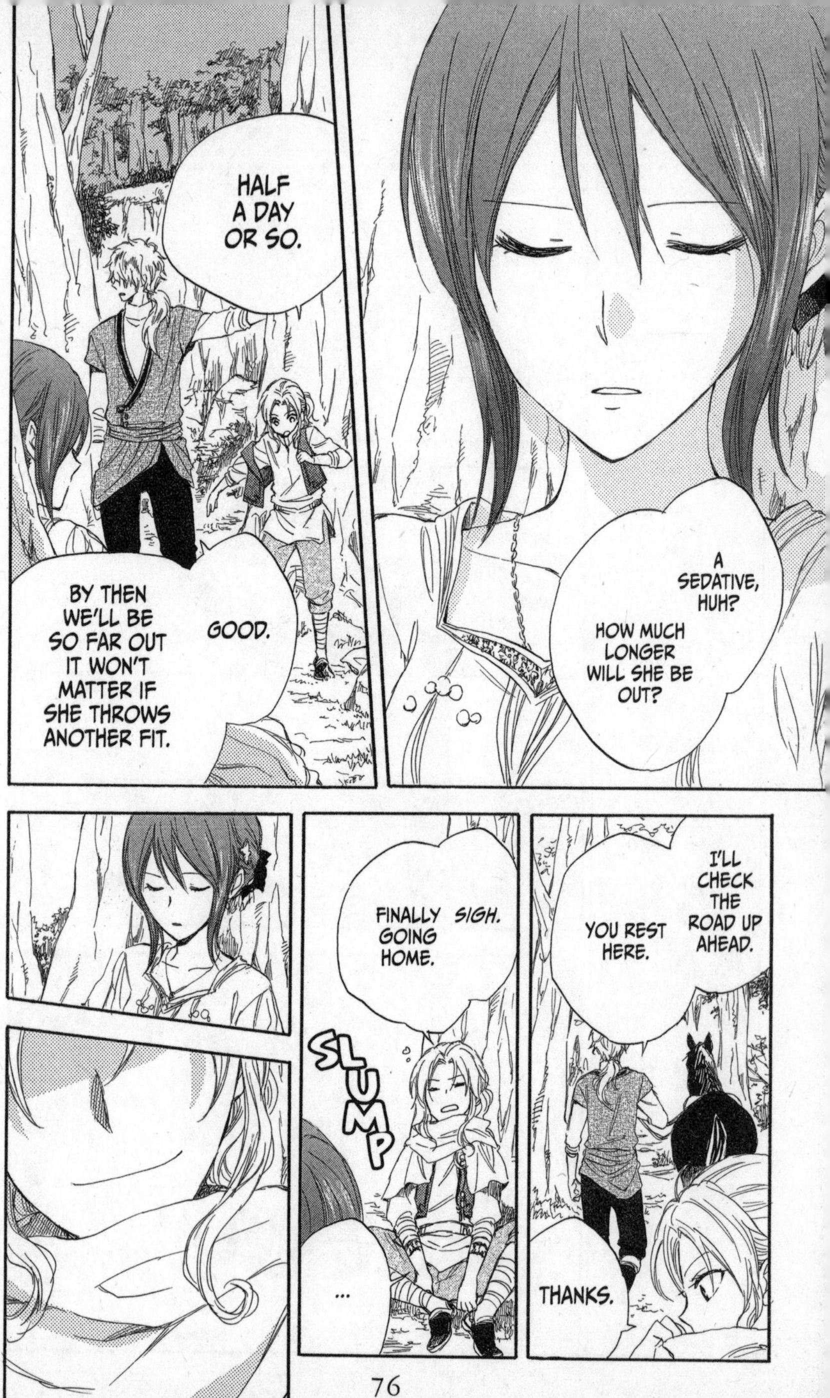

A SEDATIVE, HUH?
HOW MUCH LONGER WILL SHE BE OUT?
HALF A DAY OR SO.
GOOD.
BY THEN WE'LL BE SO FAR OUT IT WON'T MATTER IF SHE THROWS ANOTHER FIT.
I'LL CHECK THE ROAD UP AHEAD.
YOU REST HERE.
THANKS.
FINALLY GOING HOME. SIGH.
SLUMP
...

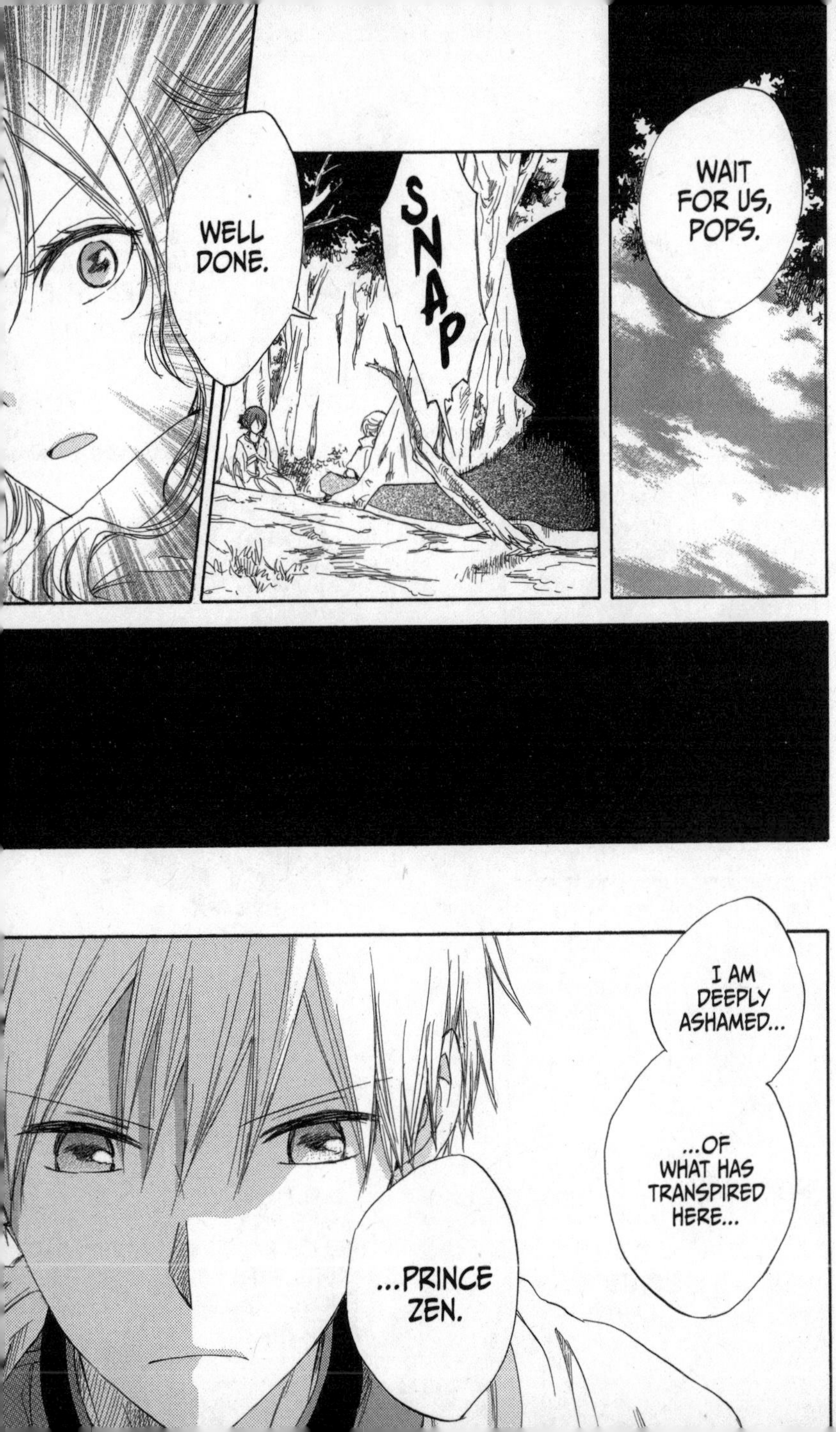
WAIT FOR US, POPS.
SNAP
WELL DONE.
I AM DEEPLY ASHAMED...
...OF WHAT HAS TRANSPIRED HERE...
...PRINCE ZEN.

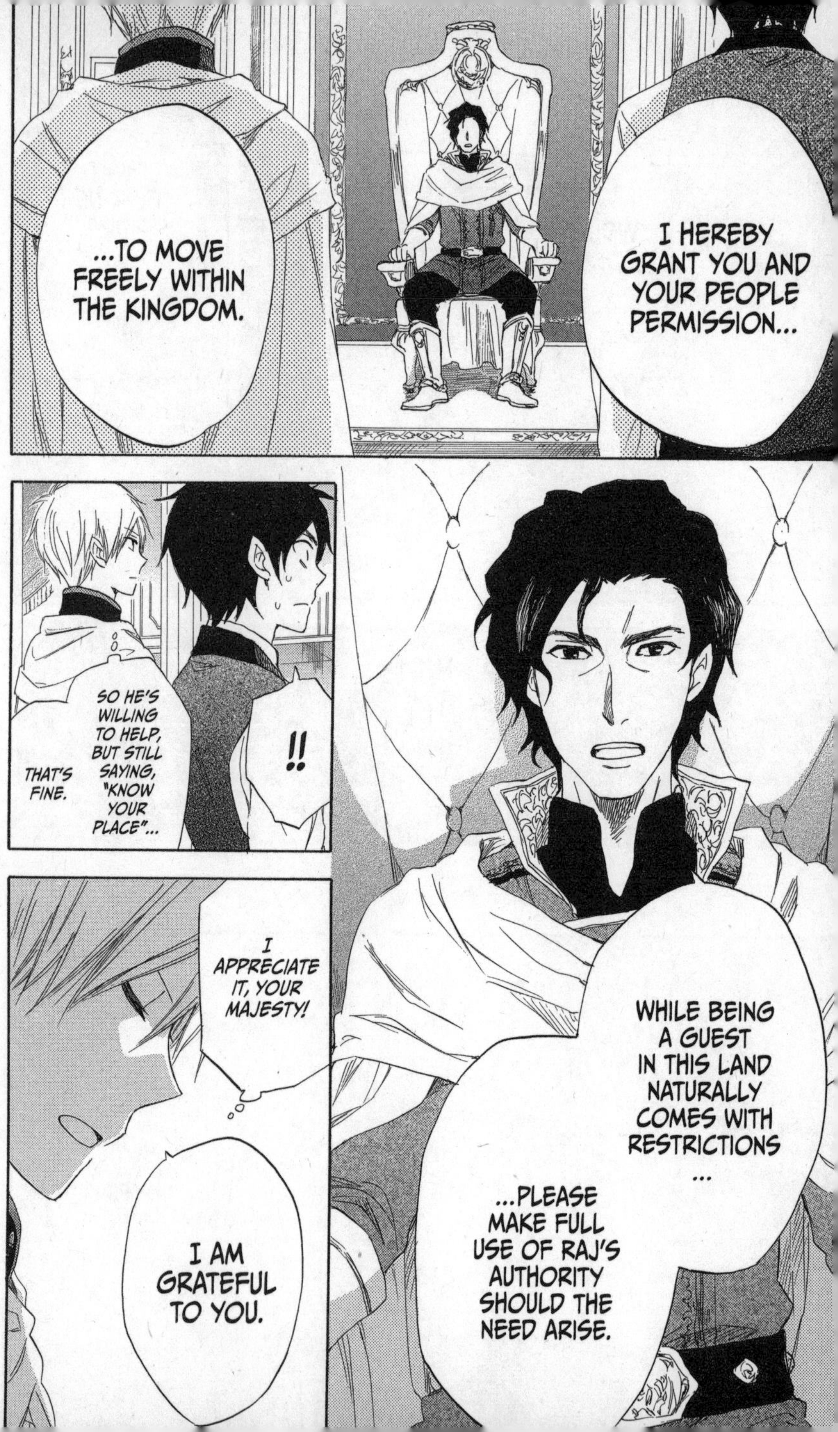
I HEREBY GRANT YOU AND YOUR PEOPLE PERMISSION...
...TO MOVE FREELY WITHIN THE KINGDOM.
WHILE BEING A GUEST IN THIS LAND NATURALLY COMES WITH RESTRICTIONS...
...PLEASE MAKE FULL USE OF RAJ'S AUTHORITY SHOULD THE NEED ARISE.
!!
SO HE'S WILLING TO HELP, BUT STILL SAYING, "KNOW YOUR PLACE"...
THAT'S FINE.
I APPRECIATE IT, YOUR MAJESTY!
I AM GRATEFUL TO YOU.

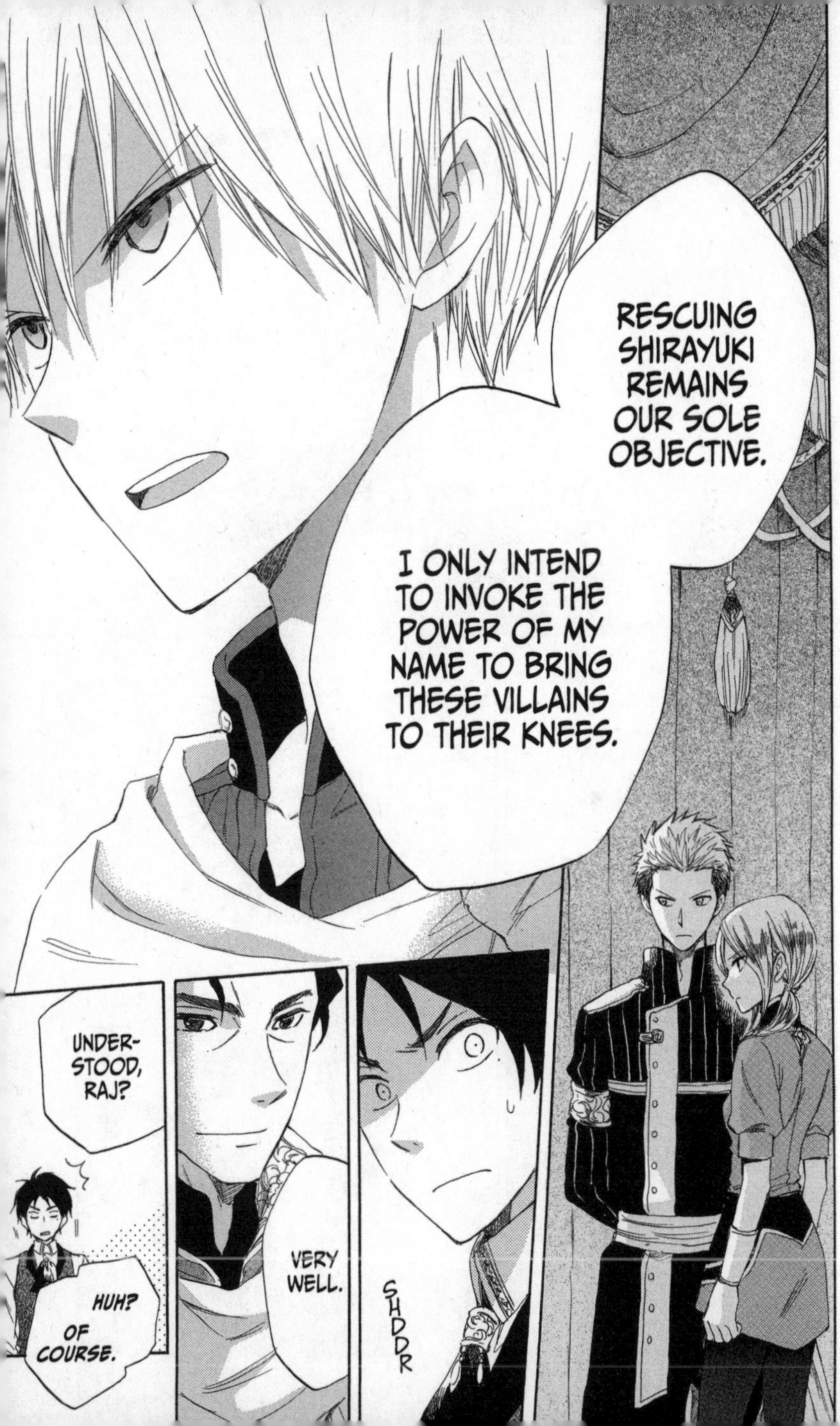
RESCUING SHIRAYUKI REMAINS OUR SOLE OBJECTIVE.
I ONLY INTEND TO INVOKE THE POWER OF MY NAME TO BRING THESE VILLAINS TO THEIR KNEES.
SHDDR
VERY WELL.
UNDER-STOOD, RAJ?
HUH? OF COURSE.

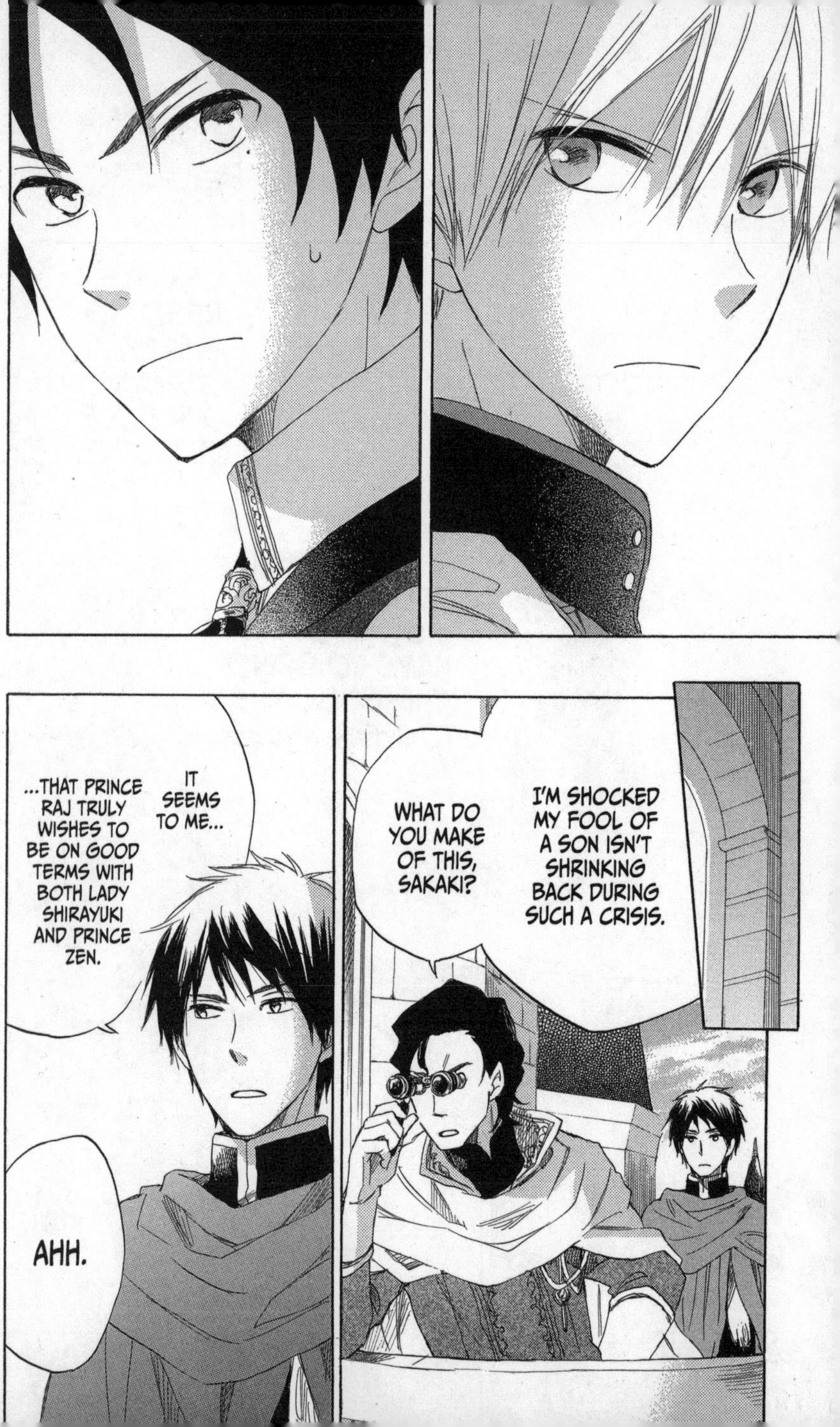
I'M SHOCKED MY FOOL OF A SON ISN'T SHRINKING BACK DURING SUCH A CRISIS.
WHAT DO YOU MAKE OF THIS, SAKAKI?
IT SEEMS TO ME...
...THAT PRINCE RAJ TRULY WISHES TO BE ON GOOD TERMS WITH BOTH LADY SHIRAYUKI AND PRINCE ZEN.
AHH.

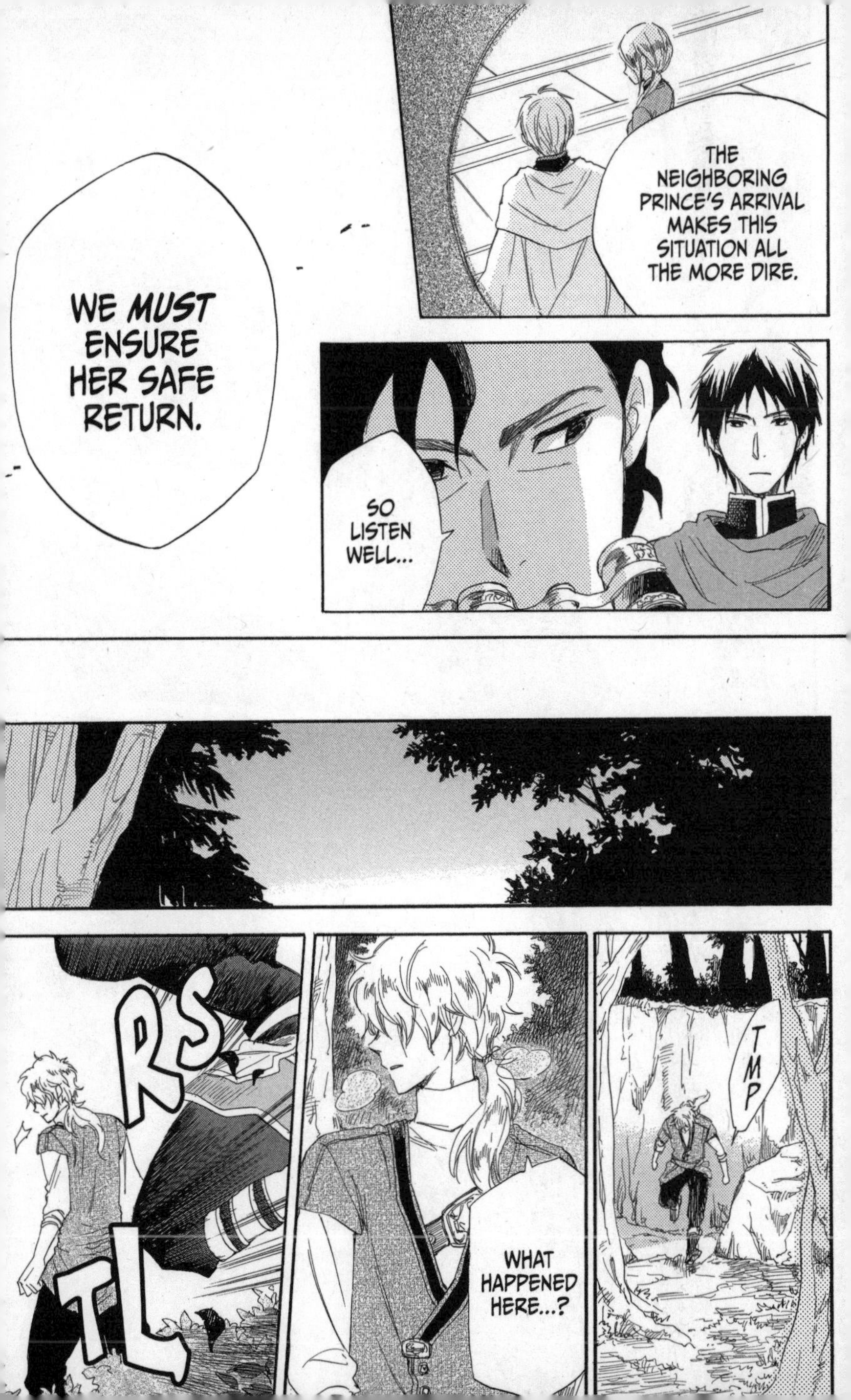
THE NEIGHBORING PRINCE'S ARRIVAL MAKES THIS SITUATION ALL THE MORE DIRE.
SO LISTEN WELL...
WE *MUST* ENSURE HER SAFE RETURN.
TMP
WHAT HAPPENED HERE...?
RS
TL

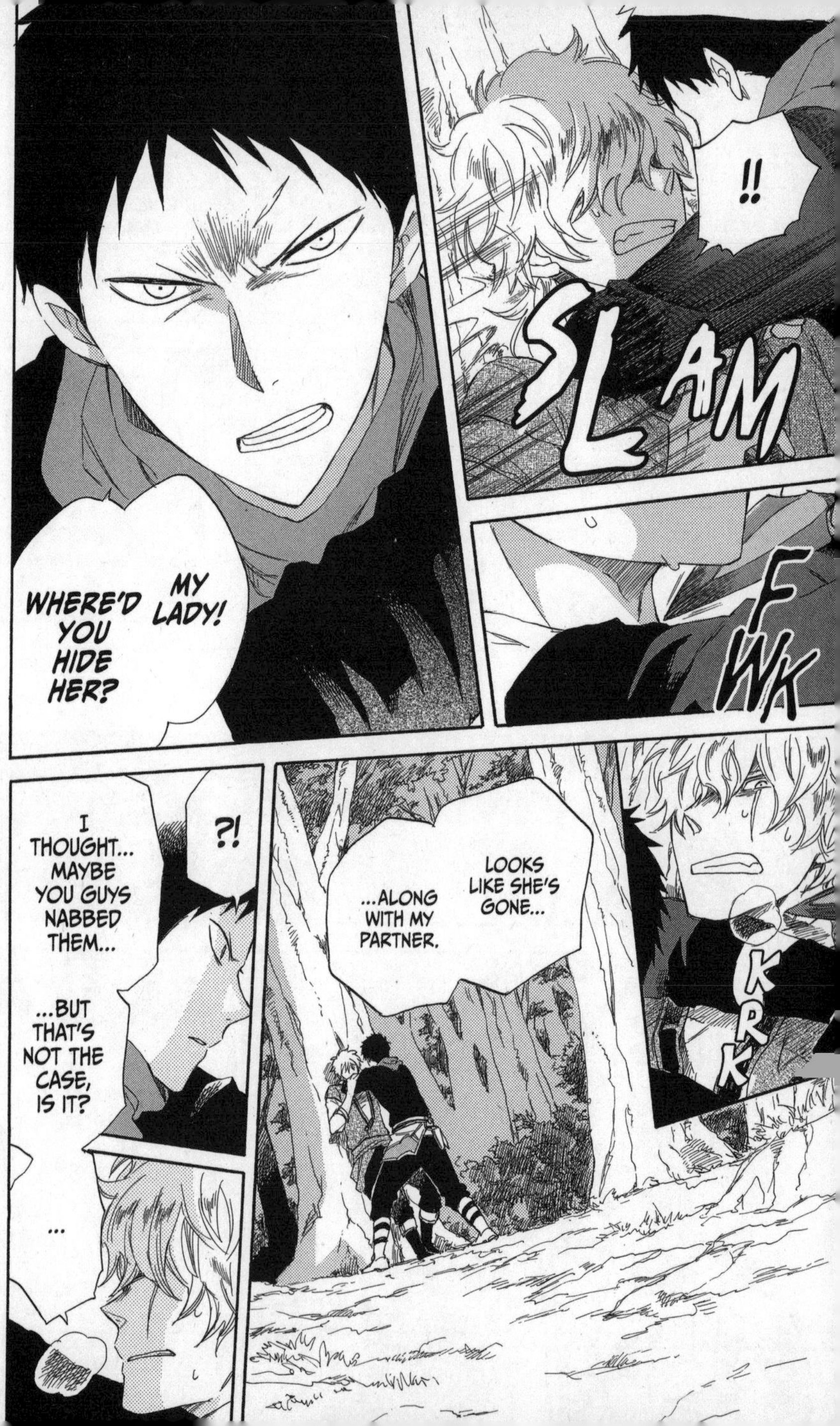
!!
SLAM
FWK
MY LADY!
WHERE'D YOU HIDE HER?
KRK
LOOKS LIKE SHE'S GONE...
...ALONG WITH MY PARTNER.
?!
I THOUGHT... MAYBE YOU GUYS NABBED THEM...
...BUT THAT'S NOT THE CASE, IS IT?
...

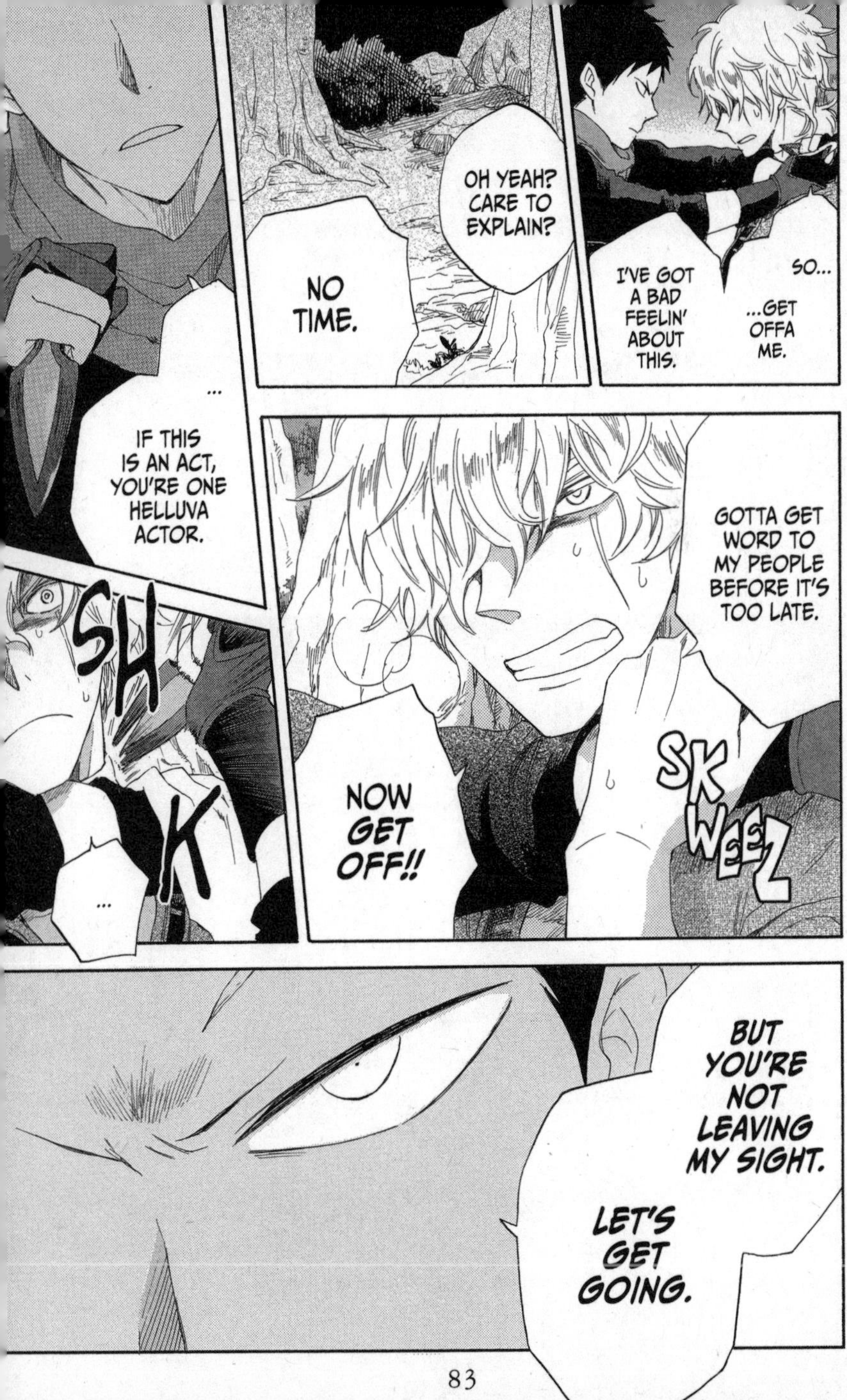
I'VE GOT A BAD FEELIN' ABOUT THIS.
SO...
...GET OFFA ME.
OH YEAH? CARE TO EXPLAIN?
NO TIME.
...
IF THIS IS AN ACT, YOU'RE ONE HELLUVA ACTOR.
GOTTA GET WORD TO MY PEOPLE BEFORE IT'S TOO LATE.
SKWEEZ
NOW GET OFF!!
SHK
...
BUT YOU'RE NOT LEAVING MY SIGHT.
LET'S GET GOING.

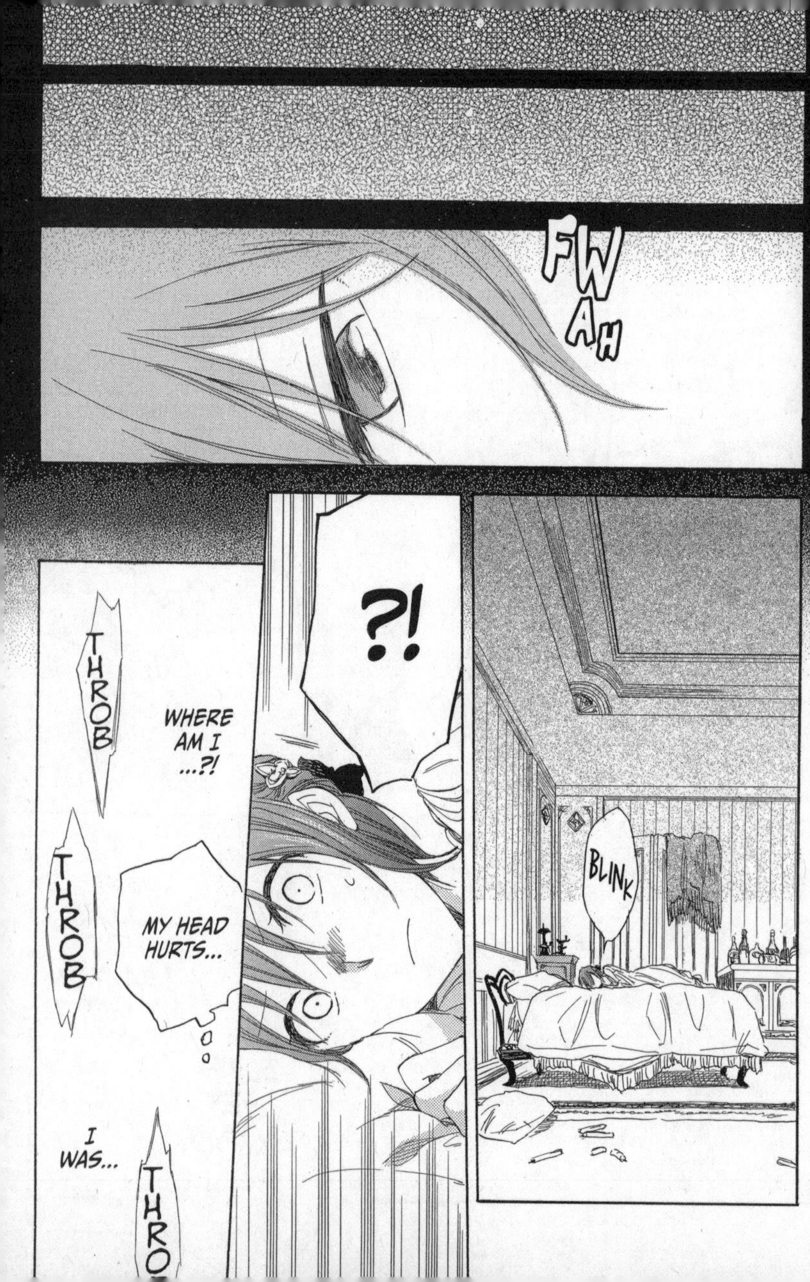
FWAH
BLINK
?!
WHERE AM I ...?!
THROB
THROB
MY HEAD HURTS...
I WAS...
THRO

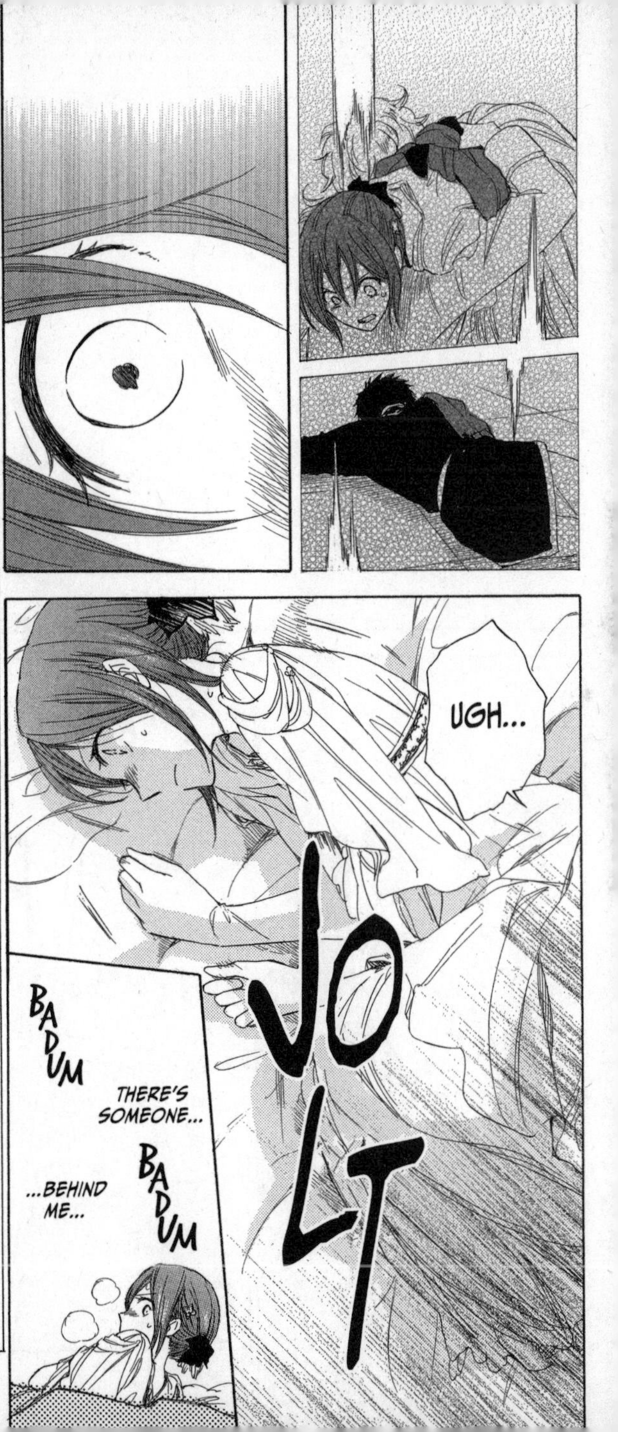
UGH...
JOLT
BADUM
THERE'S SOMEONE...
BADUM
...BEHIND ME...

Q: "What are the names of the two guards at Poet's Gate?"

Gate Guard (1)

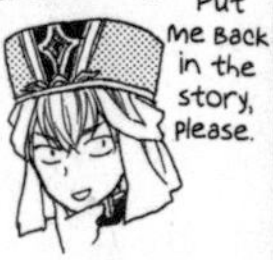
Put me back in the story, please.

Kai Ulkir

He often gets bored, so he wishes he were stationed at a busier gate. His senior guard, however, tells him that'll never happen. He wants to surprise Kiki with something special.

Or, rather, he wishes she would surprise him with a nice gift instead.

6

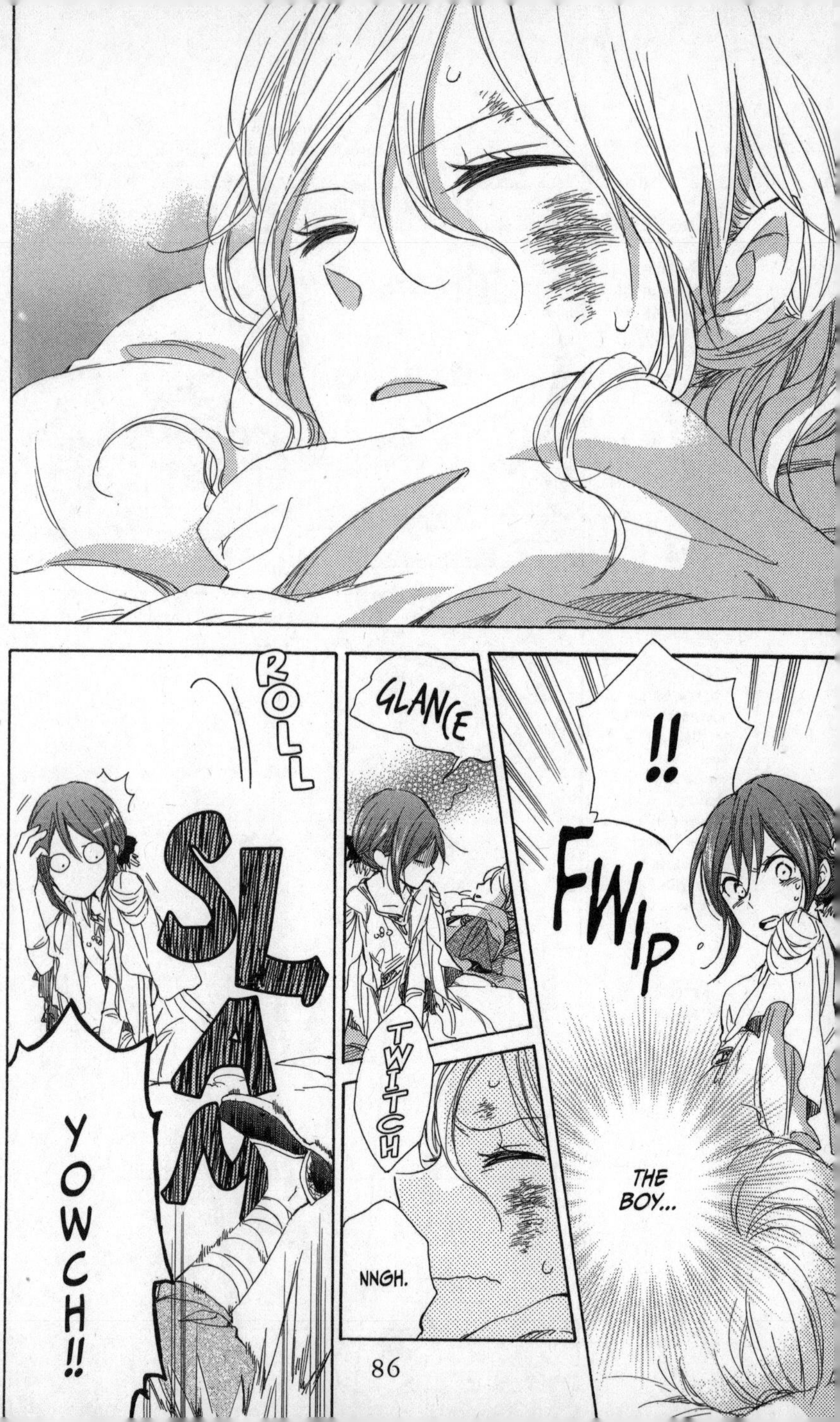
!!
FWIP
THE BOY...
GLANCE
TWITCH
NNGH.
ROLL
SLAM
YOWCH!!

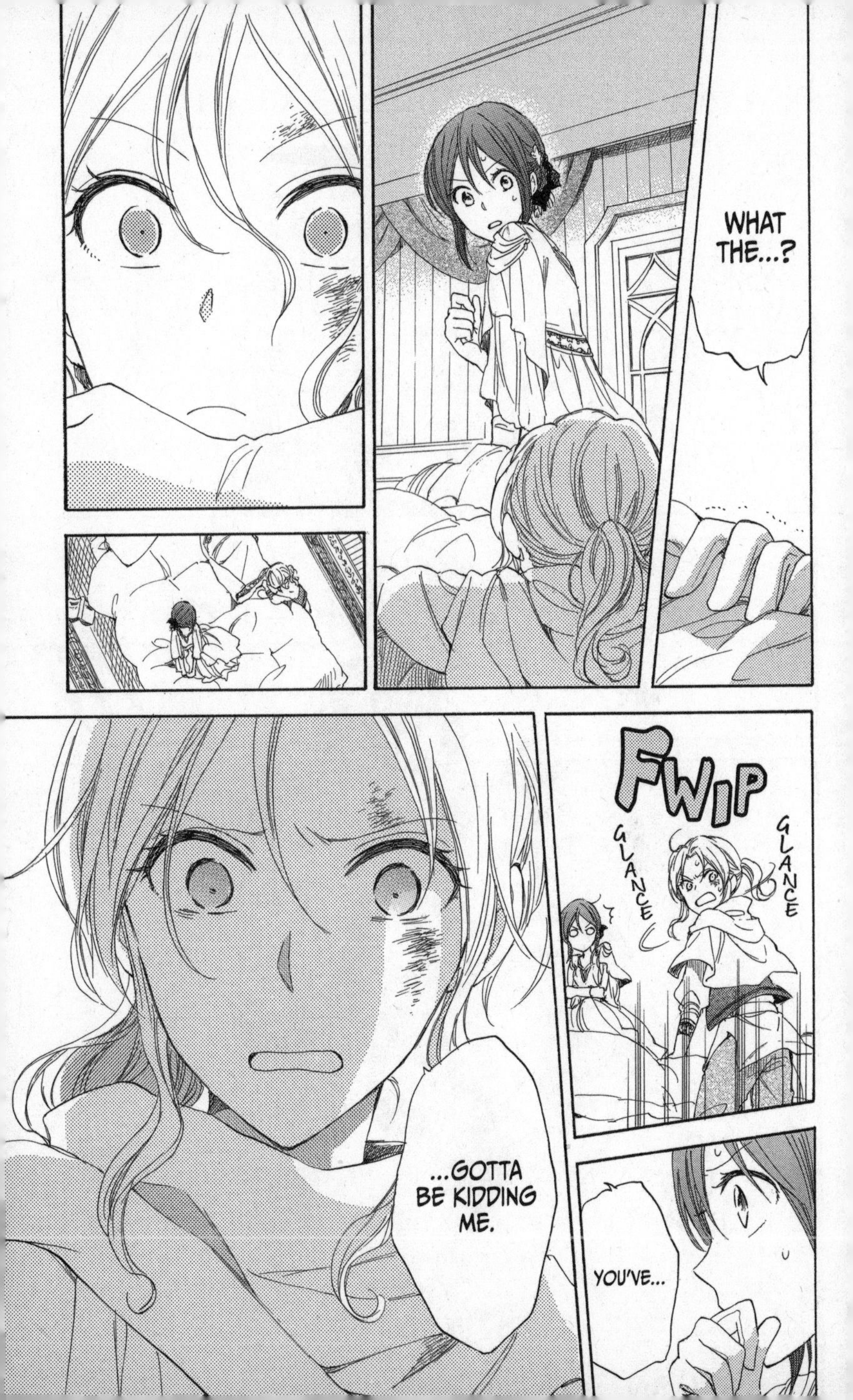
WHAT THE...?
FWIP
GLANCE
GLANCE
YOU'VE...
...GOTTA BE KIDDING ME.

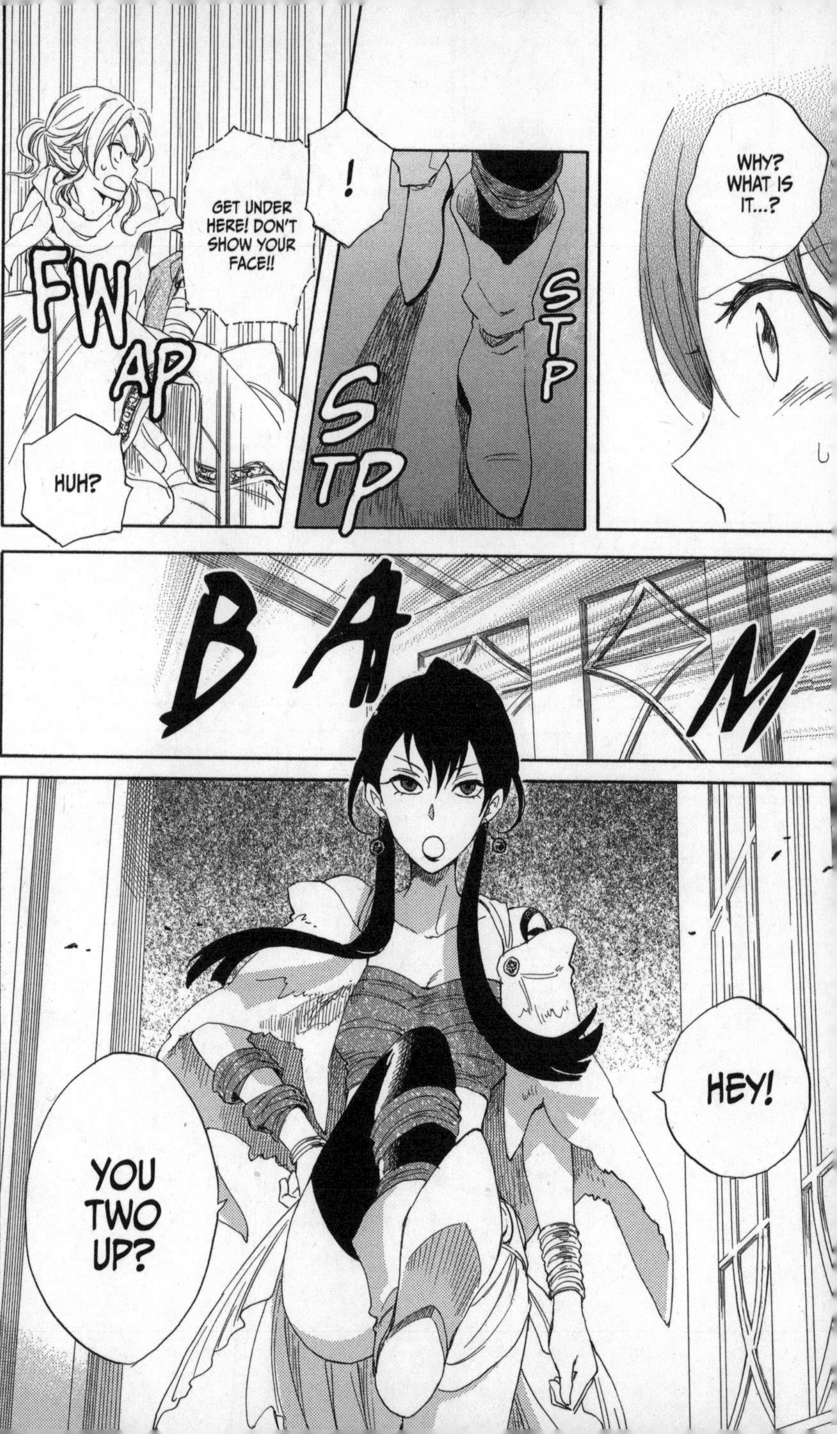
WHY? WHAT IS IT...?
!
STP
STP
GET UNDER HERE! DON'T SHOW YOUR FACE!!
FWAP
HUH?
BAM
HEY!
YOU TWO UP?

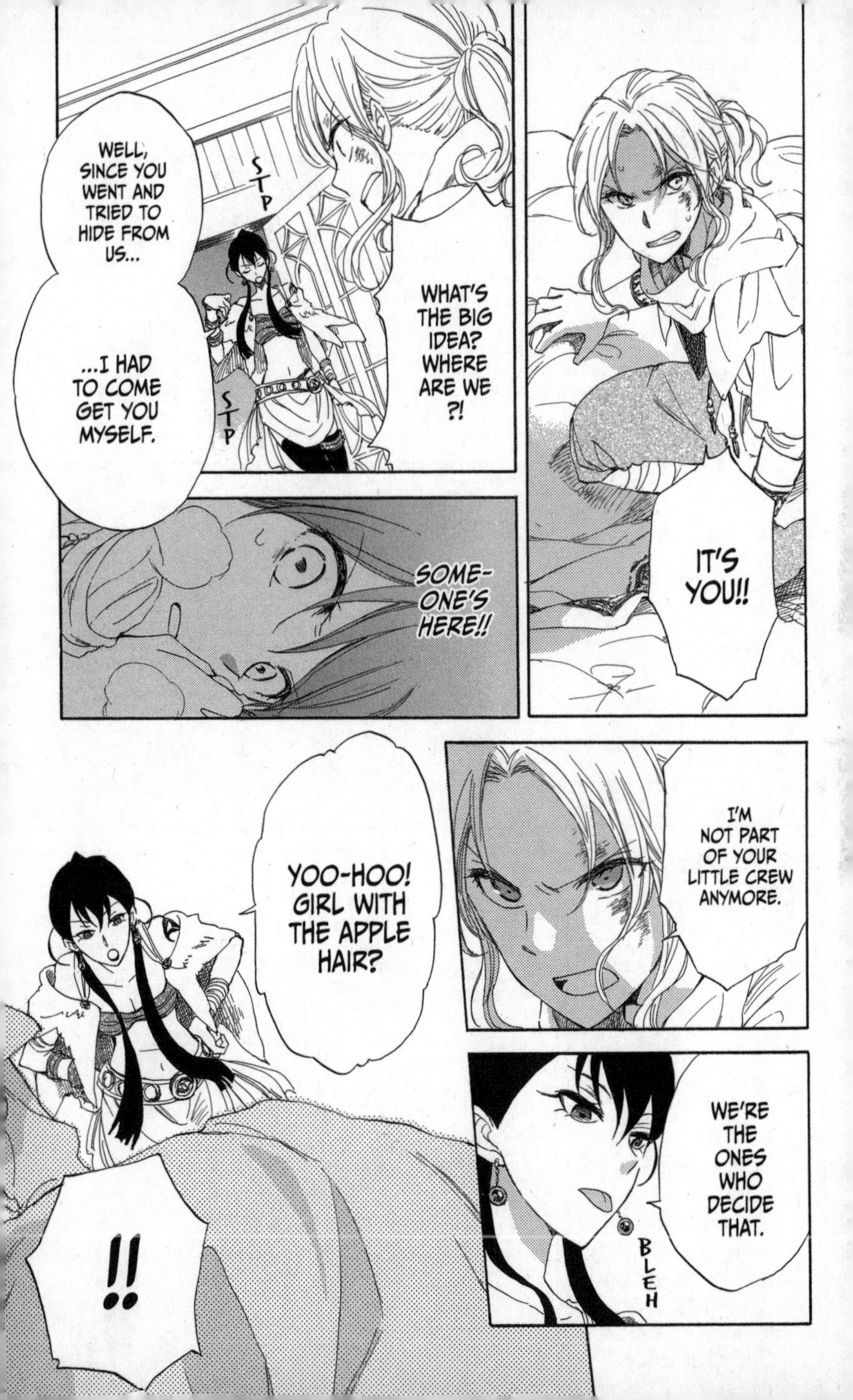
IT'S YOU!!
WHAT'S THE BIG IDEA? WHERE ARE WE ?!
STP
WELL, SINCE YOU WENT AND TRIED TO HIDE FROM US...
...I HAD TO COME GET YOU MYSELF.
STP
SOME-ONE'S HERE!!
I'M NOT PART OF YOUR LITTLE CREW ANYMORE.
WE'RE THE ONES WHO DECIDE THAT.
BLEH
YOO-HOO! GIRL WITH THE APPLE HAIR?
!!

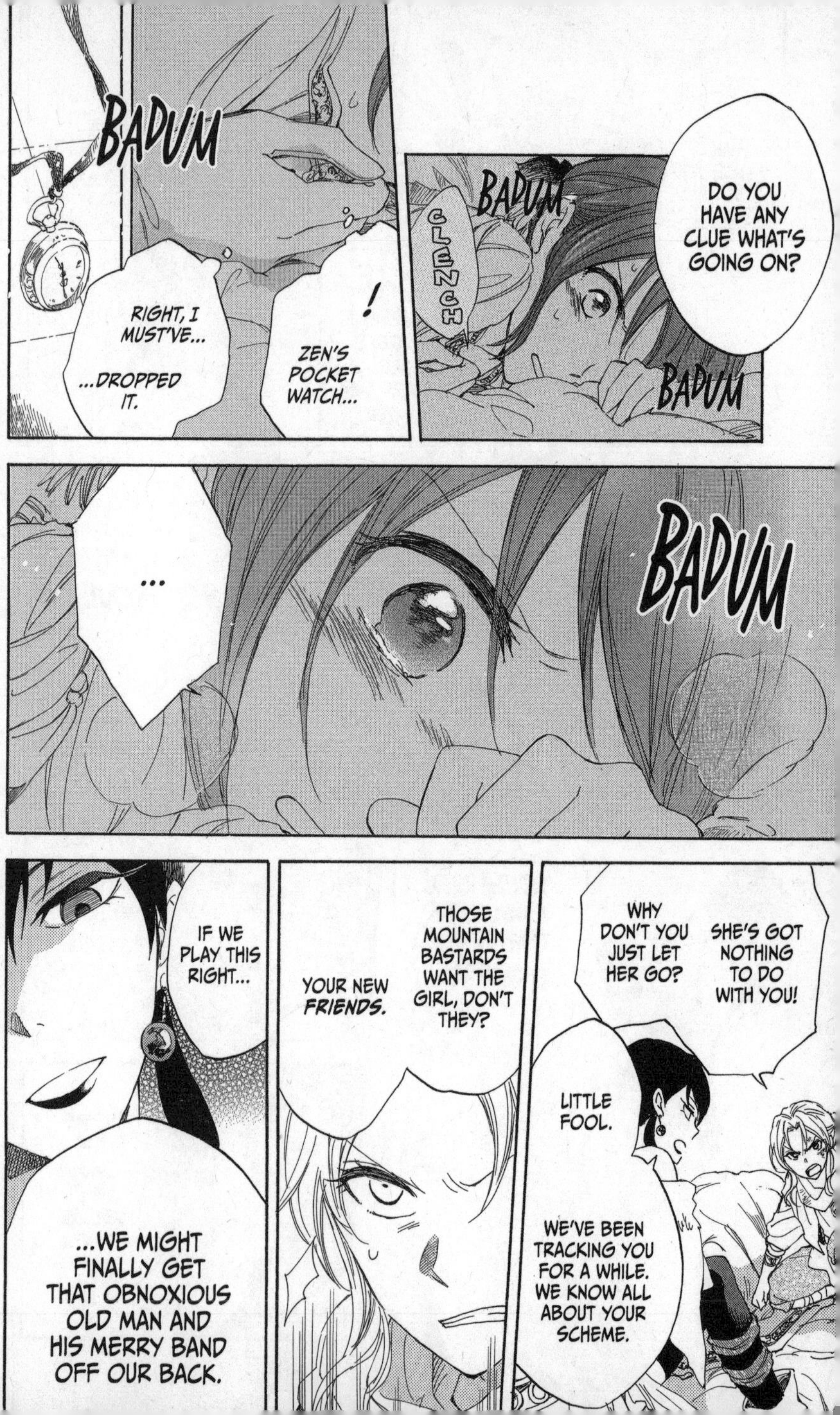
DO YOU HAVE ANY CLUE WHAT'S GOING ON?
BADUM
CLENCH
BADUM
BADUM
!
ZEN'S POCKET WATCH...
RIGHT, I MUST'VE...
...DROPPED IT.
BADUM
...
SHE'S GOT NOTHING TO DO WITH YOU!
WHY DON'T YOU JUST LET HER GO?
LITTLE FOOL.
WE'VE BEEN TRACKING YOU FOR A WHILE. WE KNOW ALL ABOUT YOUR SCHEME.
THOSE MOUNTAIN BASTARDS WANT THE GIRL, DON'T THEY?
YOUR NEW FRIENDS.
IF WE PLAY THIS RIGHT...
...WE MIGHT FINALLY GET THAT OBNOXIOUS OLD MAN AND HIS MERRY BAND OFF OUR BACK.

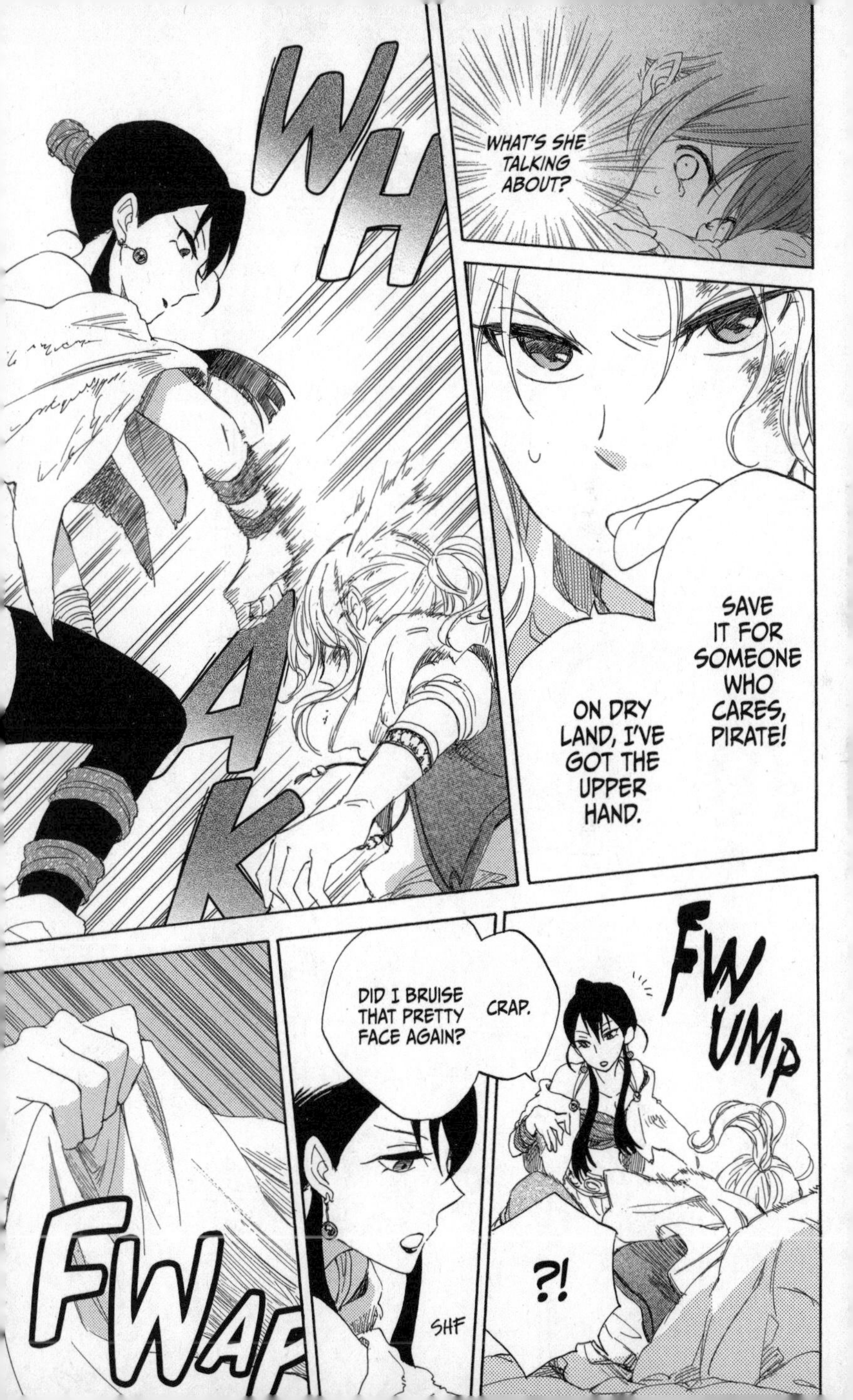
WHAT'S SHE TALKING ABOUT?
SAVE IT FOR SOMEONE WHO CARES, PIRATE!
ON DRY LAND, I'VE GOT THE UPPER HAND.
WHAK
FWUMP
CRAP.
?!
DID I BRUISE THAT PRETTY FACE AGAIN?
SHF
FWAP

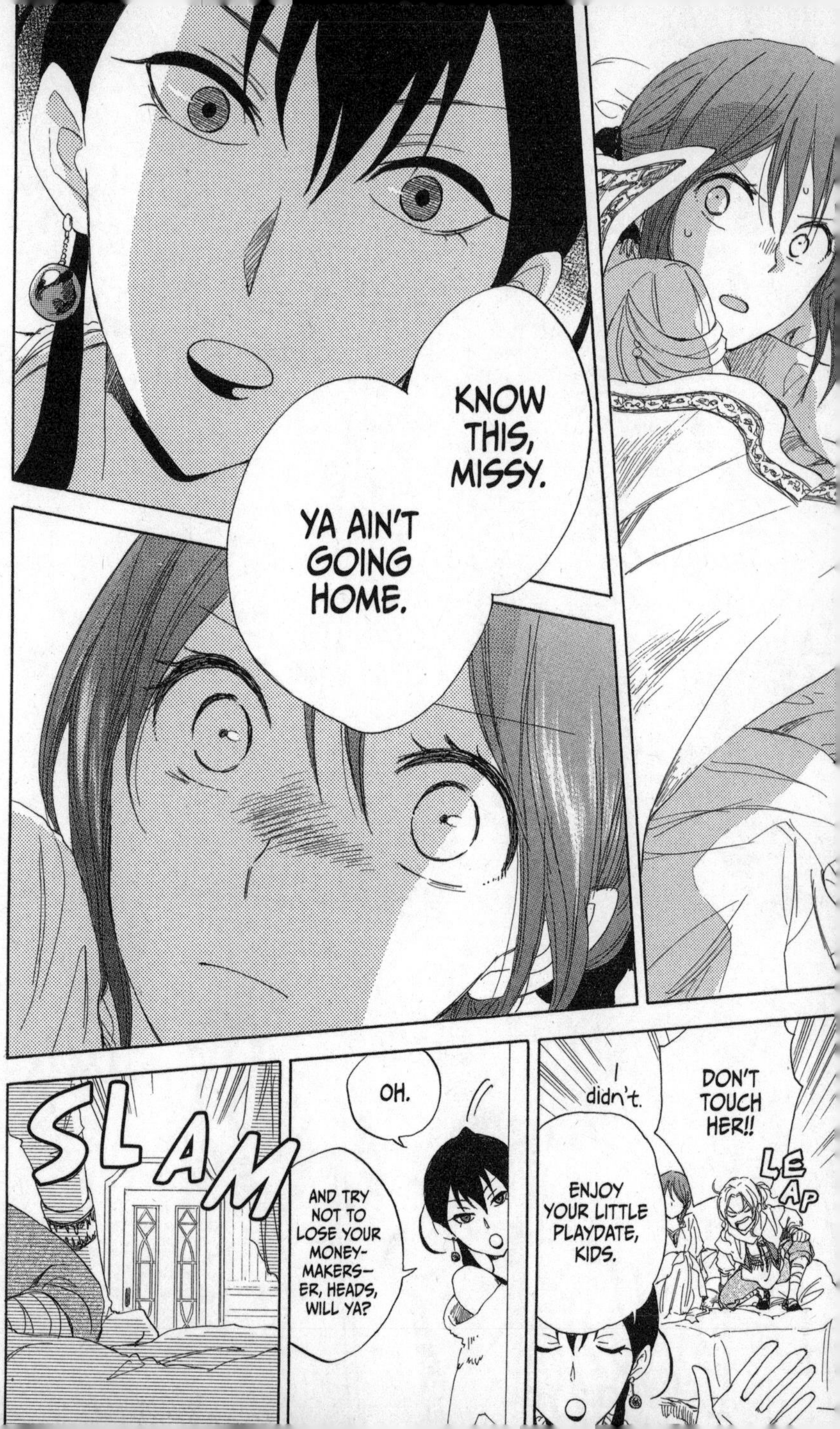
KNOW THIS, MISSY.
YA AIN'T GOING HOME.
DON'T TOUCH HER!!
LEAP
I didn't.
ENJOY YOUR LITTLE PLAYDATE, KIDS.
OH.
AND TRY NOT TO LOSE YOUR MONEY-MAKERS—ER, HEADS, WILL YA?
SLAM

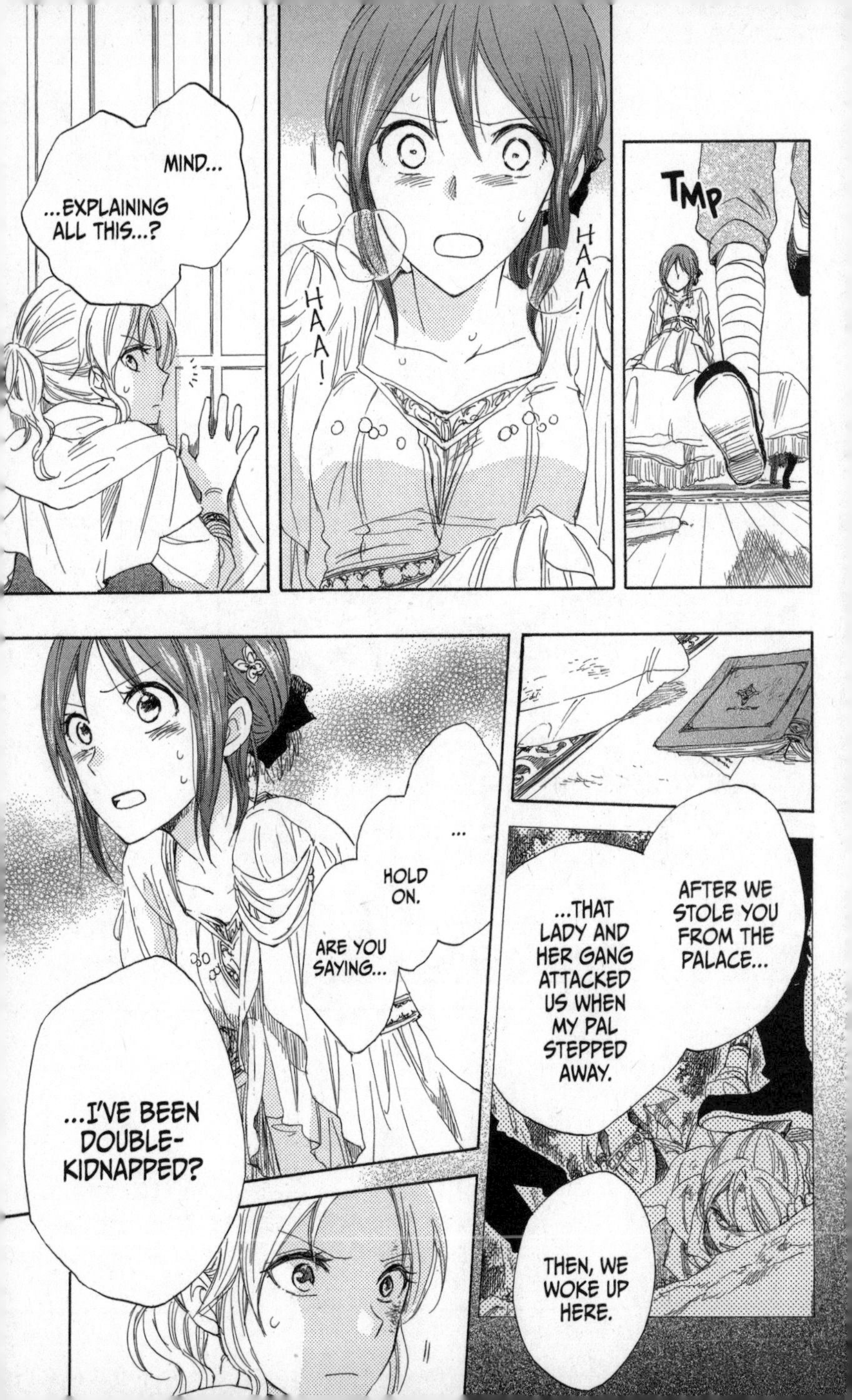

TMP
HAA!
HAA!
MIND...
...EXPLAINING ALL THIS...?
AFTER WE STOLE YOU FROM THE PALACE...
...THAT LADY AND HER GANG ATTACKED US WHEN MY PAL STEPPED AWAY.
THEN, WE WOKE UP HERE.
...
HOLD ON.
ARE YOU SAYING...
...I'VE BEEN DOUBLE-KIDNAPPED?

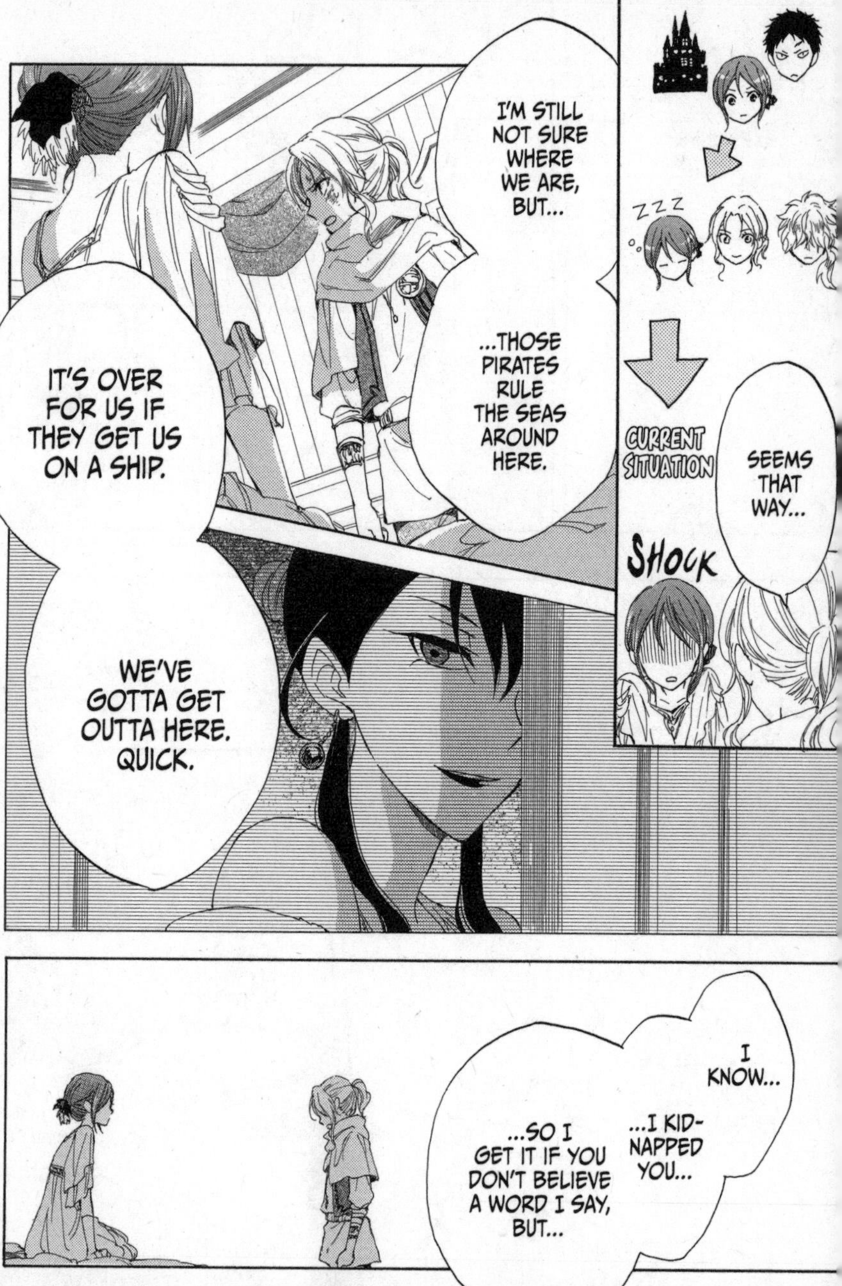
CURRENT SITUATION
SEEMS THAT WAY...
SHOCK
I'M STILL NOT SURE WHERE WE ARE, BUT...
...THOSE PIRATES RULE THE SEAS AROUND HERE.
IT'S OVER FOR US IF THEY GET US ON A SHIP.
WE'VE GOTTA GET OUTTA HERE. QUICK.
I KNOW...
...I KID-NAPPED YOU...
...SO I GET IT IF YOU DON'T BELIEVE A WORD I SAY, BUT...

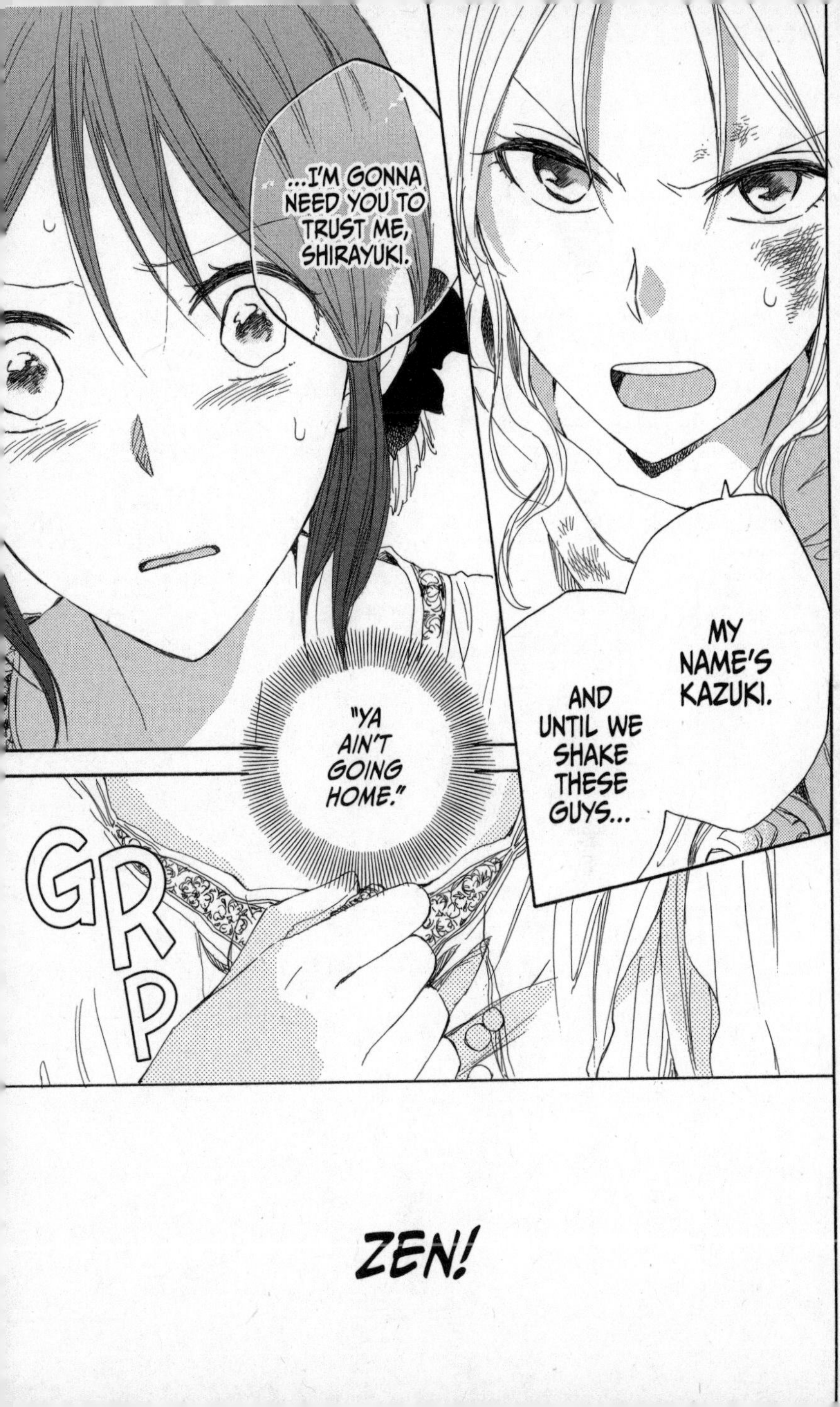
MY NAME'S KAZUKI.
AND UNTIL WE SHAKE THESE GUYS...
...I'M GONNA NEED YOU TO TRUST ME, SHIRAYUKI.
"YA AIN'T GOING HOME."
GRP
ZEN!

"Unrelated to the Main Plot" Theater #2

BUT, MASTER, IF YOU CASUALLY MENTION HOW CUTE YOUR MAIDS ARE...
WINK
...MY LADY MAY GET JEALOUS AND SHOW YOU SOME EXTRA LOVE.
SHIRAYUKI... IT'S BEEN BROUGHT TO MY ATTENTION HOW...
Prince Zen, Forging Ahead
HUH?
...AT THE PALACE... I'M SURROUNDED BY...BEAUTIFUL MAIDS.
WELL, SURE.
"Sure" ...?
IF WE'RE TALKING ABOUT THE LADIES IN YOUR LIFE...
...WE CAN'T FORGET KIKI, WHO'S COOL AND PRETTY.
HER EYES, HER VOICE, HER WHOLE DEMEANOR ...
I'D LOVE TO TRY TALKING TO HER MORE, IN GENERAL.
SO YOU ENDED UP BEING JEALOUS OF KIKI?
HOW DO THINGS ALWAYS WIND UP LIKE THIS?
BE-GONE.

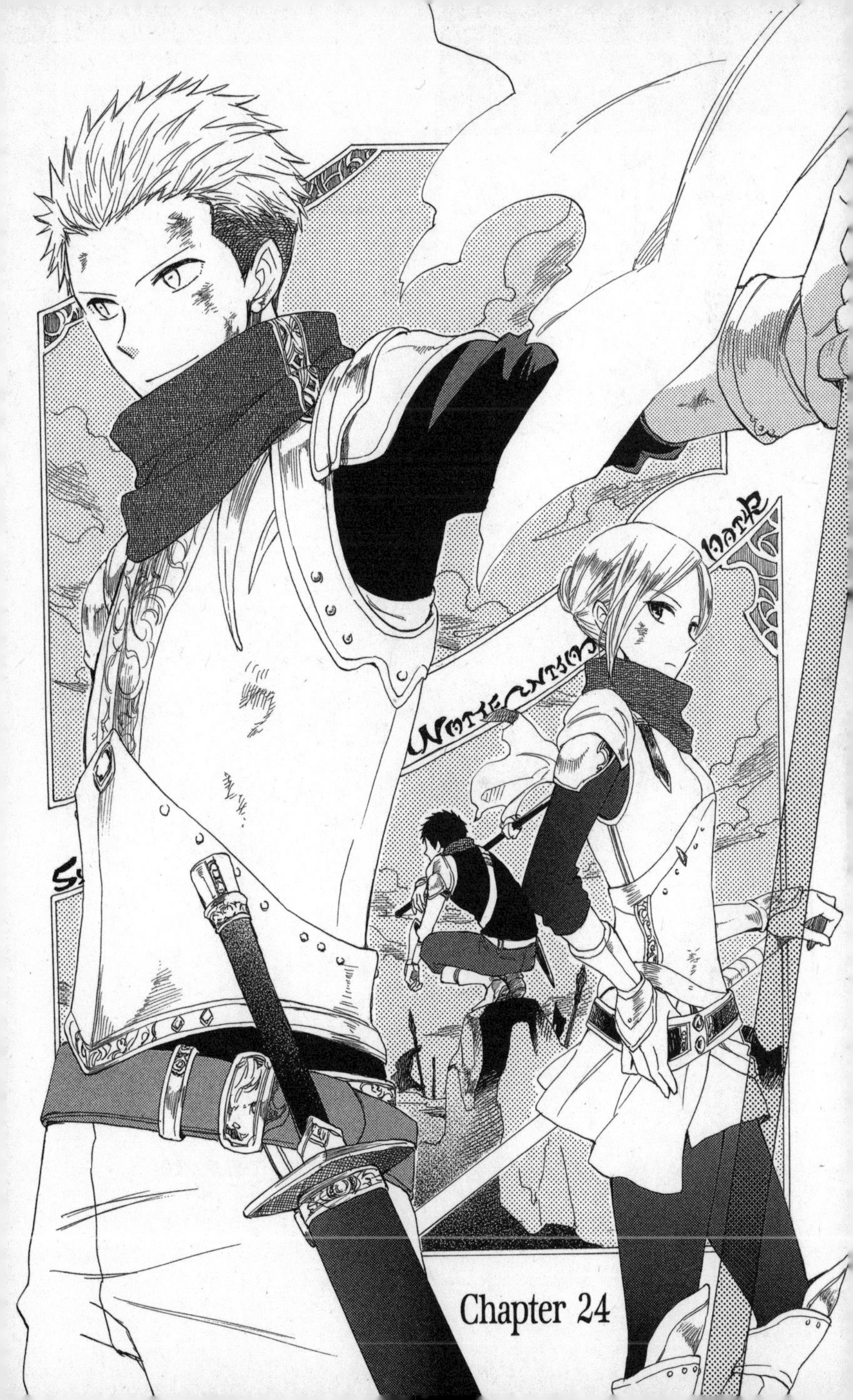

Chapter 24

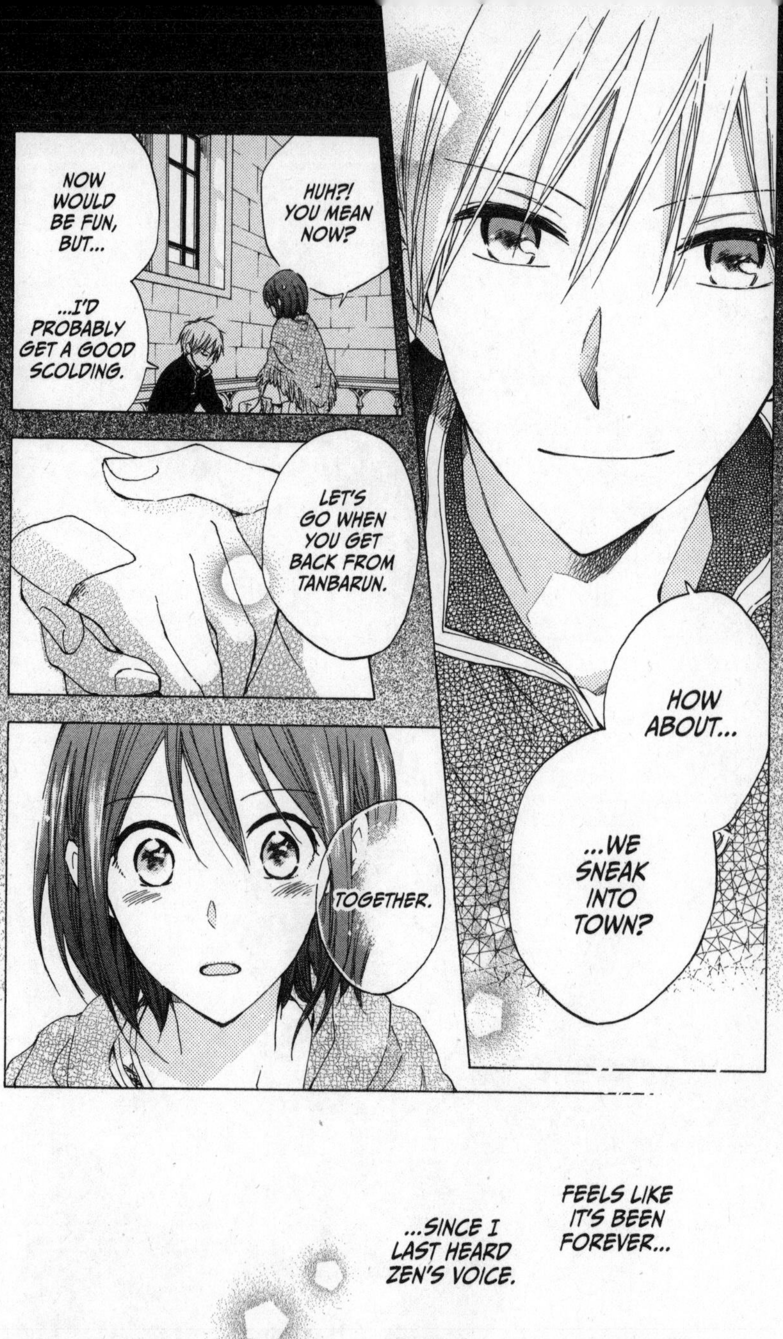
HOW ABOUT...
...WE SNEAK INTO TOWN?
HUH?! YOU MEAN NOW?
NOW WOULD BE FUN, BUT...
...I'D PROBABLY GET A GOOD SCOLDING.
LET'S GO WHEN YOU GET BACK FROM TANBARUN.
TOGETHER.
FEELS LIKE IT'S BEEN FOREVER...
...SINCE I LAST HEARD ZEN'S VOICE.

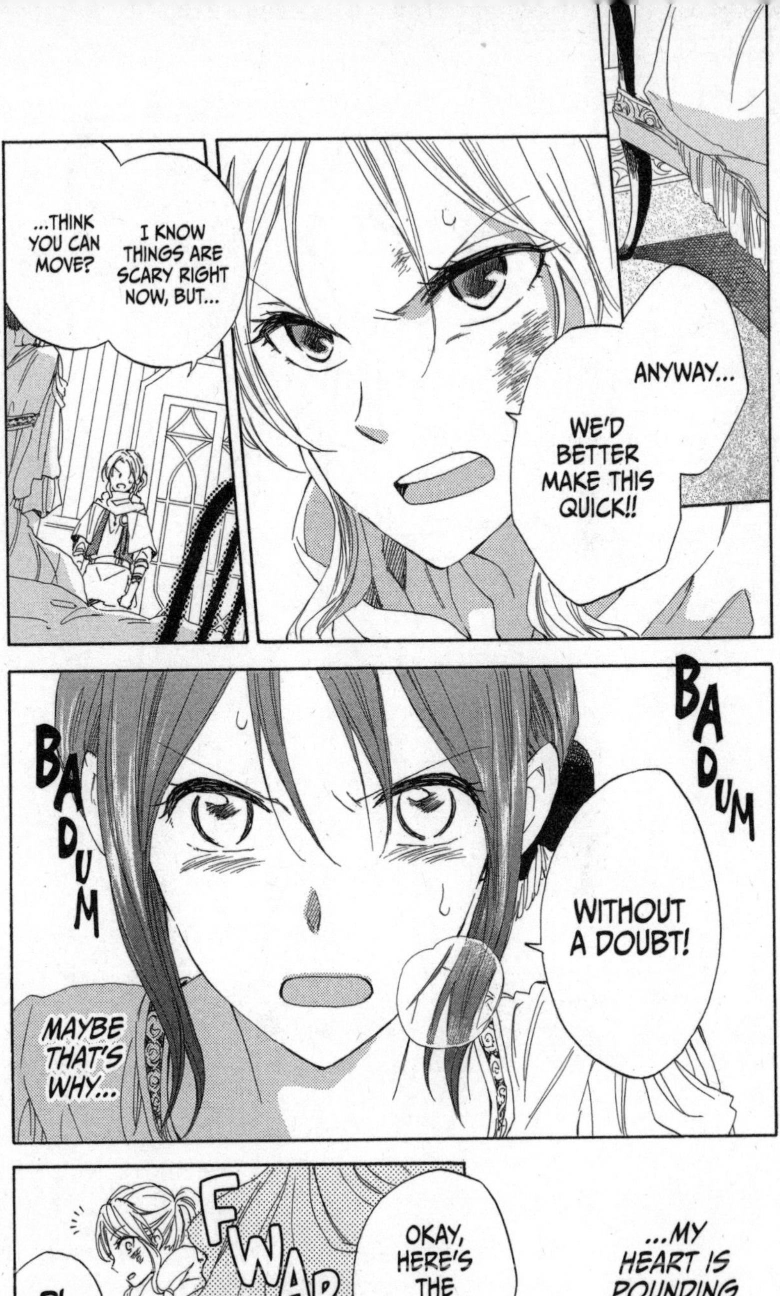
ANYWAY...
WE'D BETTER MAKE THIS QUICK!!
I KNOW THINGS ARE SCARY RIGHT NOW, BUT...
...THINK YOU CAN MOVE?
BADUM
WITHOUT A DOUBT!
BADUM
MAYBE THAT'S WHY...
...MY HEART IS POUNDING LIKE THIS.
OKAY, HERE'S THE PLAN...
FWAP
?!

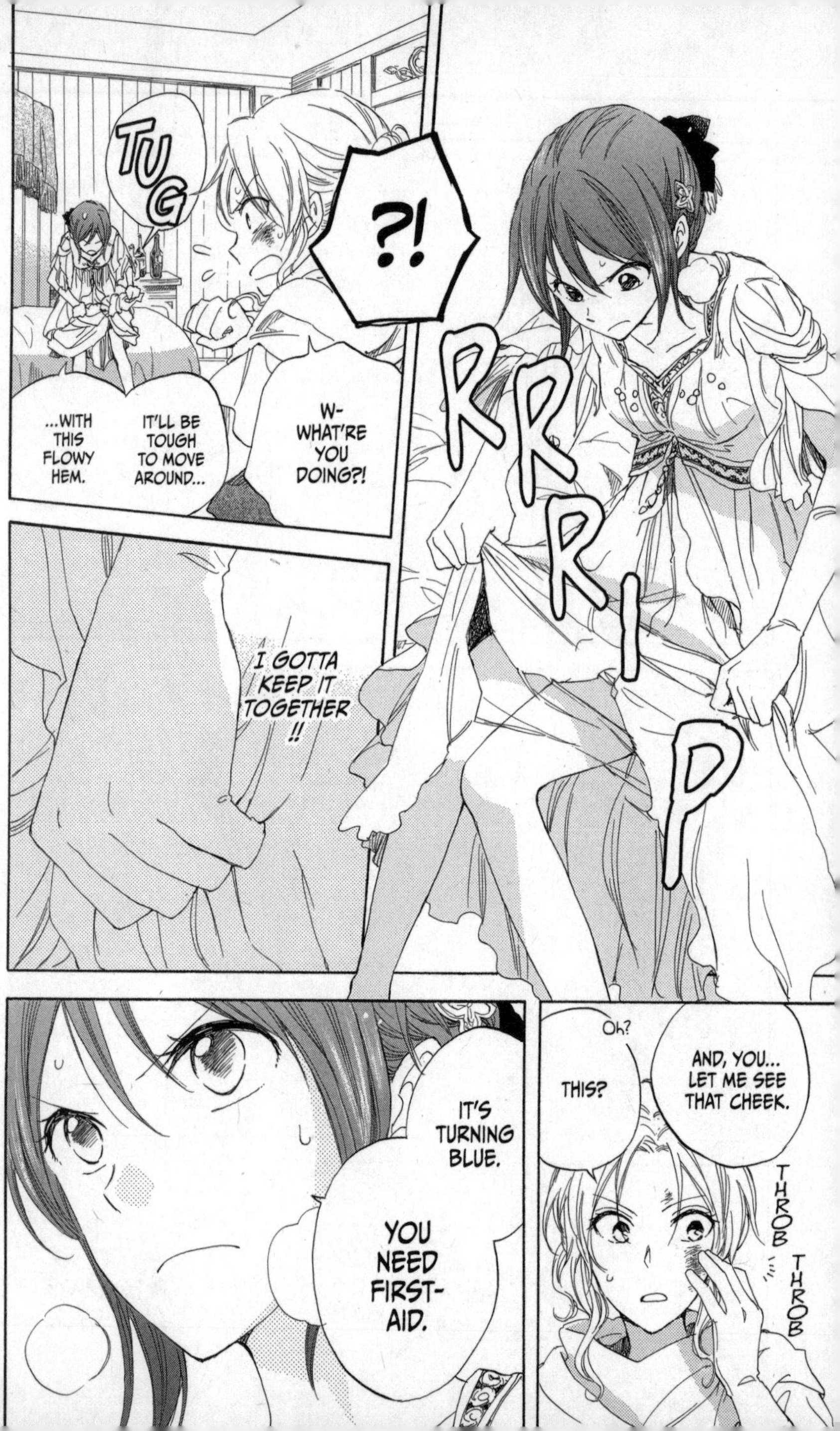
?!
RRRIP
TUG
W-WHAT'RE YOU DOING?!
IT'LL BE TOUGH TO MOVE AROUND...
...WITH THIS FLOWY HEM.
I GOTTA KEEP IT TOGETHER!!
AND, YOU... LET ME SEE THAT CHEEK.
Oh?
THIS?
THROB THROB
IT'S TURNING BLUE.
YOU NEED FIRST-AID.

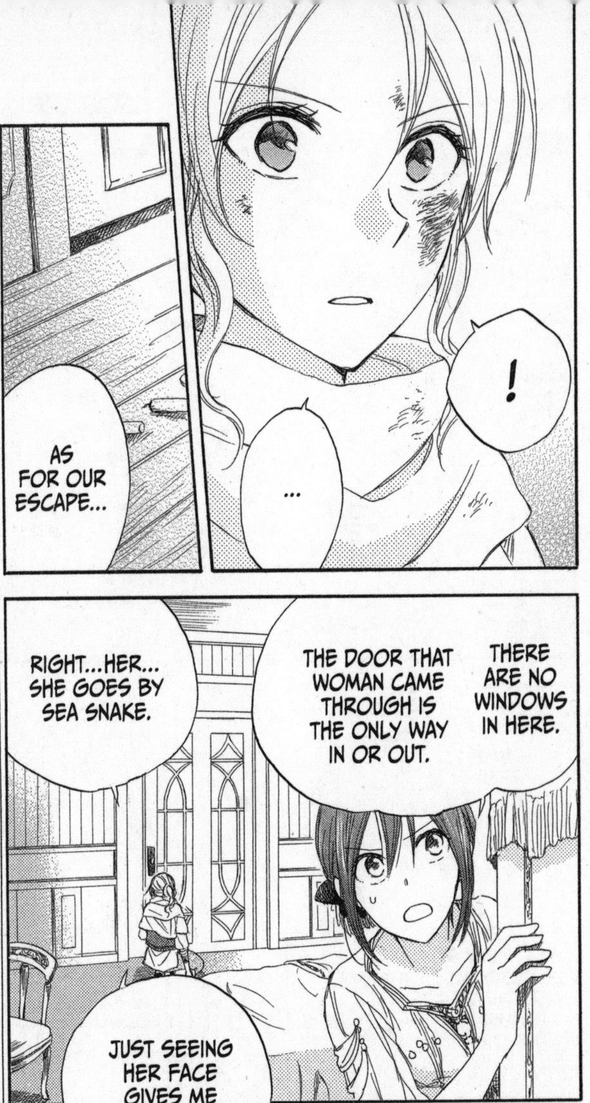
!
...
AS FOR OUR ESCAPE...
THERE ARE NO WINDOWS IN HERE.
THE DOOR THAT WOMAN CAME THROUGH IS THE ONLY WAY IN OR OUT.
RIGHT...HER... SHE GOES BY SEA SNAKE.
JUST SEEING HER FACE GIVES ME CHILLS...
WAIT! DID YOU SAY NO WINDOWS?

Gate Guard (2)

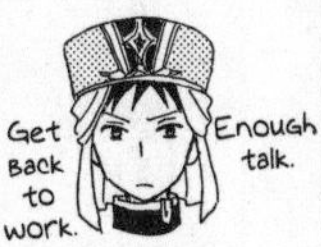
Enough talk.
Get back to work.

Shila Eigan

Ulkir's senior colleague. He's serious about the job, but he often gets roped into pointless chats with Ulkir that he later regrets.

The day Zen actually asked him for his name, Eigan was so thrilled that he went out drinking with Ulkir. Maybe they really do get along after all?

7

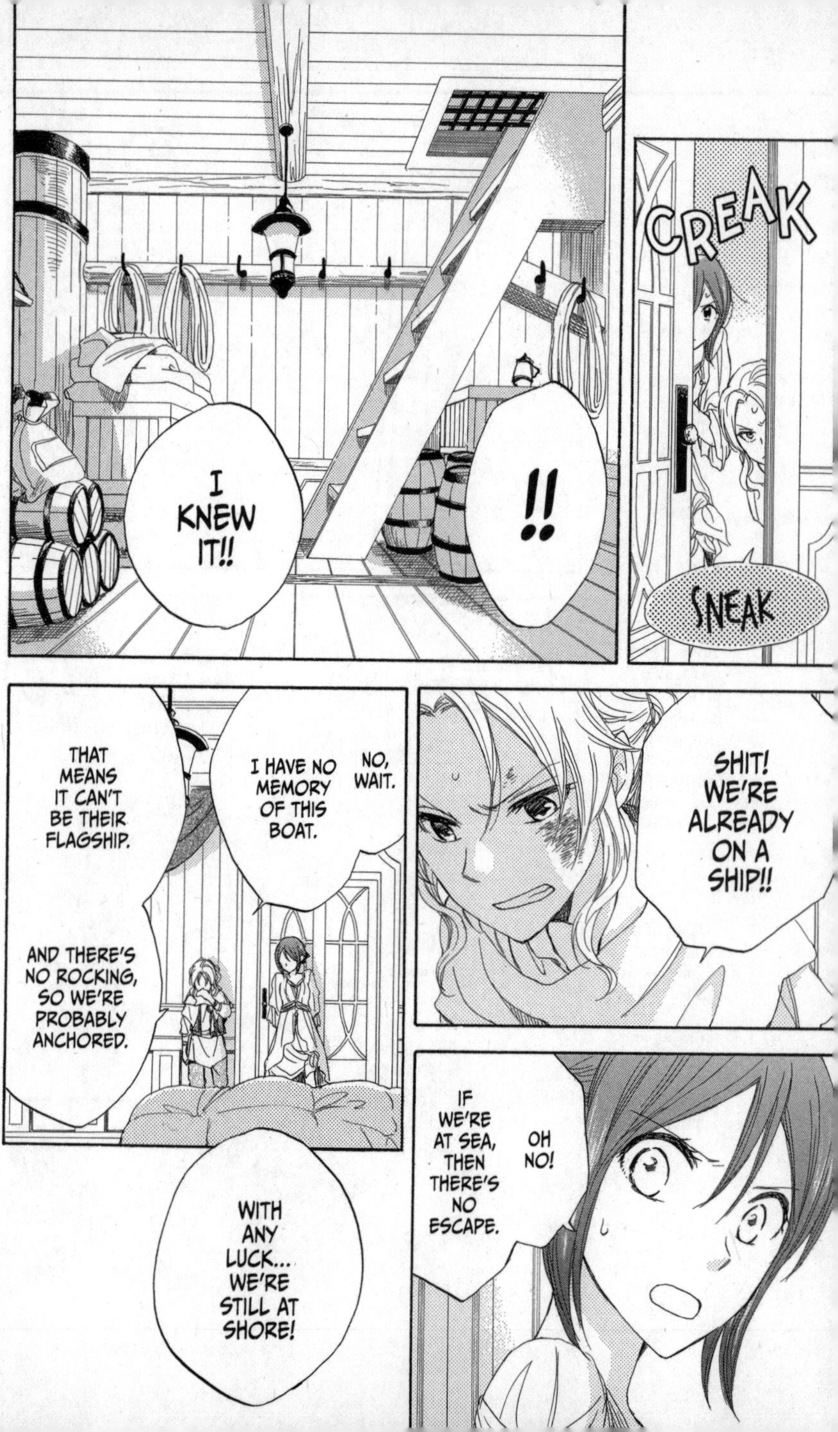
CREAK
SNEAK
!!
I KNEW IT!!
SHIT! WE'RE ALREADY ON A SHIP!!
NO, WAIT.
I HAVE NO MEMORY OF THIS BOAT.
THAT MEANS IT CAN'T BE THEIR FLAGSHIP.
AND THERE'S NO ROCKING, SO WE'RE PROBABLY ANCHORED.
OH NO!
IF WE'RE AT SEA, THEN THERE'S NO ESCAPE.
WITH ANY LUCK... WE'RE STILL AT SHORE!

Q: "How do the characters bathe?"

I'd like to portray them bathing at some point. Maybe... probably... someday...

The waitstaff and soldiers have their own bathing areas.

Of course, Izana and Zen have the largest baths in the palace. Although they probably don't have rose petals floating on the water. (That's a distinct possibility with Raj, though).

We've gotta have a bath scene sooner or later, right, Your Highness?

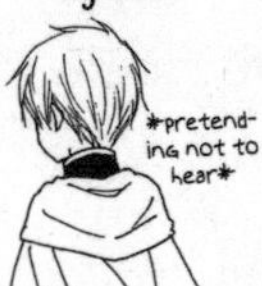
pretending not to hear

8

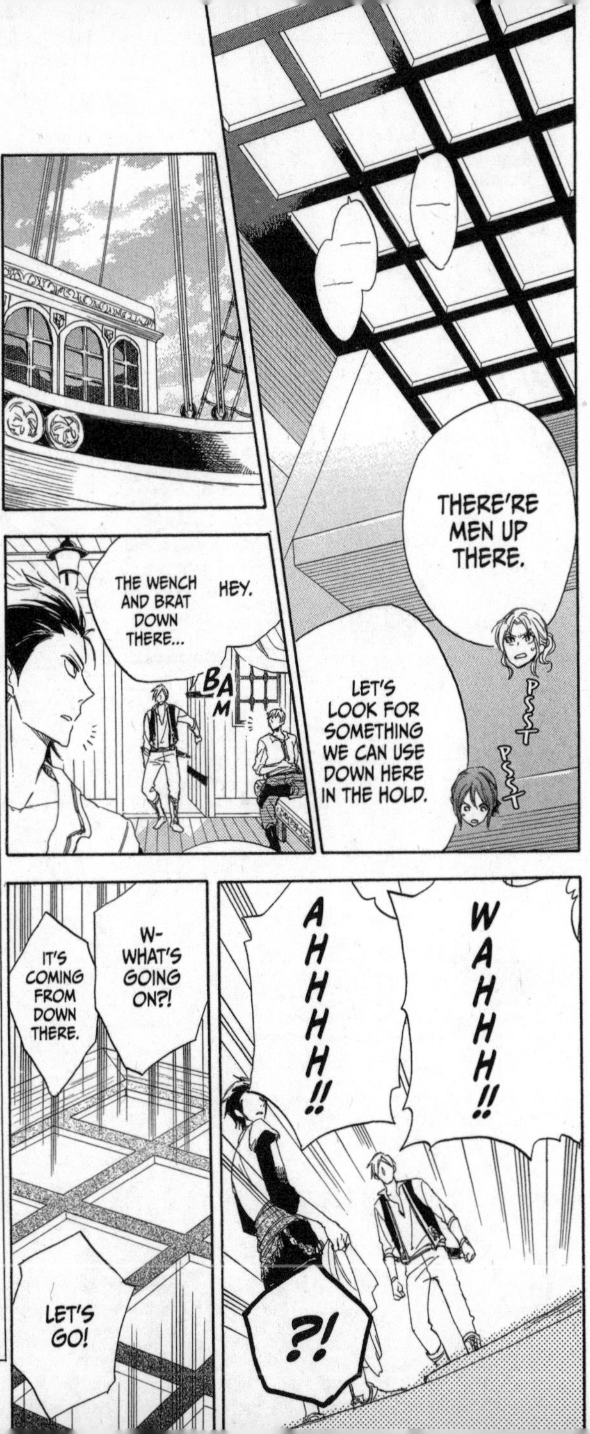
THERE'RE MEN UP THERE.
LET'S LOOK FOR SOMETHING WE CAN USE DOWN HERE IN THE HOLD.
PSST
PSST
HEY.
THE WENCH AND BRAT DOWN THERE...
BAM
WAHHHH!!
AHHHHH!!
?!
W-WHAT'S GOING ON?!
IT'S COMING FROM DOWN THERE.
LET'S GO!

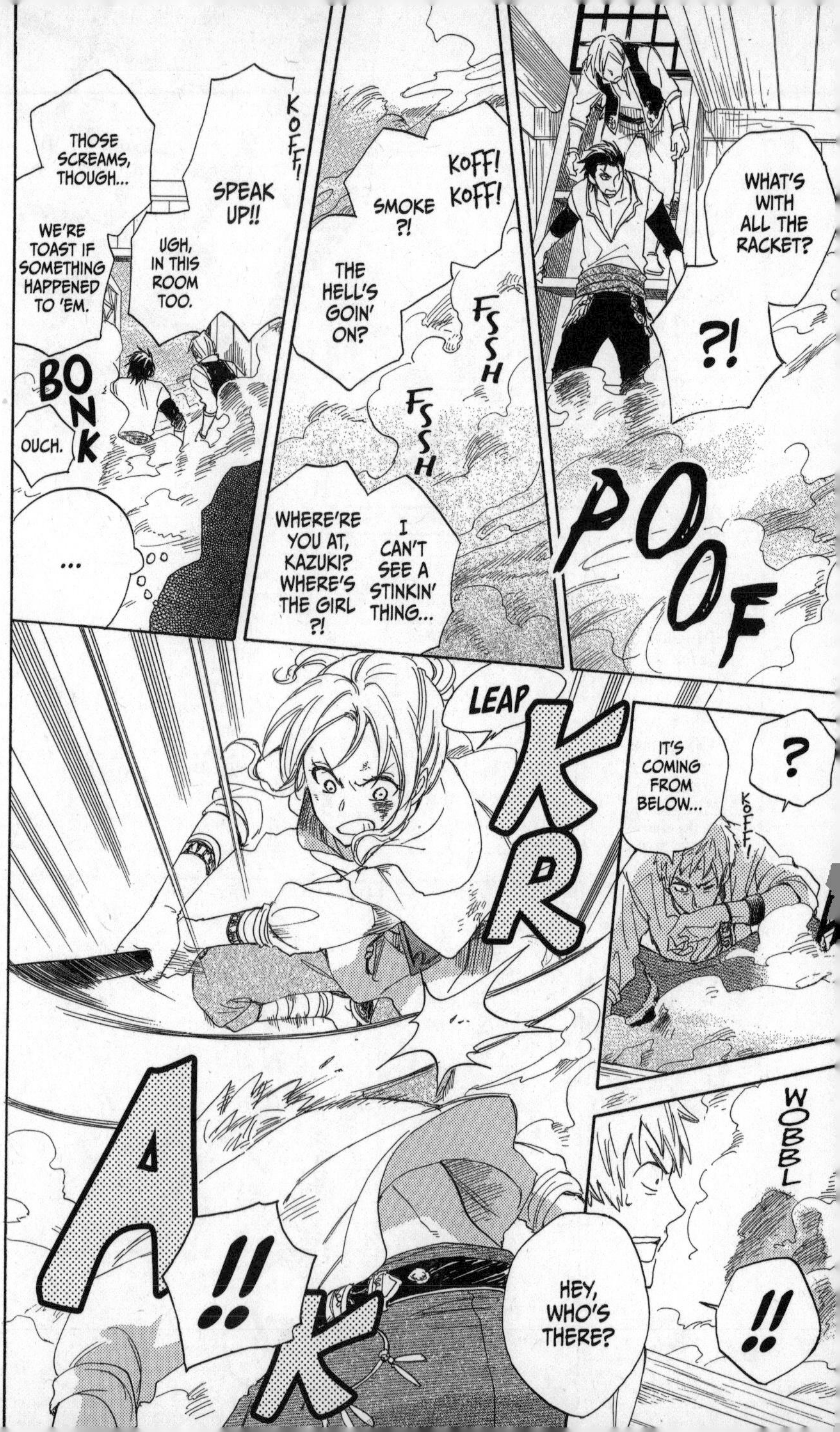
WHAT'S WITH ALL THE RACKET?
?!
POOF
KOFF! KOFF!
SMOKE?!
THE HELL'S GOIN' ON?
FSSH
FSSH
I CAN'T SEE A STINKIN' THING...
WHERE'RE YOU AT, KAZUKI? WHERE'S THE GIRL?!
KOFF!
SPEAK UP!!
UGH, IN THIS ROOM TOO.
THOSE SCREAMS, THOUGH...
WE'RE TOAST IF SOMETHING HAPPENED TO 'EM.
BONK
OUCH.
...
?
IT'S COMING FROM BELOW...
KOFF!
WOBBL
!!
HEY, WHO'S THERE?
LEAP
KRAK
!!

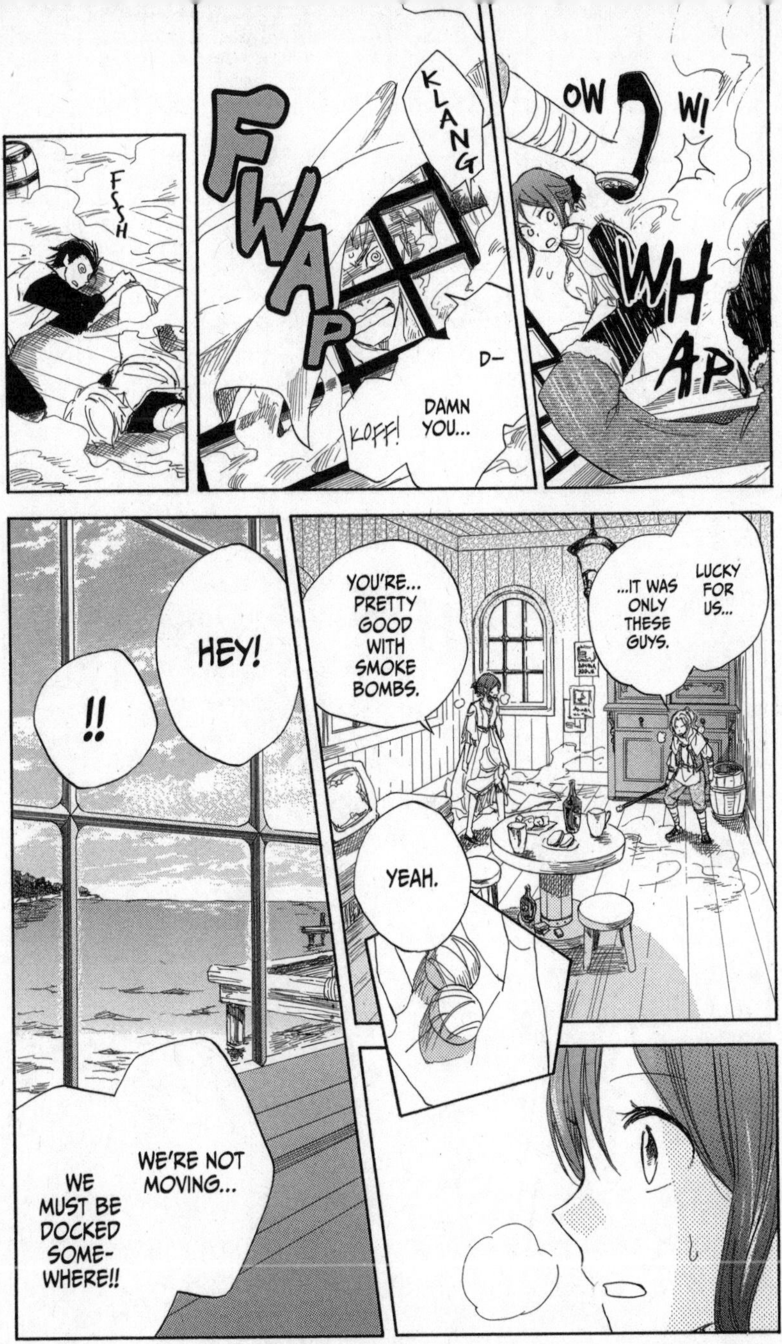

OW WI!
WHAP
KLANG
FWAP
D–
DAMN YOU...
KOFF!
FSSH
LUCKY FOR US...
...IT WAS ONLY THESE GUYS.
YOU'RE... PRETTY GOOD WITH SMOKE BOMBS.
YEAH.
HEY!
!!
WE'RE NOT MOVING...
WE MUST BE DOCKED SOME-WHERE!!

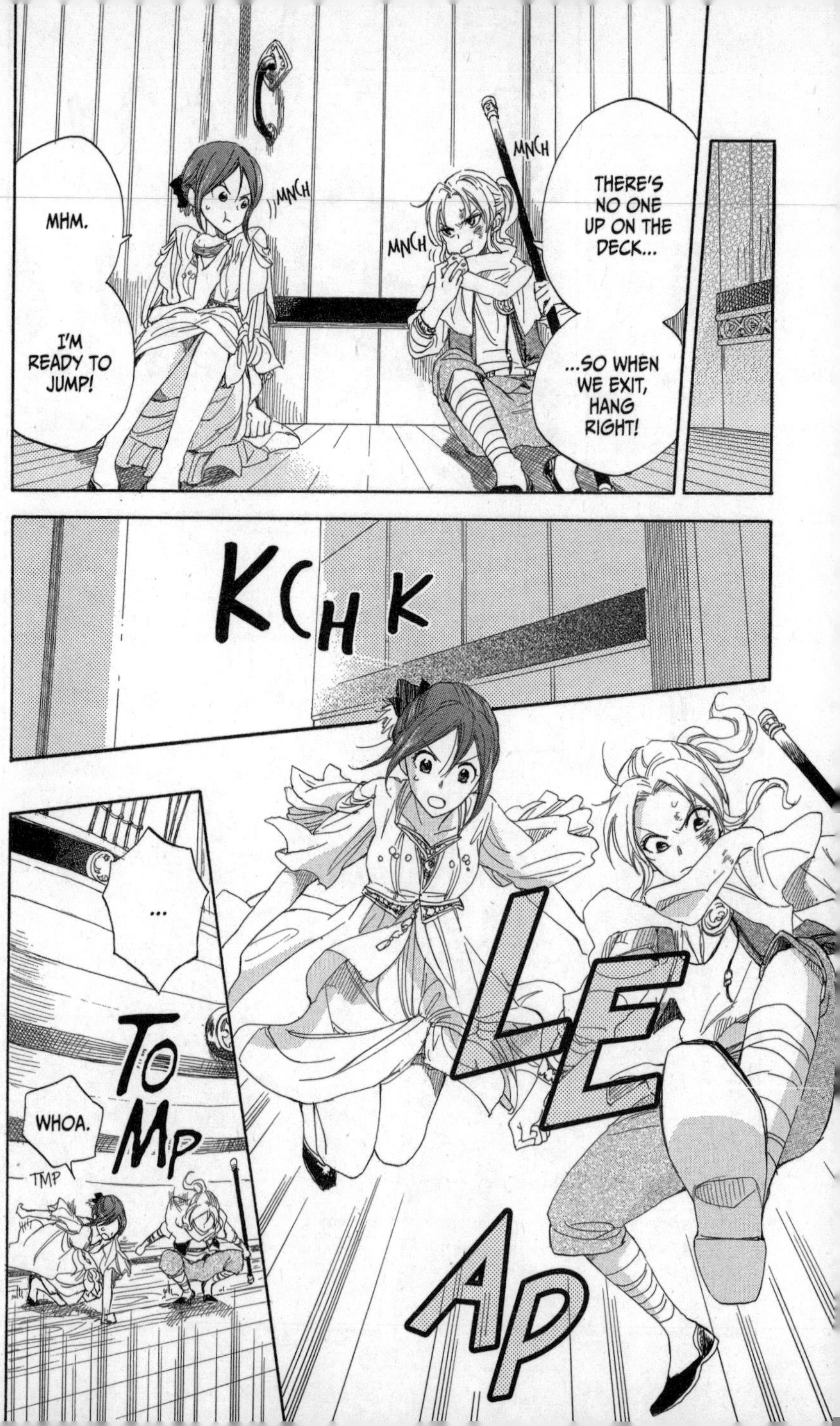
MNCH
MNCH
THERE'S NO ONE UP ON THE DECK...
...SO WHEN WE EXIT, HANG RIGHT!
MNCH
MHM.
I'M READY TO JUMP!
KCHK
LEAP
...
TOMP
WHOA.
TMP

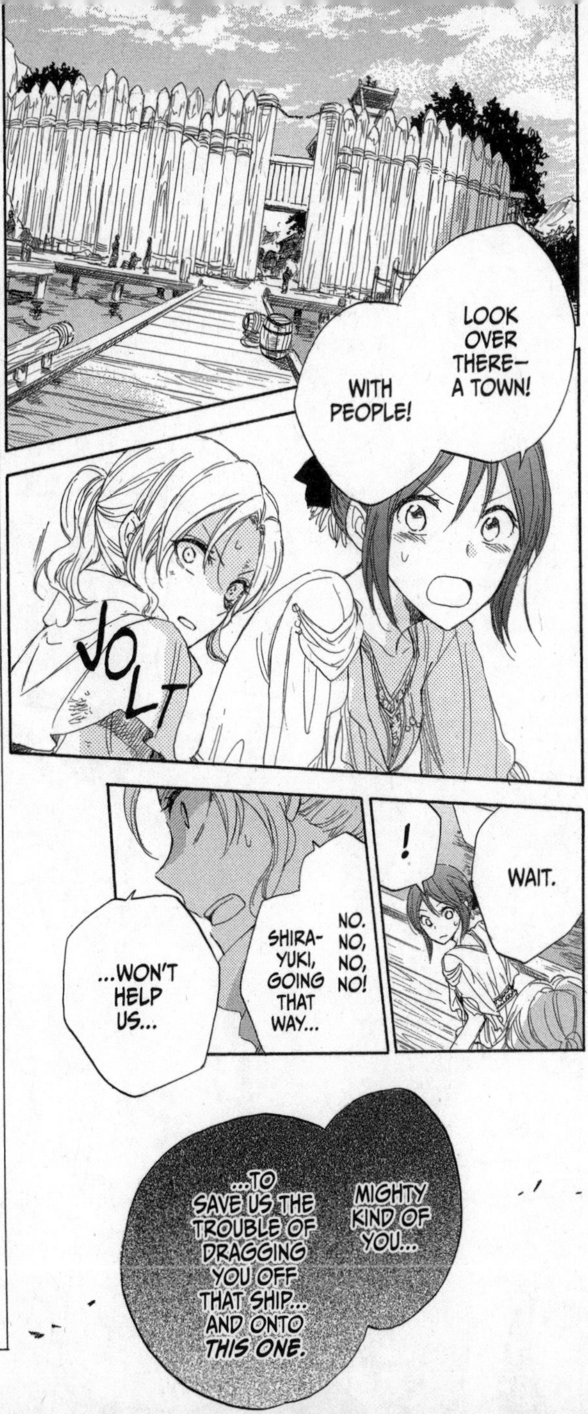
LOOK OVER THERE— A TOWN!
WITH PEOPLE!
JOLT
!
WAIT.
NO. NO, NO, NO!
SHIRA-YUKI, GOING THAT WAY...
...WON'T HELP US...
MIGHTY KIND OF YOU...
...TO SAVE US THE TROUBLE OF DRAGGING YOU OFF THAT SHIP... AND ONTO THIS ONE.

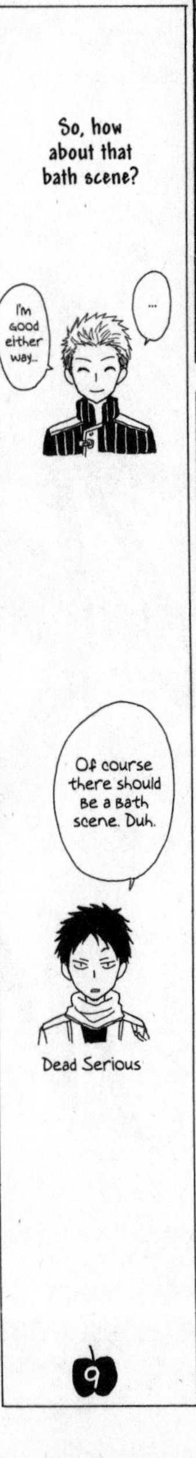
So, how about that bath scene?
...
I'm good either way...
Of course there should be a bath scene. Duh.
Dead Serious
9

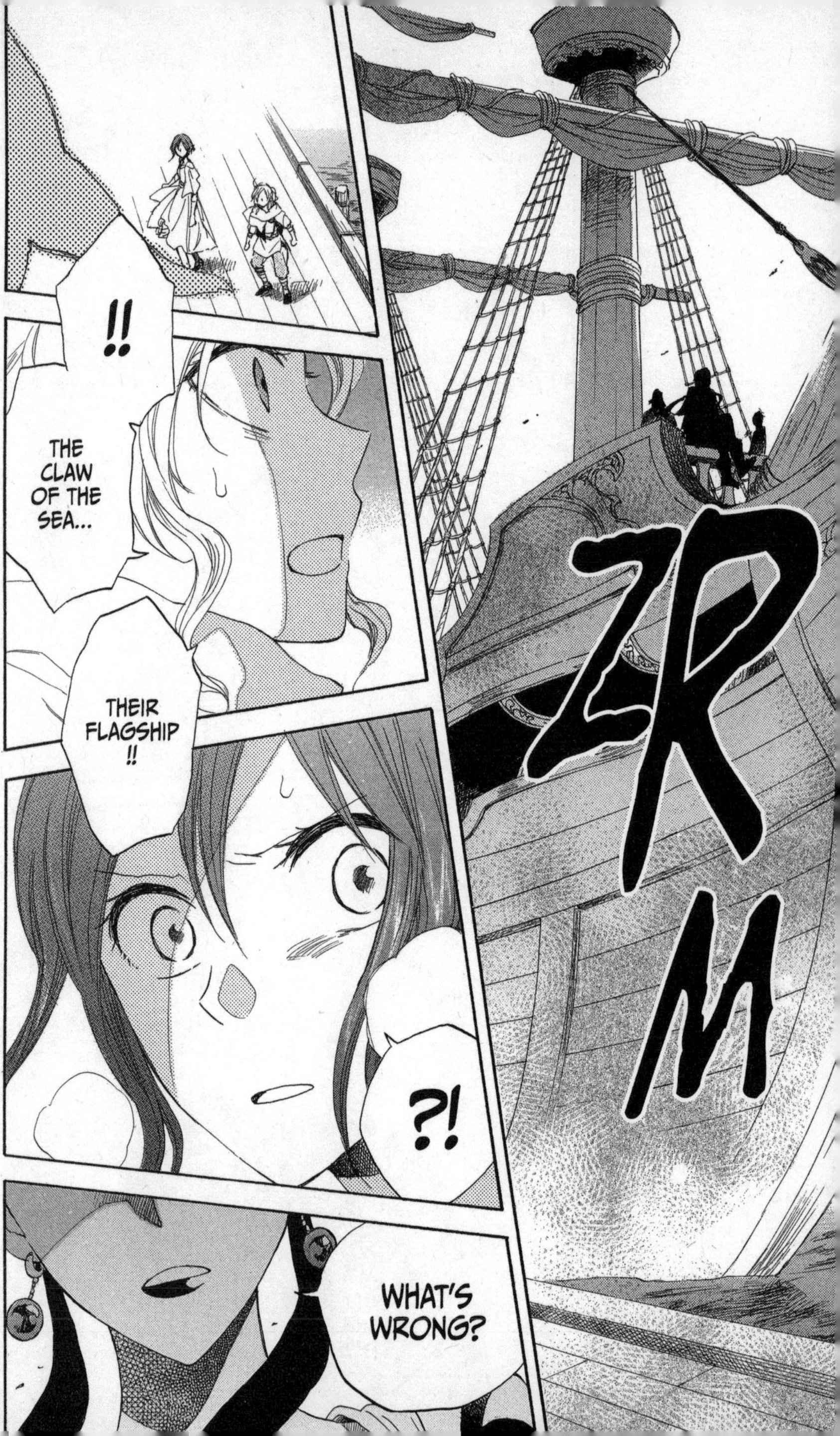
ZRM
!!
THE CLAW OF THE SEA...
THEIR FLAGSHIP !!
?!
WHAT'S WRONG?

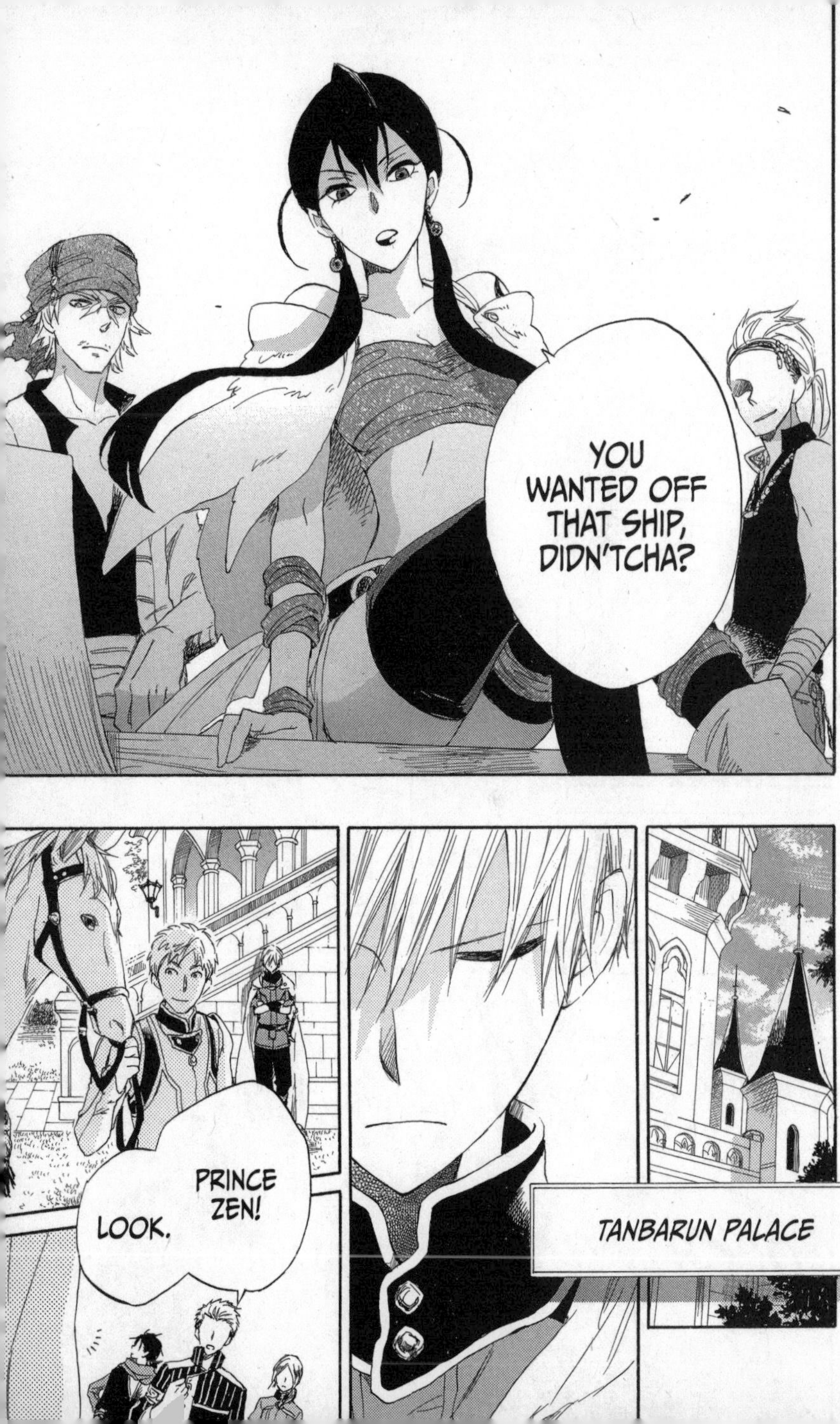
YOU WANTED OFF THAT SHIP, DIDN'TCHA?
TANBARUN PALACE
PRINCE ZEN!
LOOK.

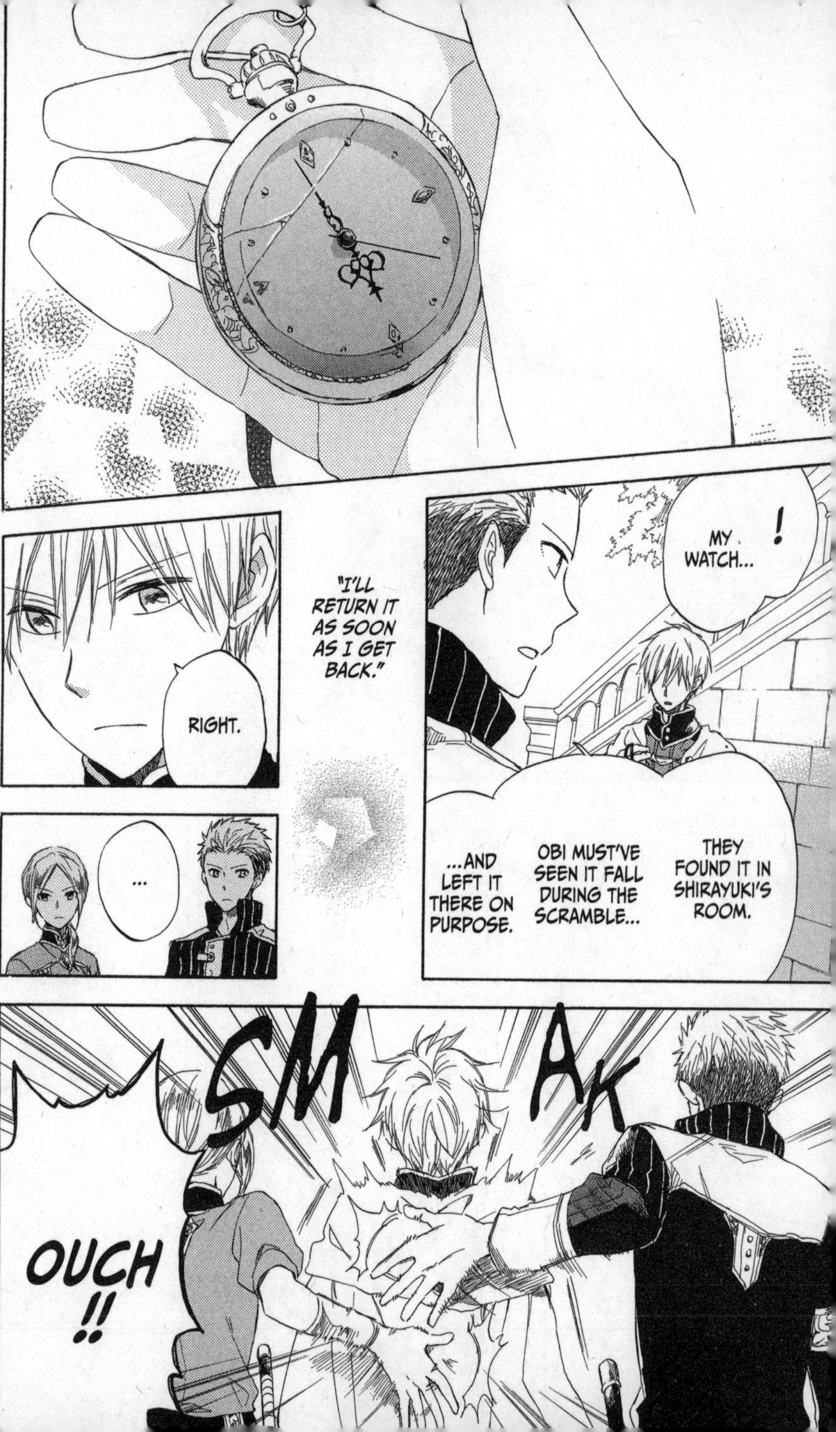
MY WATCH...
!
THEY FOUND IT IN SHIRAYUKI'S ROOM.
OBI MUST'VE SEEN IT FALL DURING THE SCRAMBLE...
...AND LEFT IT THERE ON PURPOSE.
"I'LL RETURN IT AS SOON AS I GET BACK."
RIGHT.
...
SMAK
OUCH!!

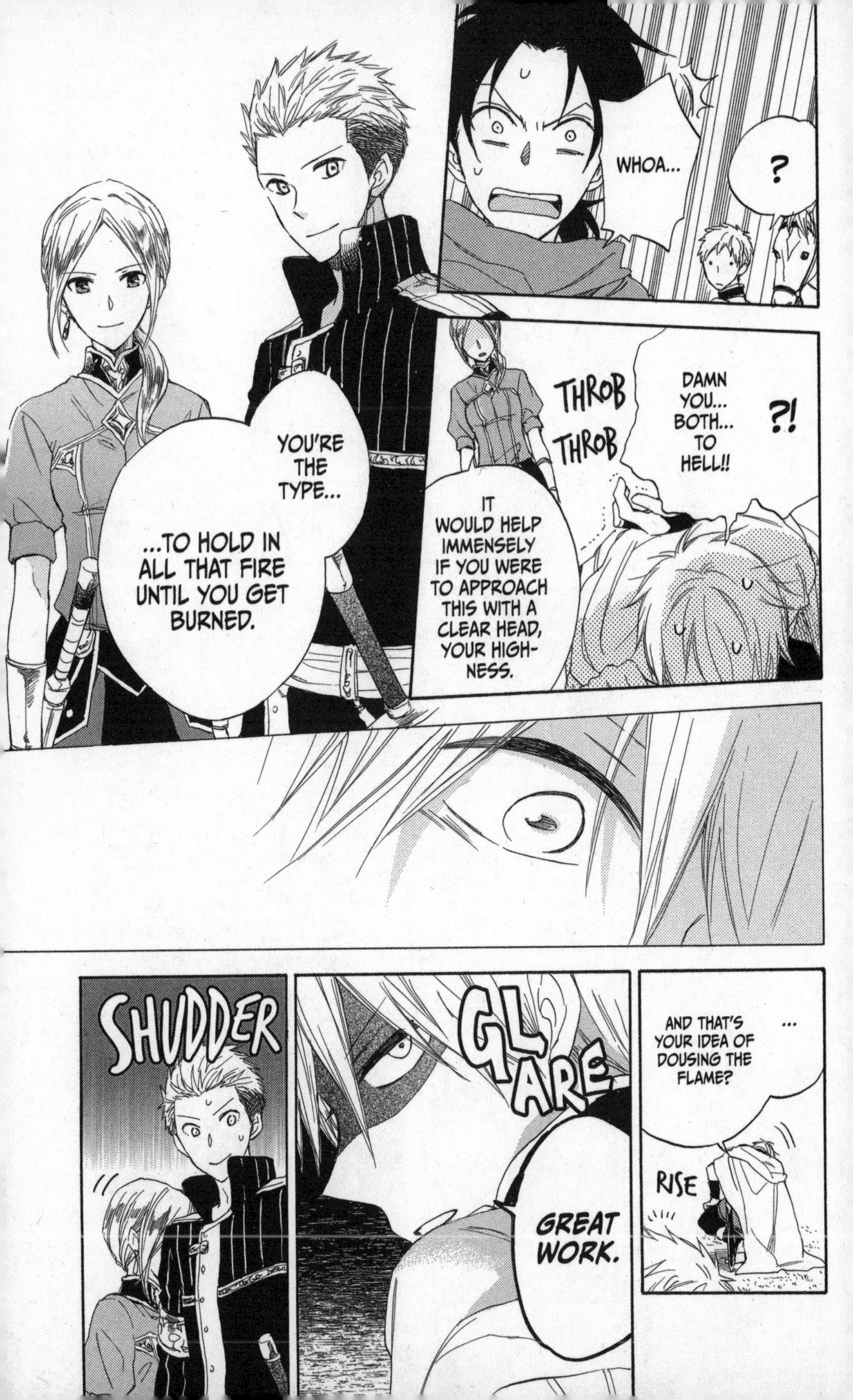
?
WHOA...
?!
DAMN YOU... BOTH... TO HELL!!
THROB
THROB
IT WOULD HELP IMMENSELY IF YOU WERE TO APPROACH THIS WITH A CLEAR HEAD, YOUR HIGHNESS.
YOU'RE THE TYPE...
...TO HOLD IN ALL THAT FIRE UNTIL YOU GET BURNED.
...
AND THAT'S YOUR IDEA OF DOUSING THE FLAME?
RISE
GLARE
GREAT WORK.
SHUDDER

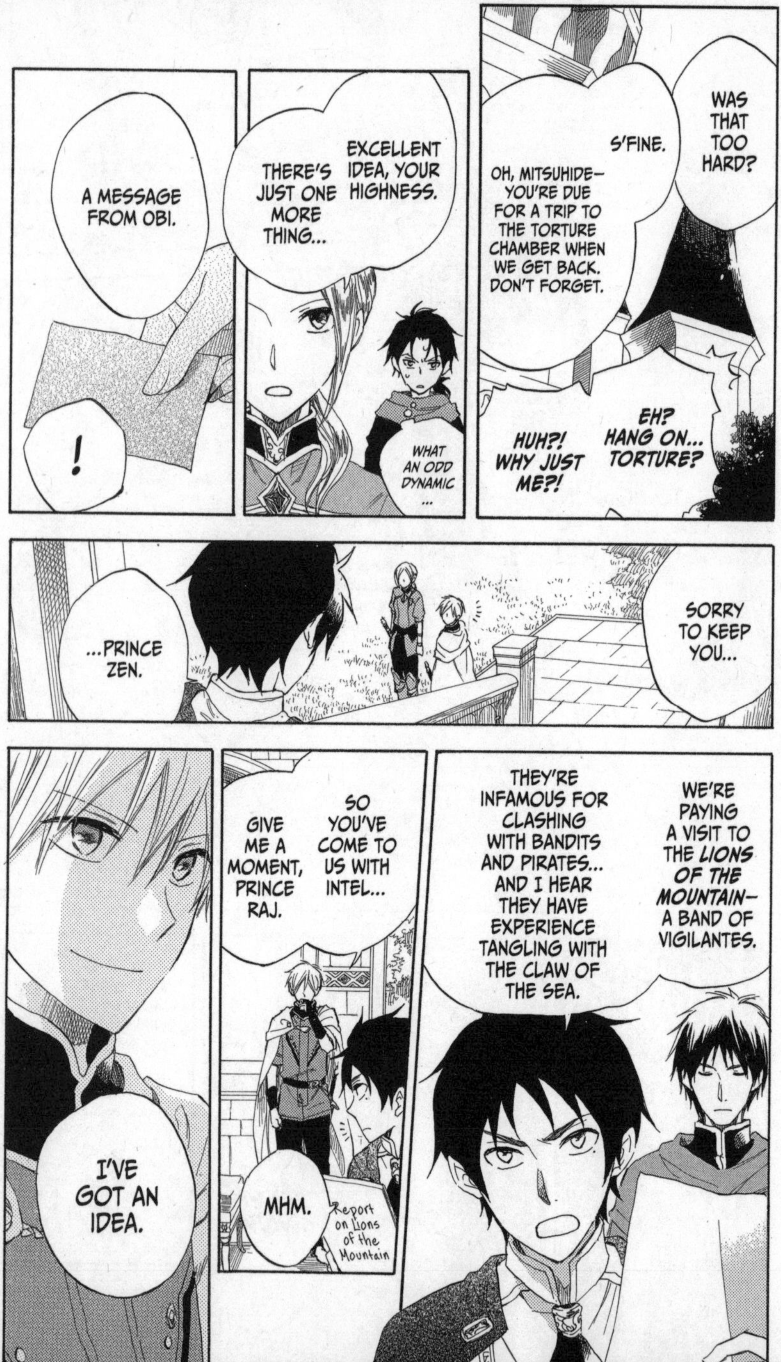
WAS THAT TOO HARD?
S'FINE.
OH, MITSUHIDE—YOU'RE DUE FOR A TRIP TO THE TORTURE CHAMBER WHEN WE GET BACK. DON'T FORGET.
EH? HANG ON... TORTURE?
HUH?! WHY JUST ME?!
EXCELLENT IDEA, YOUR HIGHNESS.
THERE'S JUST ONE MORE THING...
WHAT AN ODD DYNAMIC...
A MESSAGE FROM OBI.
!
SORRY TO KEEP YOU...
...PRINCE ZEN.
WE'RE PAYING A VISIT TO THE *LIONS OF THE MOUNTAIN*—A BAND OF VIGILANTES.
THEY'RE INFAMOUS FOR CLASHING WITH BANDITS AND PIRATES... AND I HEAR THEY HAVE EXPERIENCE TANGLING WITH THE CLAW OF THE SEA.
SO YOU'VE COME TO US WITH INTEL...
GIVE ME A MOMENT, PRINCE RAJ.
MHM.
Report on Lions of the Mountain
I'VE GOT AN IDEA.

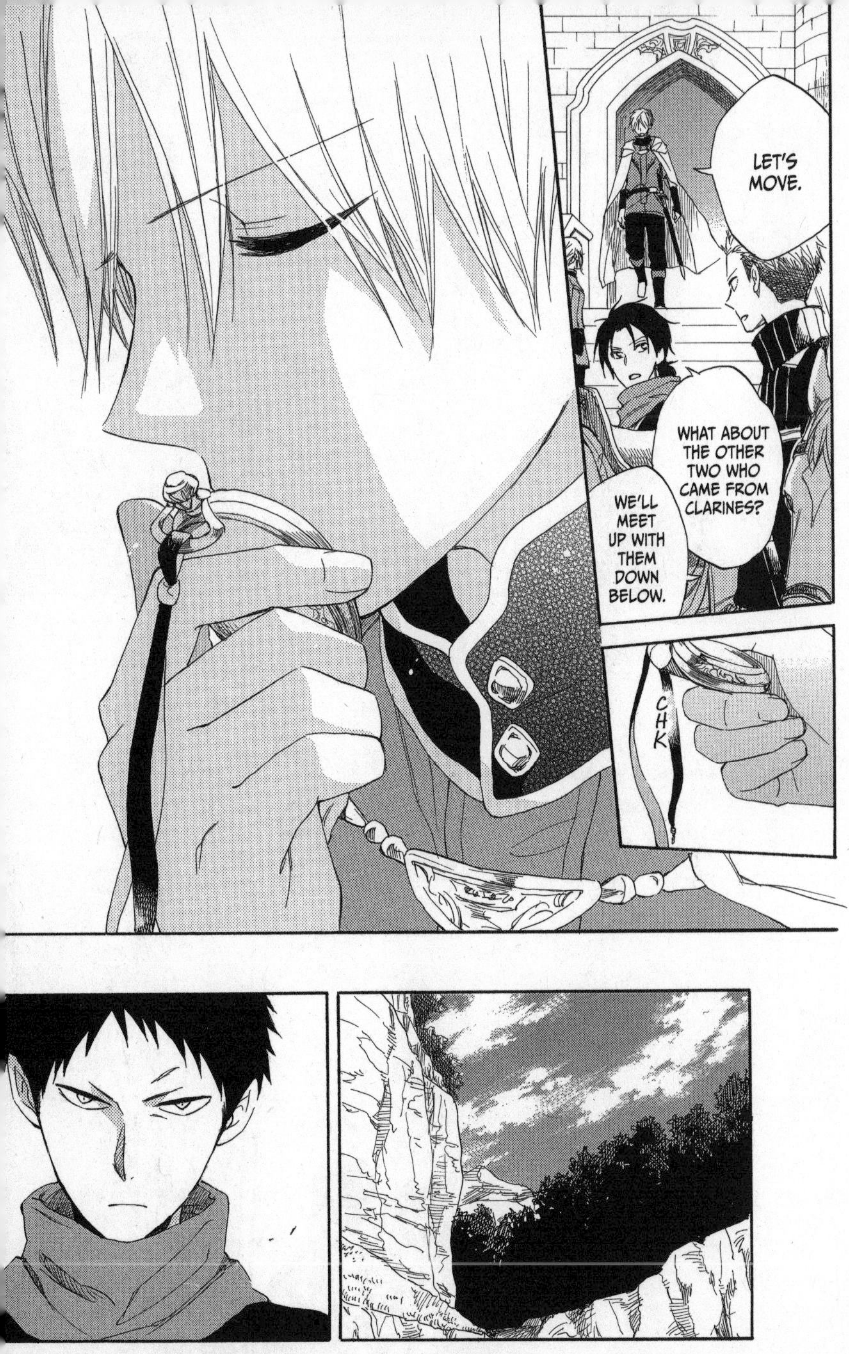
LET'S MOVE.
WHAT ABOUT THE OTHER TWO WHO CAME FROM CLARINES?
WE'LL MEET UP WITH THEM DOWN BELOW.
CHK

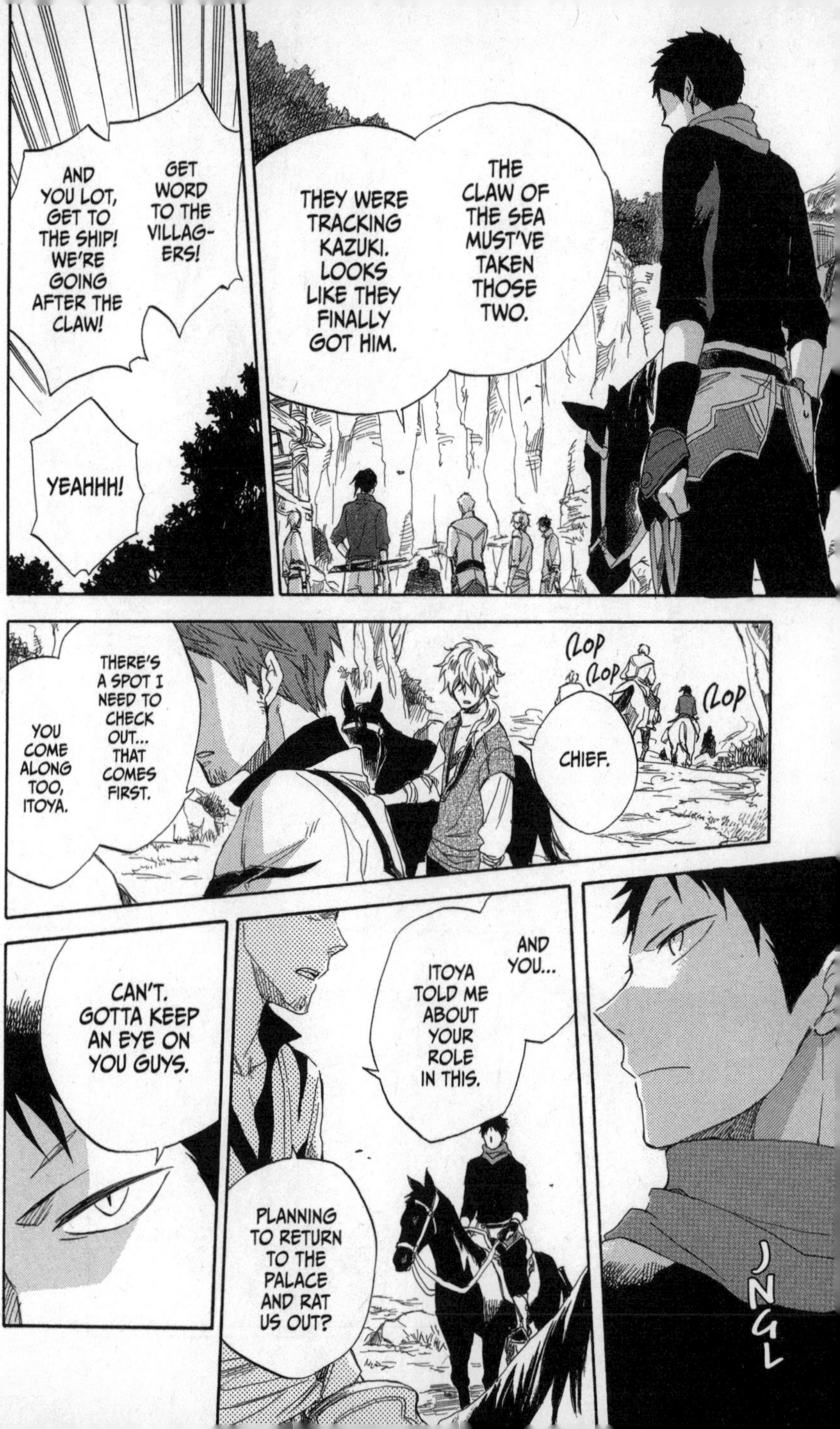
THE CLAW OF THE SEA MUST'VE TAKEN THOSE TWO.
THEY WERE TRACKING KAZUKI. LOOKS LIKE THEY FINALLY GOT HIM.
GET WORD TO THE VILLAG-ERS!
AND YOU LOT, GET TO THE SHIP! WE'RE GOING AFTER THE CLAW!
YEAHHH!
CLOP
CLOP
CLOP
CHIEF.
THERE'S A SPOT I NEED TO CHECK OUT... THAT COMES FIRST.
YOU COME ALONG TOO, ITOYA.
AND YOU...
JNGL
ITOYA TOLD ME ABOUT YOUR ROLE IN THIS.
PLANNING TO RETURN TO THE PALACE AND RAT US OUT?
CAN'T. GOTTA KEEP AN EYE ON YOU GUYS.

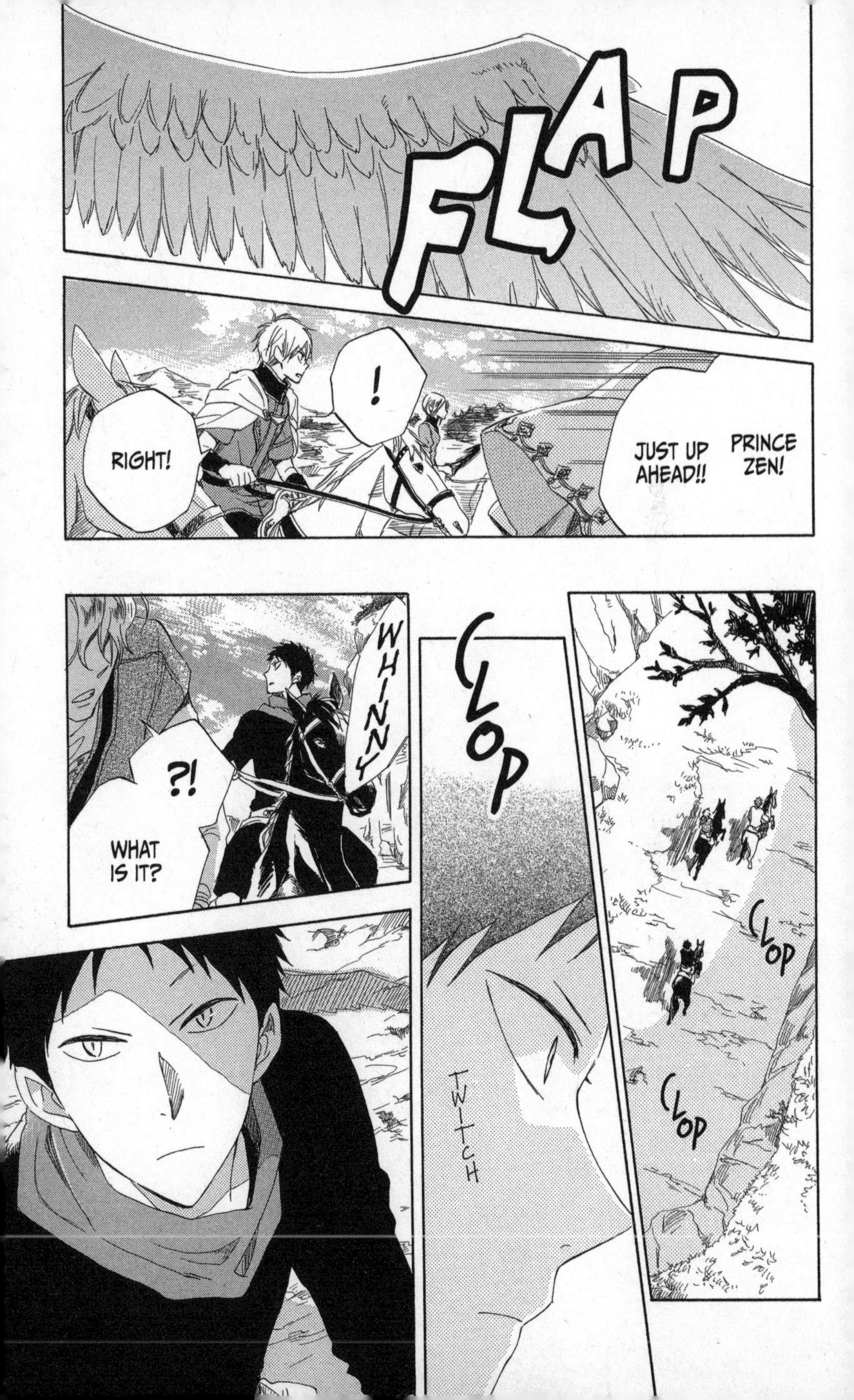
FLAP
PRINCE ZEN!
JUST UP AHEAD!!
!
RIGHT!
CLOP
CLOP
CLOP
TWITCH
WHINNY
?!
WHAT IS IT?

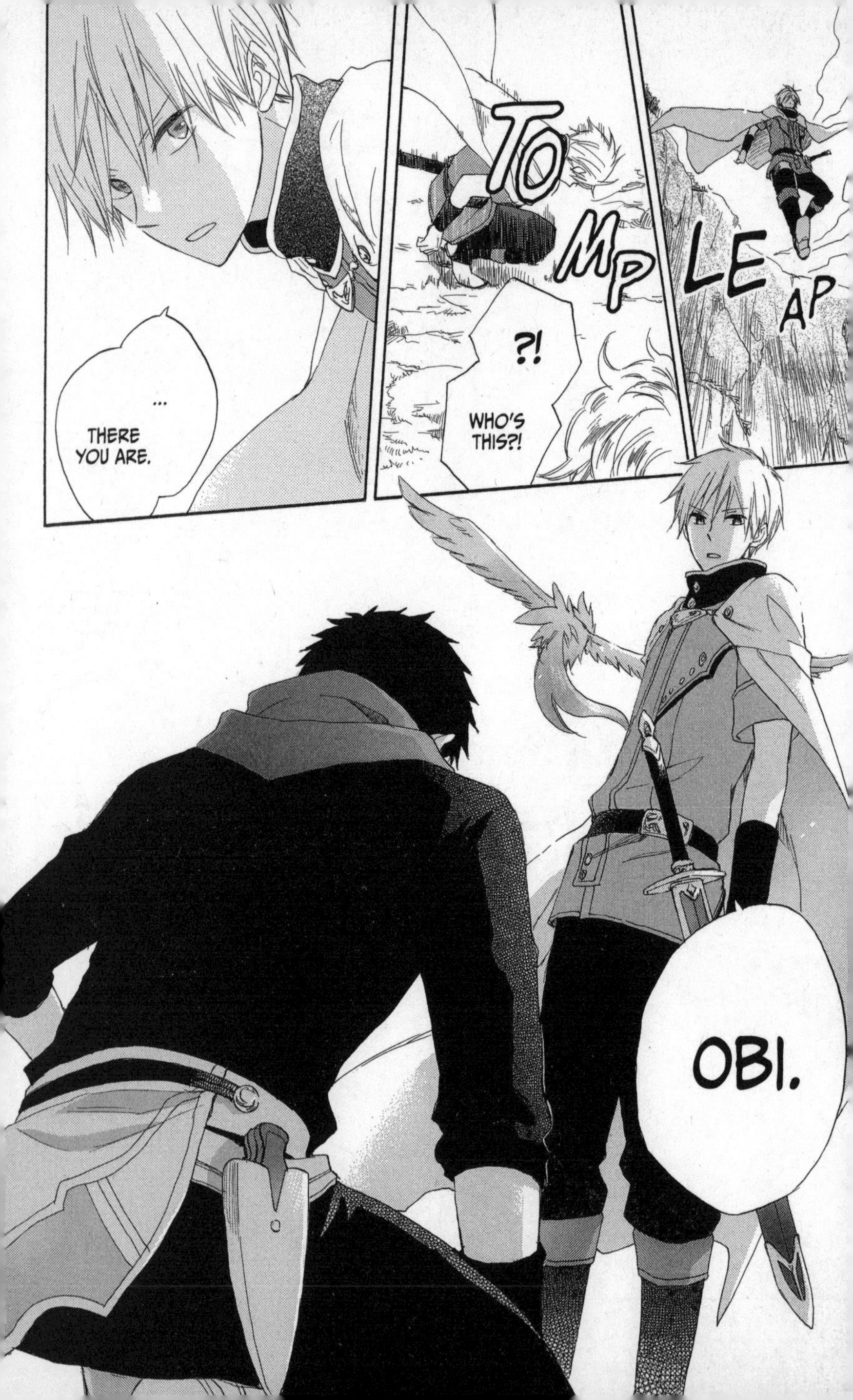
LEAP
TOMP
?!
WHO'S THIS?!
...
THERE YOU ARE.
OBI.

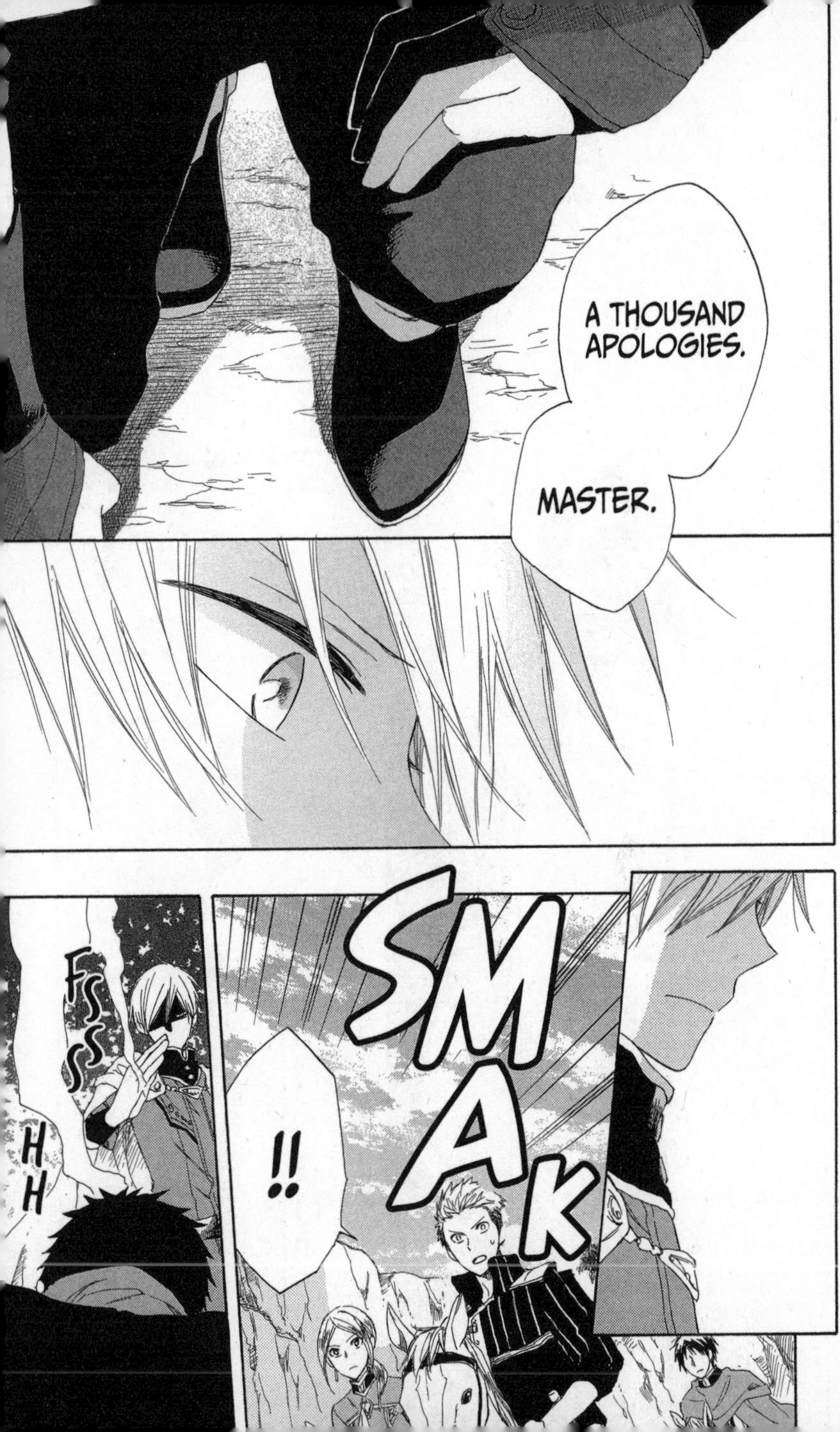
A THOUSAND APOLOGIES.
MASTER.
SMAK
!!
FSSSHH

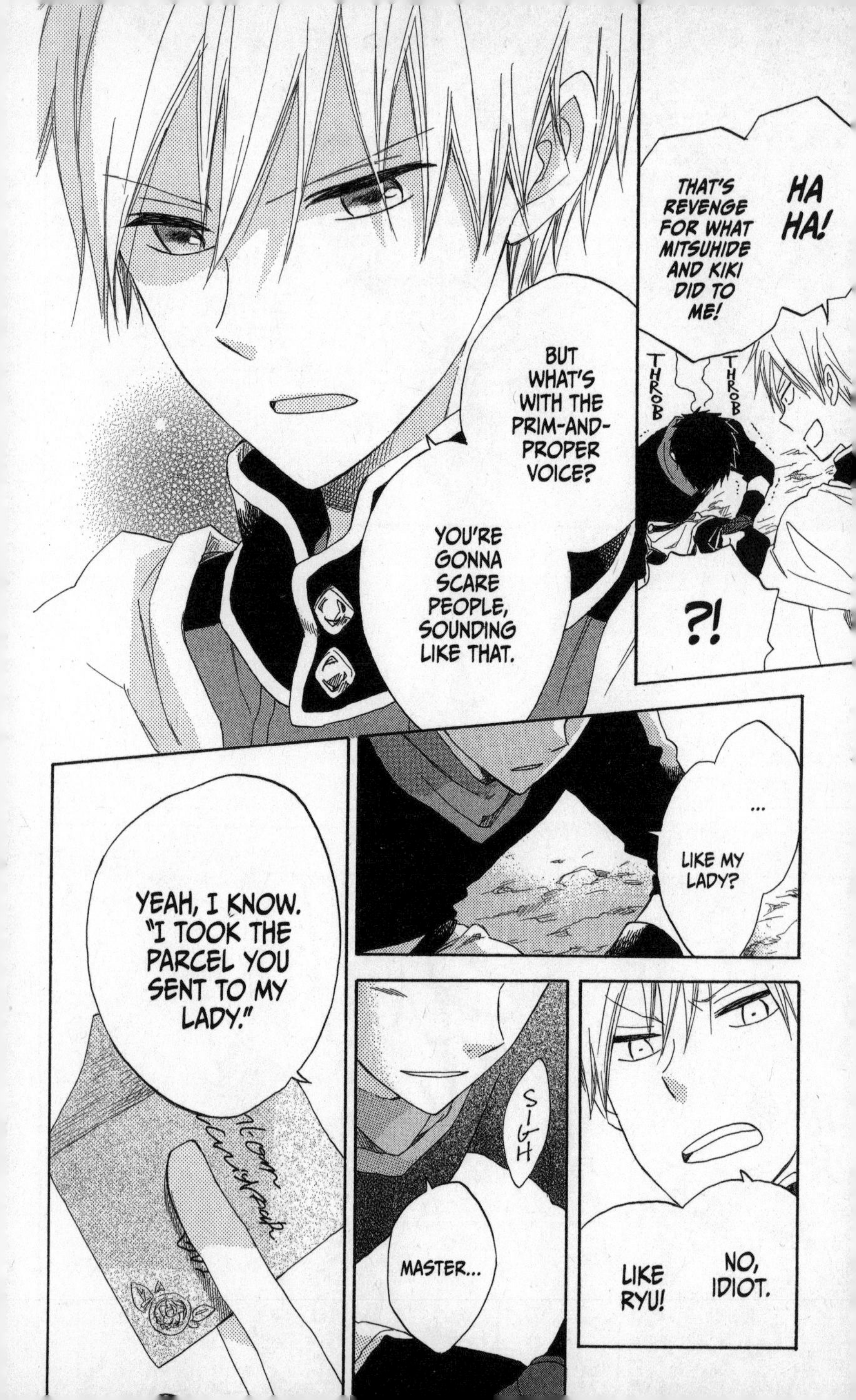
HA HA!
THAT'S REVENGE FOR WHAT MITSUHIDE AND KIKI DID TO ME!
THROB
THROB
?!
BUT WHAT'S WITH THE PRIM-AND-PROPER VOICE?
YOU'RE GONNA SCARE PEOPLE, SOUNDING LIKE THAT.
...
LIKE MY LADY?
NO, IDIOT.
LIKE RYU!
SIGH
MASTER...
YEAH, I KNOW. "I TOOK THE PARCEL YOU SENT TO MY LADY."

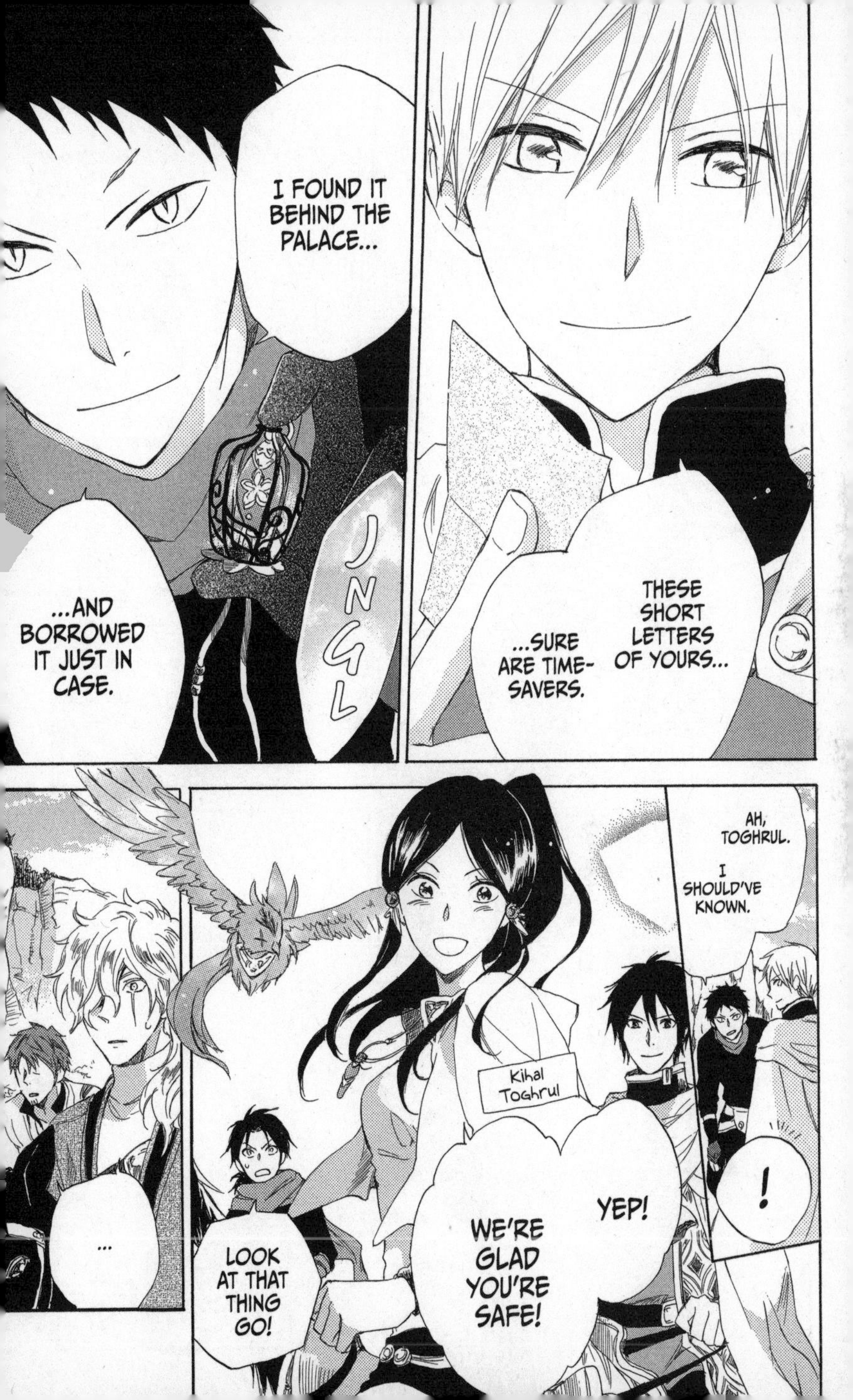
THESE SHORT LETTERS OF YOURS...
...SURE ARE TIME-SAVERS.
I FOUND IT BEHIND THE PALACE...
JINGL
...AND BORROWED IT JUST IN CASE.
AH, TOGHRUL.
I SHOULD'VE KNOWN.
!
Kihal Toghrul
YEP!
WE'RE GLAD YOU'RE SAFE!
LOOK AT THAT THING GO!
...

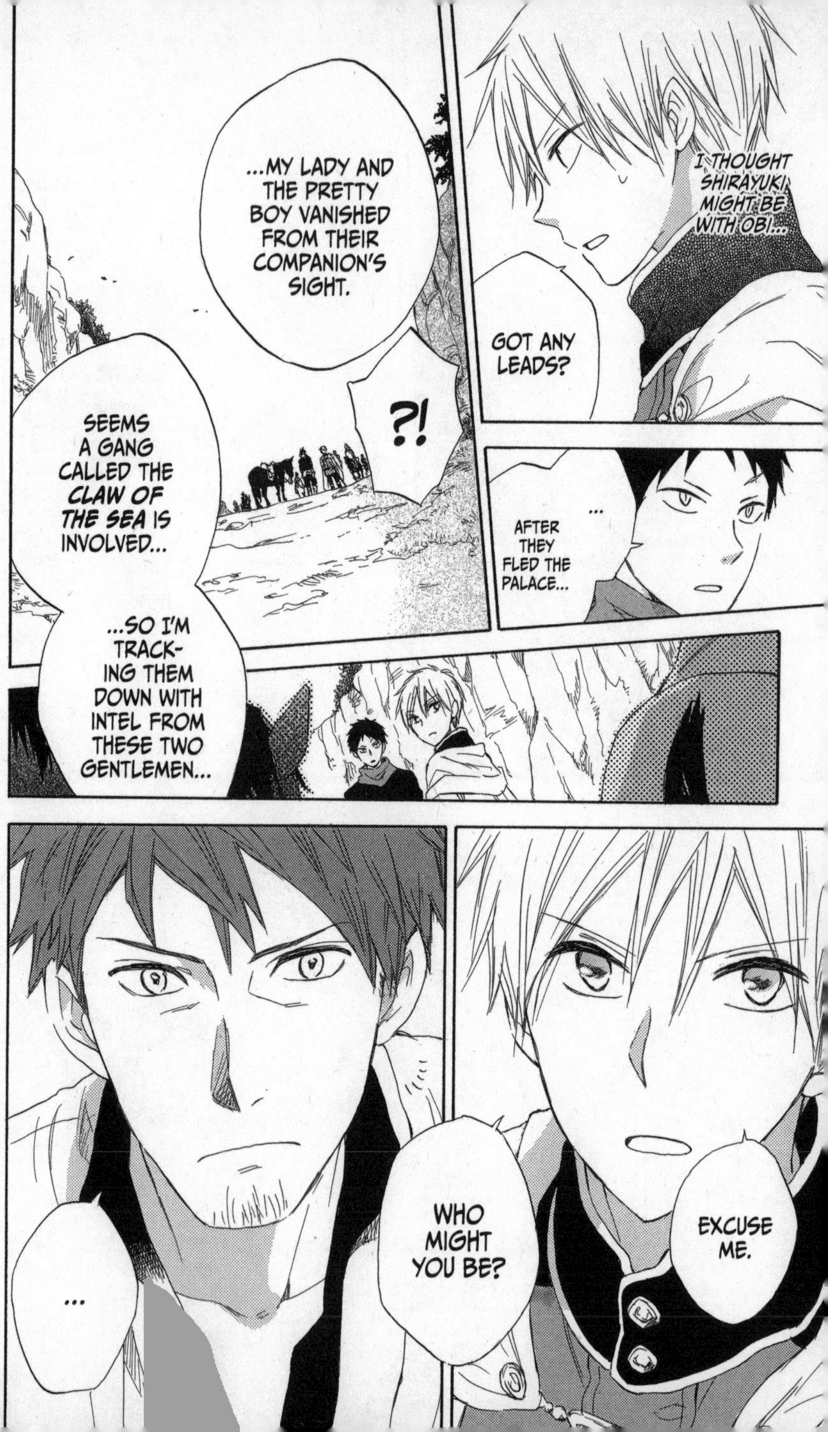
I THOUGHT SHIRAYUKI MIGHT BE WITH OBI...
GOT ANY LEADS?
...
AFTER THEY FLED THE PALACE...
...MY LADY AND THE PRETTY BOY VANISHED FROM THEIR COMPANION'S SIGHT.
?!
SEEMS A GANG CALLED THE *CLAW OF THE SEA* IS INVOLVED...
...SO I'M TRACKING THEM DOWN WITH INTEL FROM THESE TWO GENTLEMEN...
EXCUSE ME.
WHO MIGHT YOU BE?
...

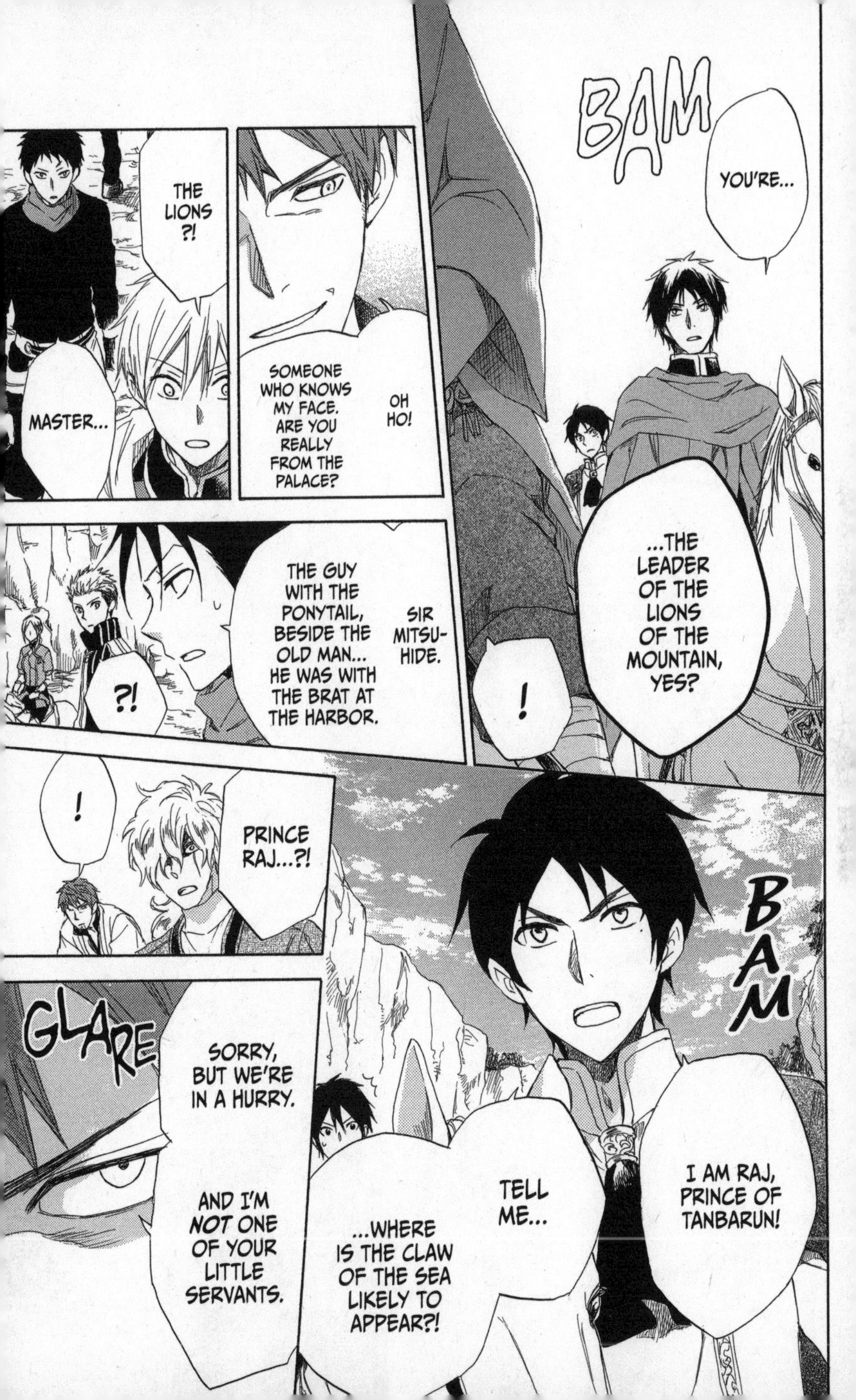
BAM
YOU'RE...
...THE LEADER OF THE LIONS OF THE MOUNTAIN, YES?
!
OH HO!
SOMEONE WHO KNOWS MY FACE. ARE YOU REALLY FROM THE PALACE?
THE LIONS ?!
MASTER...
SIR MITSUHIDE.
THE GUY WITH THE PONYTAIL, BESIDE THE OLD MAN... HE WAS WITH THE BRAT AT THE HARBOR.
?!
BAM
I AM RAJ, PRINCE OF TANBARUN!
TELL ME...
...WHERE IS THE CLAW OF THE SEA LIKELY TO APPEAR?!
PRINCE RAJ...?!
!
GLARE
SORRY, BUT WE'RE IN A HURRY.
AND I'M NOT ONE OF YOUR LITTLE SERVANTS.

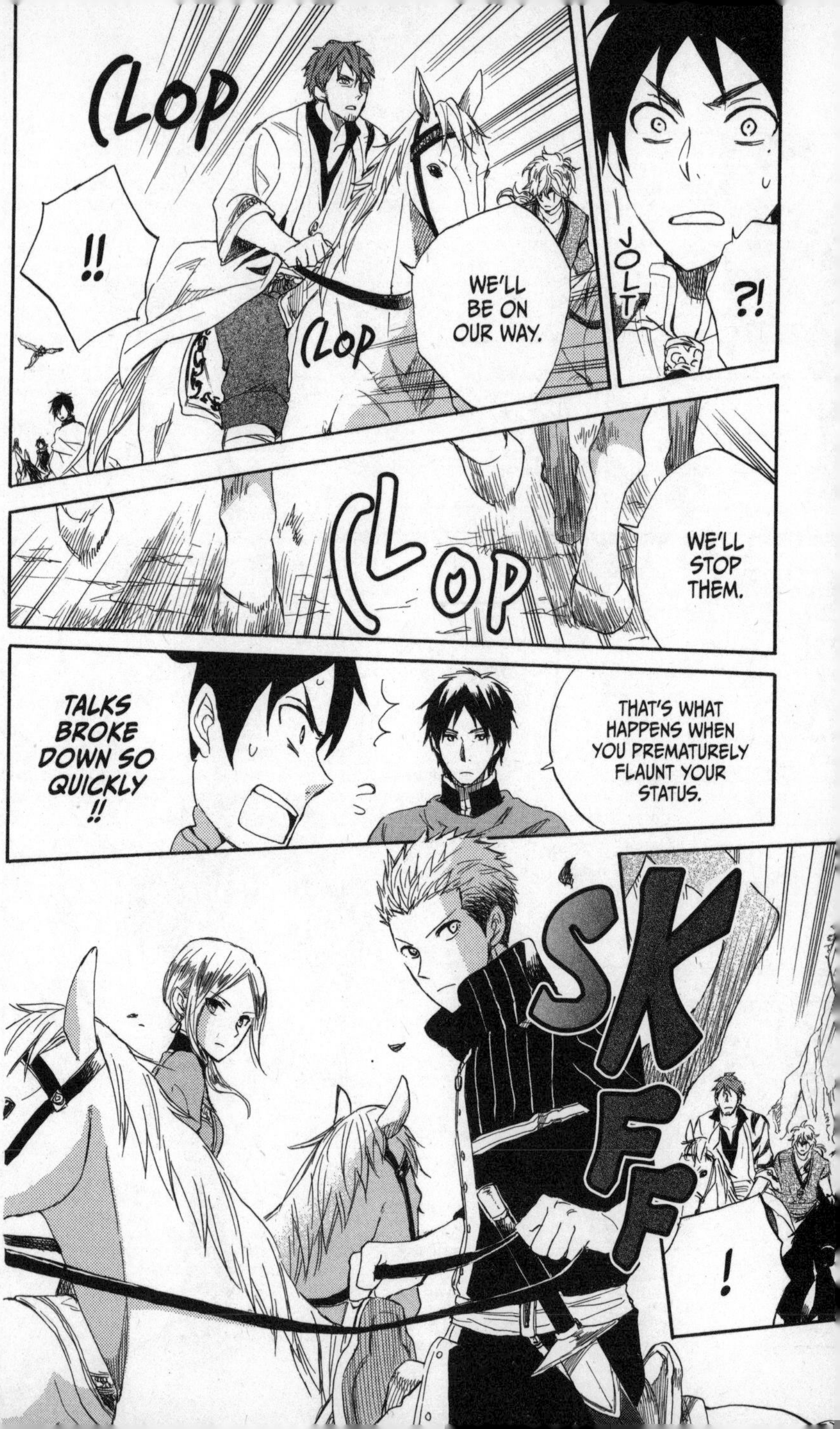
JOLT
?!
WE'LL BE ON OUR WAY.
CLOP
CLOP
!!
WE'LL STOP THEM.
CLOP
THAT'S WHAT HAPPENS WHEN YOU PREMATURELY FLAUNT YOUR STATUS.
TALKS BROKE DOWN SO QUICKLY !!
SKFF
!

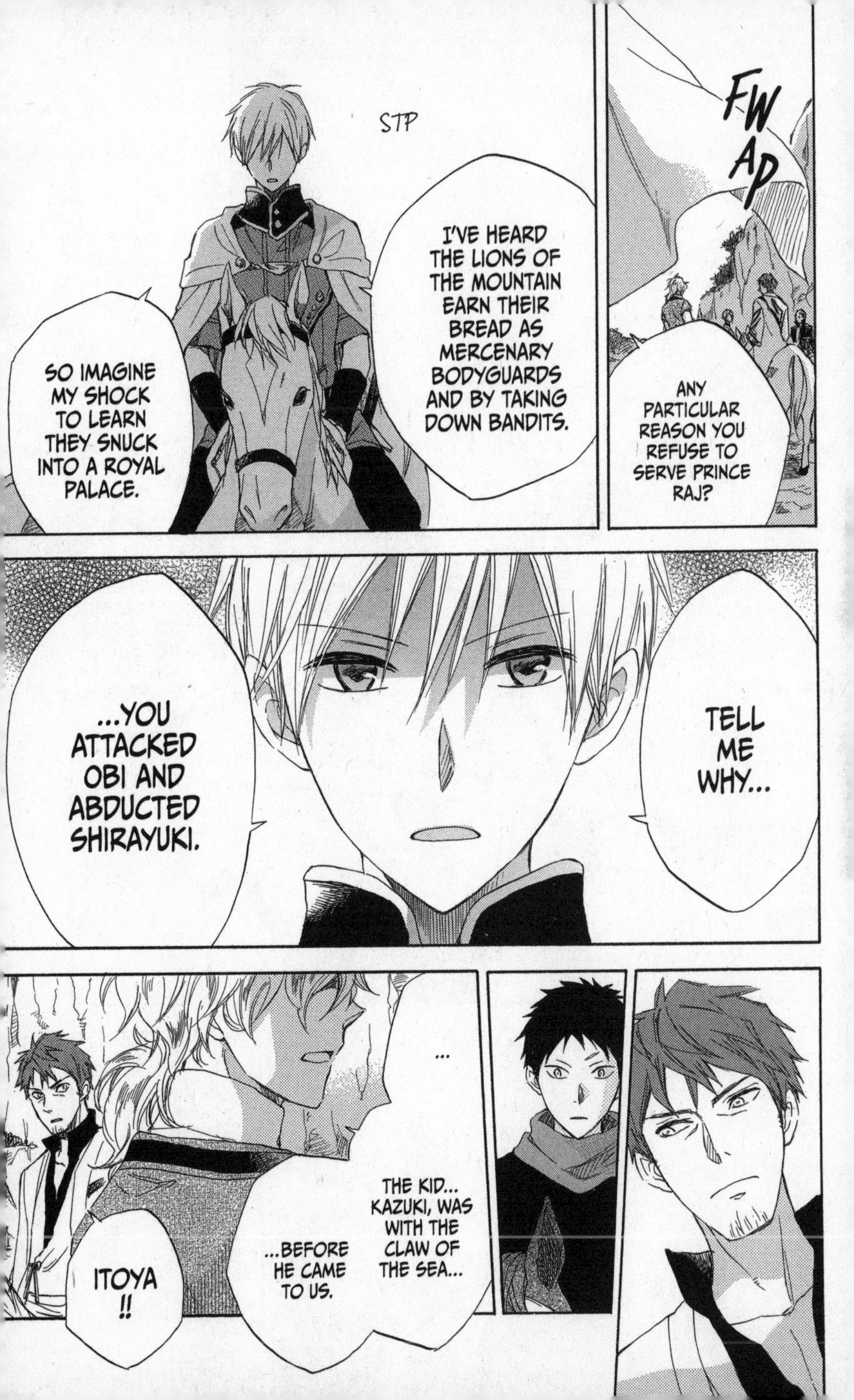
FWAP
ANY PARTICULAR REASON YOU REFUSE TO SERVE PRINCE RAJ?
STP
I'VE HEARD THE LIONS OF THE MOUNTAIN EARN THEIR BREAD AS MERCENARY BODYGUARDS AND BY TAKING DOWN BANDITS.
SO IMAGINE MY SHOCK TO LEARN THEY SNUCK INTO A ROYAL PALACE.
TELL ME WHY...
...YOU ATTACKED OBI AND ABDUCTED SHIRAYUKI.
...
THE KID... KAZUKI, WAS WITH THE CLAW OF THE SEA...
...BEFORE HE CAME TO US.
ITOYA !!

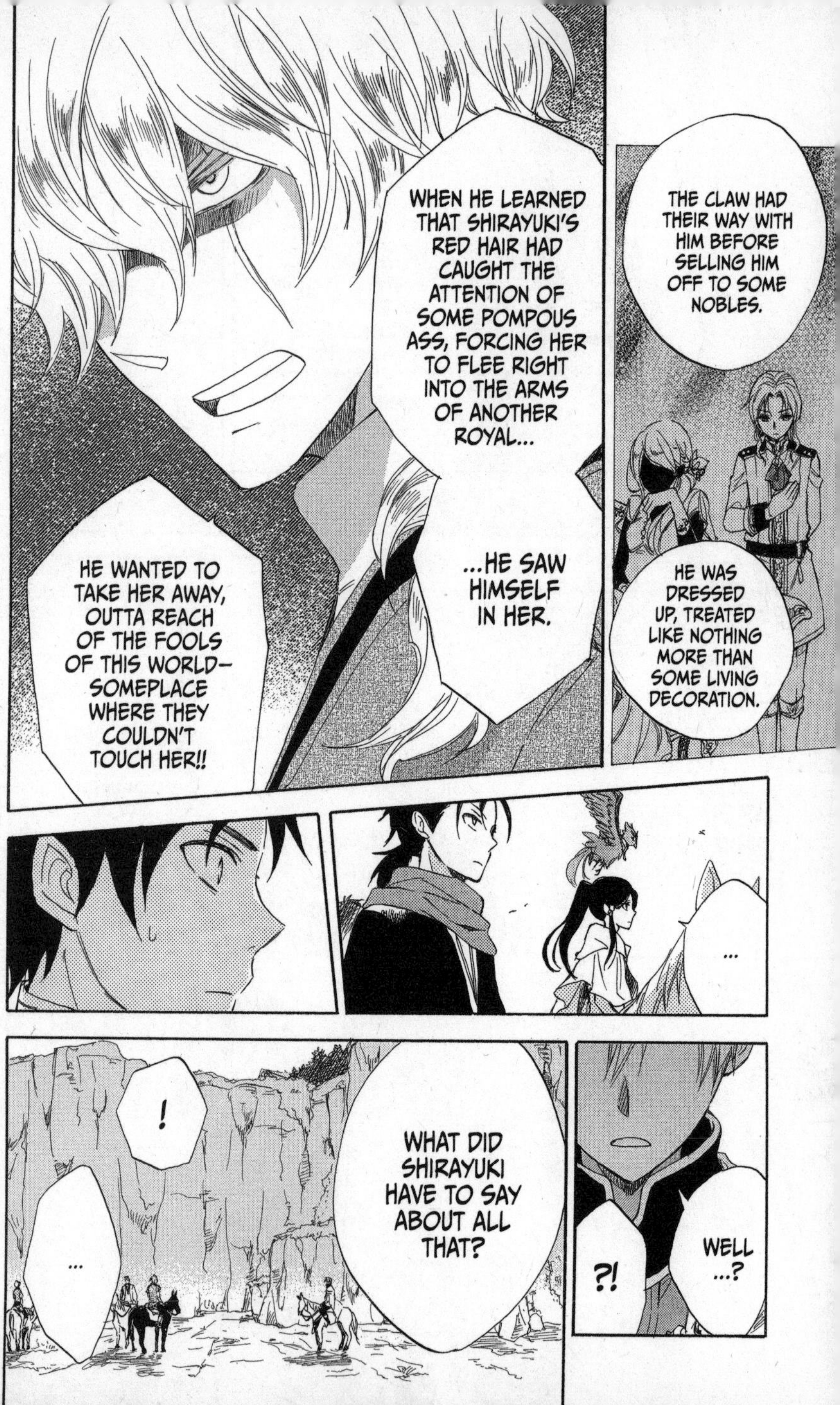
THE CLAW HAD THEIR WAY WITH HIM BEFORE SELLING HIM OFF TO SOME NOBLES.
HE WAS DRESSED UP, TREATED LIKE NOTHING MORE THAN SOME LIVING DECORATION.
WHEN HE LEARNED THAT SHIRAYUKI'S RED HAIR HAD CAUGHT THE ATTENTION OF SOME POMPOUS ASS, FORCING HER TO FLEE RIGHT INTO THE ARMS OF ANOTHER ROYAL...
...HE SAW HIMSELF IN HER.
HE WANTED TO TAKE HER AWAY, OUTTA REACH OF THE FOOLS OF THIS WORLD–SOMEPLACE WHERE THEY COULDN'T TOUCH HER!!
...
WELL ...?
?!
WHAT DID SHIRAYUKI HAVE TO SAY ABOUT ALL THAT?
!
...

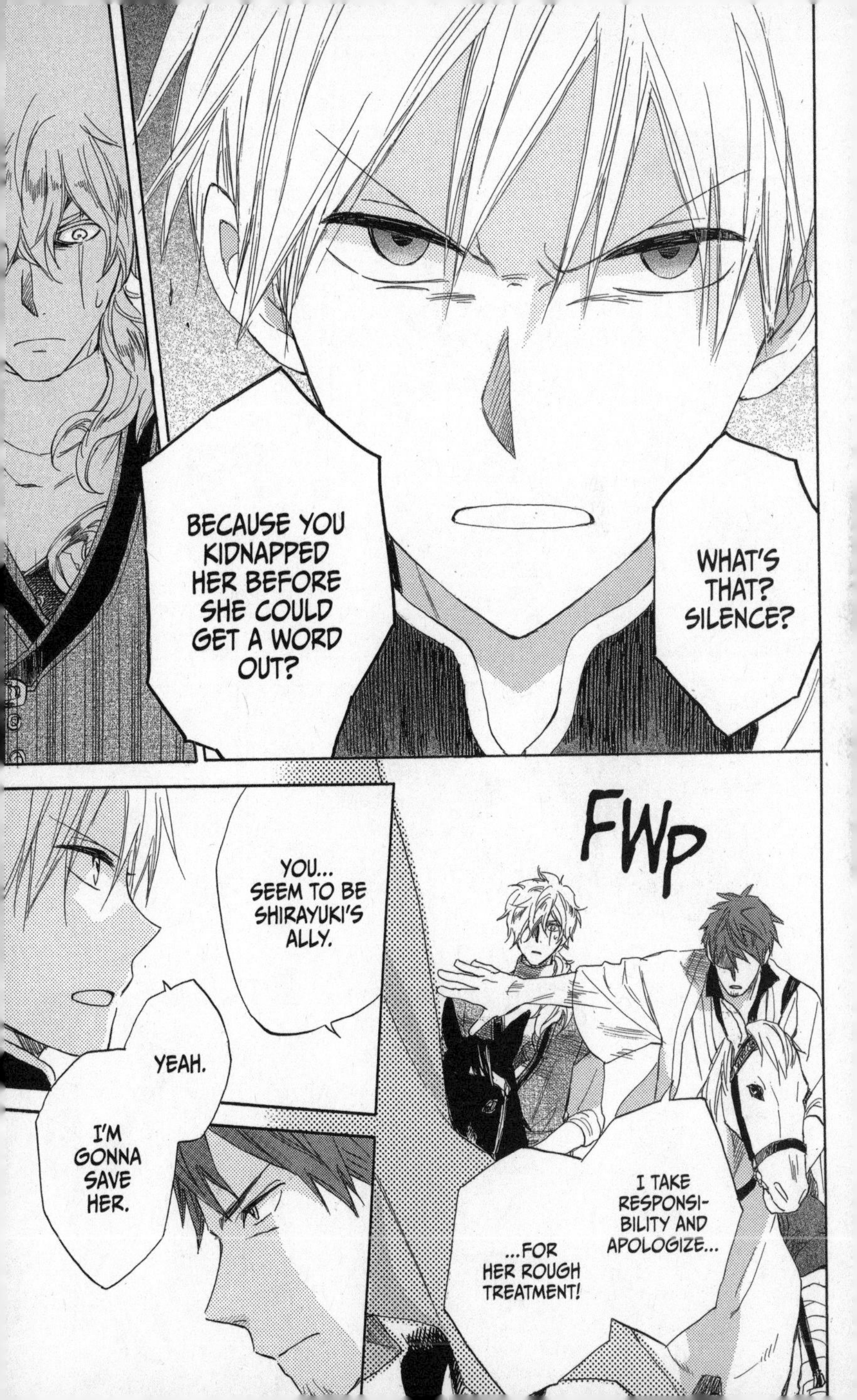
WHAT'S THAT? SILENCE?
BECAUSE YOU KIDNAPPED HER BEFORE SHE COULD GET A WORD OUT?
FWP
I TAKE RESPONSI-BILITY AND APOLOGIZE...
...FOR HER ROUGH TREATMENT!
YOU... SEEM TO BE SHIRAYUKI'S ALLY.
YEAH.
I'M GONNA SAVE HER.

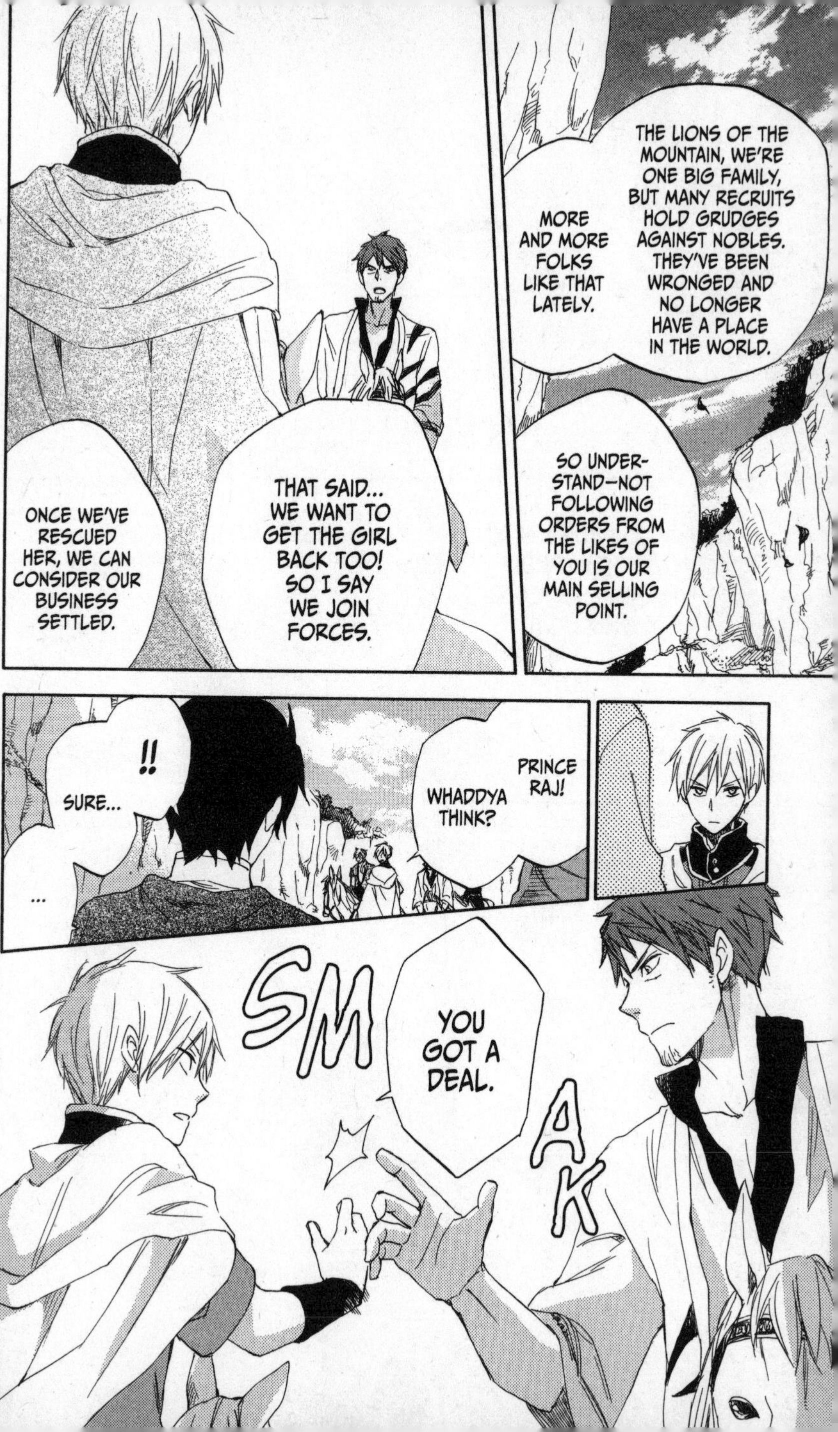
THE LIONS OF THE MOUNTAIN, WE'RE ONE BIG FAMILY, BUT MANY RECRUITS HOLD GRUDGES AGAINST NOBLES. THEY'VE BEEN WRONGED AND NO LONGER HAVE A PLACE IN THE WORLD.
MORE AND MORE FOLKS LIKE THAT LATELY.
SO UNDER-STAND—NOT FOLLOWING ORDERS FROM THE LIKES OF YOU IS OUR MAIN SELLING POINT.
THAT SAID... WE WANT TO GET THE GIRL BACK TOO! SO I SAY WE JOIN FORCES.
ONCE WE'VE RESCUED HER, WE CAN CONSIDER OUR BUSINESS SETTLED.
PRINCE RAJ!
WHADDYA THINK?
!!
SURE...
...
YOU GOT A DEAL.
SMAK

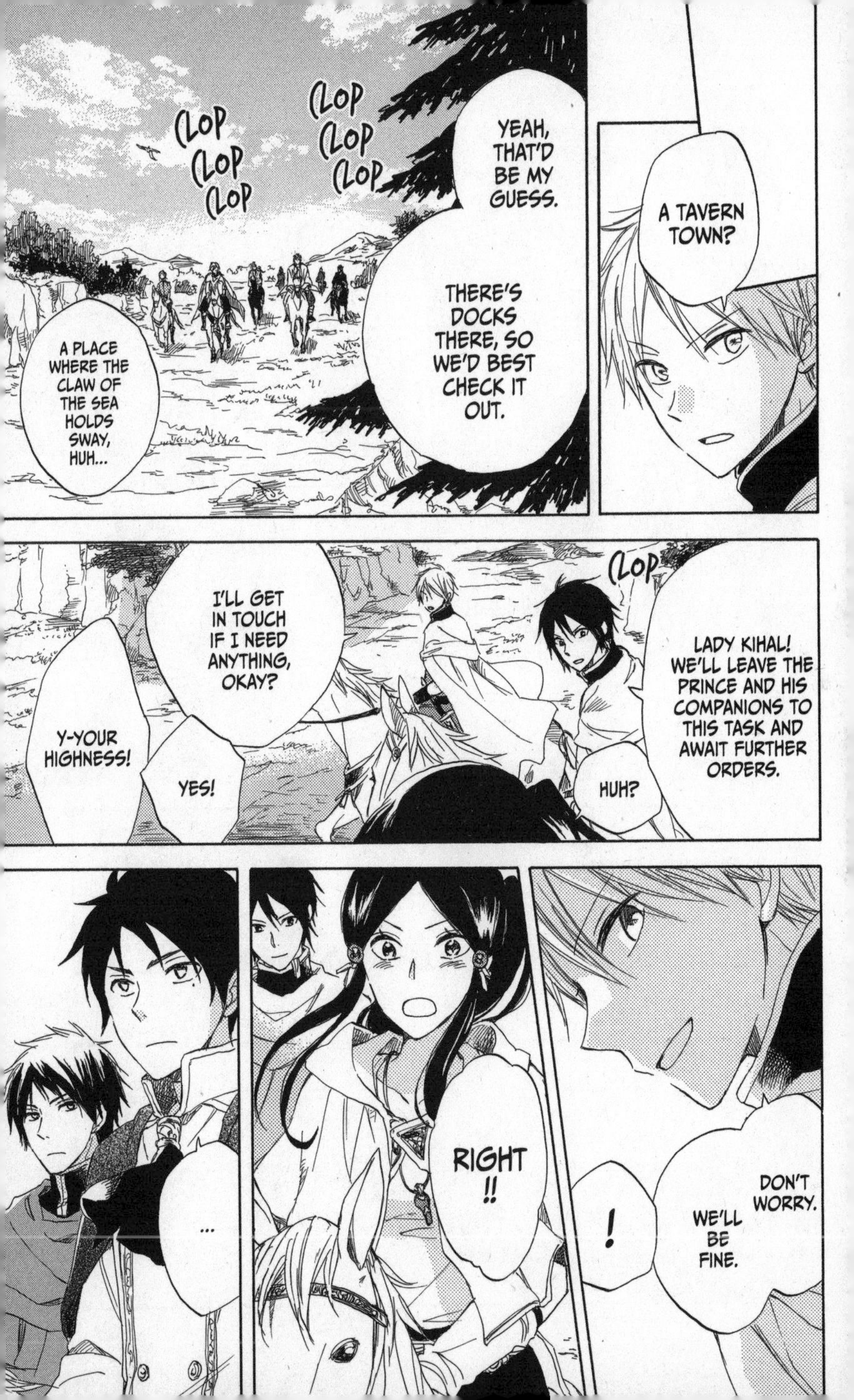
A TAVERN TOWN?
YEAH, THAT'D BE MY GUESS.
THERE'S DOCKS THERE, SO WE'D BEST CHECK IT OUT.
CLOP CLOP CLOP
CLOP CLOP CLOP
A PLACE WHERE THE CLAW OF THE SEA HOLDS SWAY, HUH...
CLOP
LADY KIHAL! WE'LL LEAVE THE PRINCE AND HIS COMPANIONS TO THIS TASK AND AWAIT FURTHER ORDERS.
HUH?
I'LL GET IN TOUCH IF I NEED ANYTHING, OKAY?
YES!
Y-YOUR HIGHNESS!
DON'T WORRY.
WE'LL BE FINE.
!
RIGHT !!
...

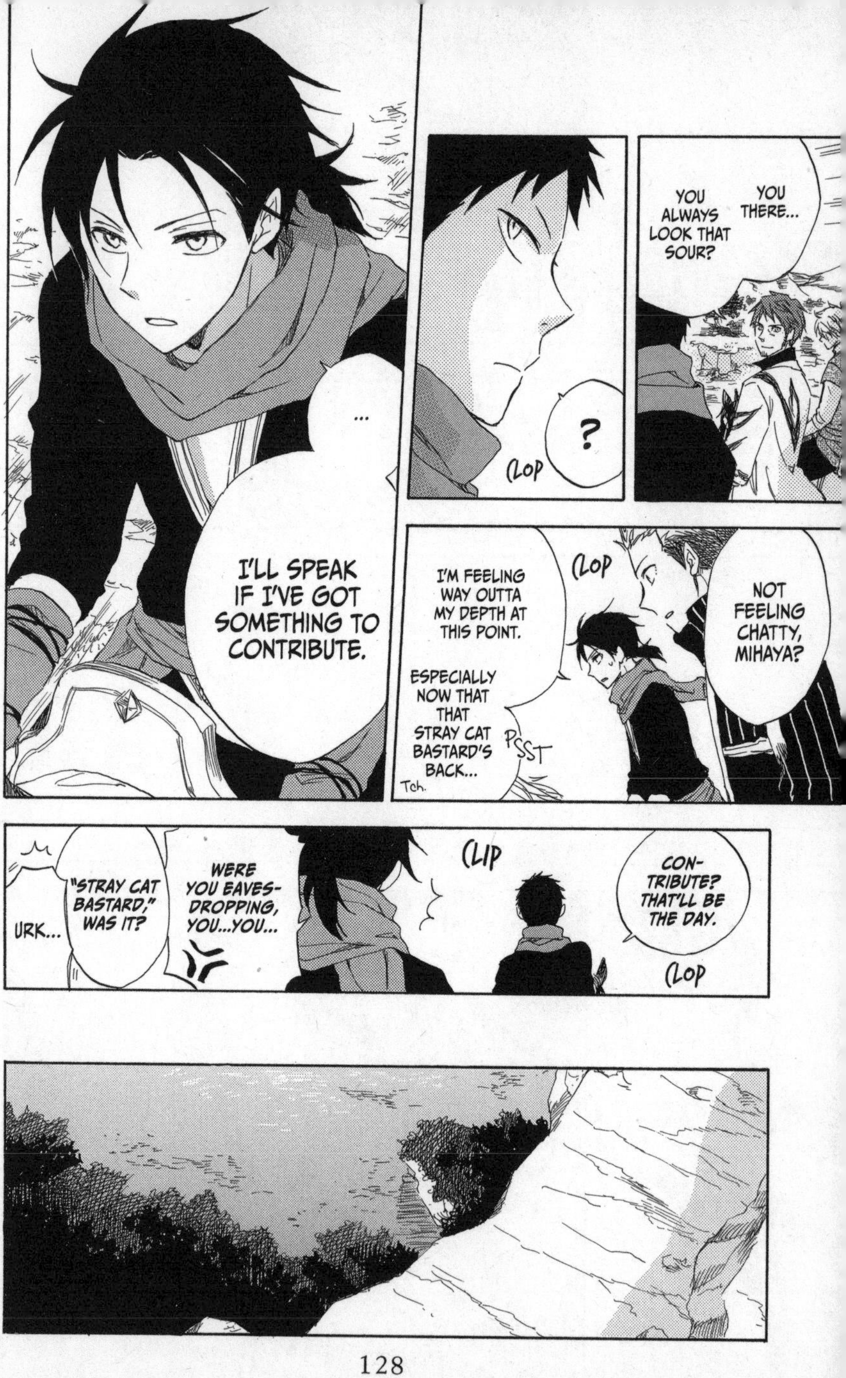
YOU THERE...
YOU ALWAYS LOOK THAT SOUR?
?
CLOP
NOT FEELING CHATTY, MIHAYA?
CLOP
I'M FEELING WAY OUTTA MY DEPTH AT THIS POINT.
ESPECIALLY NOW THAT THAT STRAY CAT BASTARD'S BACK...
PSST
Tch.
...
I'LL SPEAK IF I'VE GOT SOMETHING TO CONTRIBUTE.
CON-TRIBUTE? THAT'LL BE THE DAY.
CLIP
CLOP
WERE YOU EAVES-DROPPING, YOU...YOU...
"STRAY CAT BASTARD," WAS IT?
URK...

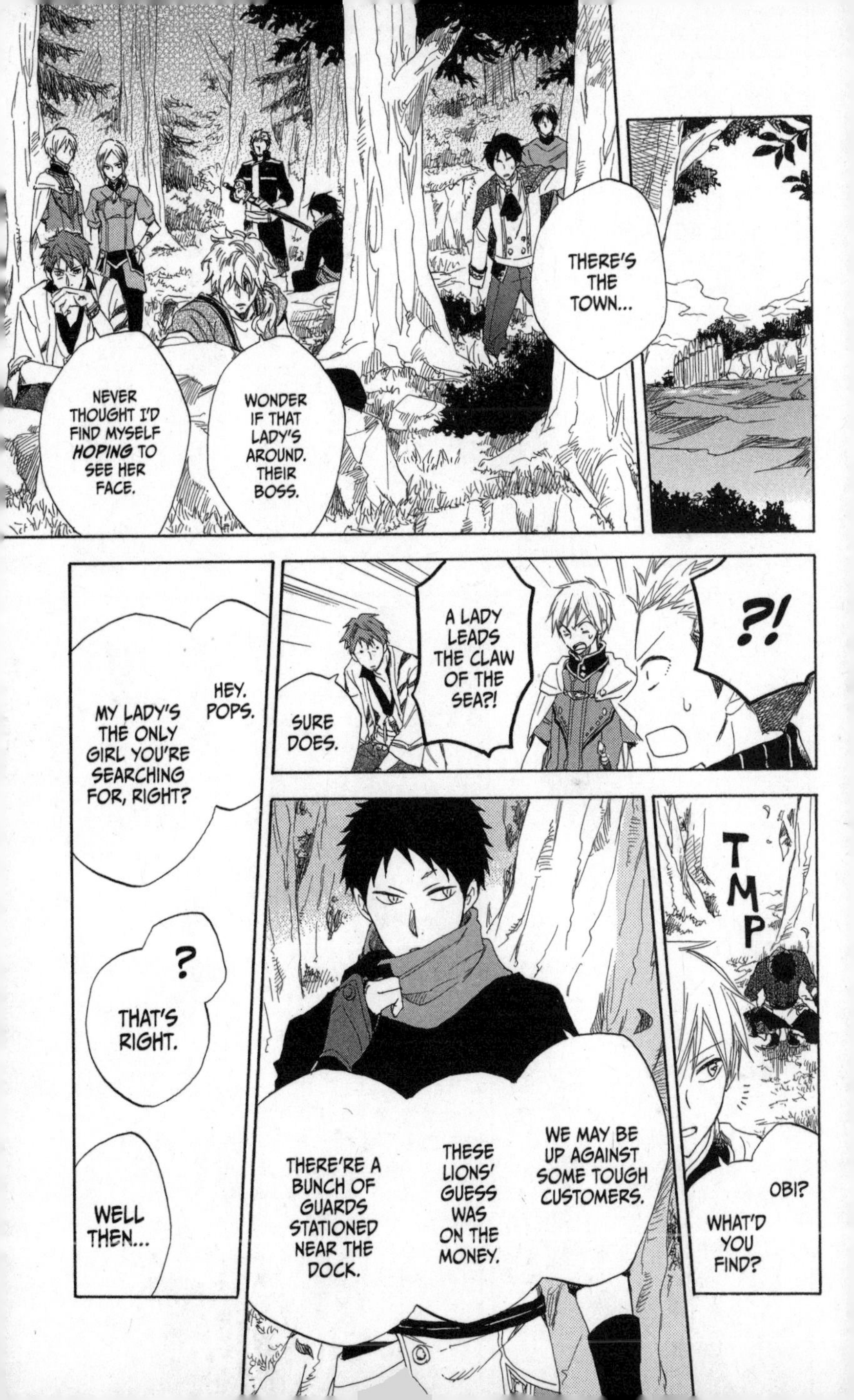
THERE'S THE TOWN...
WONDER IF THAT LADY'S AROUND. THEIR BOSS.
NEVER THOUGHT I'D FIND MYSELF *HOPING* TO SEE HER FACE.
?!
A LADY LEADS THE CLAW OF THE SEA?!
SURE DOES.
TMP
OBI?
WHAT'D YOU FIND?
WE MAY BE UP AGAINST SOME TOUGH CUSTOMERS.
THESE LIONS' GUESS WAS ON THE MONEY.
THERE'RE A BUNCH OF GUARDS STATIONED NEAR THE DOCK.
HEY. POPS.
MY LADY'S THE ONLY GIRL YOU'RE SEARCHING FOR, RIGHT?
?
THAT'S RIGHT.
WELL THEN...

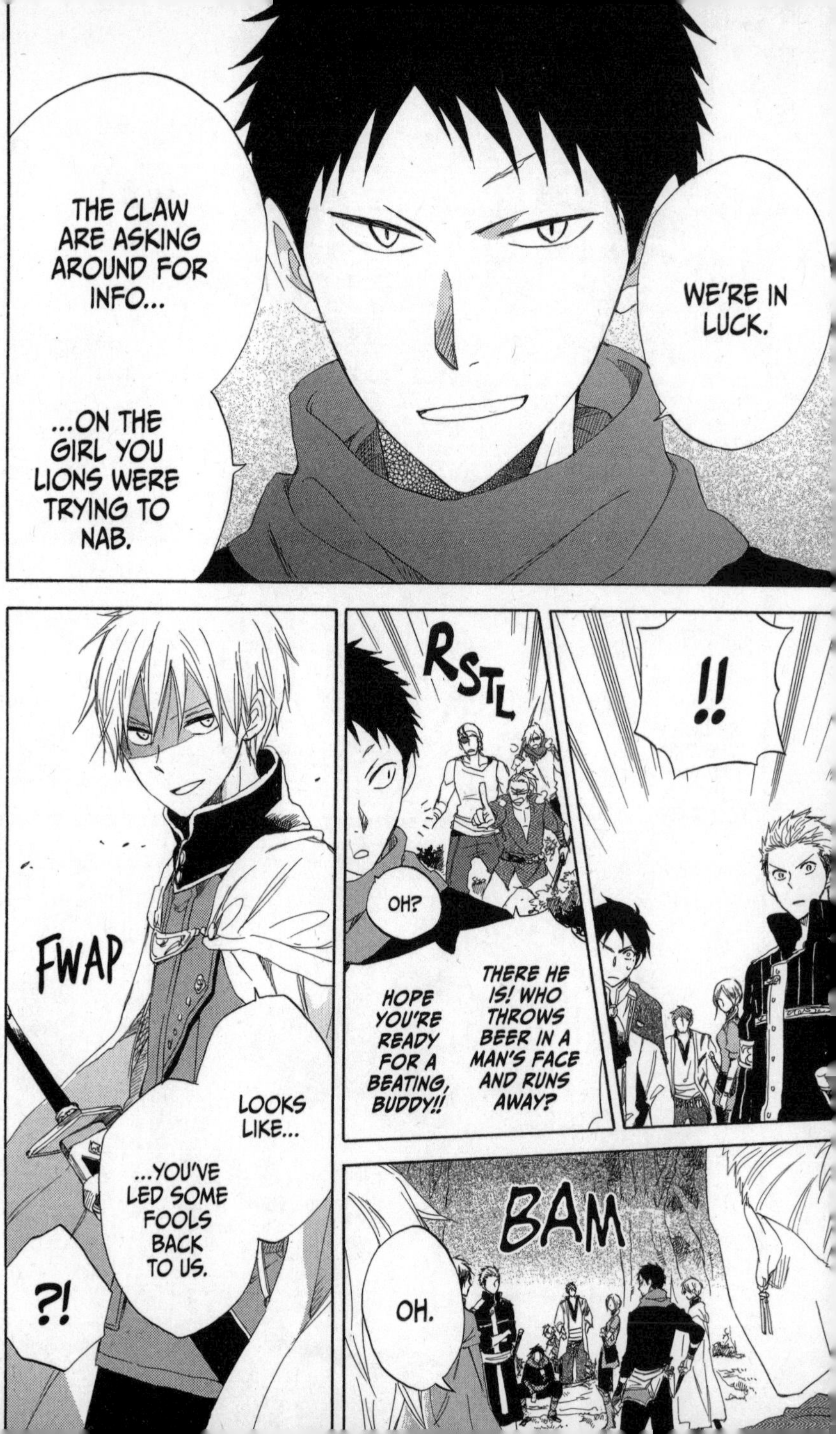
WE'RE IN LUCK.
THE CLAW ARE ASKING AROUND FOR INFO...
...ON THE GIRL YOU LIONS WERE TRYING TO NAB.
!!
RSTL
THERE HE IS! WHO THROWS BEER IN A MAN'S FACE AND RUNS AWAY?
HOPE YOU'RE READY FOR A BEATING, BUDDY!!
OH?
BAM
OH.
FWAP
LOOKS LIKE...
...YOU'VE LED SOME FOOLS BACK TO US.
?!

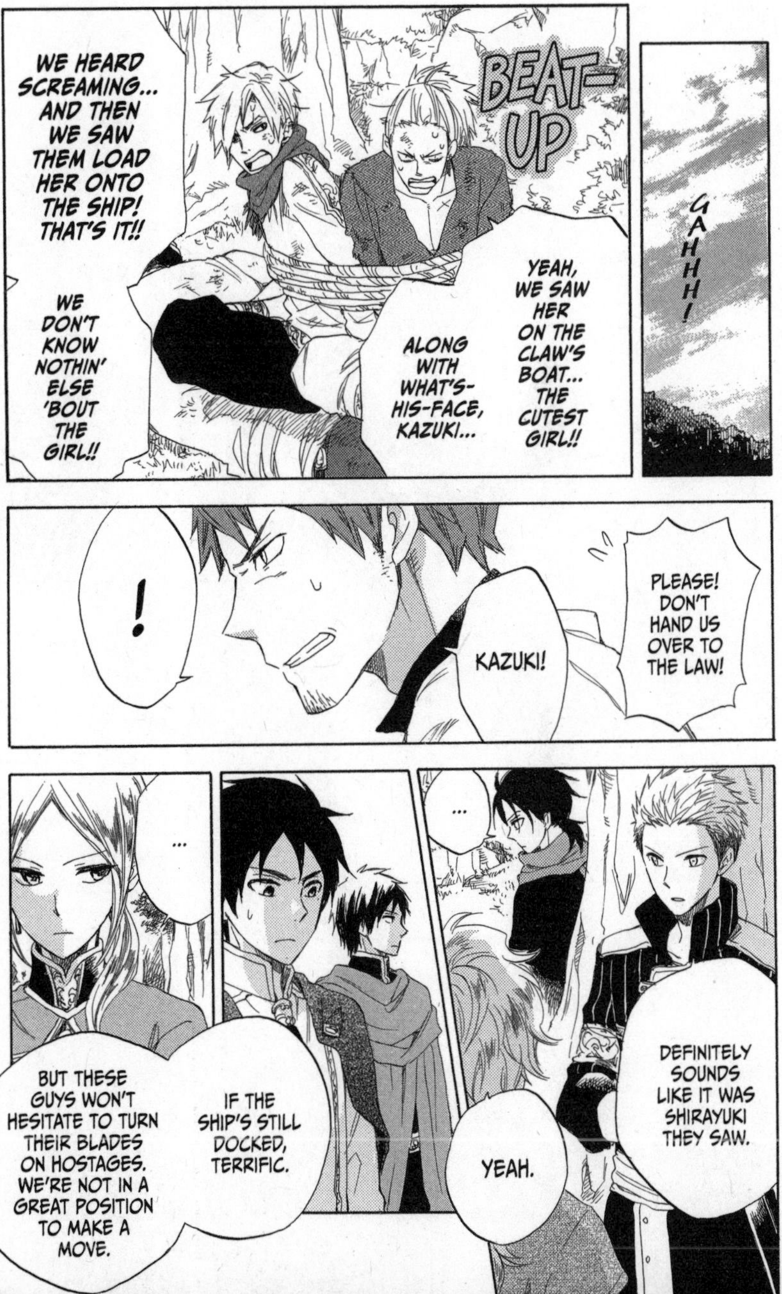
GAHHHH!
BEAT-UP
YEAH, WE SAW HER ON THE CLAW'S BOAT... THE CUTEST GIRL!!
ALONG WITH WHAT'S-HIS-FACE, KAZUKI...
WE HEARD SCREAMING... AND THEN WE SAW THEM LOAD HER ONTO THE SHIP! THAT'S IT!!
WE DON'T KNOW NOTHIN' ELSE 'BOUT THE GIRL!!
PLEASE! DON'T HAND US OVER TO THE LAW!
KAZUKI!
!
...
DEFINITELY SOUNDS LIKE IT WAS SHIRAYUKI THEY SAW.
YEAH.
IF THE SHIP'S STILL DOCKED, TERRIFIC.
...
BUT THESE GUYS WON'T HESITATE TO TURN THEIR BLADES ON HOSTAGES. WE'RE NOT IN A GREAT POSITION TO MAKE A MOVE.

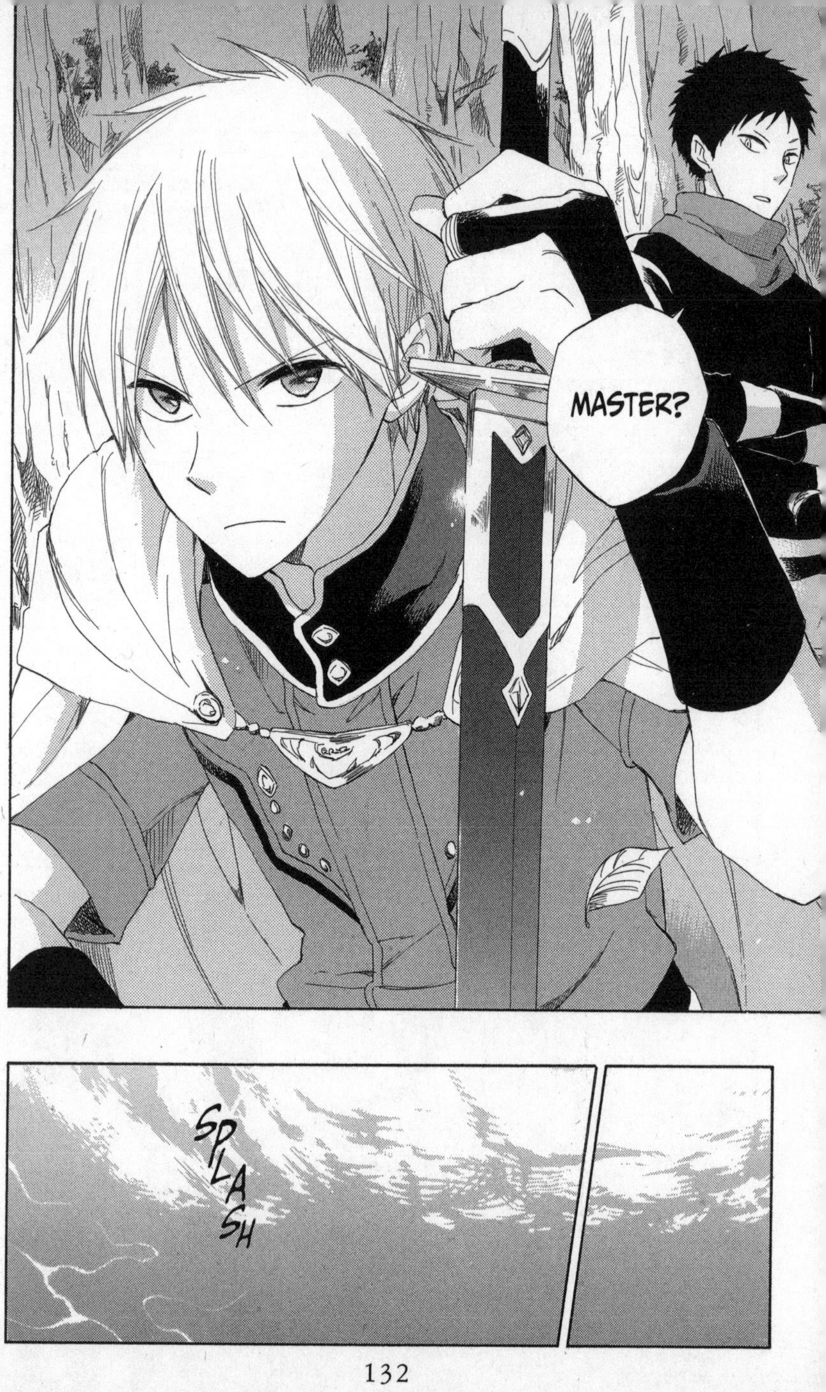
MASTER?
SPLASH

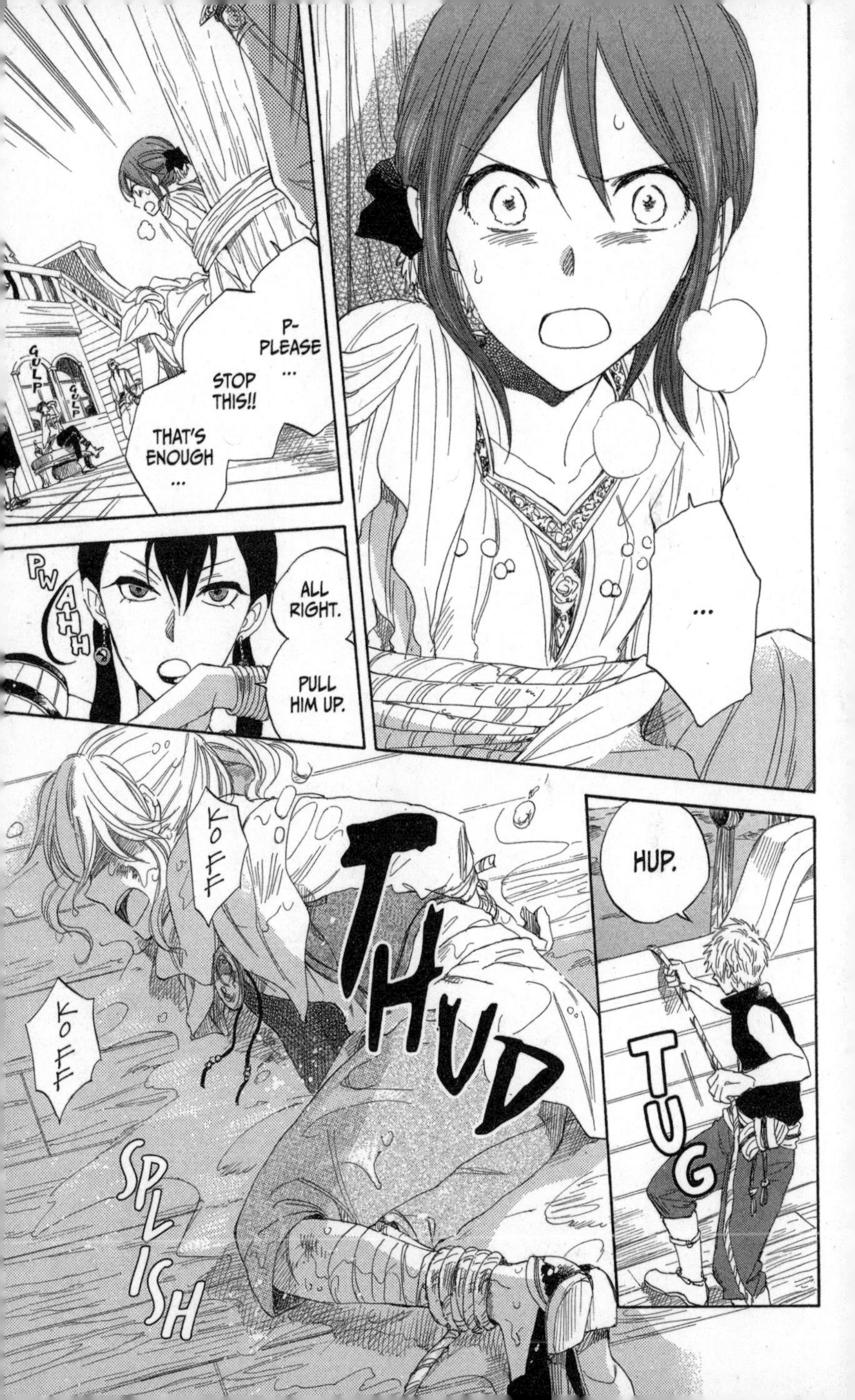
...
P-PLEASE...
STOP THIS!!
THAT'S ENOUGH...
GULP
GULP
ALL RIGHT.
PULL HIM UP.
PWAHH
HUP.
TUG
THUD
KOFF
KOFF
SPLISH

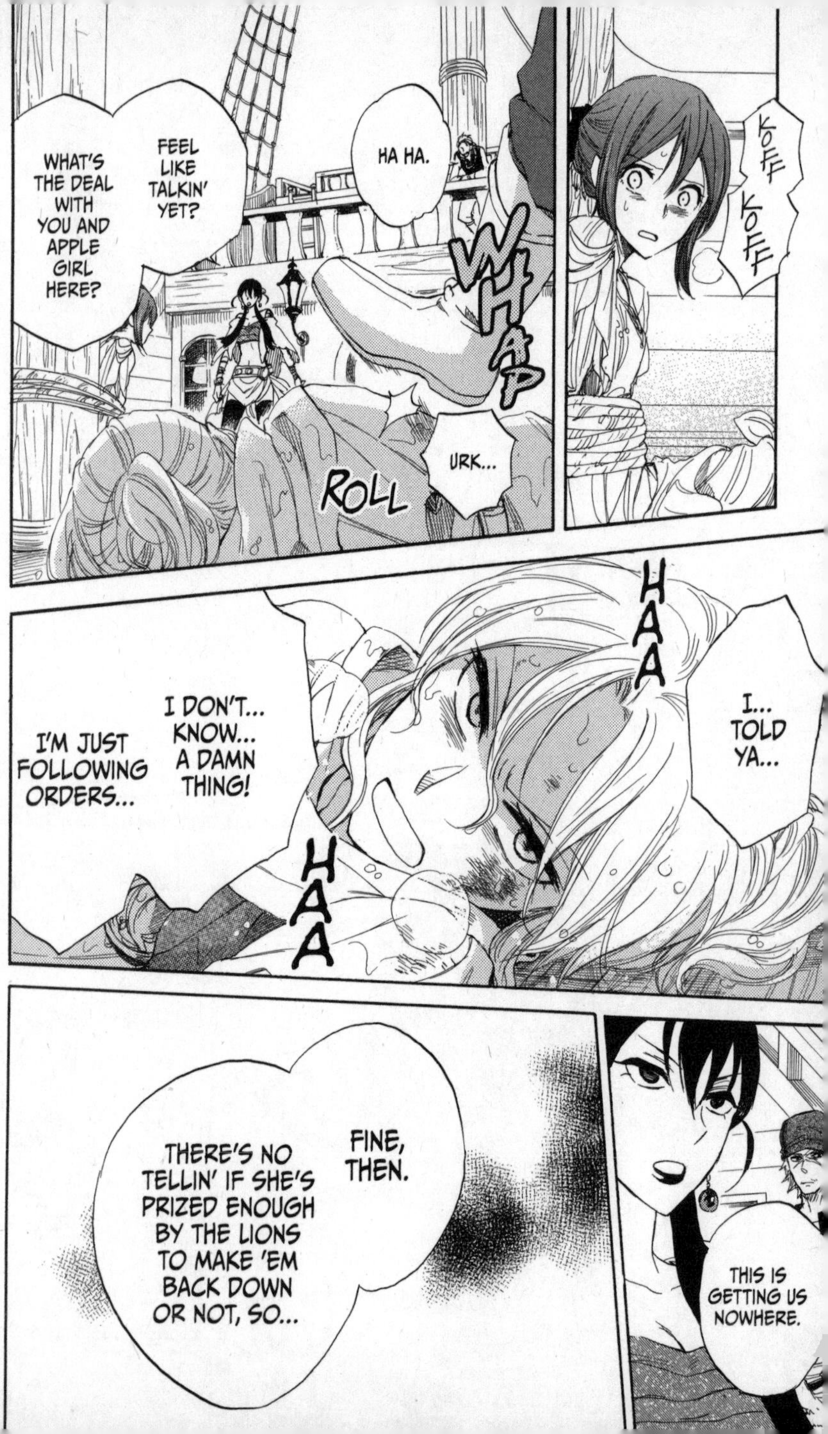
KOFF KOFF
HA HA.
WHAP
FEEL LIKE TALKIN' YET?
WHAT'S THE DEAL WITH YOU AND APPLE GIRL HERE?
URK...
ROLL
HAA
I... TOLD YA...
I DON'T... KNOW... A DAMN THING!
I'M JUST FOLLOWING ORDERS...
HAA
THIS IS GETTING US NOWHERE.
FINE, THEN.
THERE'S NO TELLIN' IF SHE'S PRIZED ENOUGH BY THE LIONS TO MAKE 'EM BACK DOWN OR NOT, SO...

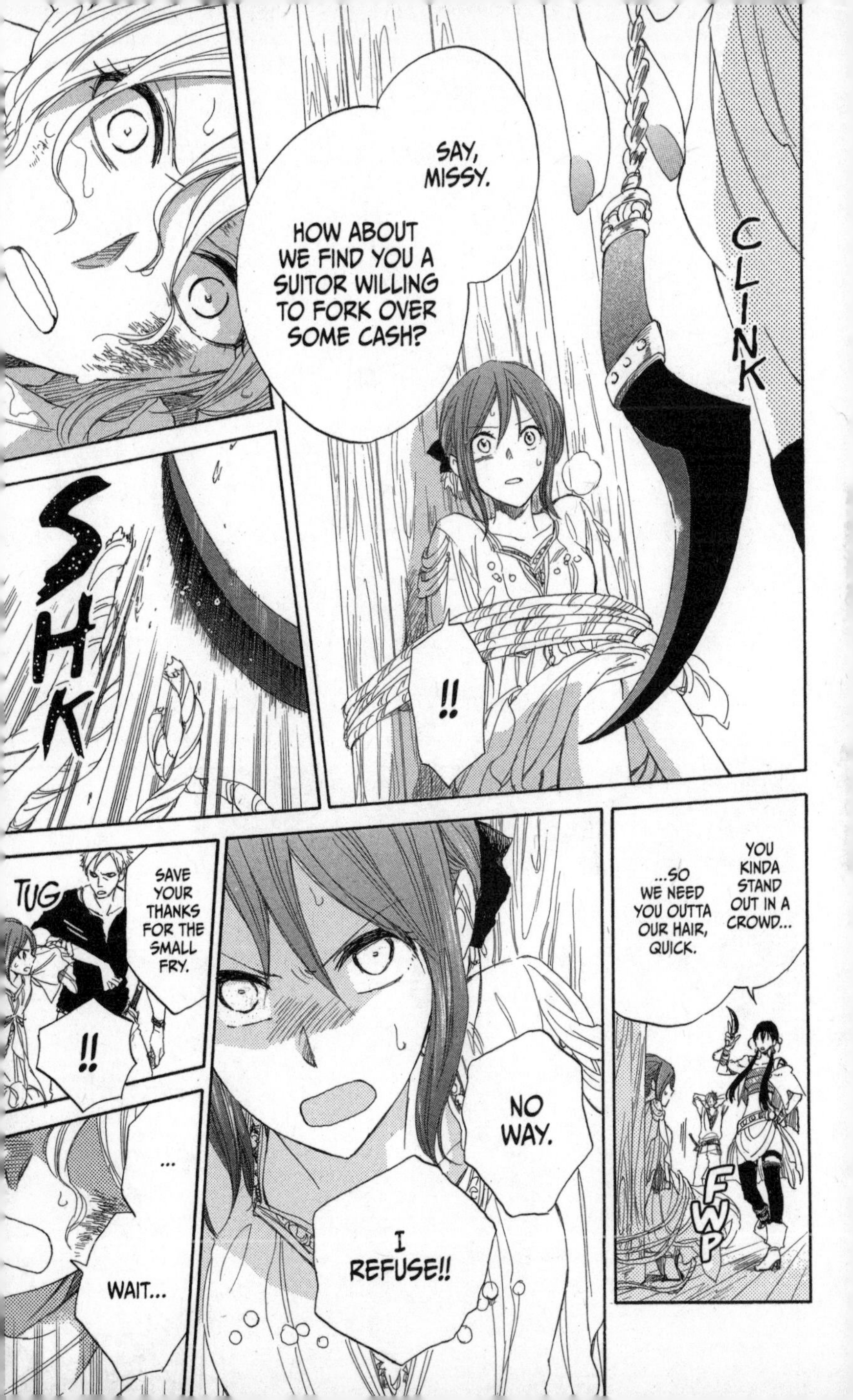
SAY, MISSY.
HOW ABOUT WE FIND YOU A SUITOR WILLING TO FORK OVER SOME CASH?
CLINK
!!
SHK
YOU KINDA STAND OUT IN A CROWD...
...SO WE NEED YOU OUTTA OUR HAIR, QUICK.
FWP
NO WAY.
I REFUSE!!
SAVE YOUR THANKS FOR THE SMALL FRY.
TUG
!!
...
WAIT...

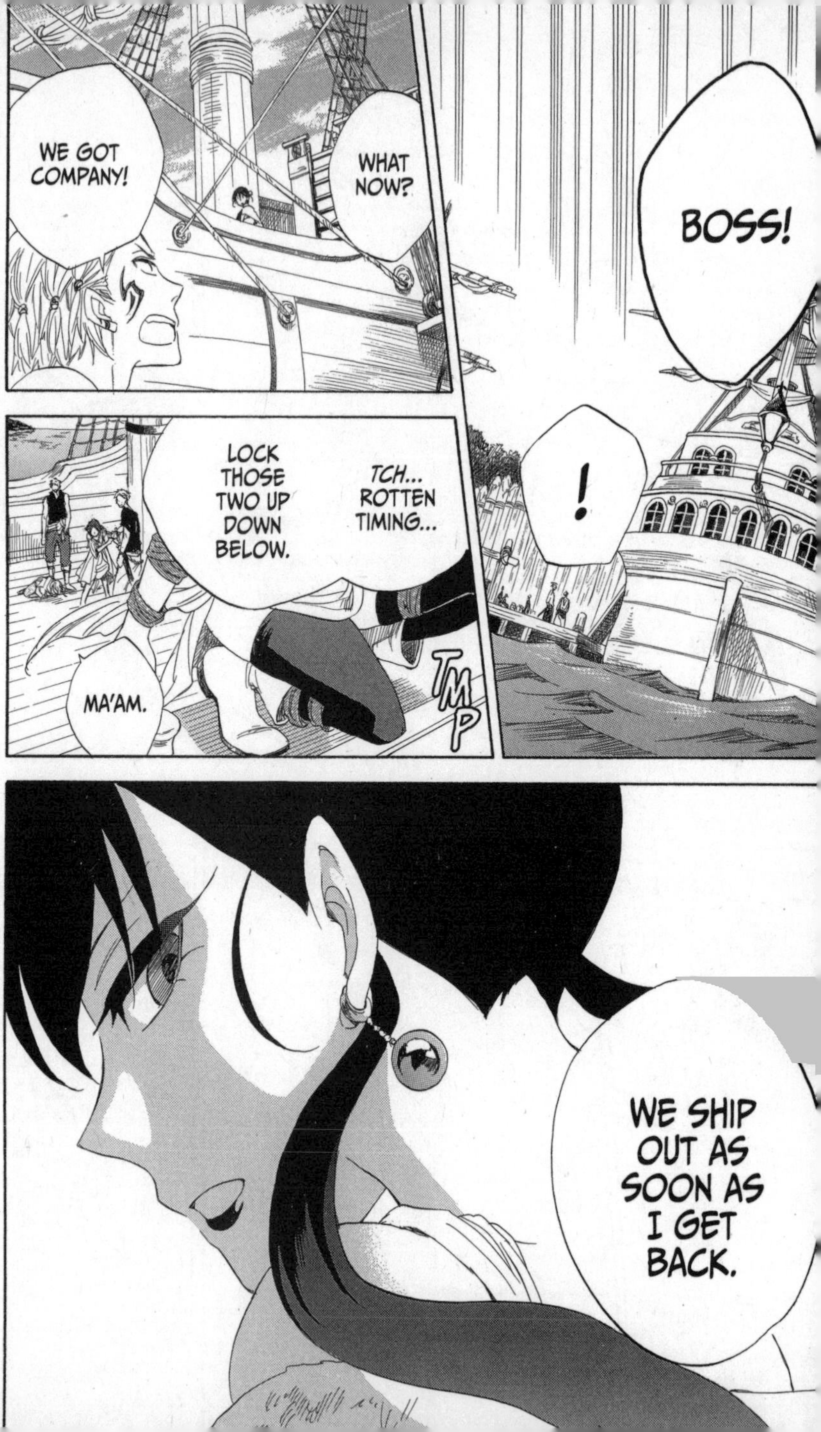
BOSS!
!
WHAT NOW?
WE GOT COMPANY!
TCH... ROTTEN TIMING...
LOCK THOSE TWO UP DOWN BELOW.
TMP
MA'AM.
WE SHIP OUT AS SOON AS I GET BACK.

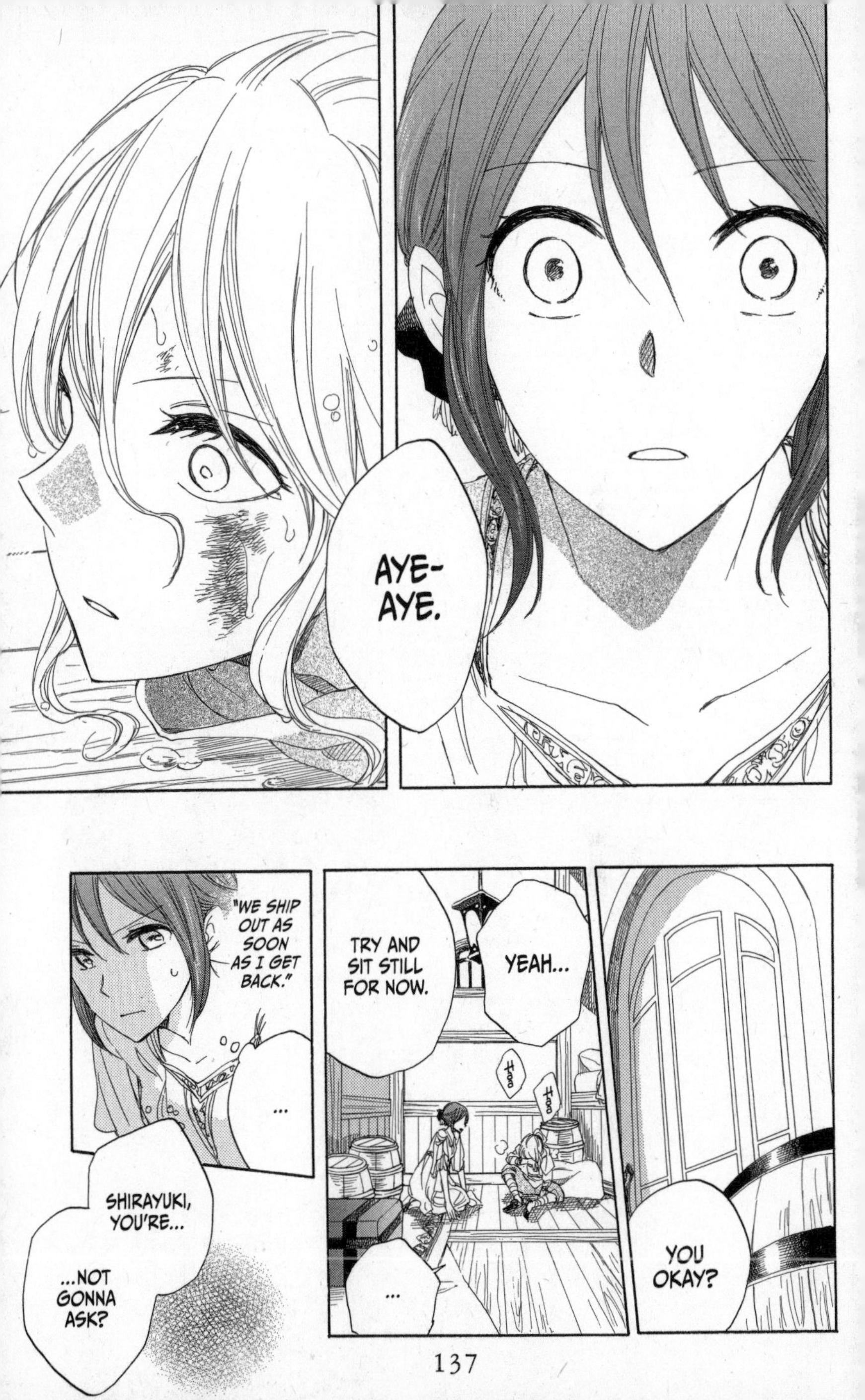
AYE-AYE.
YOU OKAY?
YEAH...
TRY AND SIT STILL FOR NOW.
...
"WE SHIP OUT AS SOON AS I GET BACK."
...
SHIRAYUKI, YOU'RE...
...NOT GONNA ASK?

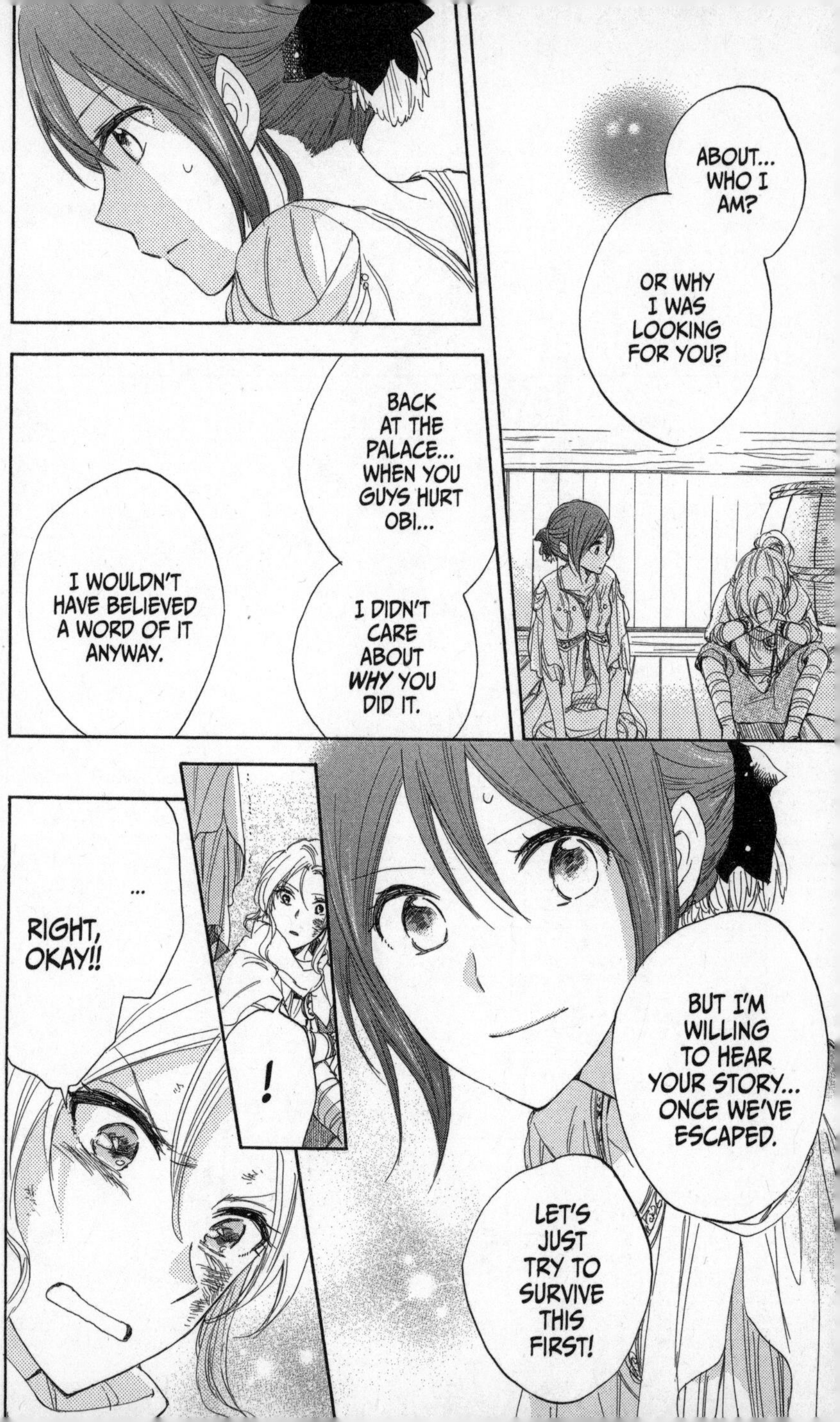
ABOUT... WHO I AM?
OR WHY I WAS LOOKING FOR YOU?
BACK AT THE PALACE... WHEN YOU GUYS HURT OBI...
I DIDN'T CARE ABOUT *WHY* YOU DID IT.
I WOULDN'T HAVE BELIEVED A WORD OF IT ANYWAY.
BUT I'M WILLING TO HEAR YOUR STORY... ONCE WE'VE ESCAPED.
LET'S JUST TRY TO SURVIVE THIS FIRST!
!
...
RIGHT, OKAY!!

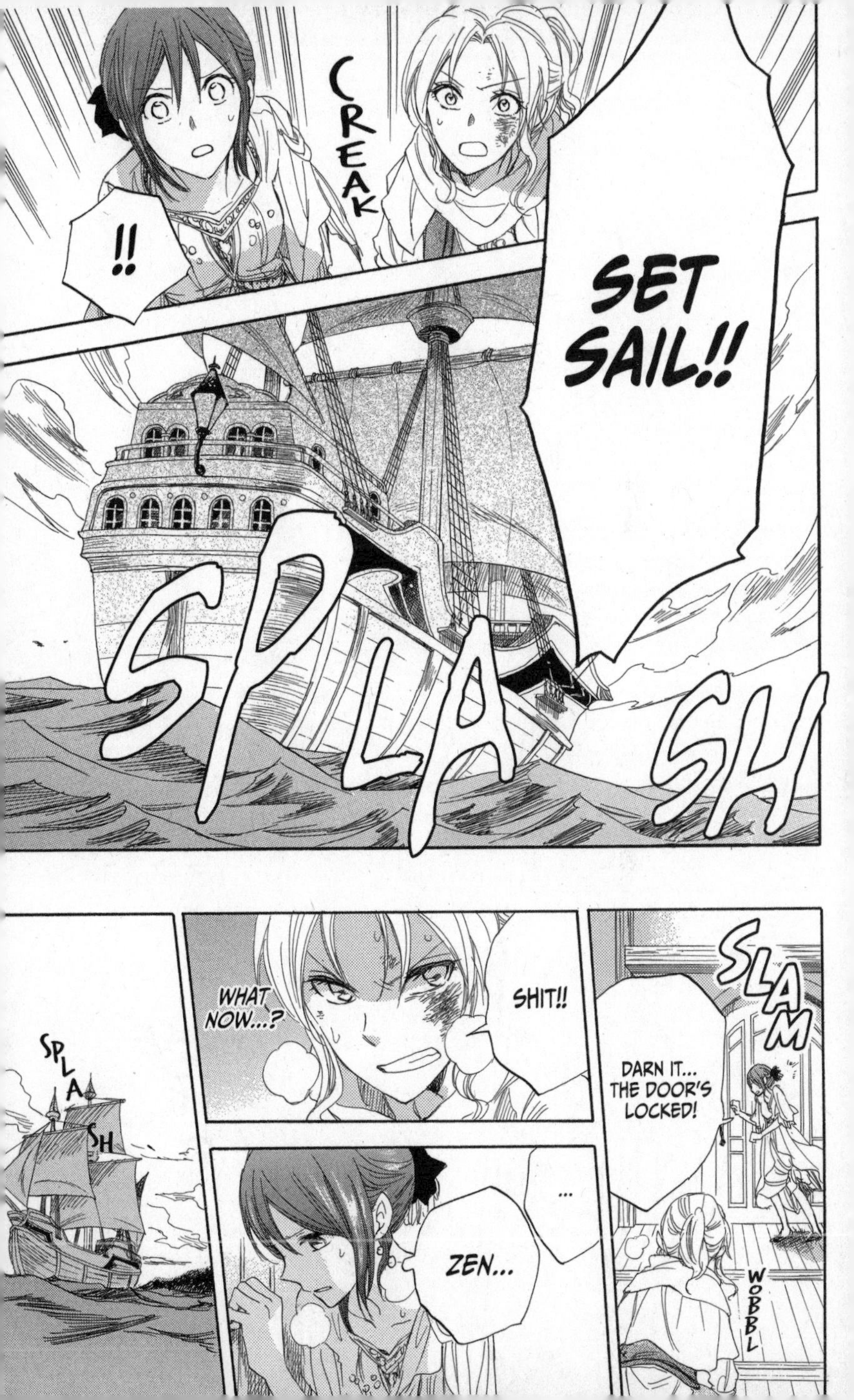
CREAK
!!
SET SAIL!!
SPLASH
SLAM
DARN IT... THE DOOR'S LOCKED!
WOBBBL
SHIT!!
WHAT NOW...?
...
ZEN...
SPLASH

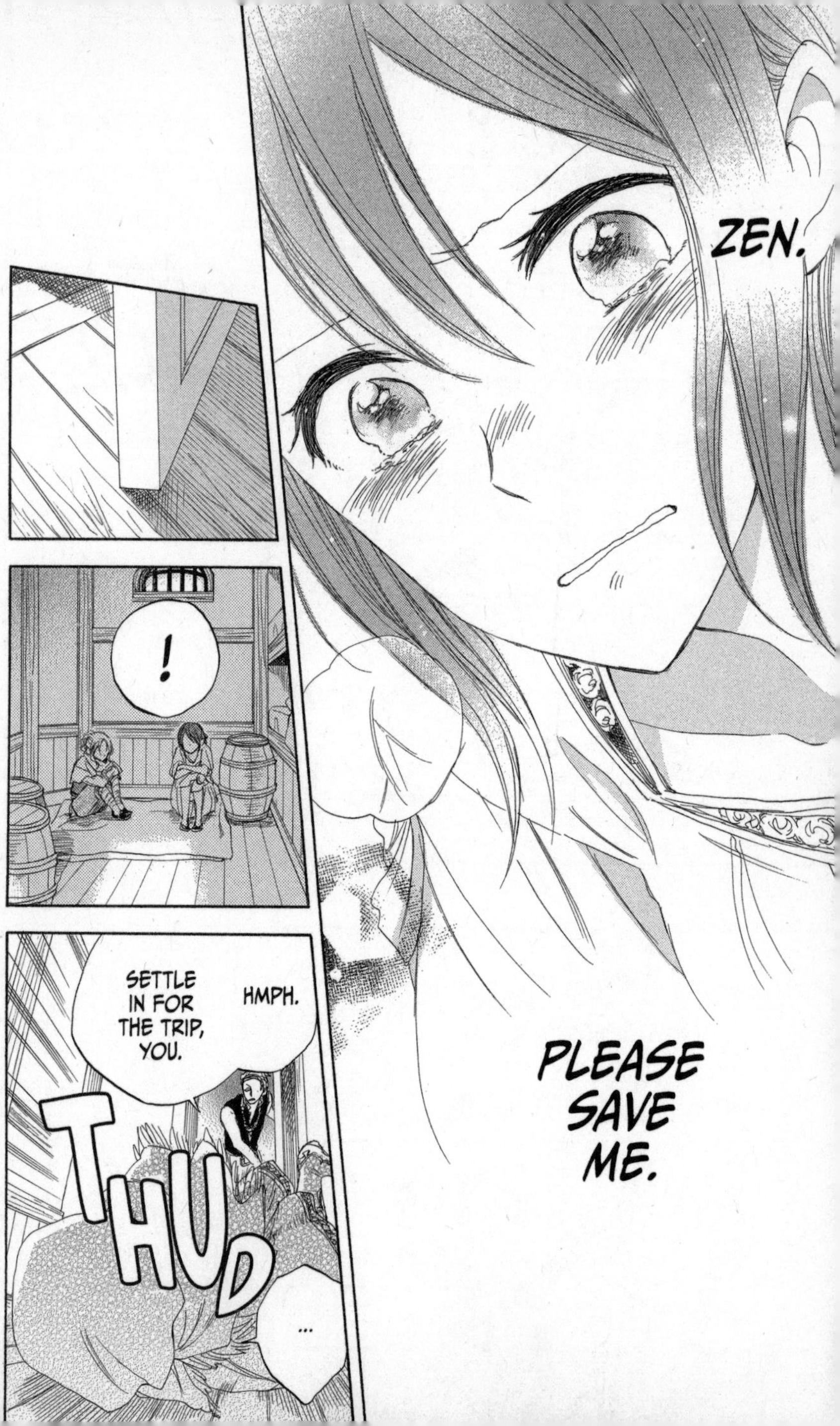
ZEN.
PLEASE SAVE ME.
!
HMPH.
SETTLE IN FOR THE TRIP, YOU.
THUD
...

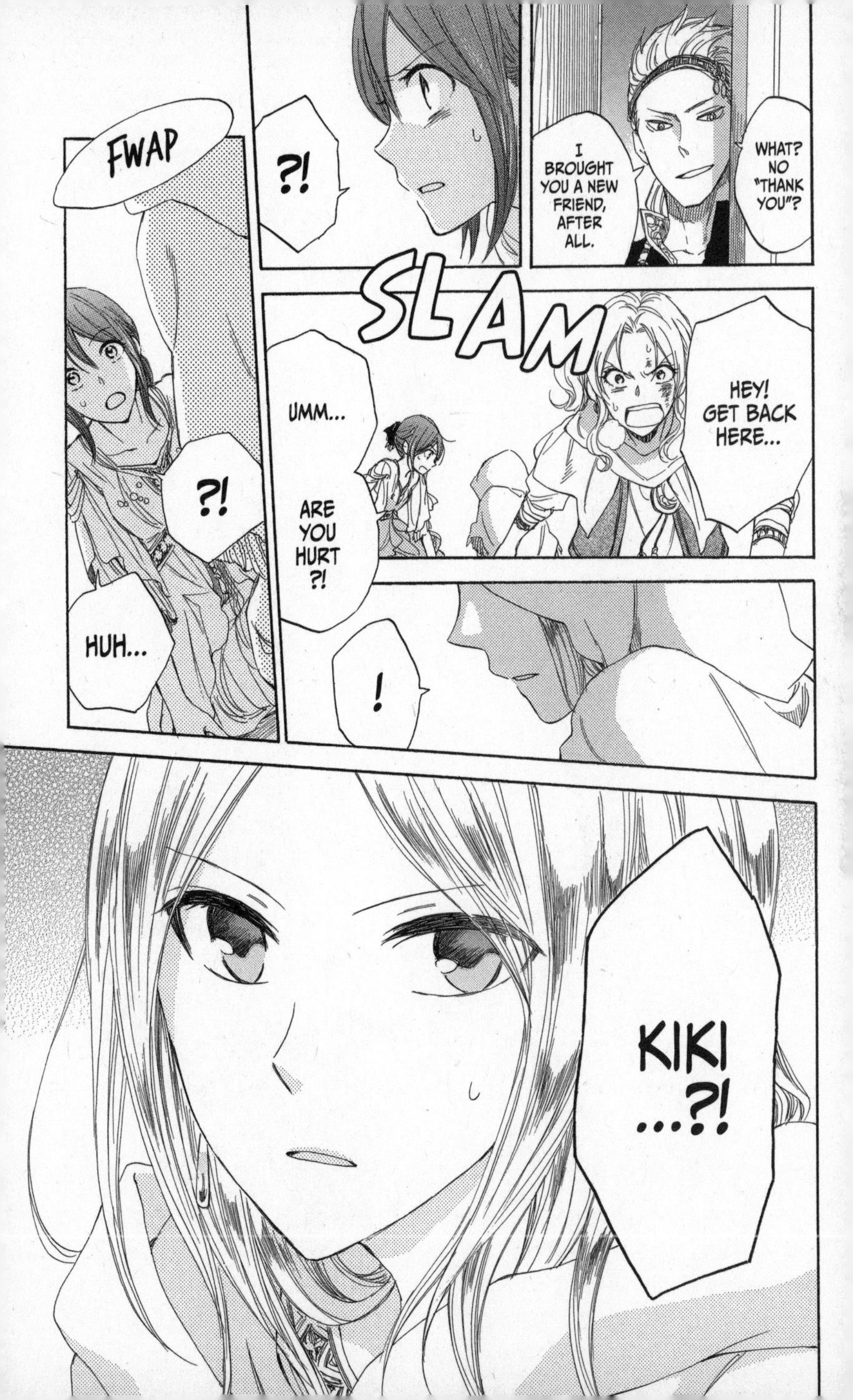
WHAT? NO "THANK YOU"?
I BROUGHT YOU A NEW FRIEND, AFTER ALL.
?!
HEY! GET BACK HERE...
SLAM
UMM... ARE YOU HURT?!
!
FWAP
?!
HUH...
KIKI...?!

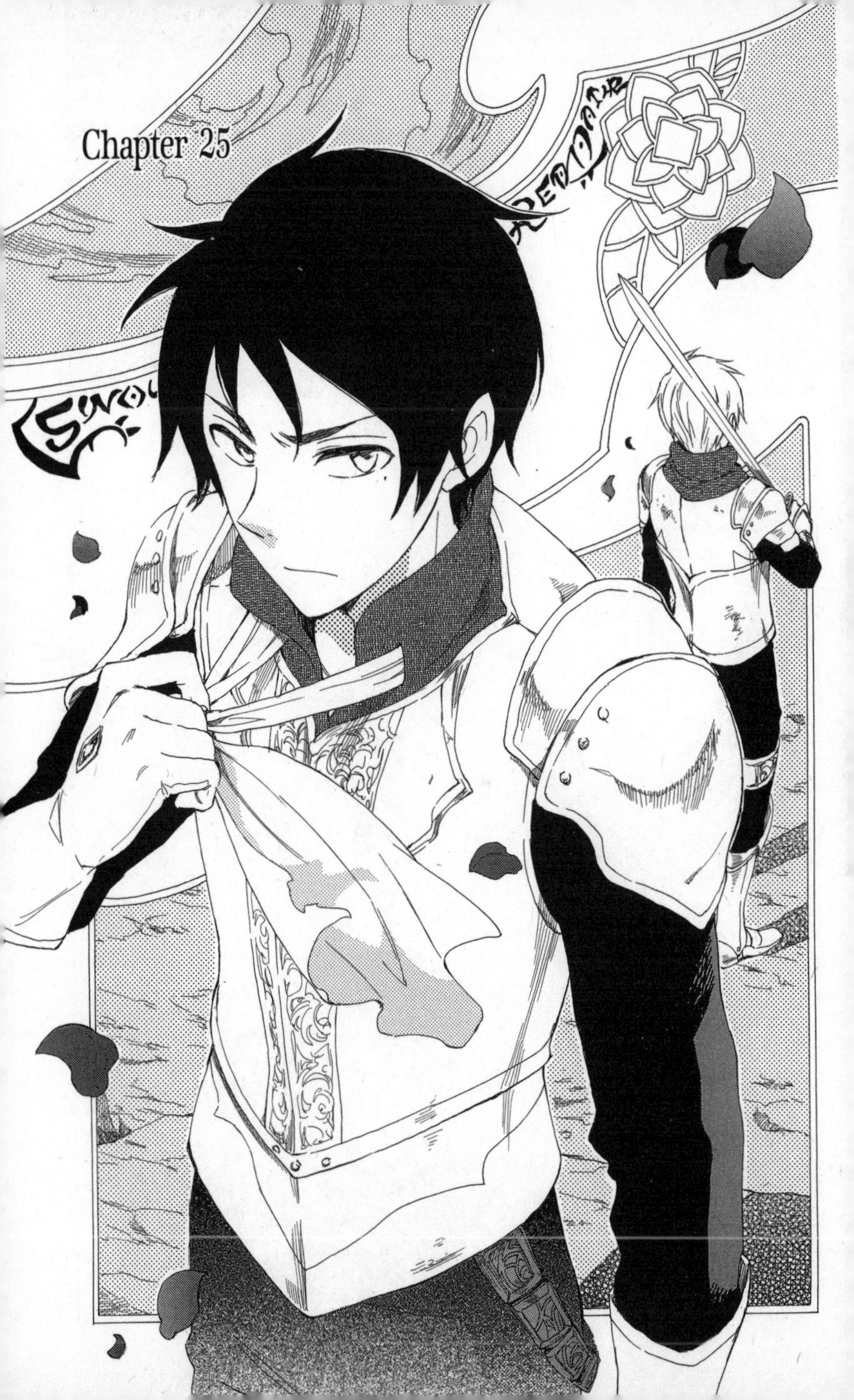
Chapter 25

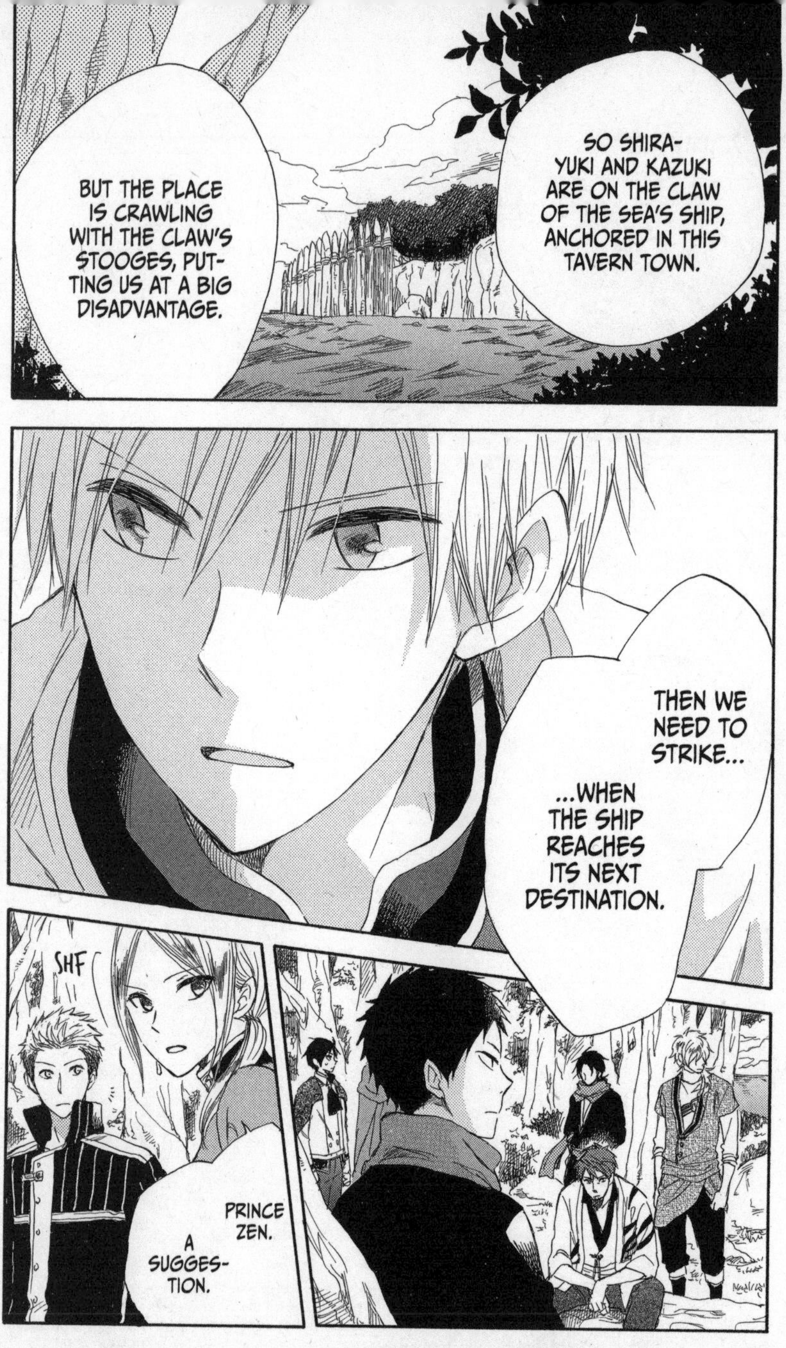
SO SHIRA-YUKI AND KAZUKI ARE ON THE CLAW OF THE SEA'S SHIP, ANCHORED IN THIS TAVERN TOWN.
BUT THE PLACE IS CRAWLING WITH THE CLAW'S STOOGES, PUT-TING US AT A BIG DISADVANTAGE.
THEN WE NEED TO STRIKE...
...WHEN THE SHIP REACHES ITS NEXT DESTINATION.
SHF
PRINCE ZEN.
A SUGGES-TION.

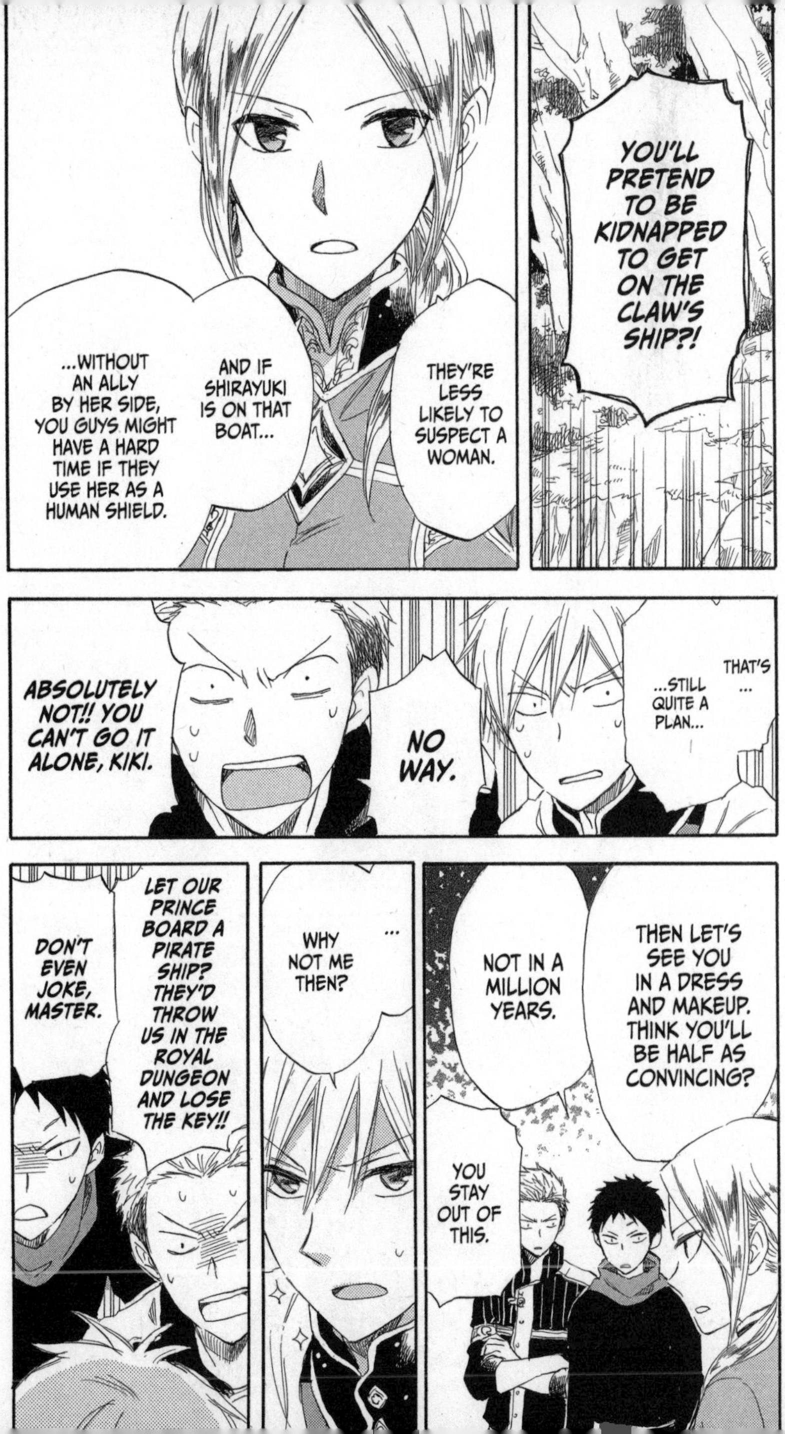
YOU'LL PRETEND TO BE KIDNAPPED TO GET ON THE CLAW'S SHIP?!
THEY'RE LESS LIKELY TO SUSPECT A WOMAN.
AND IF SHIRAYUKI IS ON THAT BOAT...
...WITHOUT AN ALLY BY HER SIDE, YOU GUYS MIGHT HAVE A HARD TIME IF THEY USE HER AS A HUMAN SHIELD.
THAT'S...
...STILL QUITE A PLAN...
NO WAY.
ABSOLUTELY NOT!! YOU CAN'T GO IT ALONE, KIKI.
THEN LET'S SEE YOU IN A DRESS AND MAKEUP. THINK YOU'LL BE HALF AS CONVINCING?
NOT IN A MILLION YEARS.
YOU STAY OUT OF THIS.
...
WHY NOT ME THEN?
LET OUR PRINCE BOARD A PIRATE SHIP? THEY'D THROW US IN THE ROYAL DUNGEON AND LOSE THE KEY!!
DON'T EVEN JOKE, MASTER.

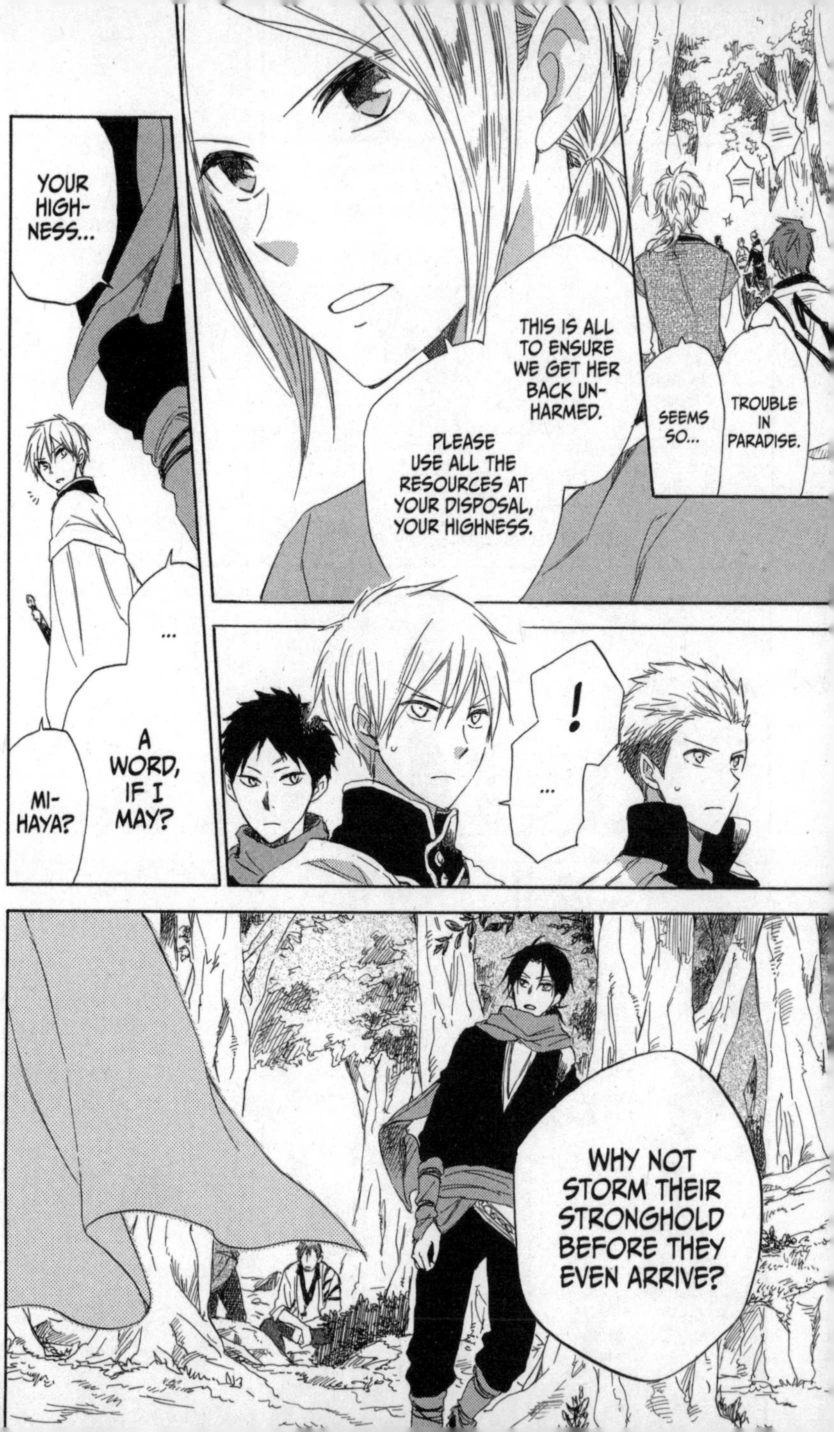
TROUBLE IN PARADISE.
SEEMS SO...
THIS IS ALL TO ENSURE WE GET HER BACK UNHARMED.
PLEASE USE ALL THE RESOURCES AT YOUR DISPOSAL, YOUR HIGHNESS.
!
...
YOUR HIGHNESS...
...
A WORD, IF I MAY?
MIHAYA?
WHY NOT STORM THEIR STRONGHOLD BEFORE THEY EVEN ARRIVE?

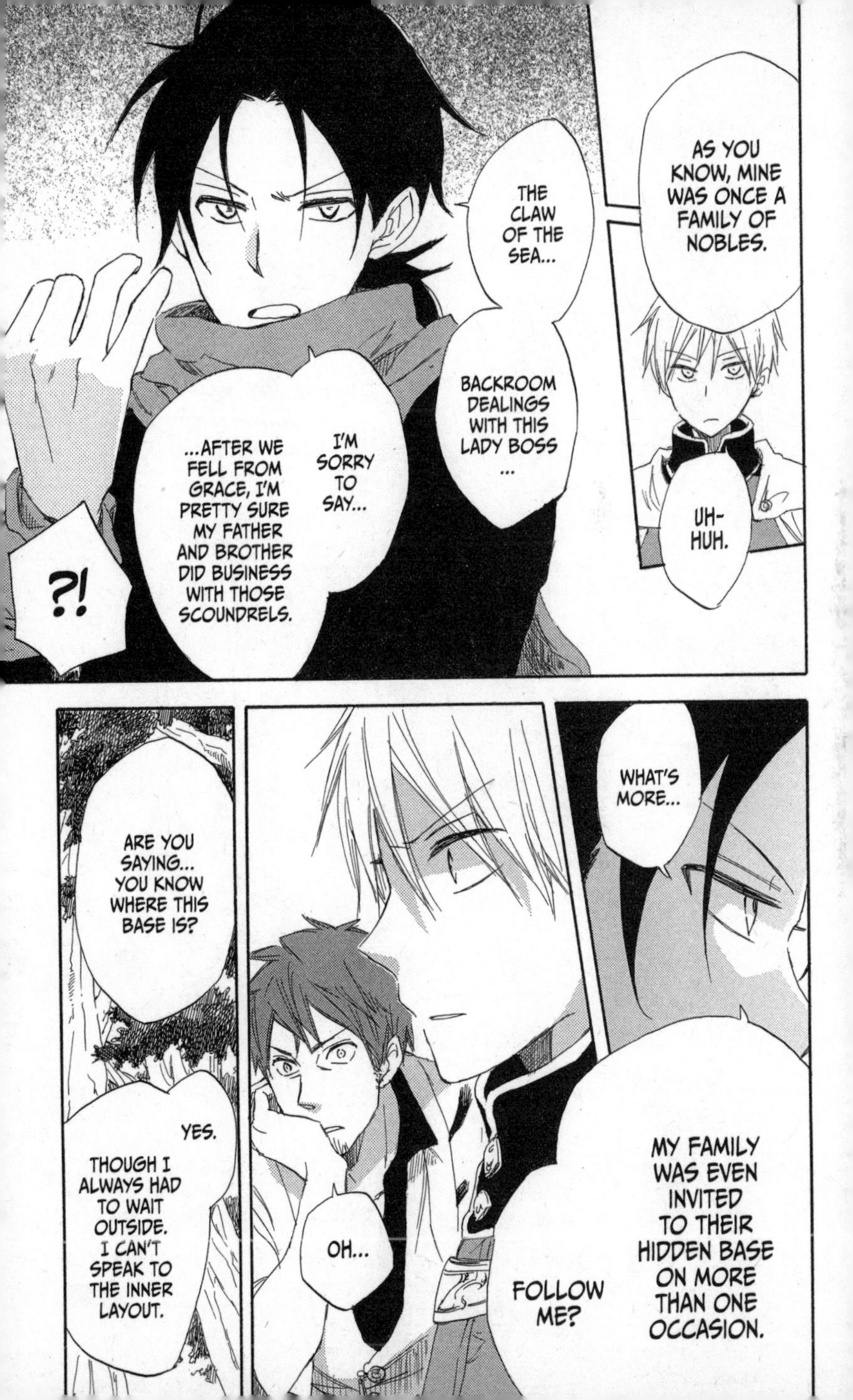
AS YOU KNOW, MINE WAS ONCE A FAMILY OF NOBLES.
UH-HUH.
THE CLAW OF THE SEA...
BACKROOM DEALINGS WITH THIS LADY BOSS ...
I'M SORRY TO SAY...
...AFTER WE FELL FROM GRACE, I'M PRETTY SURE MY FATHER AND BROTHER DID BUSINESS WITH THOSE SCOUNDRELS.
?!
WHAT'S MORE...
MY FAMILY WAS EVEN INVITED TO THEIR HIDDEN BASE ON MORE THAN ONE OCCASION.
FOLLOW ME?
OH...
ARE YOU SAYING... YOU KNOW WHERE THIS BASE IS?
YES.
THOUGH I ALWAYS HAD TO WAIT OUTSIDE. I CAN'T SPEAK TO THE INNER LAYOUT.

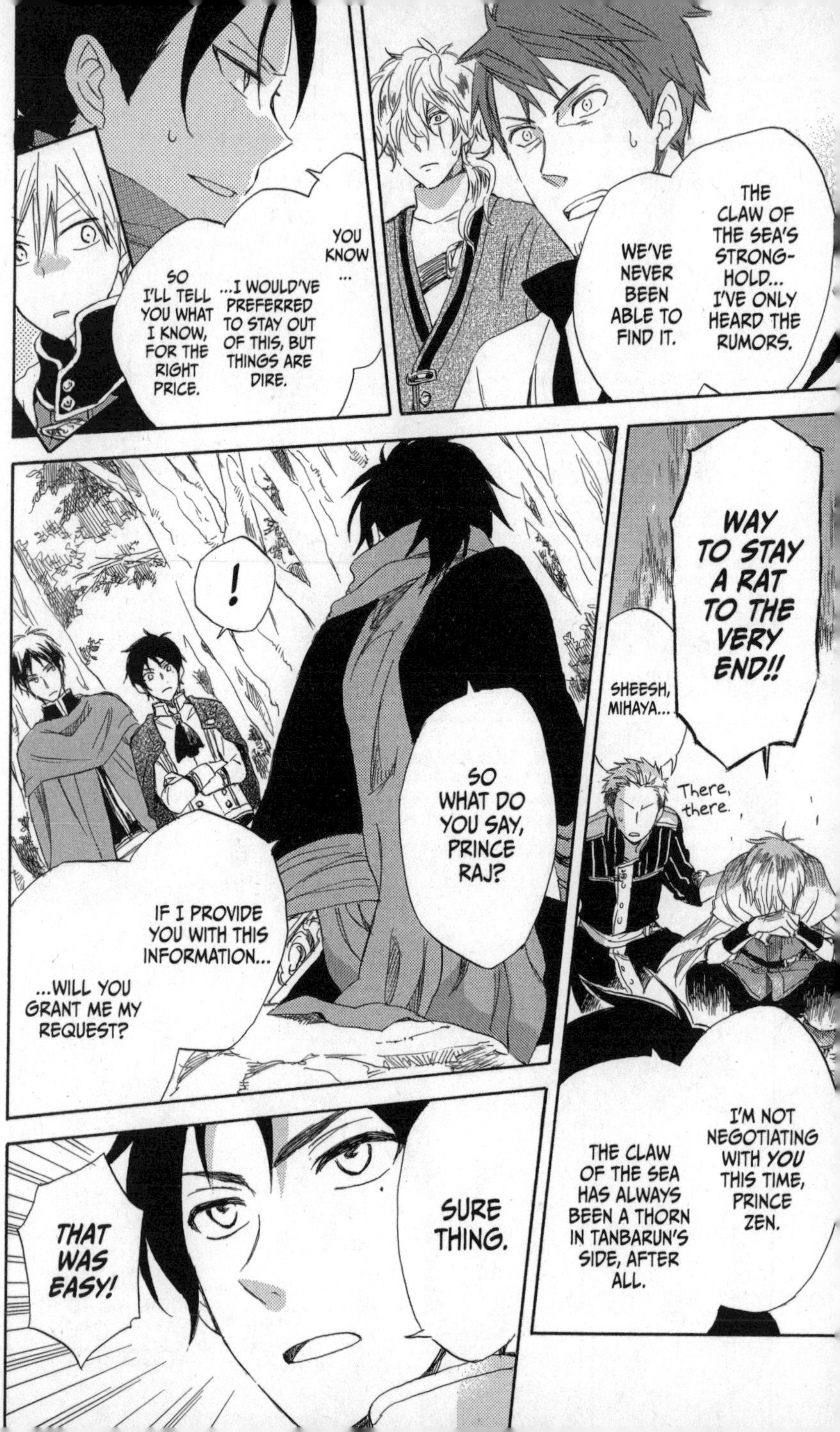
THE CLAW OF THE SEA'S STRONG-HOLD... I'VE ONLY HEARD THE RUMORS.
WE'VE NEVER BEEN ABLE TO FIND IT.
YOU KNOW...
...I WOULD'VE PREFERRED TO STAY OUT OF THIS, BUT THINGS ARE DIRE.
SO I'LL TELL YOU WHAT I KNOW, FOR THE RIGHT PRICE.
WAY TO STAY A RAT TO THE VERY END!!
SHEESH, MIHAYA...
There, there.
!
SO WHAT DO YOU SAY, PRINCE RAJ?
IF I PROVIDE YOU WITH THIS INFORMATION...
...WILL YOU GRANT ME MY REQUEST?
I'M NOT NEGOTIATING WITH *YOU* THIS TIME, PRINCE ZEN.
THE CLAW OF THE SEA HAS ALWAYS BEEN A THORN IN TANBARUN'S SIDE, AFTER ALL.
SURE THING.
THAT WAS EASY!

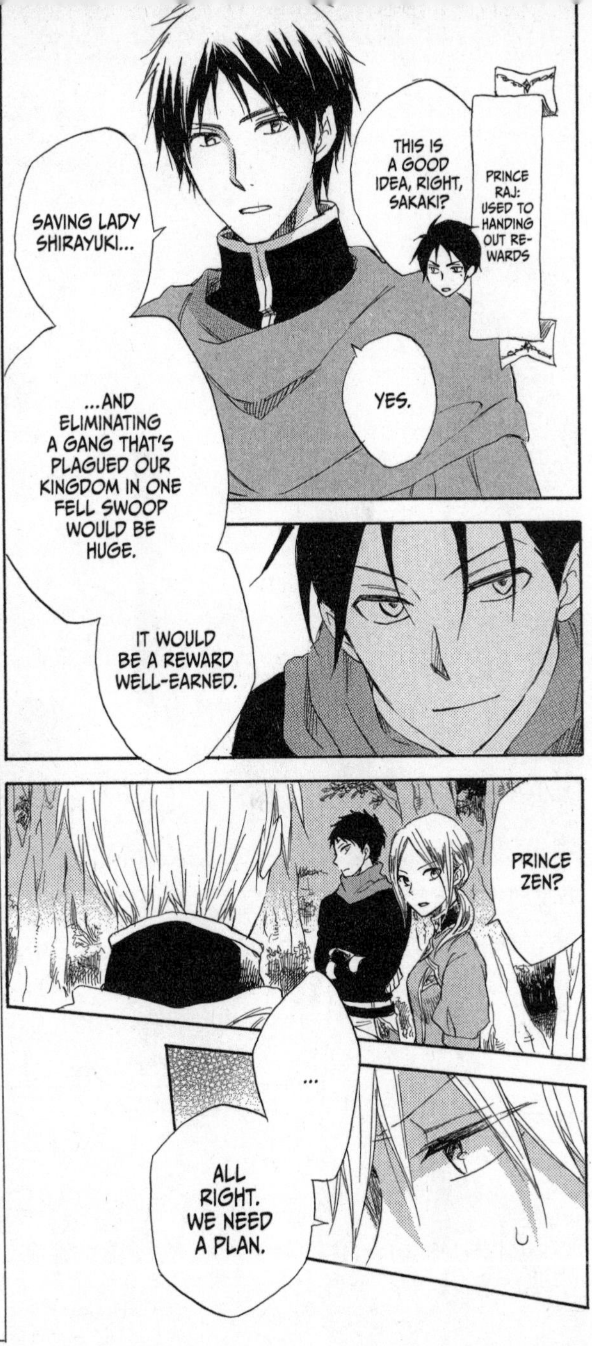
PRINCE RAJ: USED TO HANDING OUT RE-WARDS
THIS IS A GOOD IDEA, RIGHT, SAKAKI?
YES.
SAVING LADY SHIRAYUKI...
...AND ELIMINATING A GANG THAT'S PLAGUED OUR KINGDOM IN ONE FELL SWOOP WOULD BE HUGE.
IT WOULD BE A REWARD WELL-EARNED.
PRINCE ZEN?
...
ALL RIGHT. WE NEED A PLAN.

About the Title Pages for Chapters 23, 24 and 25

The Armor Series

I didn't really intend to make it a recurring theme when I was drawing Zen in armor for chapter 23, but when chapter 24 rolled around, I thought, "Why not put the aides in armor too?" and it turned into a series.

If my editor and readers start telling me to draw the characters in cuter costumes, I honestly don't know what I'll do.

But don't worry! I won't draw Shirayuki in armor for the chapter 26 title page.

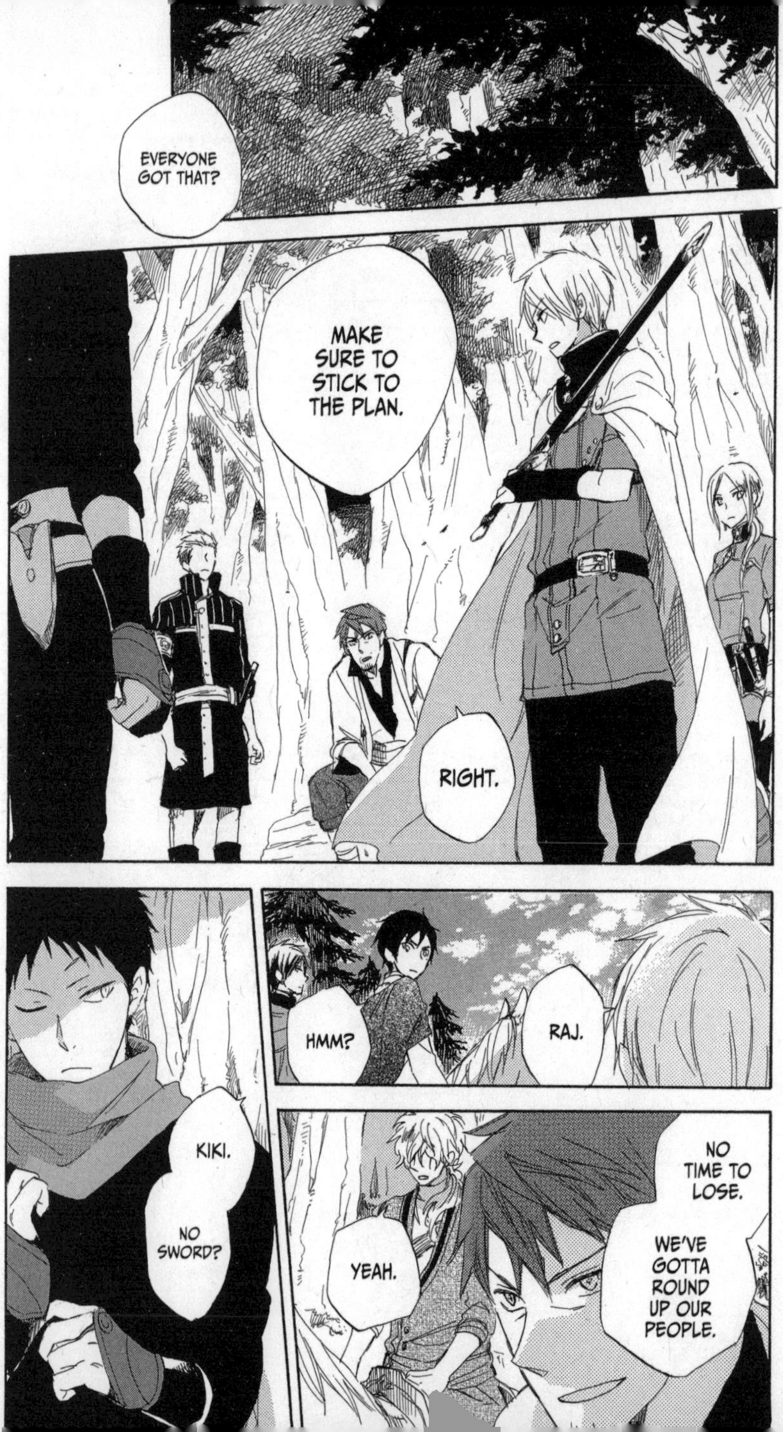

EVERYONE GOT THAT?
MAKE SURE TO STICK TO THE PLAN.
RIGHT.
RAJ.
HMM?
NO TIME TO LOSE.
WE'VE GOTTA ROUND UP OUR PEOPLE.
YEAH.
KIKI.
NO SWORD?

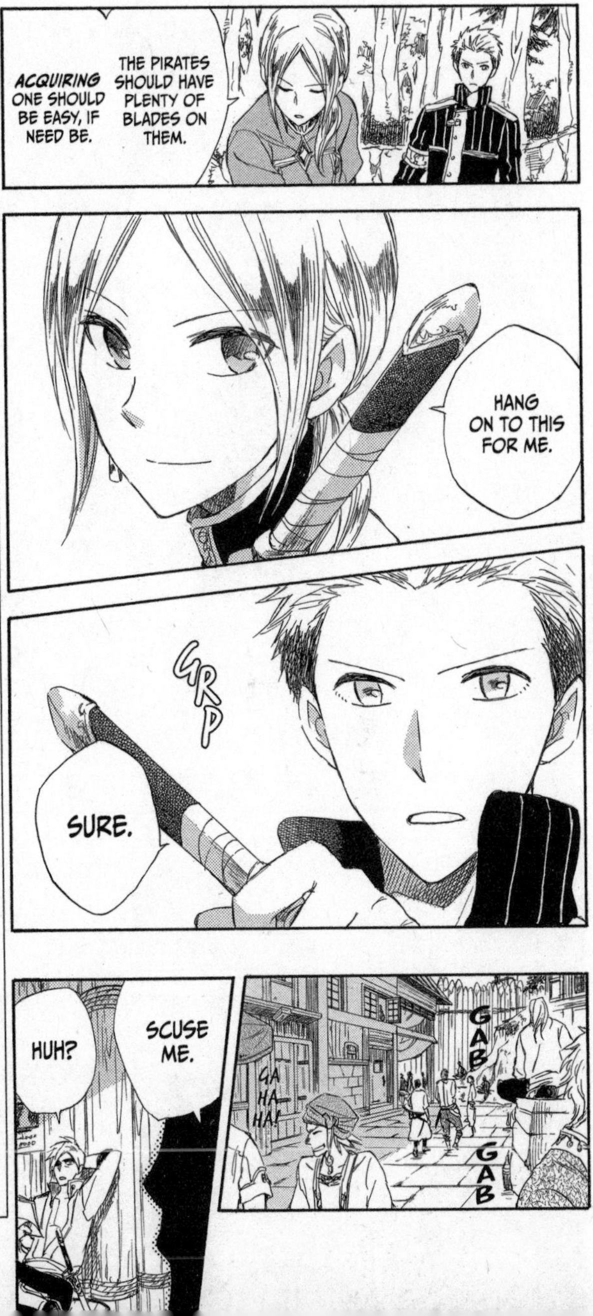
THE PIRATES SHOULD HAVE PLENTY OF BLADES ON THEM.
ACQUIRING ONE SHOULD BE EASY, IF NEED BE.
HANG ON TO THIS FOR ME.
GRP
SURE.
GAB
GA HA HA!
GAB
SCUSE ME.
HUH?

Q: "What sort of drawing materials do you use?"

I'm currently using the following:

Ink:
-Pilot products
-Manga india ink (for color pages)

Pens:
-Nikko G Pen (for 90% of characters)
-Nikko Round Pen (for hair and backgrounds)

Tone:
For character shadows, from lightest to darkest:
-30 or 40
-41
-61

I've been drawn to 31 recently, when 30 is too faint.

Color:
-Copic markers
-Watercolor paints

-Photoshop CS
↑ *Snow White with the Red Hair* is mostly digital.

11 That's about it!

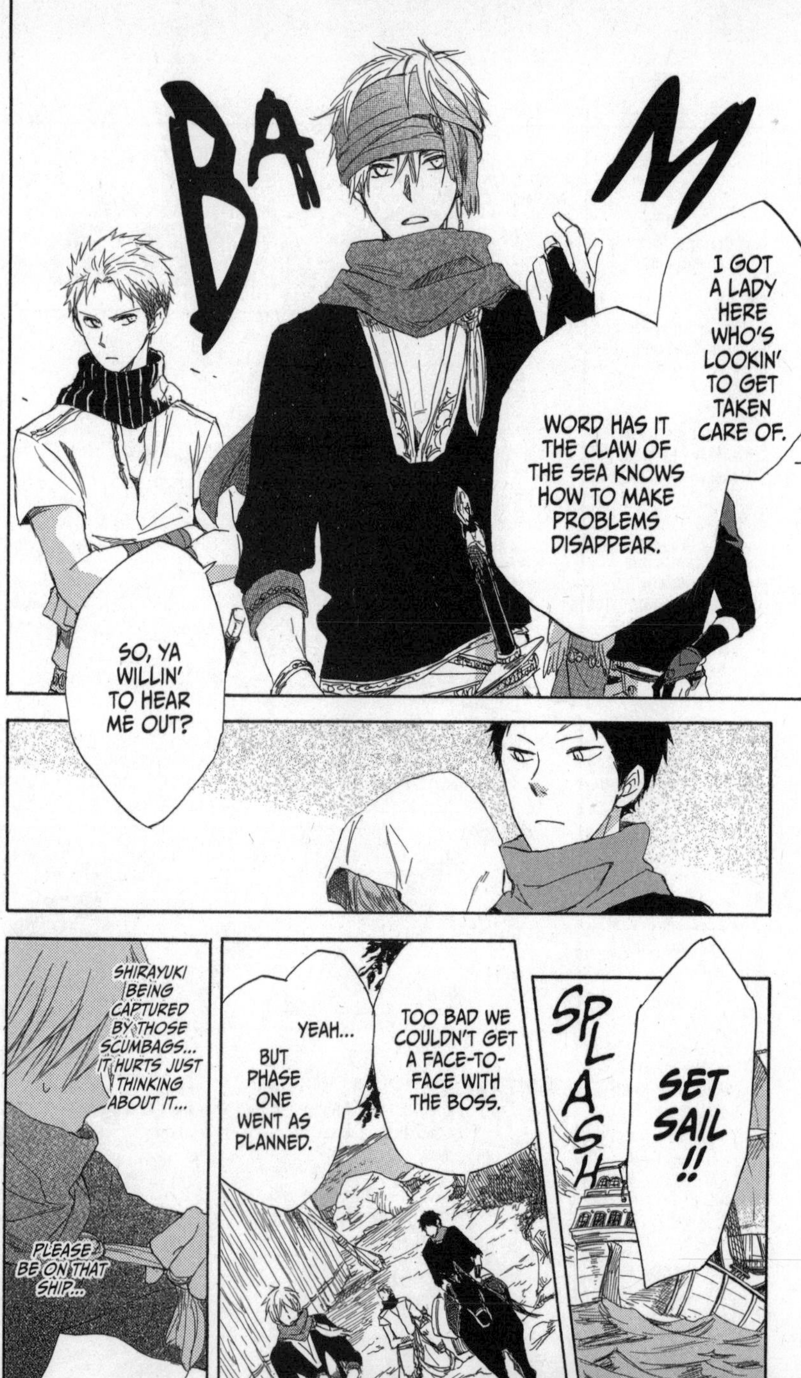
BAM
I GOT A LADY HERE WHO'S LOOKIN' TO GET TAKEN CARE OF.
WORD HAS IT THE CLAW OF THE SEA KNOWS HOW TO MAKE PROBLEMS DISAPPEAR.
SO, YA WILLIN' TO HEAR ME OUT?
SPLASH
SET SAIL!!
TOO BAD WE COULDN'T GET A FACE-TO-FACE WITH THE BOSS.
YEAH... BUT PHASE ONE WENT AS PLANNED.
SHIRAYUKI BEING CAPTURED BY THOSE SCUMBAGS... IT HURTS JUST THINKING ABOUT IT...
PLEASE BE ON THAT SHIP...

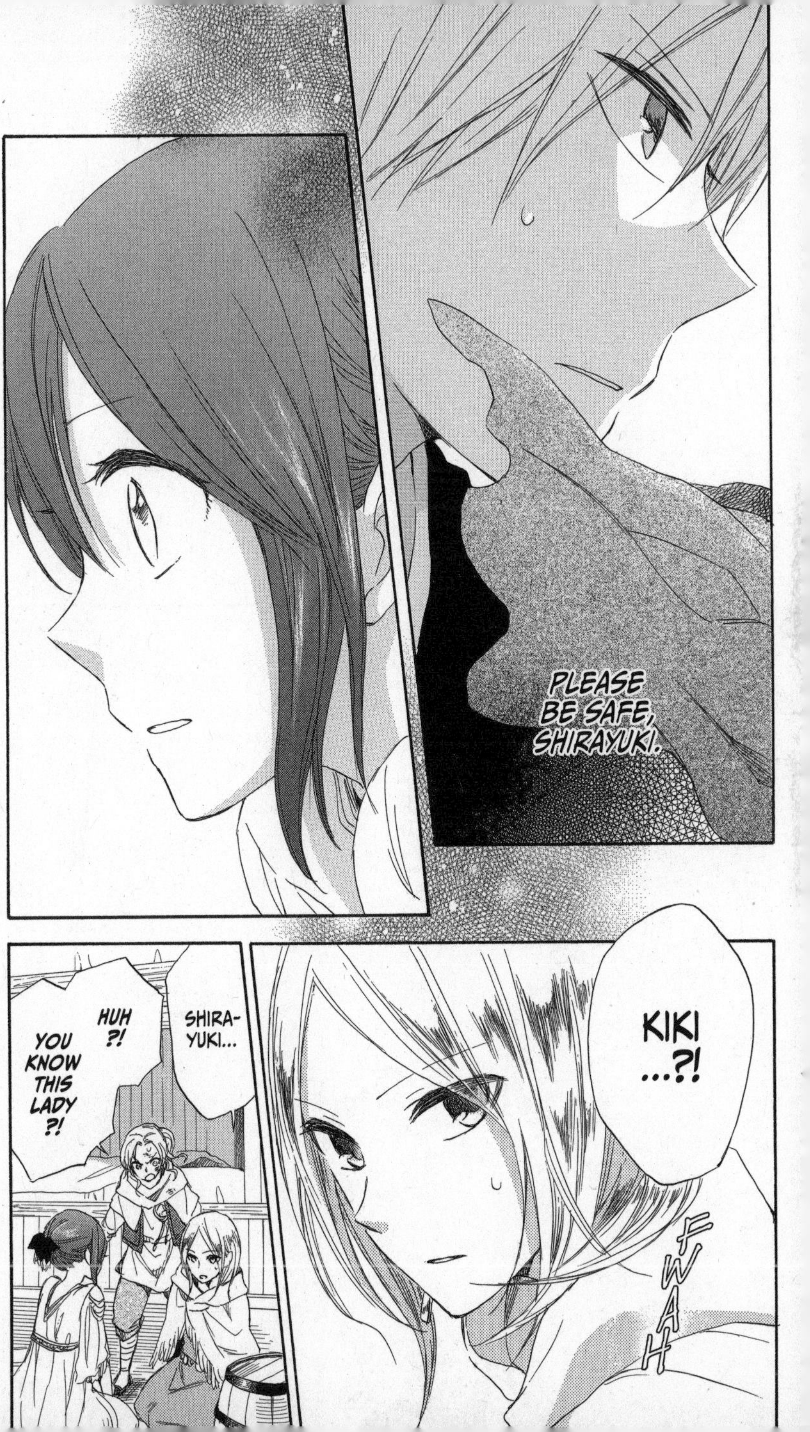
PLEASE BE SAFE, SHIRAYUKI.
KIKI ...?!
FWAH
SHIRA-YUKI...
HUH ?!
YOU KNOW THIS LADY ?!

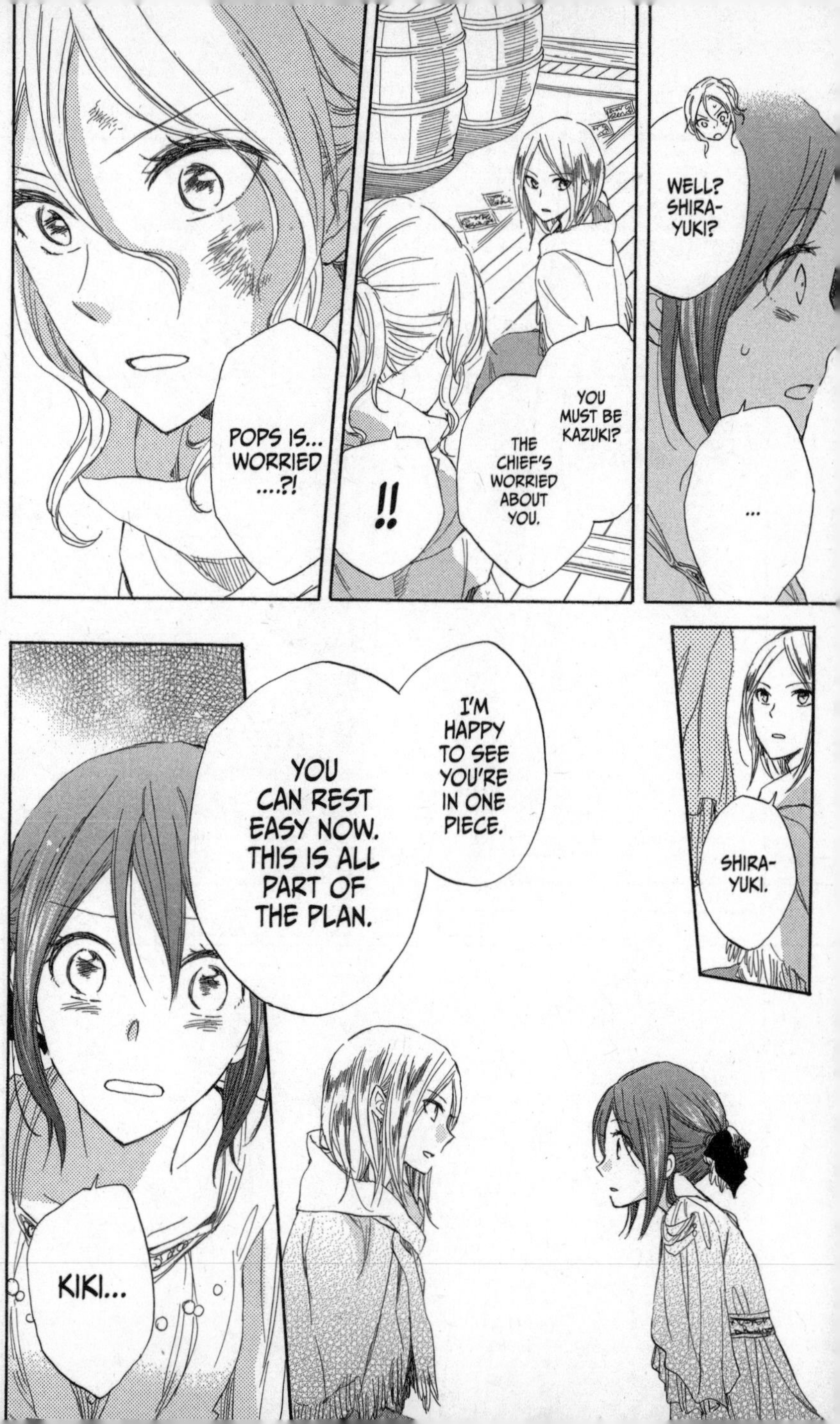
WELL? SHIRA-YUKI?
...
YOU MUST BE KAZUKI?
THE CHIEF'S WORRIED ABOUT YOU.
!!
POPS IS... WORRIED ....?!
SHIRA-YUKI.
I'M HAPPY TO SEE YOU'RE IN ONE PIECE.
YOU CAN REST EASY NOW. THIS IS ALL PART OF THE PLAN.
KIKI...

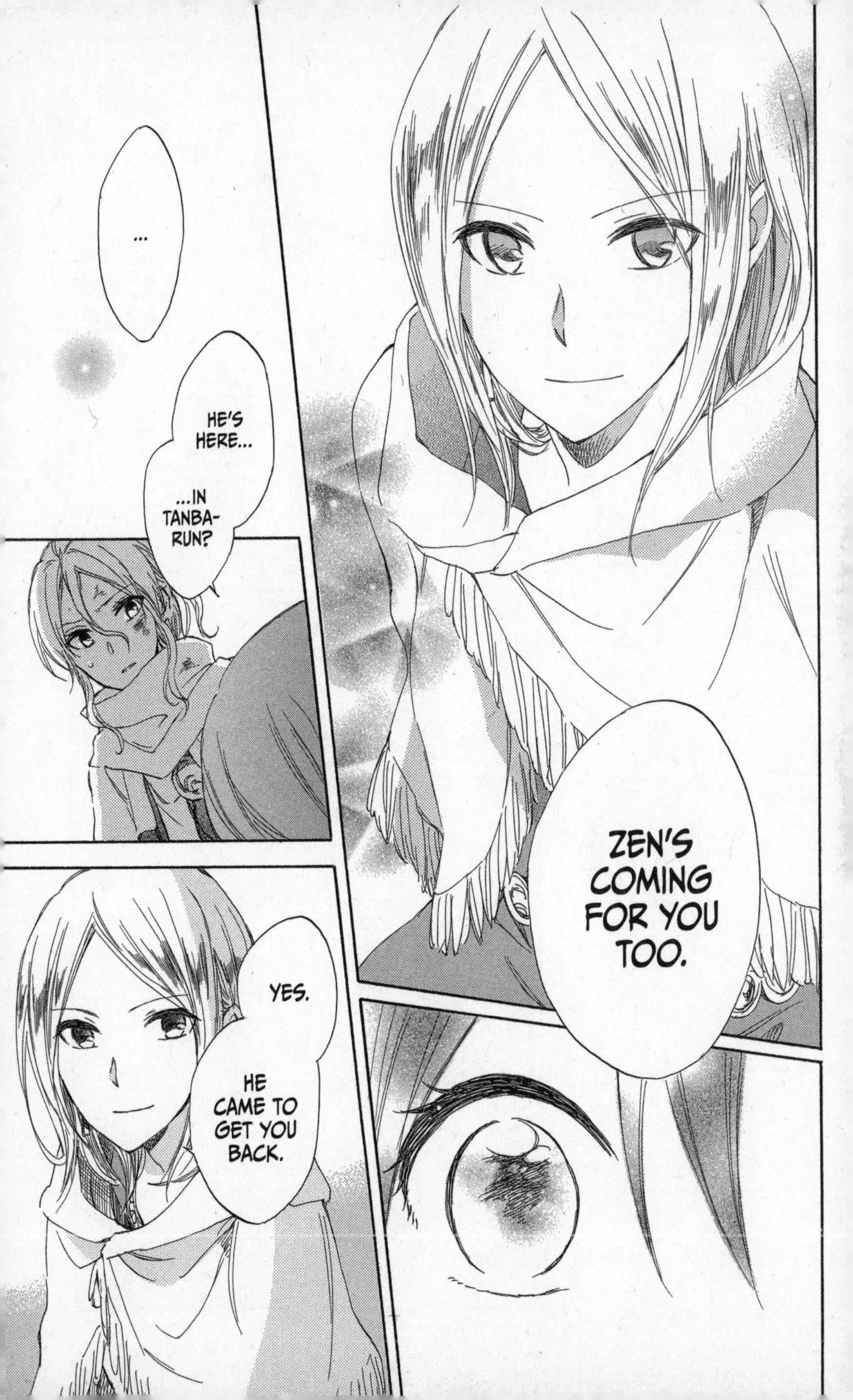
ZEN'S COMING FOR YOU TOO.
...
HE'S HERE...
...IN TANBA-RUN?
YES.
HE CAME TO GET YOU BACK.

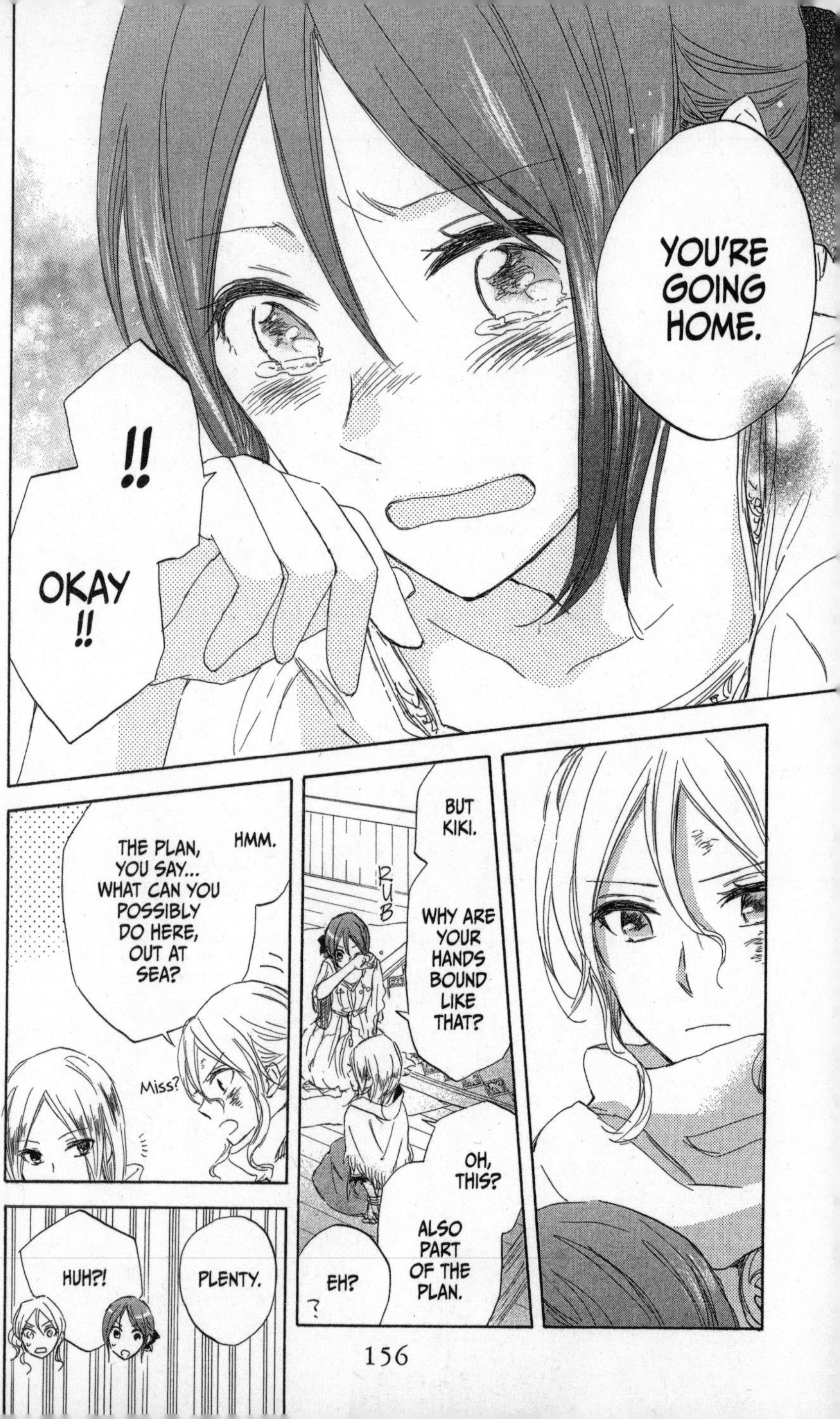
YOU'RE GOING HOME.
!!
OKAY !!
BUT KIKI.
RUB
WHY ARE YOUR HANDS BOUND LIKE THAT?
OH, THIS?
ALSO PART OF THE PLAN.
EH?
HMM.
THE PLAN, YOU SAY... WHAT CAN YOU POSSIBLY DO HERE, OUT AT SEA?
Miss?
PLENTY.
HUH?!

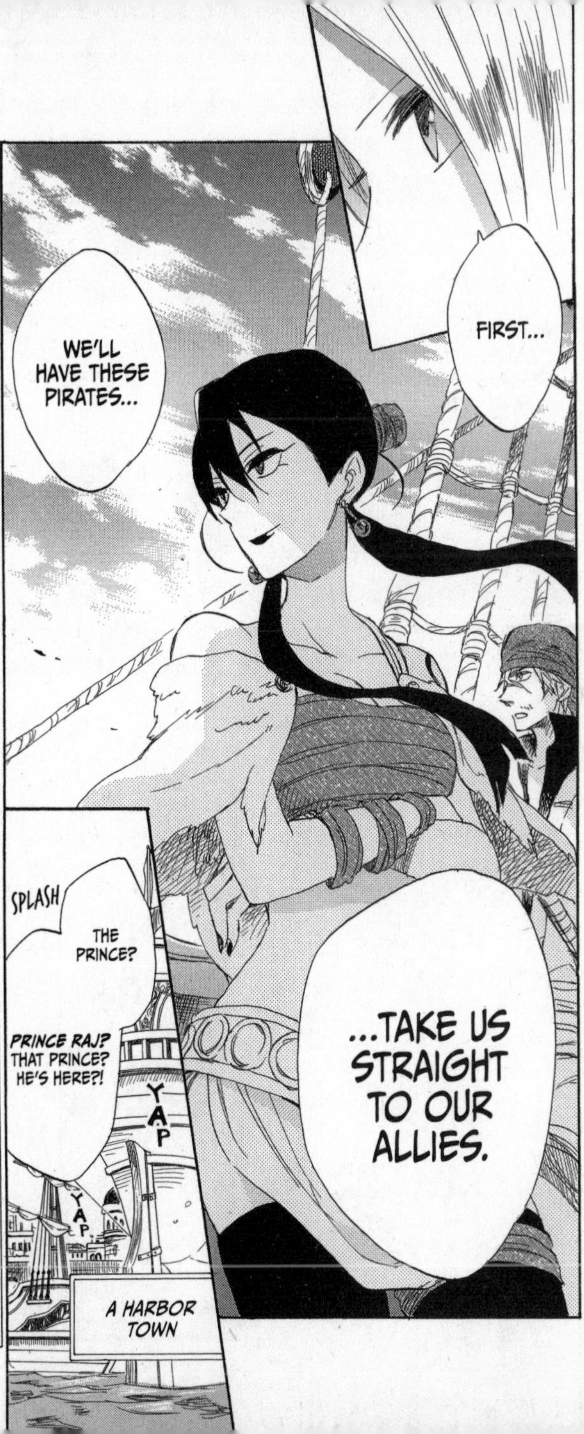
FIRST...
WE'LL HAVE THESE PIRATES...
...TAKE US STRAIGHT TO OUR ALLIES.
A HARBOR TOWN
SPLASH
THE PRINCE?
PRINCE RAJ? THAT PRINCE? HE'S HERE?!
YAP
YAP

Finally, the last sidebar.

I didn't get to include much additional art last volume, so this book has some four-panel comics and an additional bonus bit at the end.

Tensions are running high in the main plot, so the four-panels are a lot more lighthearted!

Oh, Christ.

I hope you enjoy them.

See you again at the end of the volume.

12 END

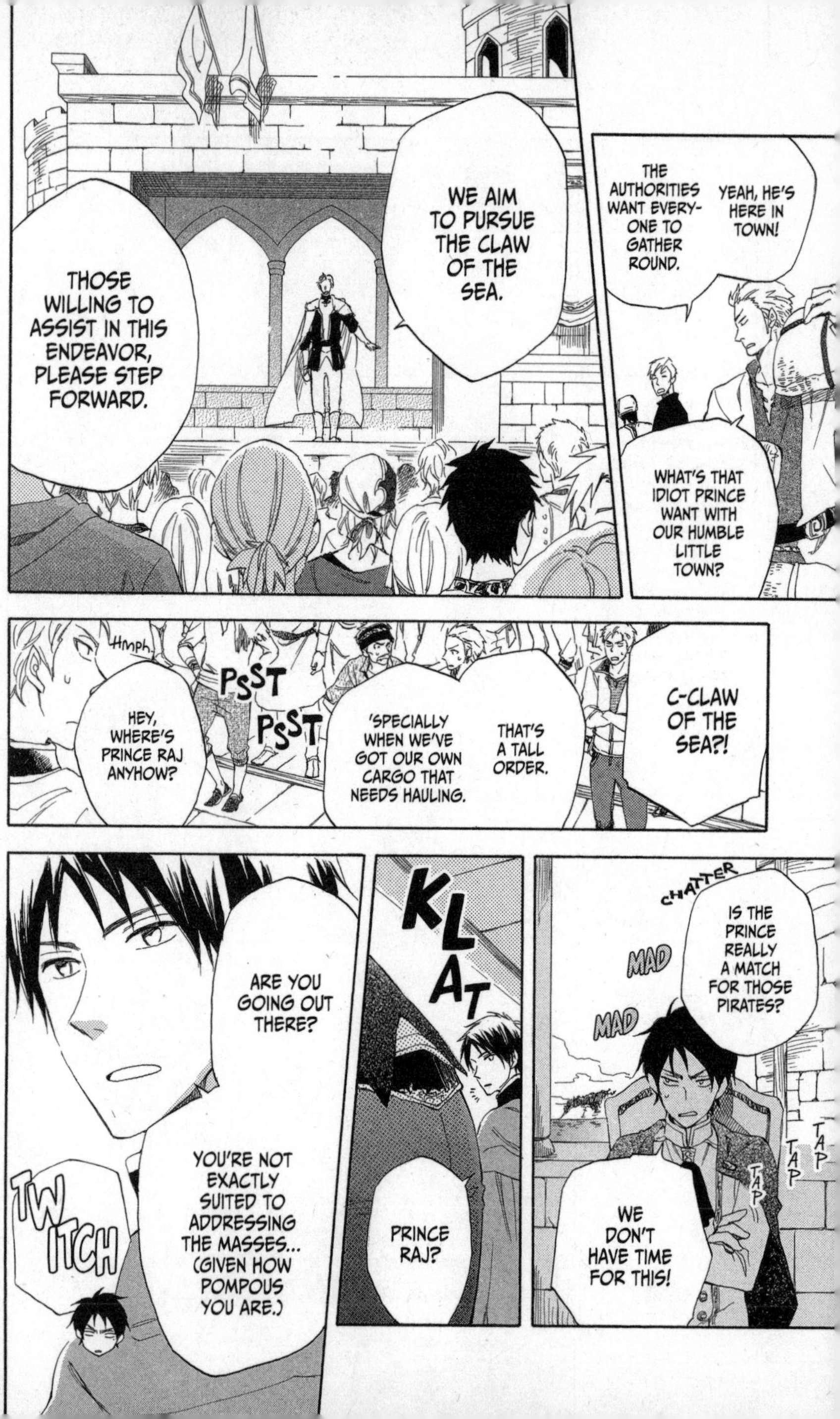
YEAH, HE'S HERE IN TOWN!
THE AUTHORITIES WANT EVERY-ONE TO GATHER ROUND.
WHAT'S THAT IDIOT PRINCE WANT WITH OUR HUMBLE LITTLE TOWN?
WE AIM TO PURSUE THE CLAW OF THE SEA.
THOSE WILLING TO ASSIST IN THIS ENDEAVOR, PLEASE STEP FORWARD.
C-CLAW OF THE SEA?!
THAT'S A TALL ORDER.
'SPECIALLY WHEN WE'VE GOT OUR OWN CARGO THAT NEEDS HAULING.
PSST
PSST
Hmph.
HEY, WHERE'S PRINCE RAJ ANYHOW?
CHATTER
IS THE PRINCE REALLY A MATCH FOR THOSE PIRATES?
MAD
MAD
TAP
TAP
TAP
WE DON'T HAVE TIME FOR THIS!
KLAT
PRINCE RAJ?
ARE YOU GOING OUT THERE?
YOU'RE NOT EXACTLY SUITED TO ADDRESSING THE MASSES... (GIVEN HOW POMPOUS YOU ARE.)
TWITCH

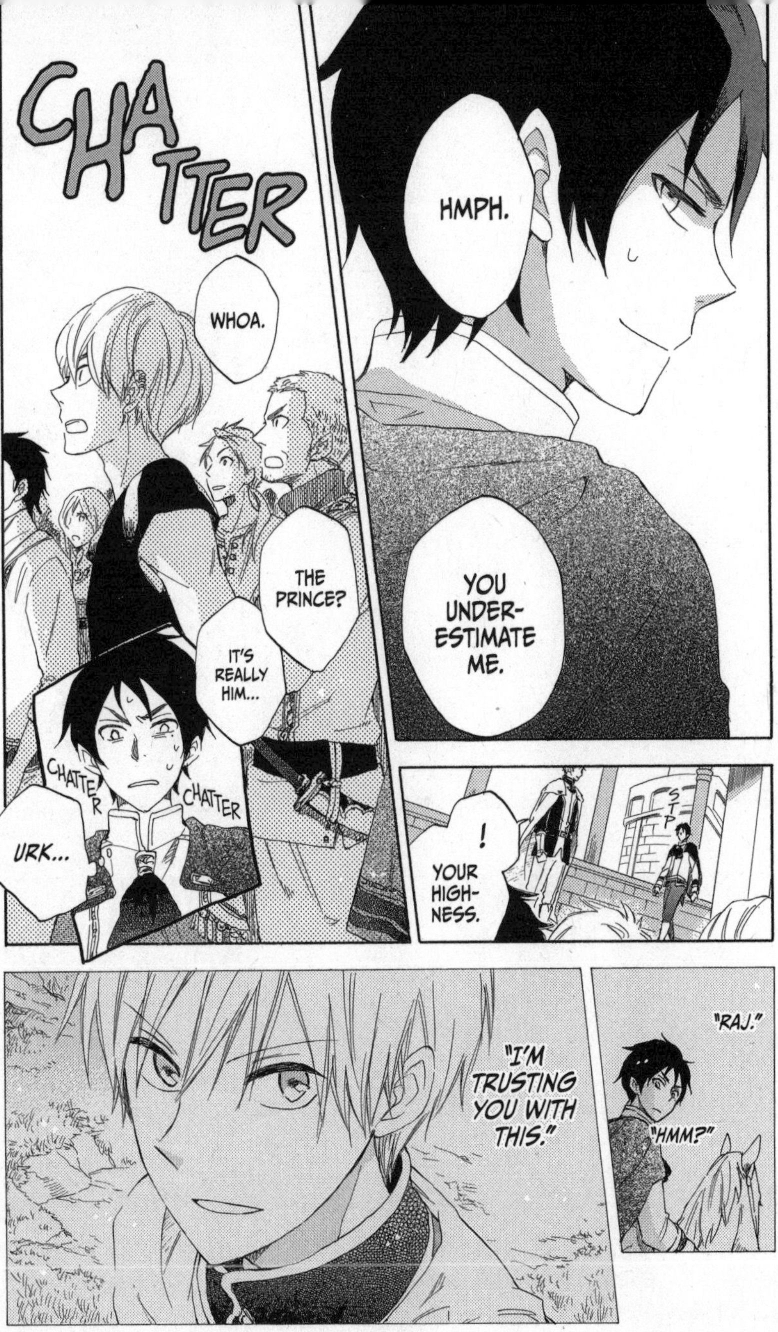
HMPH.
YOU UNDER-ESTIMATE ME.
!
YOUR HIGH-NESS.
STP
CHATTER
WHOA.
THE PRINCE?
IT'S REALLY HIM...
CHATTER
CHATTER
URK...
"RAJ."
"HMM?"
"I'M TRUSTING YOU WITH THIS."

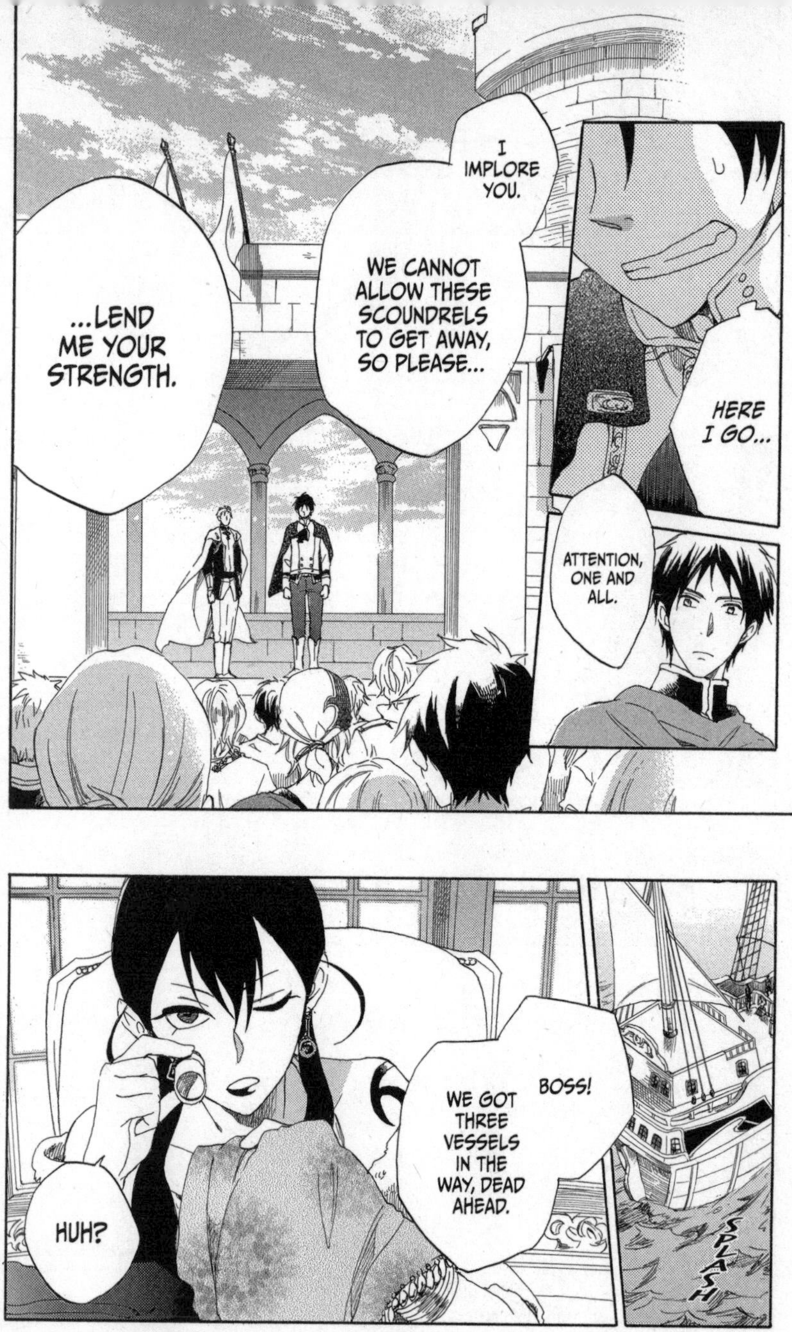
HERE I GO...
ATTENTION, ONE AND ALL.
I IMPLORE YOU.
WE CANNOT ALLOW THESE SCOUNDRELS TO GET AWAY, SO PLEASE...
...LEND ME YOUR STRENGTH.
SPLASH
BOSS!
WE GOT THREE VESSELS IN THE WAY, DEAD AHEAD.
HUH?

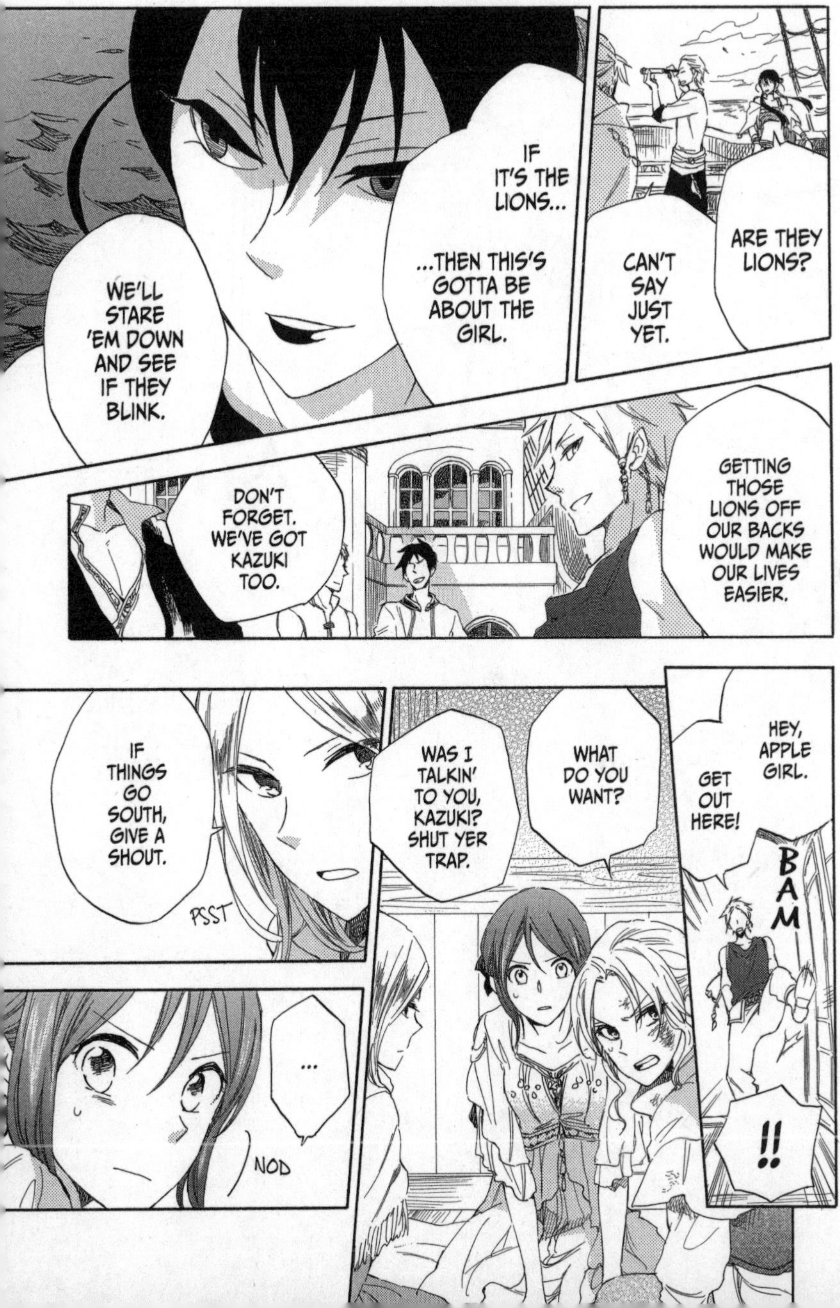
ARE THEY LIONS?
CAN'T SAY JUST YET.
IF IT'S THE LIONS...
...THEN THIS'S GOTTA BE ABOUT THE GIRL.
WE'LL STARE 'EM DOWN AND SEE IF THEY BLINK.
GETTING THOSE LIONS OFF OUR BACKS WOULD MAKE OUR LIVES EASIER.
DON'T FORGET. WE'VE GOT KAZUKI TOO.
HEY, APPLE GIRL.
GET OUT HERE!
BAM
!!
WHAT DO YOU WANT?
WAS I TALKIN' TO YOU, KAZUKI? SHUT YER TRAP.
IF THINGS GO SOUTH, GIVE A SHOUT.
PSST
...
NOD

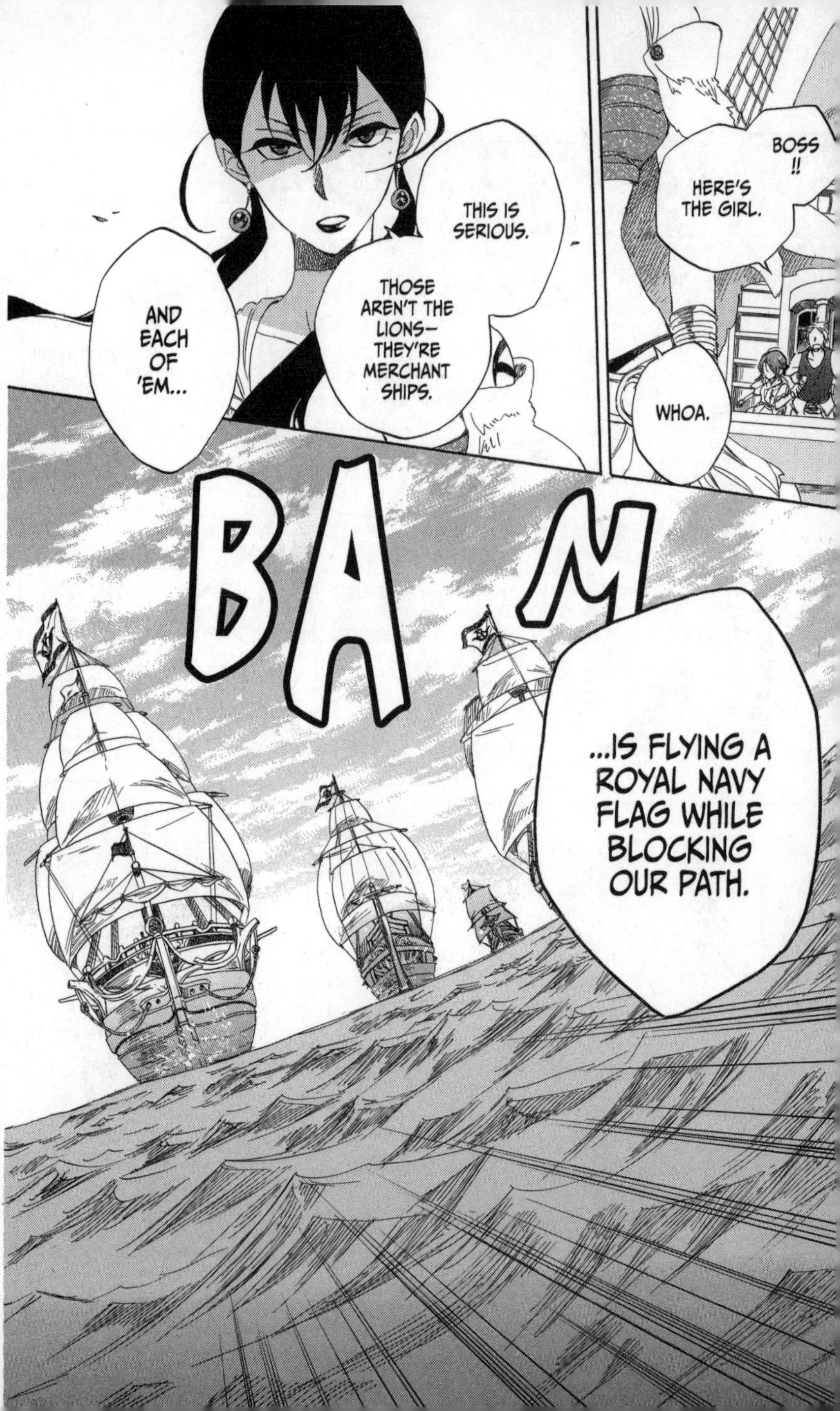
BOSS!! HERE'S THE GIRL.
WHOA.
THIS IS SERIOUS.
THOSE AREN'T THE LIONS—THEY'RE MERCHANT SHIPS.
AND EACH OF 'EM...
BAM
...IS FLYING A ROYAL NAVY FLAG WHILE BLOCKING OUR PATH.

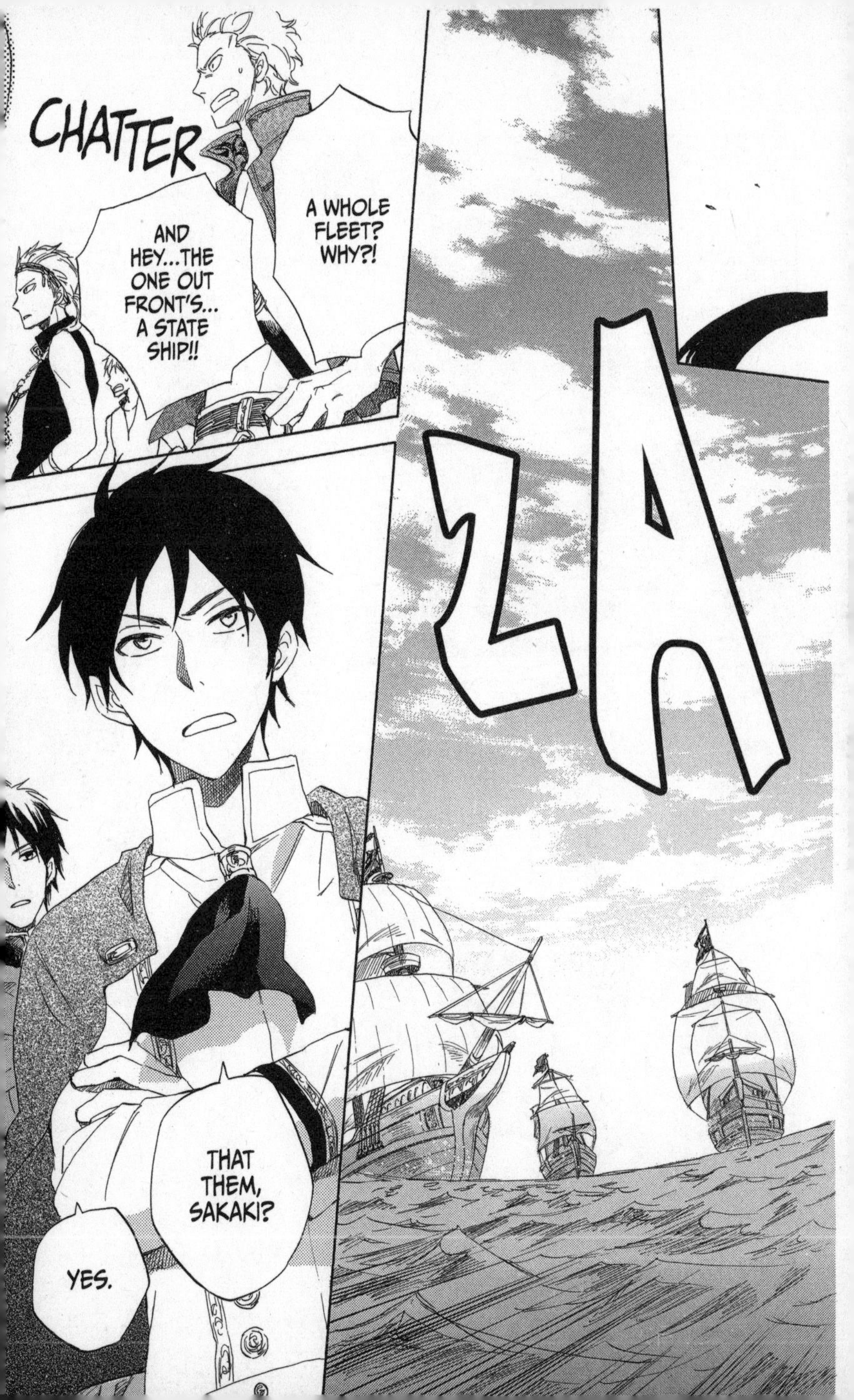
ZA
A WHOLE FLEET? WHY?!
CHATTER
AND HEY...THE ONE OUT FRONT'S... A STATE SHIP!!
THAT THEM, SAKAKI?
YES.

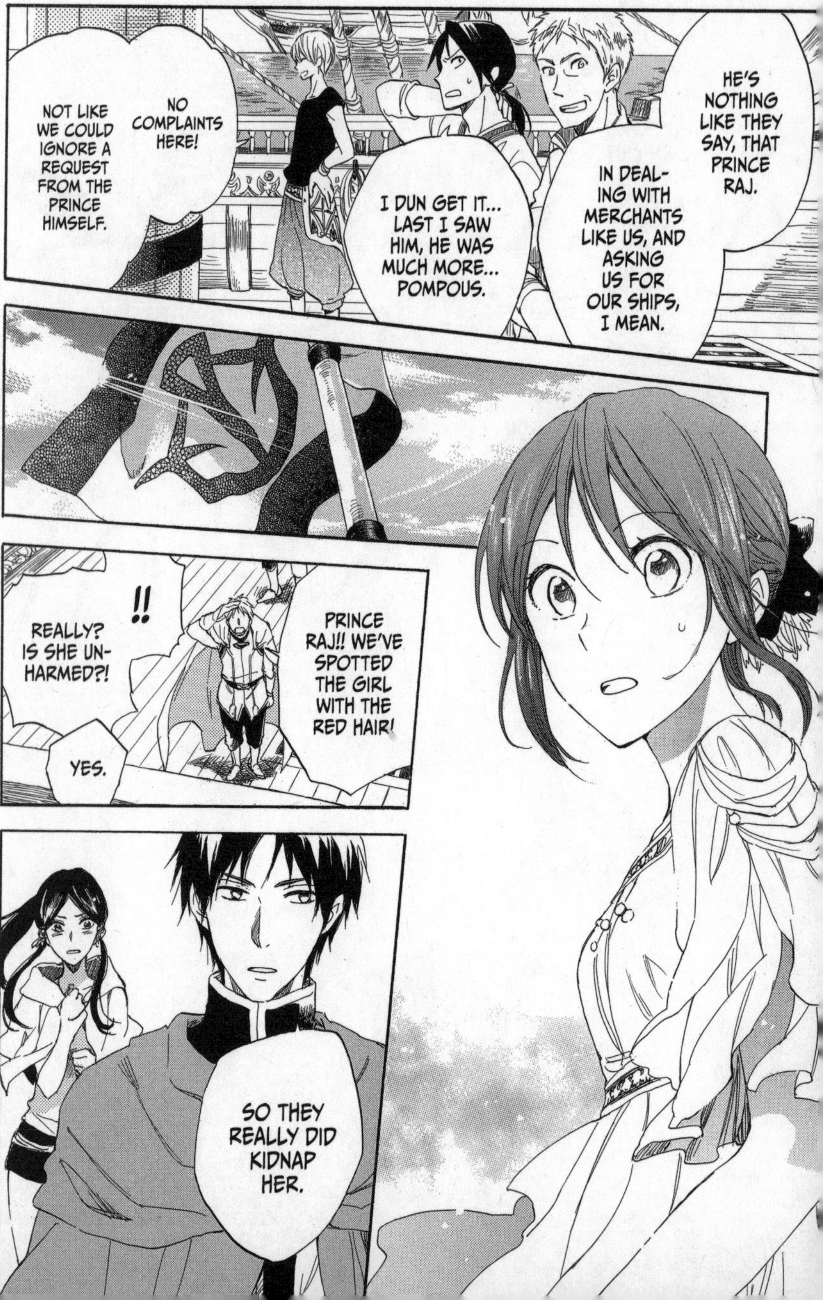
HE'S NOTHING LIKE THEY SAY, THAT PRINCE RAJ.
IN DEAL-ING WITH MERCHANTS LIKE US, AND ASKING US FOR OUR SHIPS, I MEAN.
I DUN GET IT... LAST I SAW HIM, HE WAS MUCH MORE... POMPOUS.
NO COMPLAINTS HERE!
NOT LIKE WE COULD IGNORE A REQUEST FROM THE PRINCE HIMSELF.
PRINCE RAJ!! WE'VE SPOTTED THE GIRL WITH THE RED HAIR!
!!
REALLY? IS SHE UN-HARMED?!
YES.
SO THEY REALLY DID KIDNAP HER.

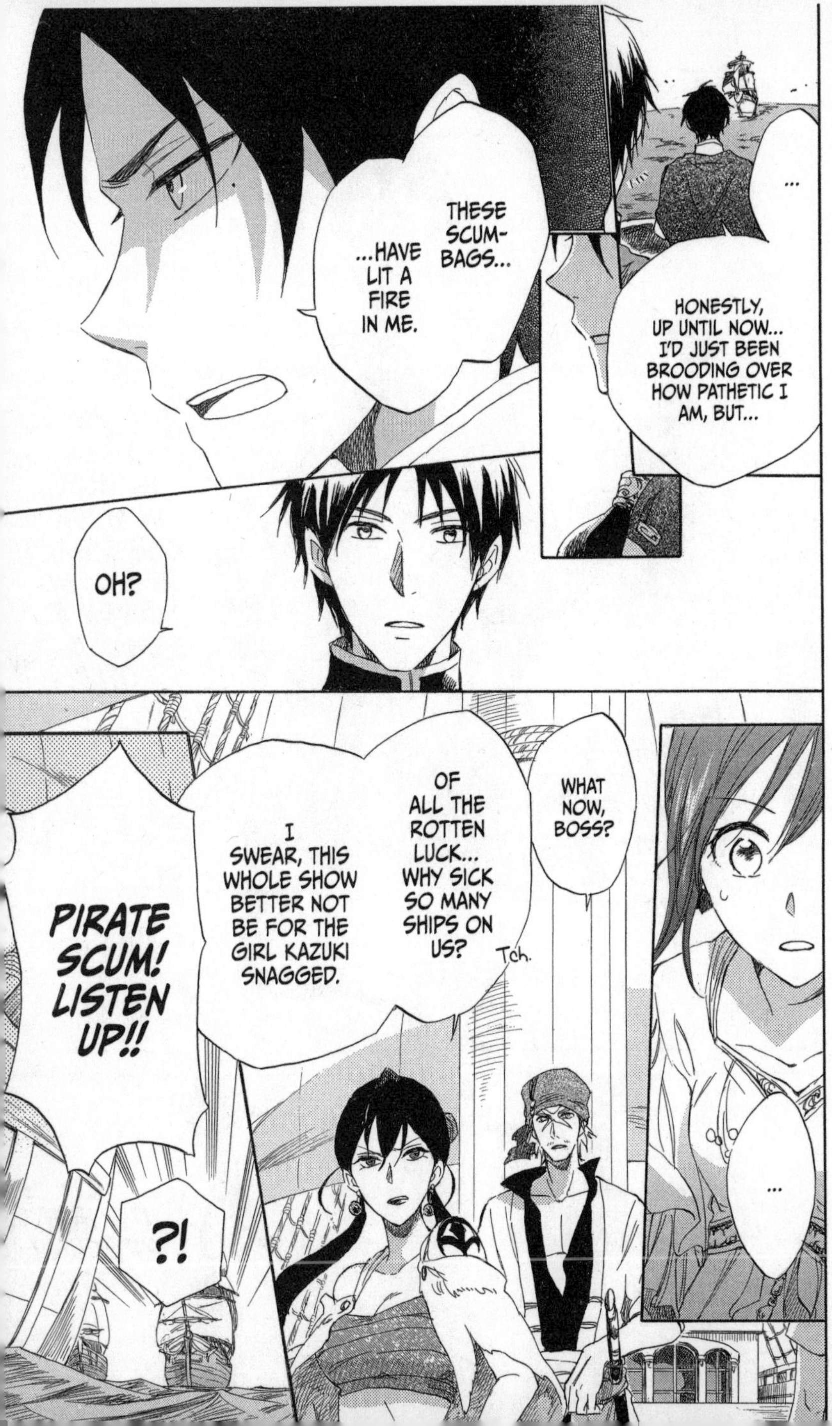
...
HONESTLY, UP UNTIL NOW... I'D JUST BEEN BROODING OVER HOW PATHETIC I AM, BUT...
THESE SCUM-BAGS...
...HAVE LIT A FIRE IN ME.
OH?
...
WHAT NOW, BOSS?
OF ALL THE ROTTEN LUCK... WHY SICK SO MANY SHIPS ON US?
Tch.
I SWEAR, THIS WHOLE SHOW BETTER NOT BE FOR THE GIRL KAZUKI SNAGGED.
PIRATE SCUM! LISTEN UP!!
?!

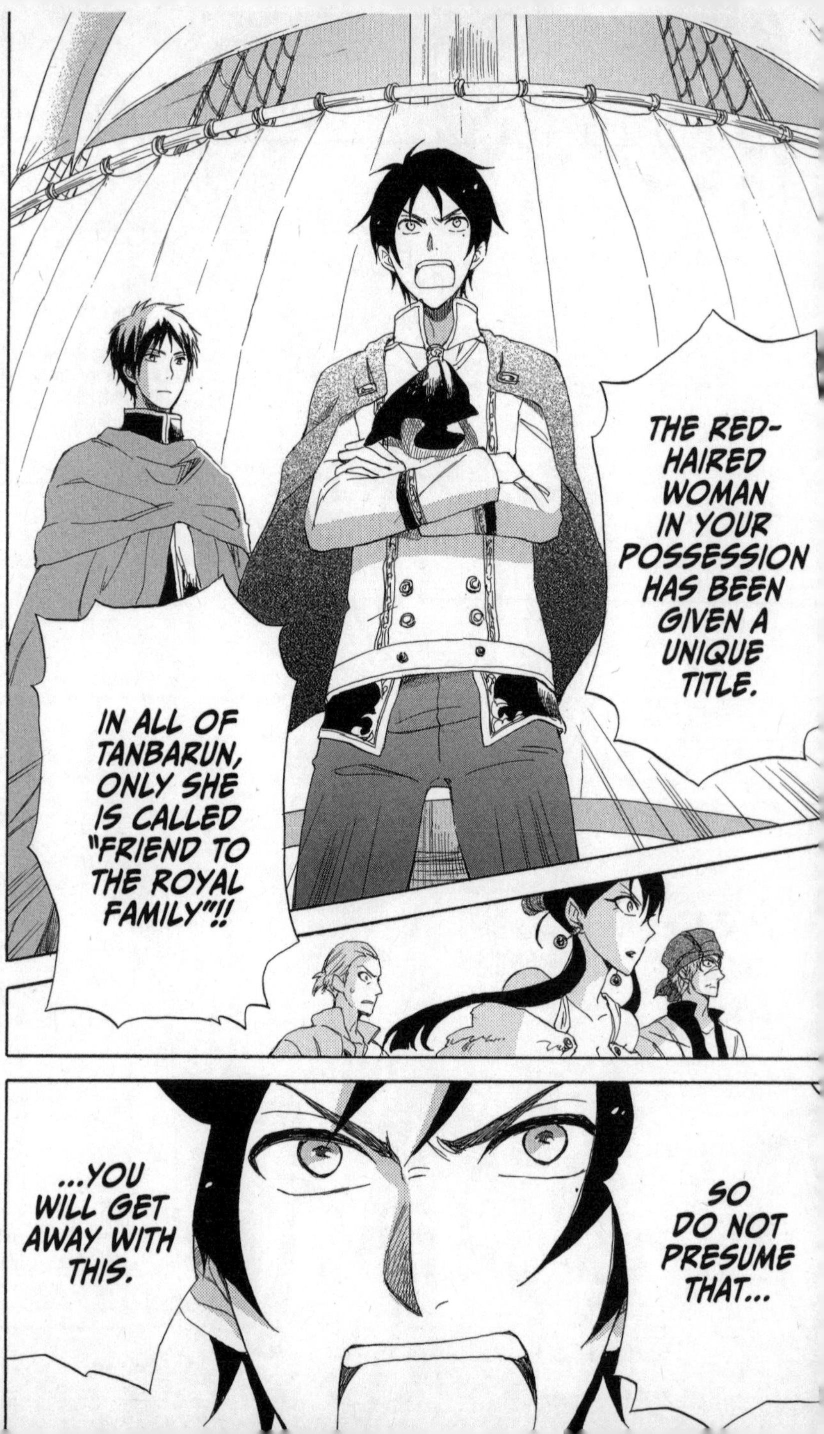
THE RED-HAIRED WOMAN IN YOUR POSSESSION HAS BEEN GIVEN A UNIQUE TITLE.
IN ALL OF TANBARUN, ONLY SHE IS CALLED "FRIEND TO THE ROYAL FAMILY"!!
SO DO NOT PRESUME THAT...
...YOU WILL GET AWAY WITH THIS.

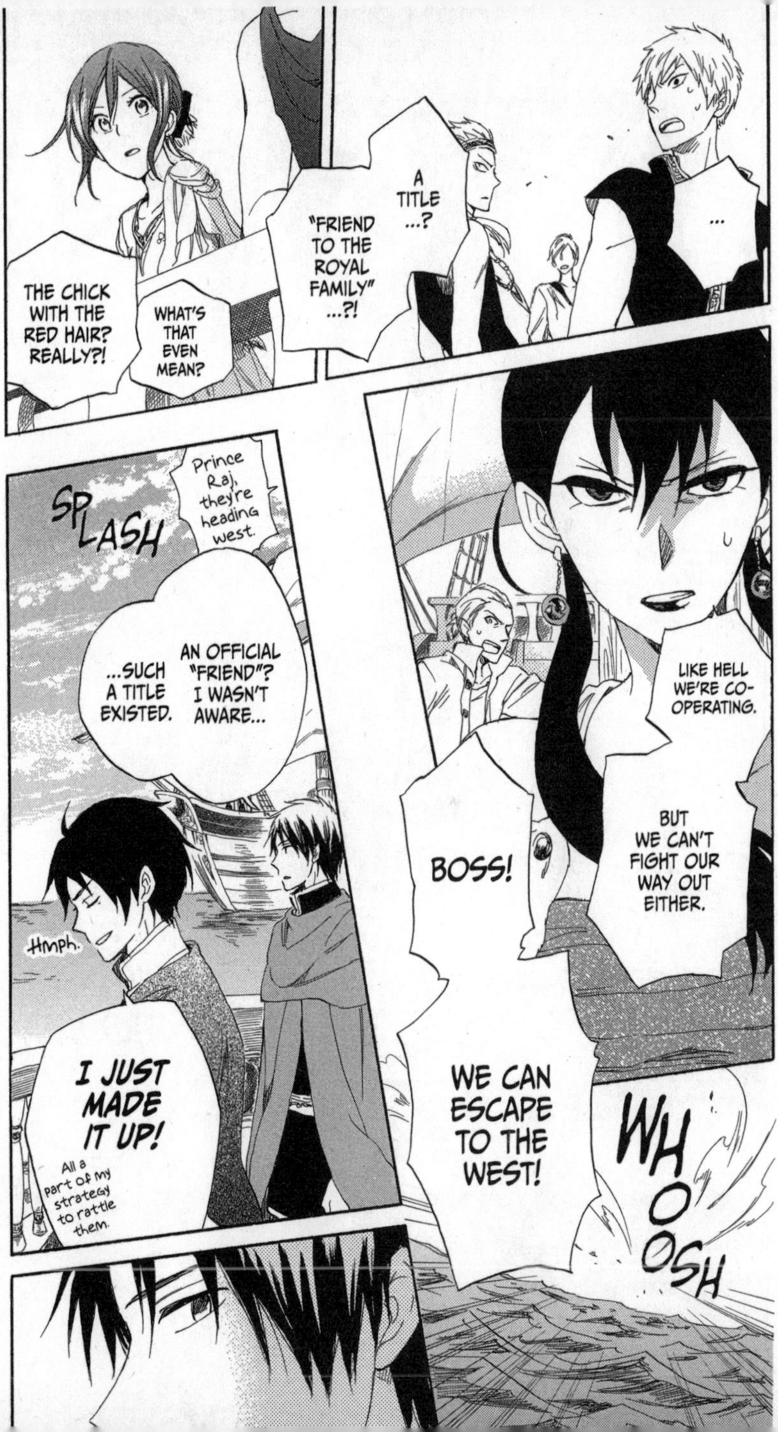

...
A TITLE ...?
"FRIEND TO THE ROYAL FAMILY" ...?!
WHAT'S THAT EVEN MEAN?
THE CHICK WITH THE RED HAIR? REALLY?!
LIKE HELL WE'RE CO-OPERATING.
BUT WE CAN'T FIGHT OUR WAY OUT EITHER.
BOSS!
WE CAN ESCAPE TO THE WEST!
WHOOSH
Prince Raj, they're heading west.
SPLASH
AN OFFICIAL "FRIEND"? I WASN'T AWARE...
...SUCH A TITLE EXISTED.
Hmph.
I JUST MADE IT UP!
All a part of my strategy to rattle them.

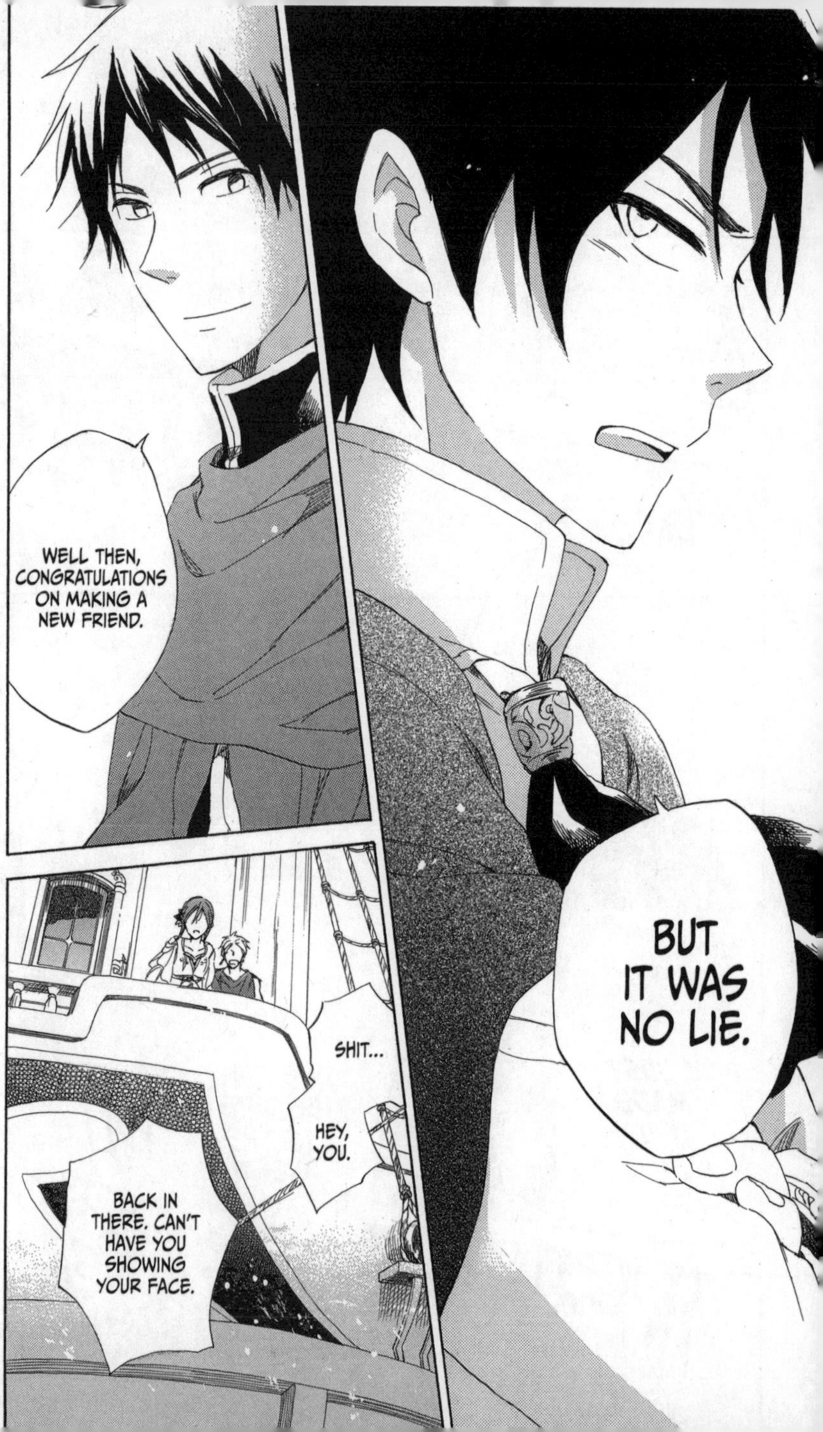
BUT IT WAS NO LIE.
WELL THEN, CONGRATULATIONS ON MAKING A NEW FRIEND.
SHIT...
HEY, YOU.
BACK IN THERE. CAN'T HAVE YOU SHOWING YOUR FACE.

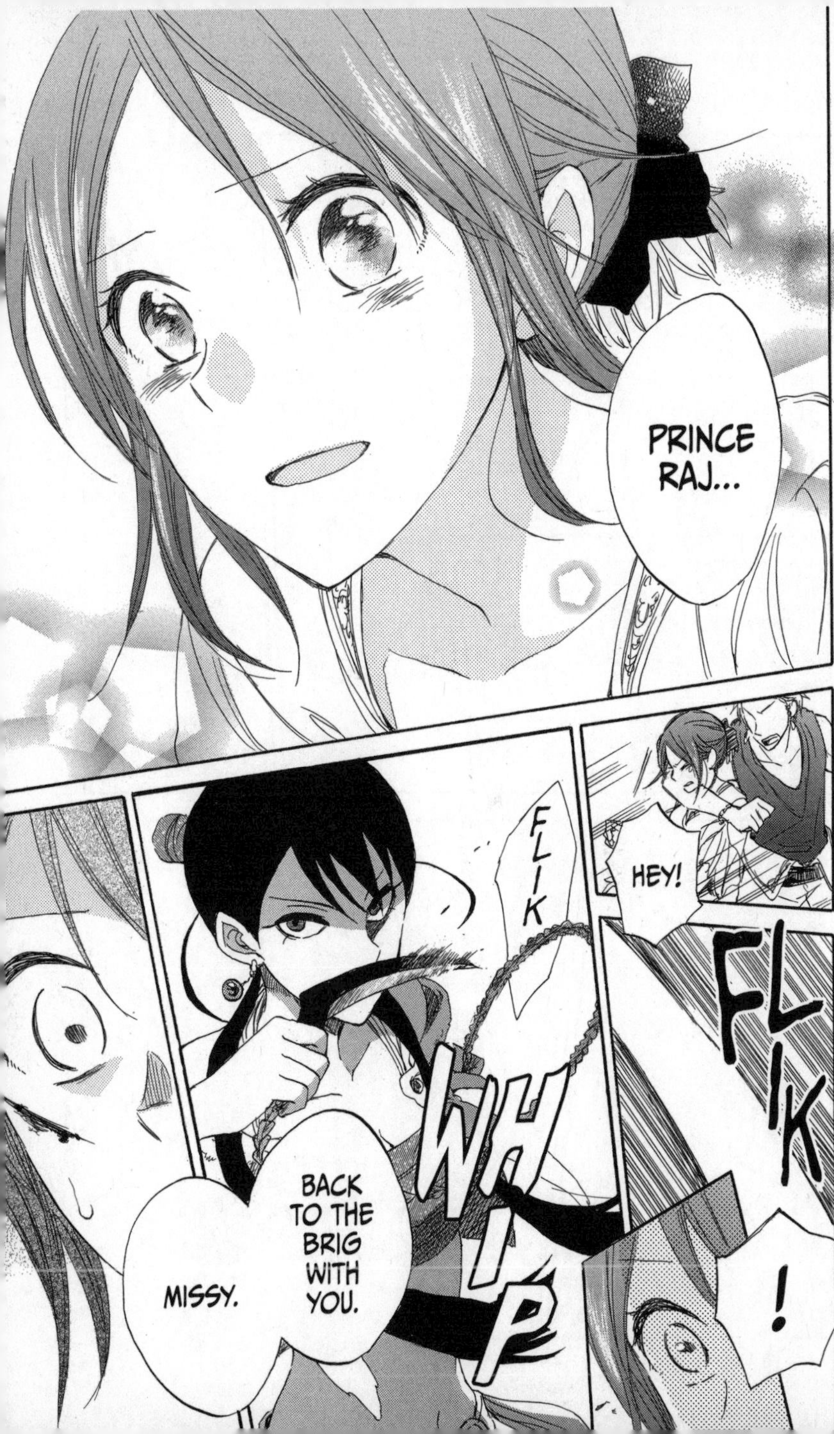
PRINCE RAJ...
HEY!
FLIK
!
FLIK
WHIP
BACK TO THE BRIG WITH YOU.
MISSY.

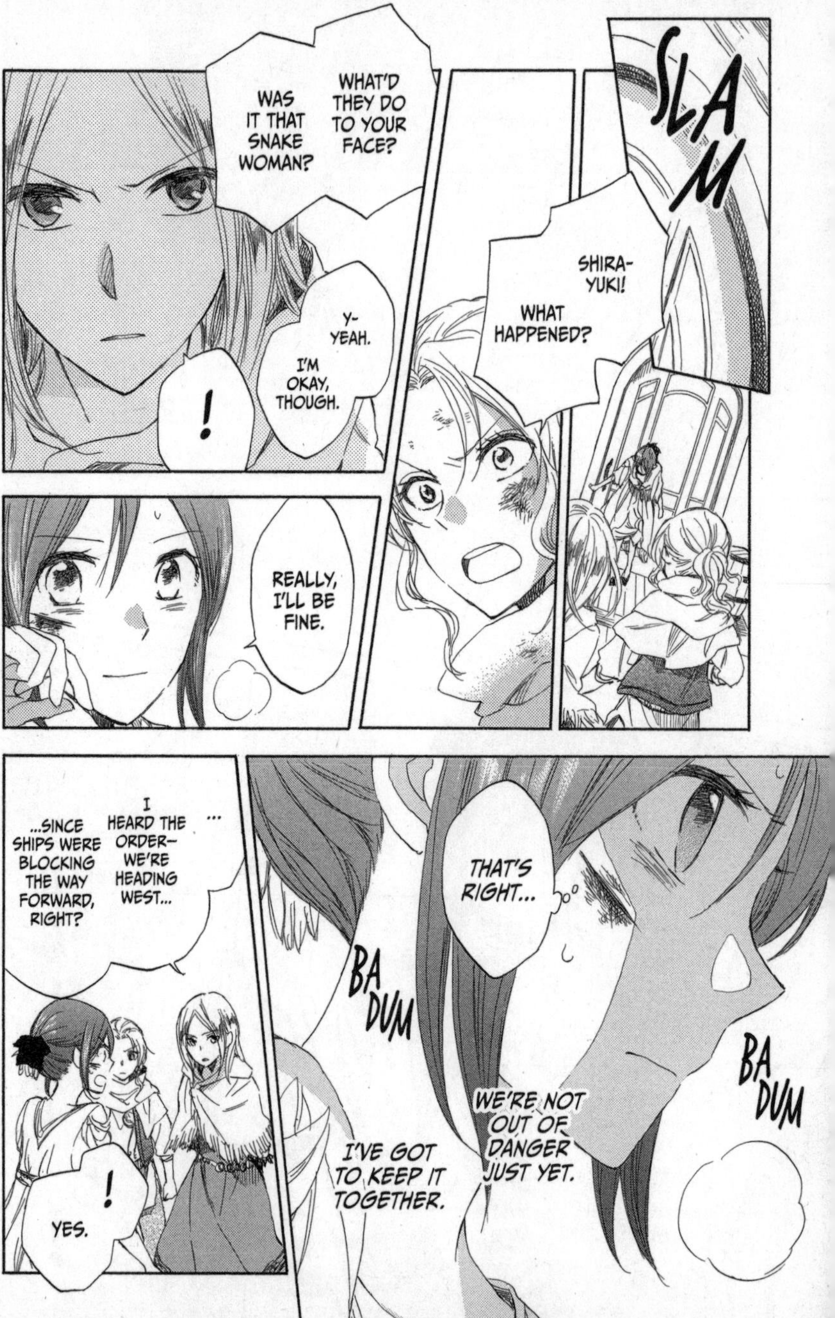
SLAM
SHIRAYUKI!
WHAT HAPPENED?
WHAT'D THEY DO TO YOUR FACE?
WAS IT THAT SNAKE WOMAN?
!
Y-YEAH.
I'M OKAY, THOUGH.
REALLY, I'LL BE FINE.
THAT'S RIGHT...
BA DUM
BA DUM
WE'RE NOT OUT OF DANGER JUST YET.
I'VE GOT TO KEEP IT TOGETHER.
...
I HEARD THE ORDER— WE'RE HEADING WEST...
...SINCE SHIPS WERE BLOCKING THE WAY FORWARD, RIGHT?
!
YES.

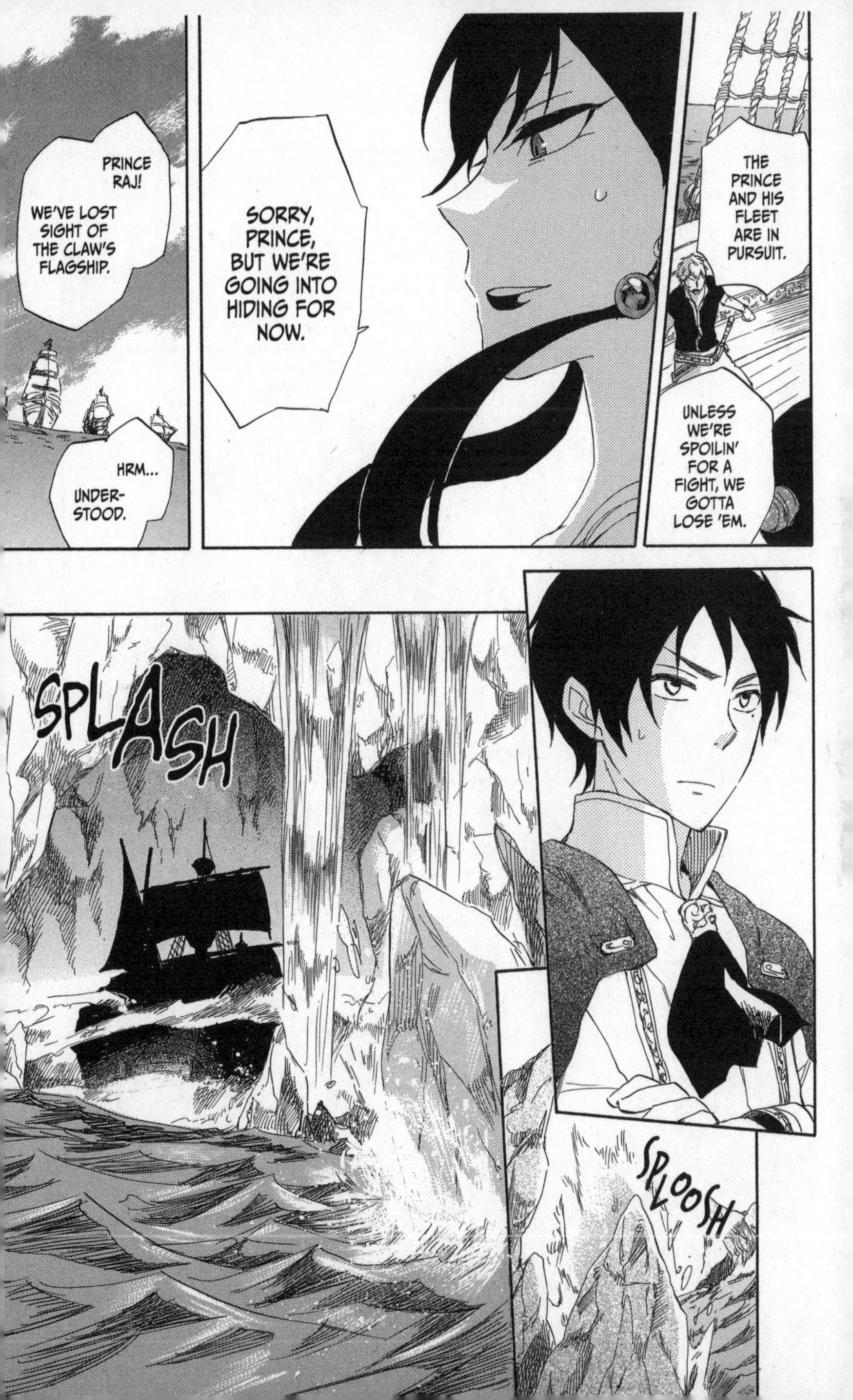
THE PRINCE AND HIS FLEET ARE IN PURSUIT.
UNLESS WE'RE SPOILIN' FOR A FIGHT, WE GOTTA LOSE 'EM.
SORRY, PRINCE, BUT WE'RE GOING INTO HIDING FOR NOW.
PRINCE RAJ! WE'VE LOST SIGHT OF THE CLAW'S FLAGSHIP.
HRM... UNDER-STOOD.
SPLOOSH
SPLASH

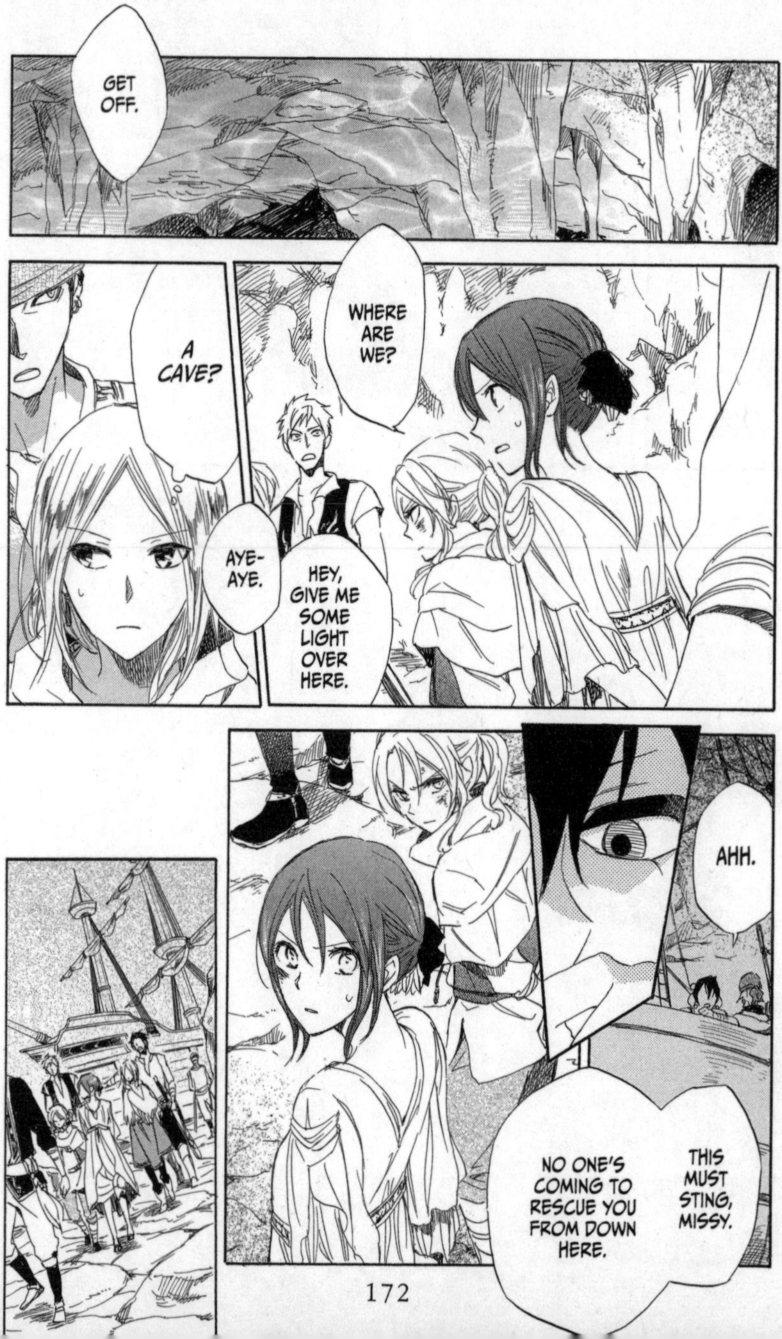
GET OFF.
WHERE ARE WE?
HEY, GIVE ME SOME LIGHT OVER HERE.
A CAVE?
AYE-AYE.
AHH.
THIS MUST STING, MISSY.
NO ONE'S COMING TO RESCUE YOU FROM DOWN HERE.

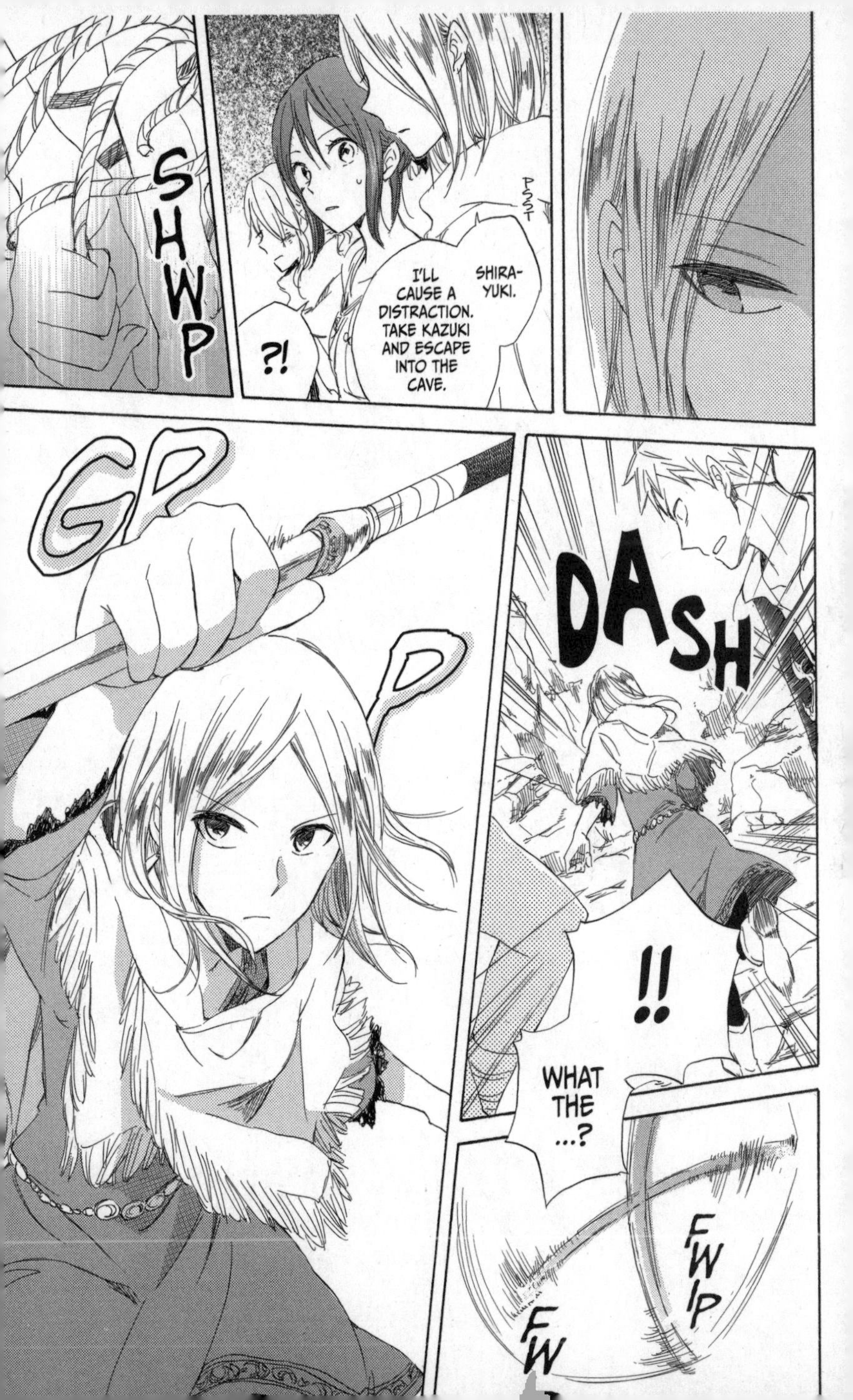
PSST
SHIRA-YUKI.
I'LL CAUSE A DISTRACTION. TAKE KAZUKI AND ESCAPE INTO THE CAVE.
?!
SHWP
DASH
!!
WHAT THE ...?
FWIP
FW
GP

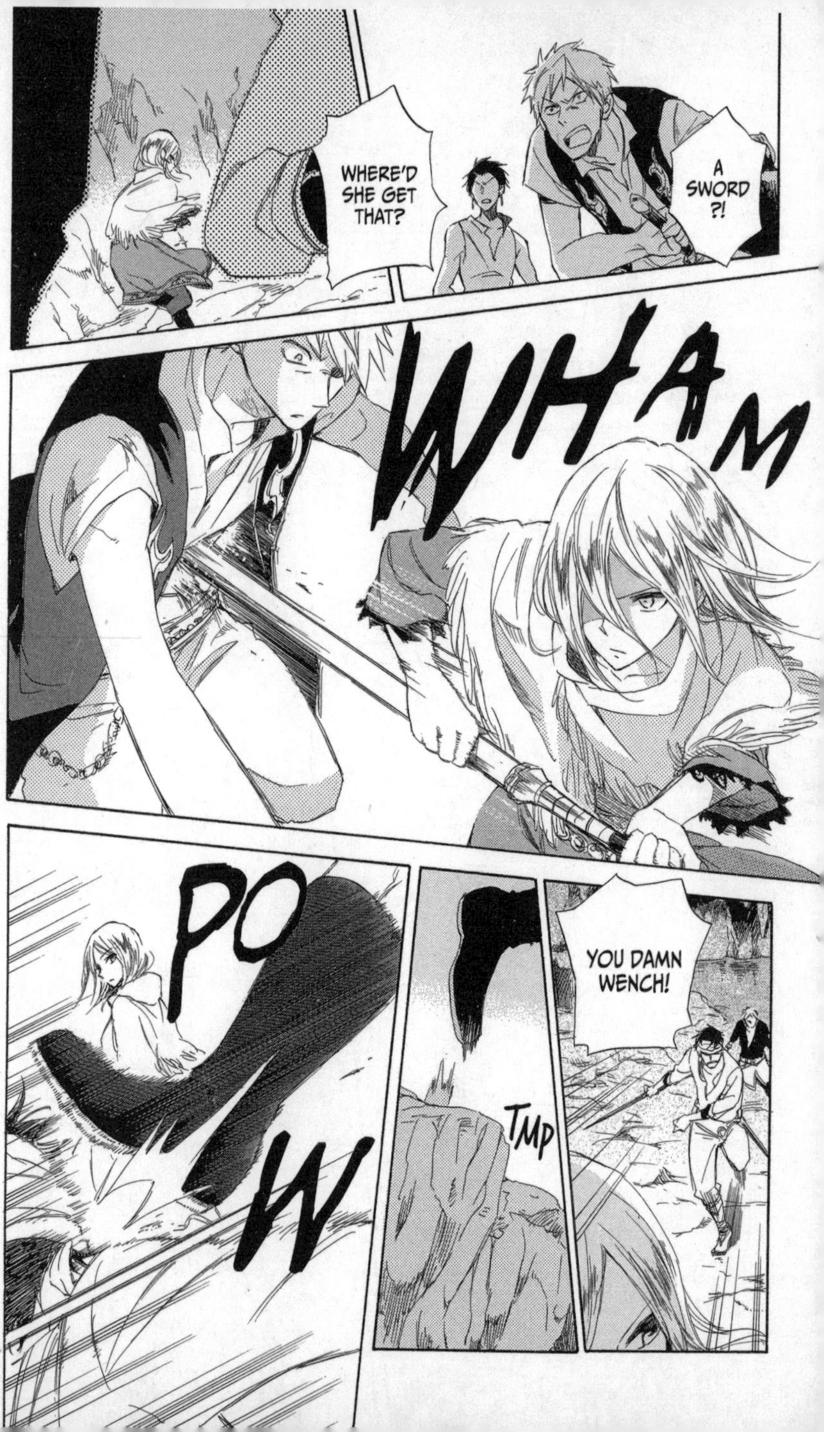
A SWORD ?!
WHERE'D SHE GET THAT?
WHAM
YOU DAMN WENCH!
TMP
POW

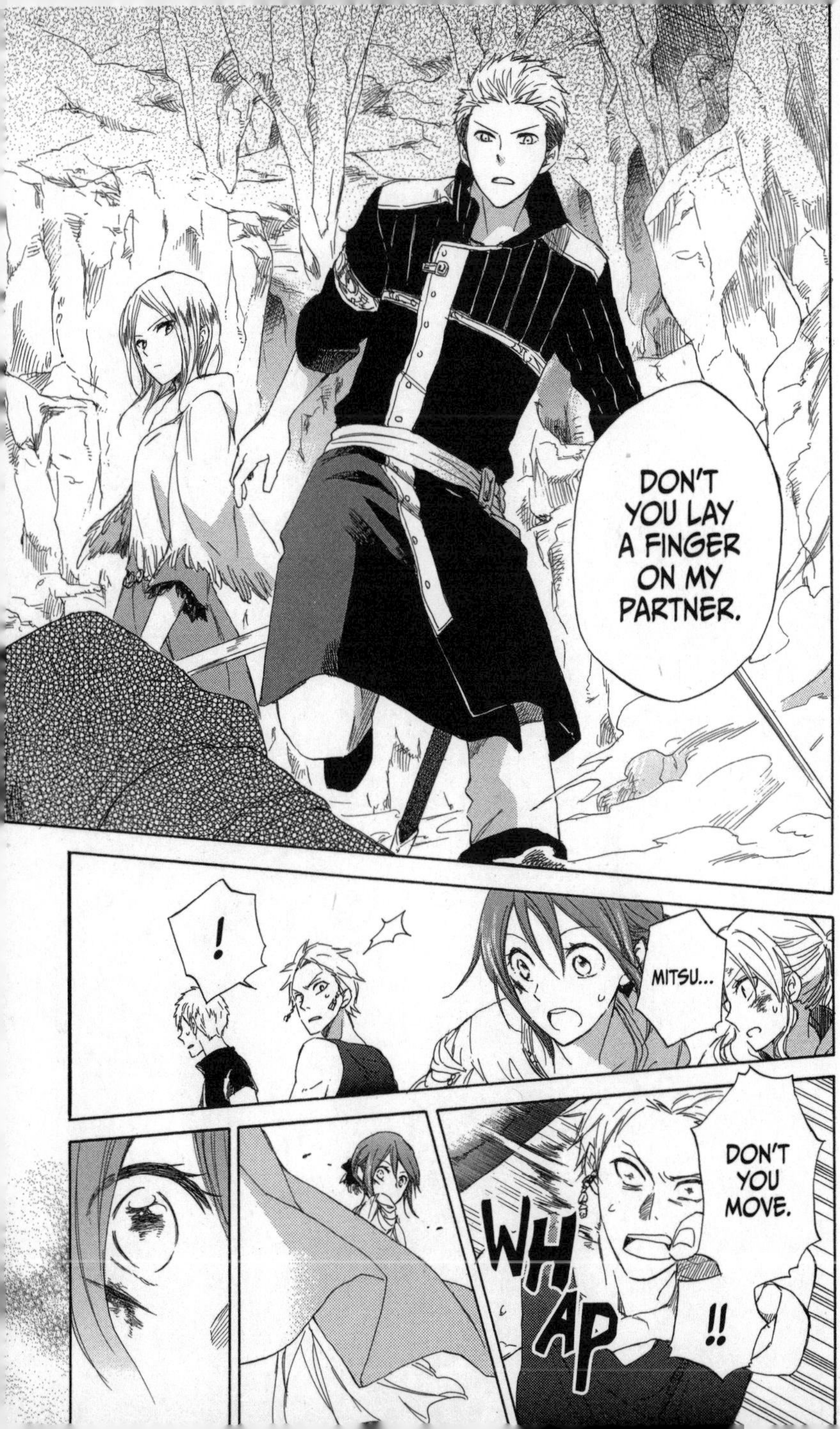
DON'T YOU LAY A FINGER ON MY PARTNER.
MITSU...
!
DON'T YOU MOVE.
WHAP
!!

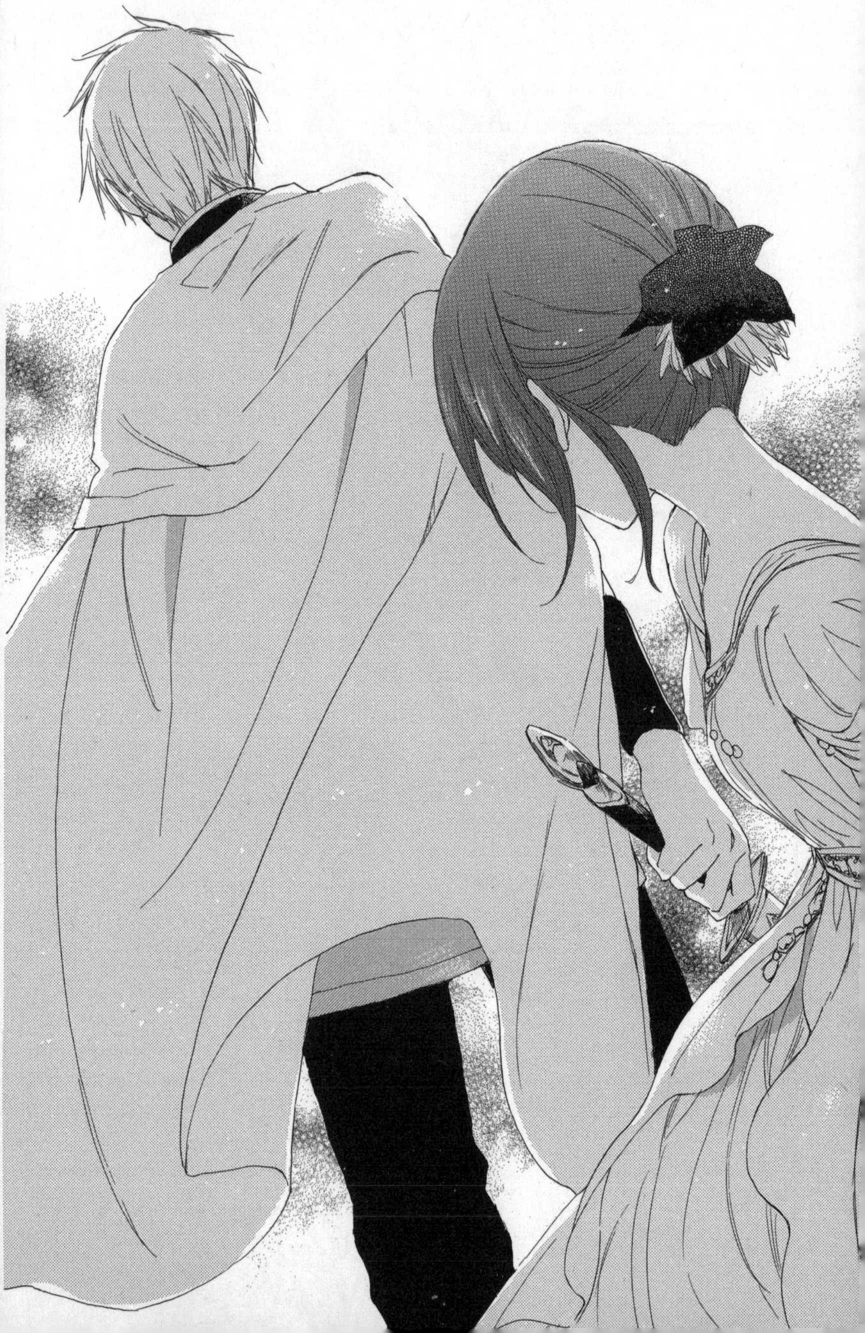

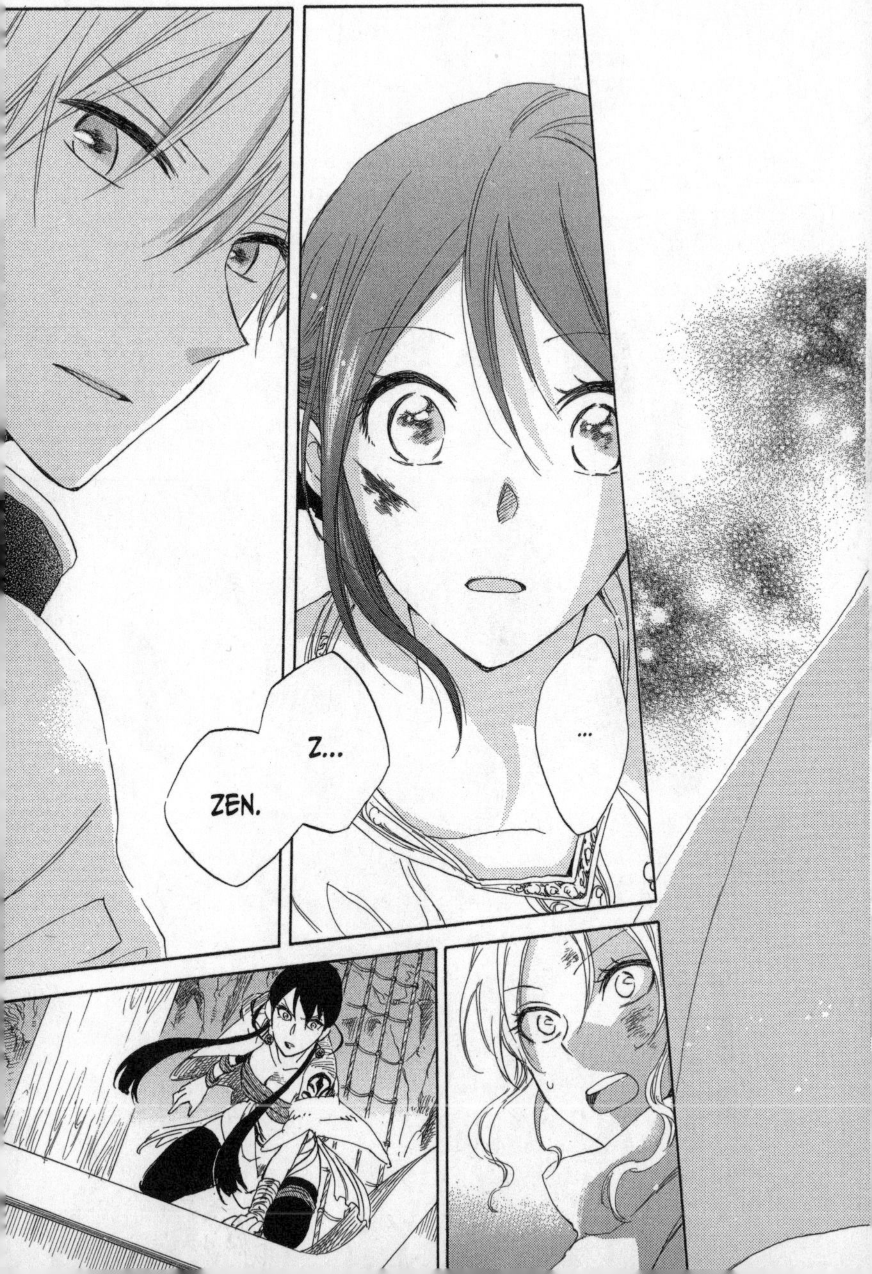
...
Z...
ZEN.

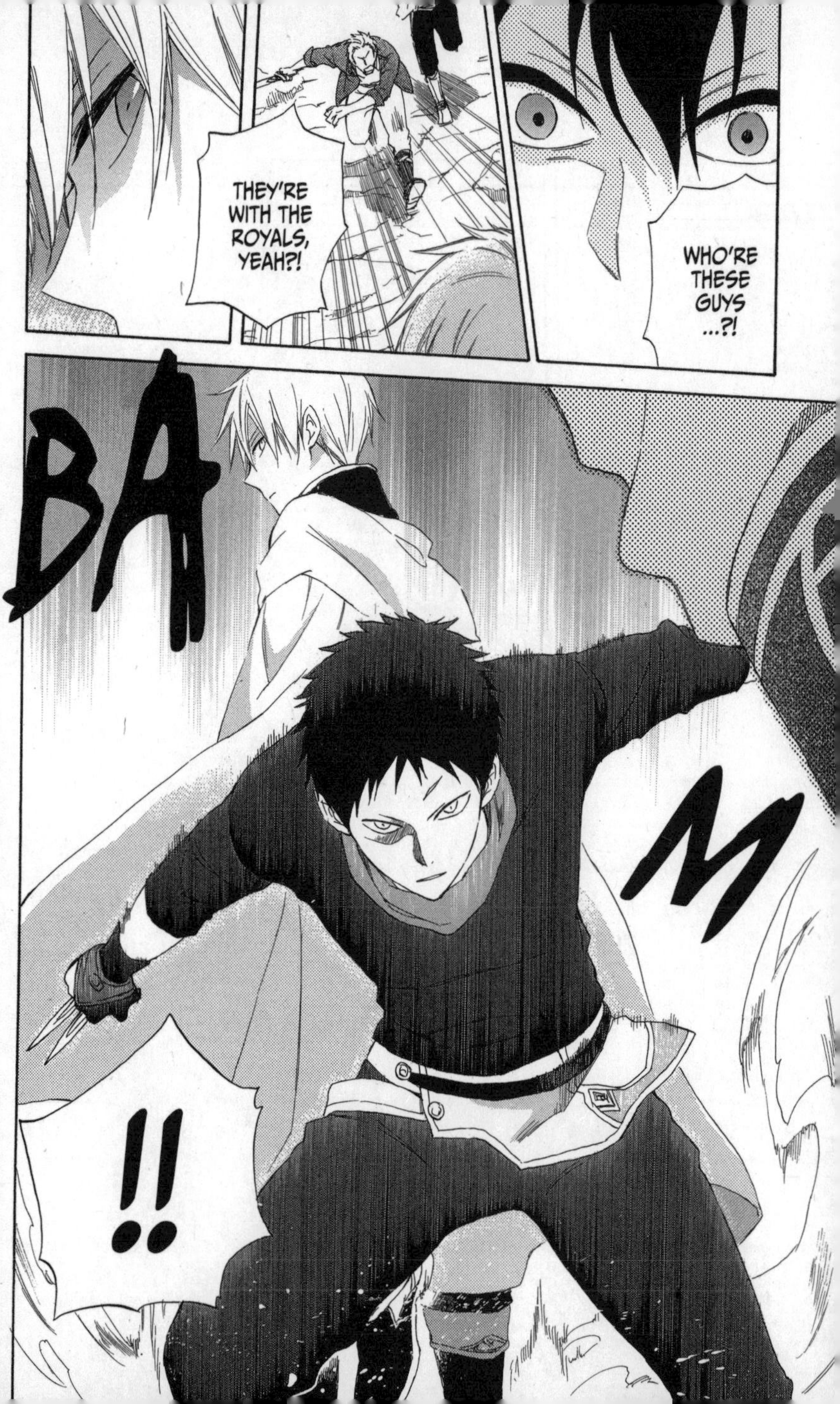
WHO'RE THESE GUYS ...?!
THEY'RE WITH THE ROYALS, YEAH?!
BAM
!!

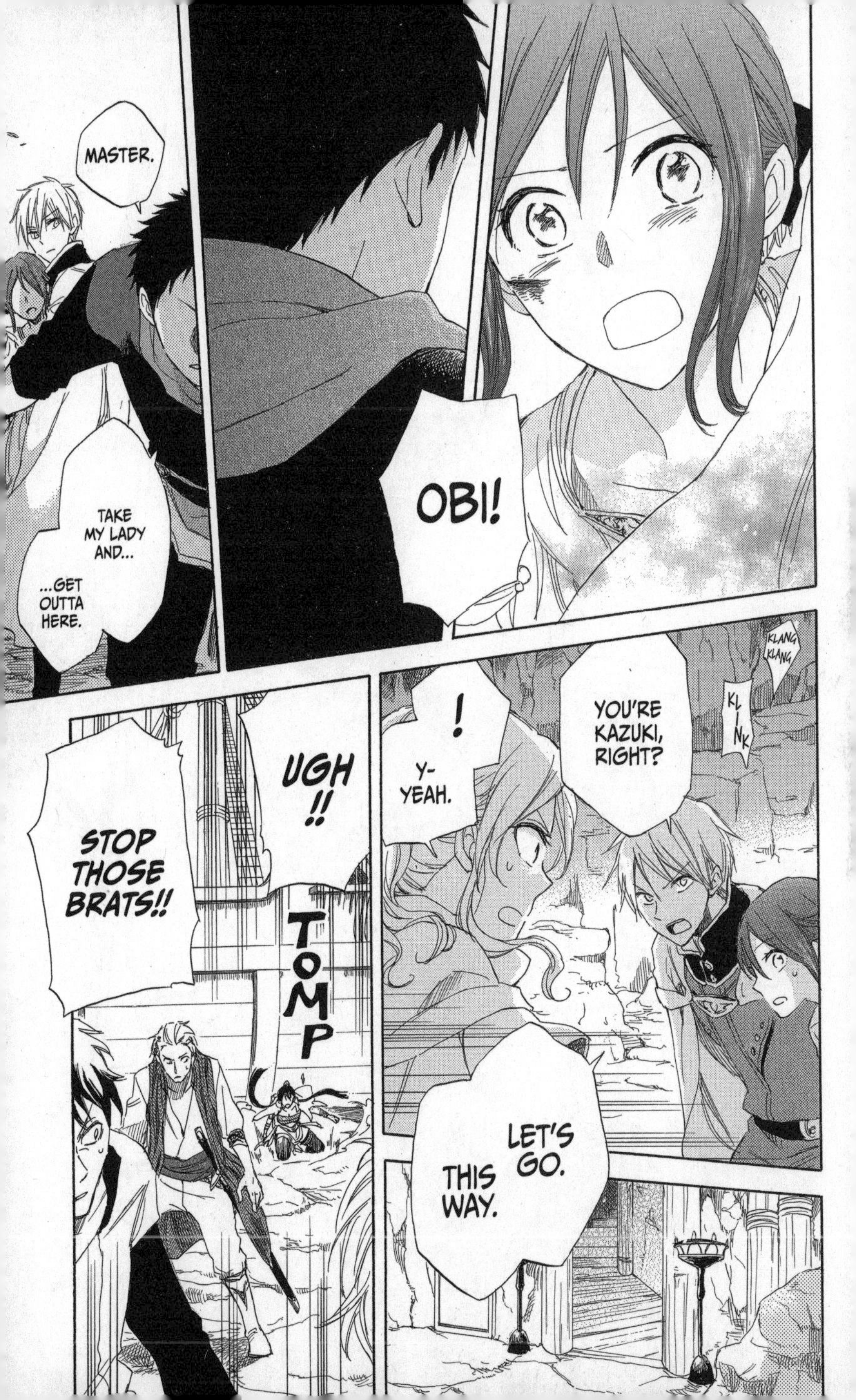
OBI!
MASTER.
TAKE MY LADY AND...
...GET OUTTA HERE.
KLANG KLANG
KLINK
YOU'RE KAZUKI, RIGHT?
!
Y- YEAH.
LET'S GO.
THIS WAY.
UGH!!
STOP THOSE BRATS!!
TOMP

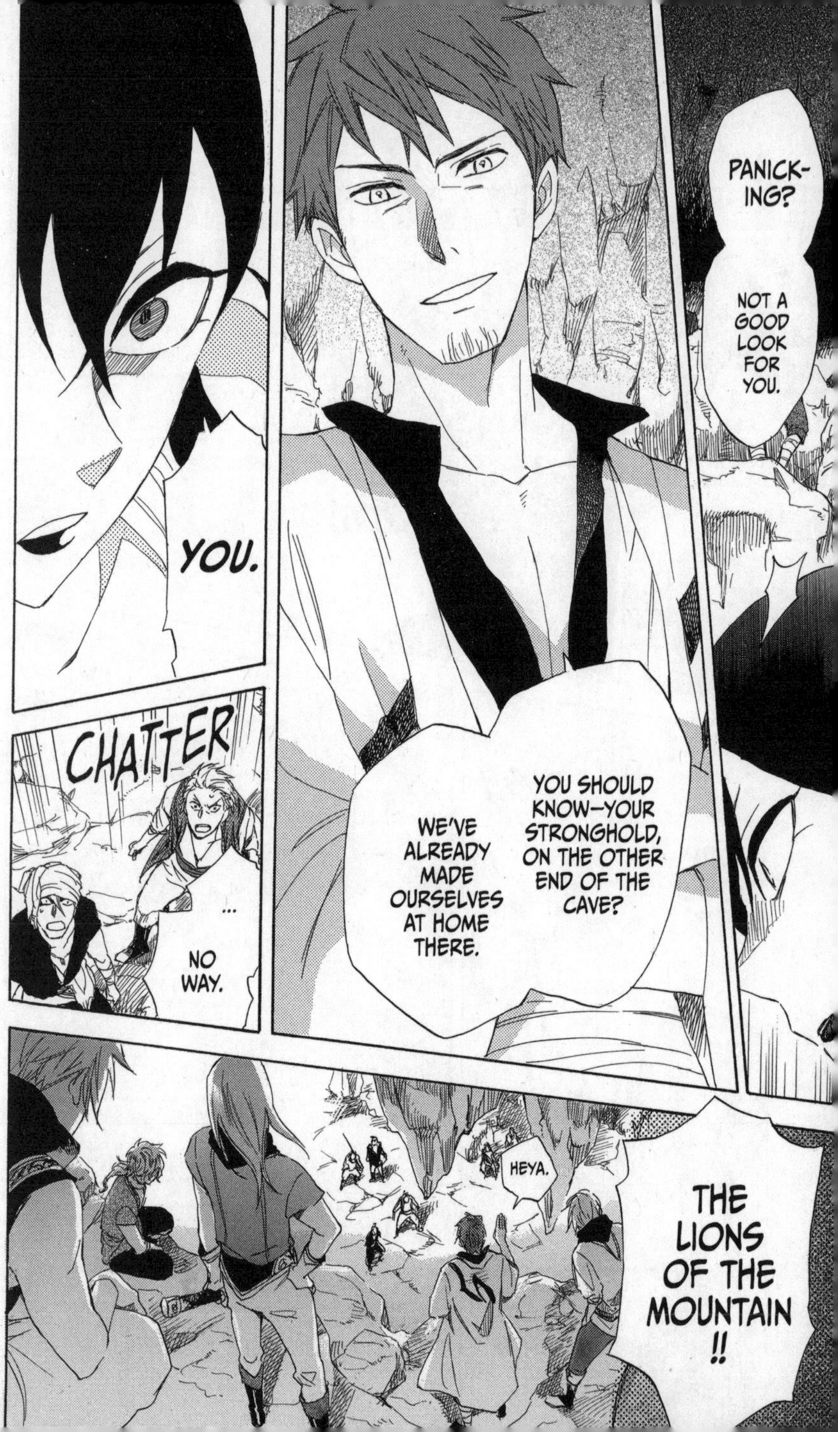
PANICK-ING?
NOT A GOOD LOOK FOR YOU.
YOU SHOULD KNOW—YOUR STRONGHOLD, ON THE OTHER END OF THE CAVE?
WE'VE ALREADY MADE OURSELVES AT HOME THERE.
YOU.
CHATTER
...
NO WAY.
HEYA.
THE LIONS OF THE MOUNTAIN!!

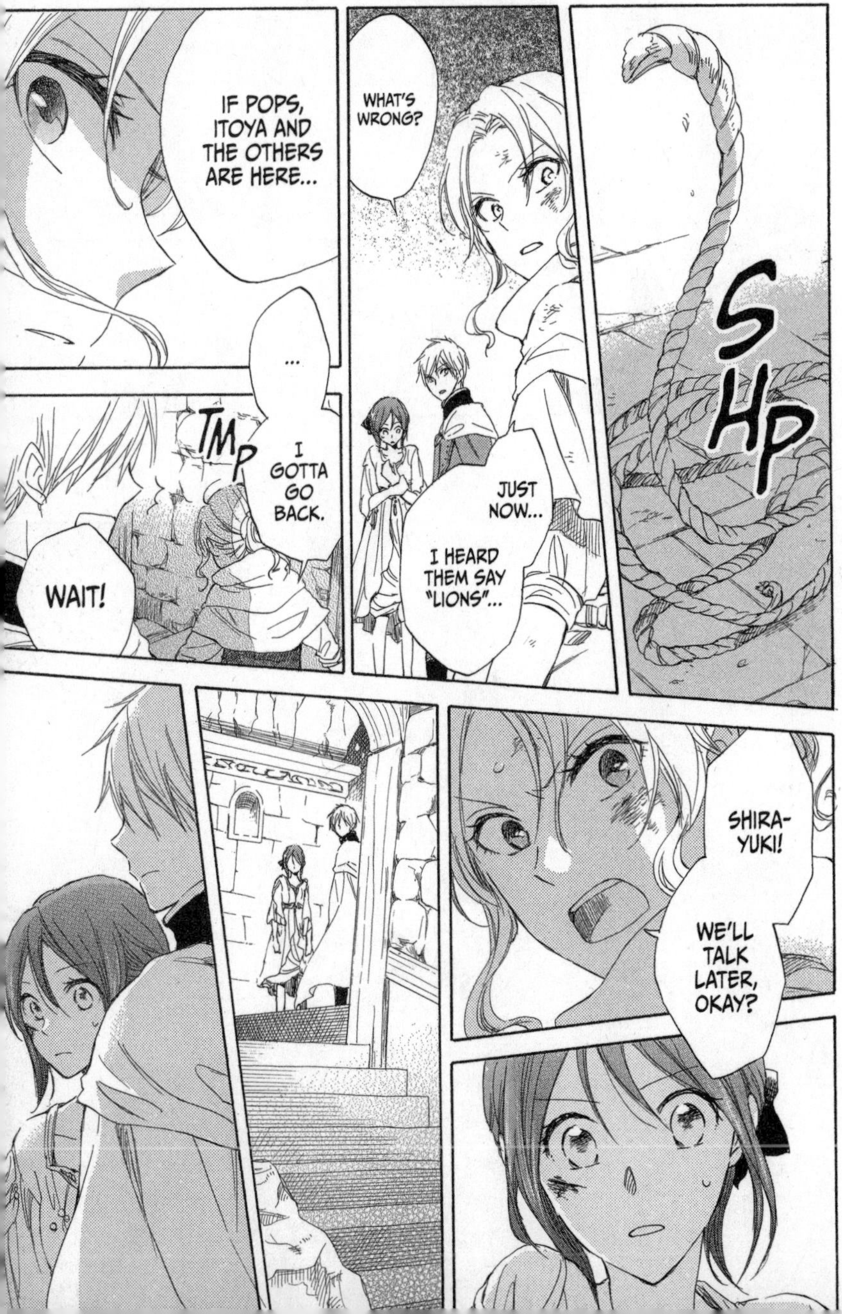
SHP
WHAT'S WRONG?
JUST NOW...
I HEARD THEM SAY "LIONS"...
IF POPS, ITOYA AND THE OTHERS ARE HERE...
...
TMP
I GOTTA GO BACK.
WAIT!
SHIRA-YUKI!
WE'LL TALK LATER, OKAY?

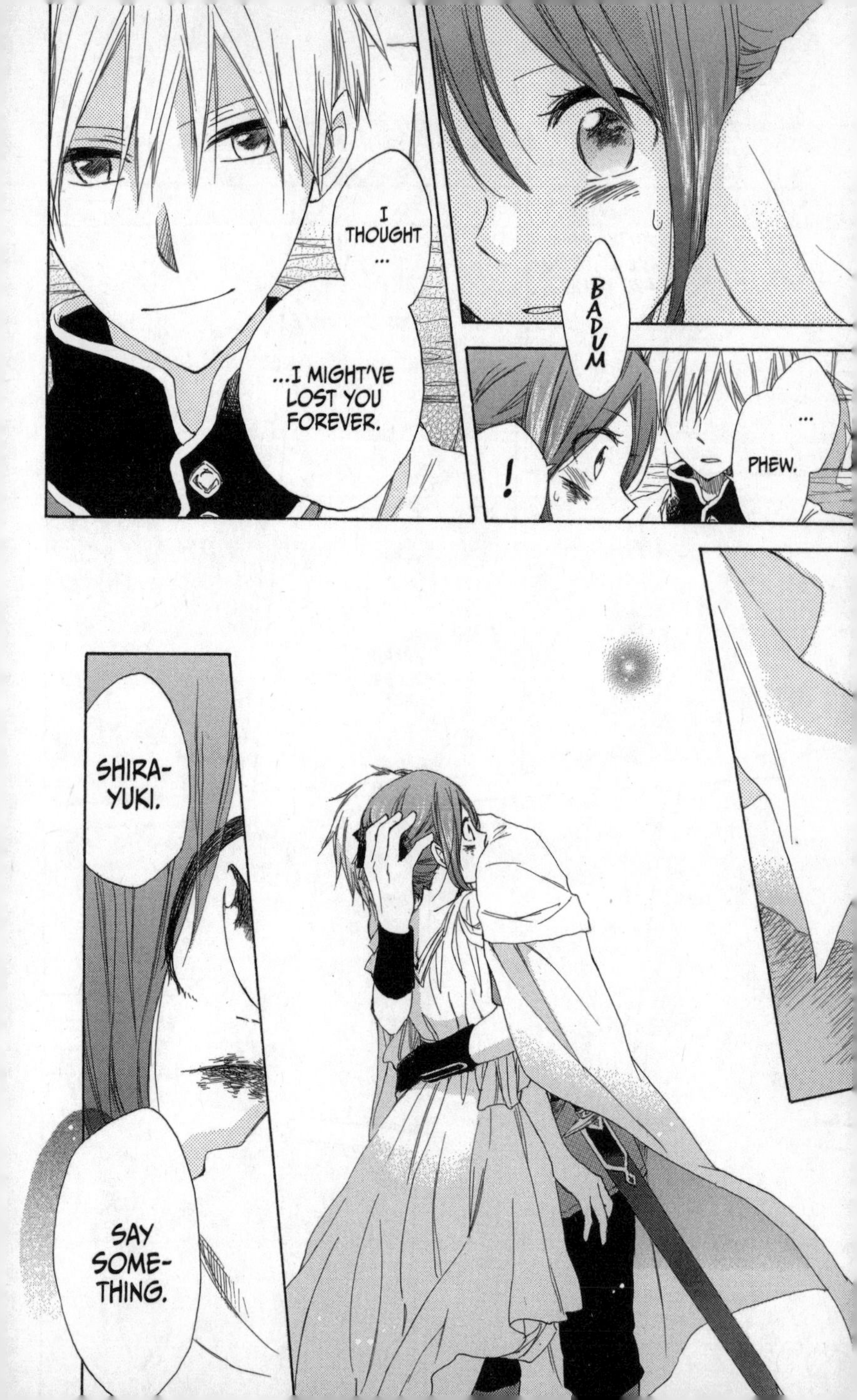
BADUM
... PHEW.
!
I THOUGHT ...
...I MIGHT'VE LOST YOU FOREVER.
SHIRA-YUKI.
SAY SOME-THING.

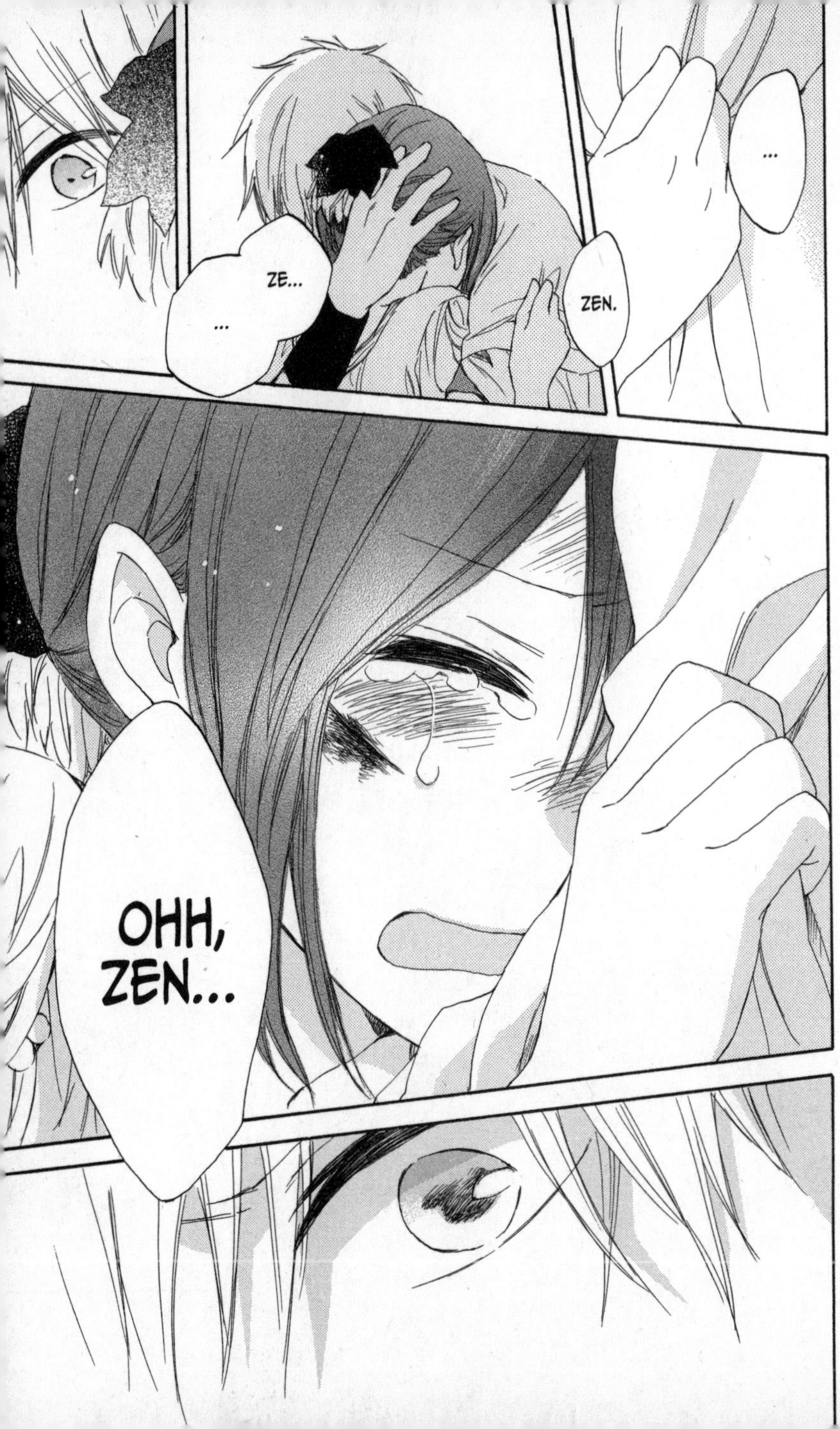
...
ZEN.
ZE...
...
OHH, ZEN...

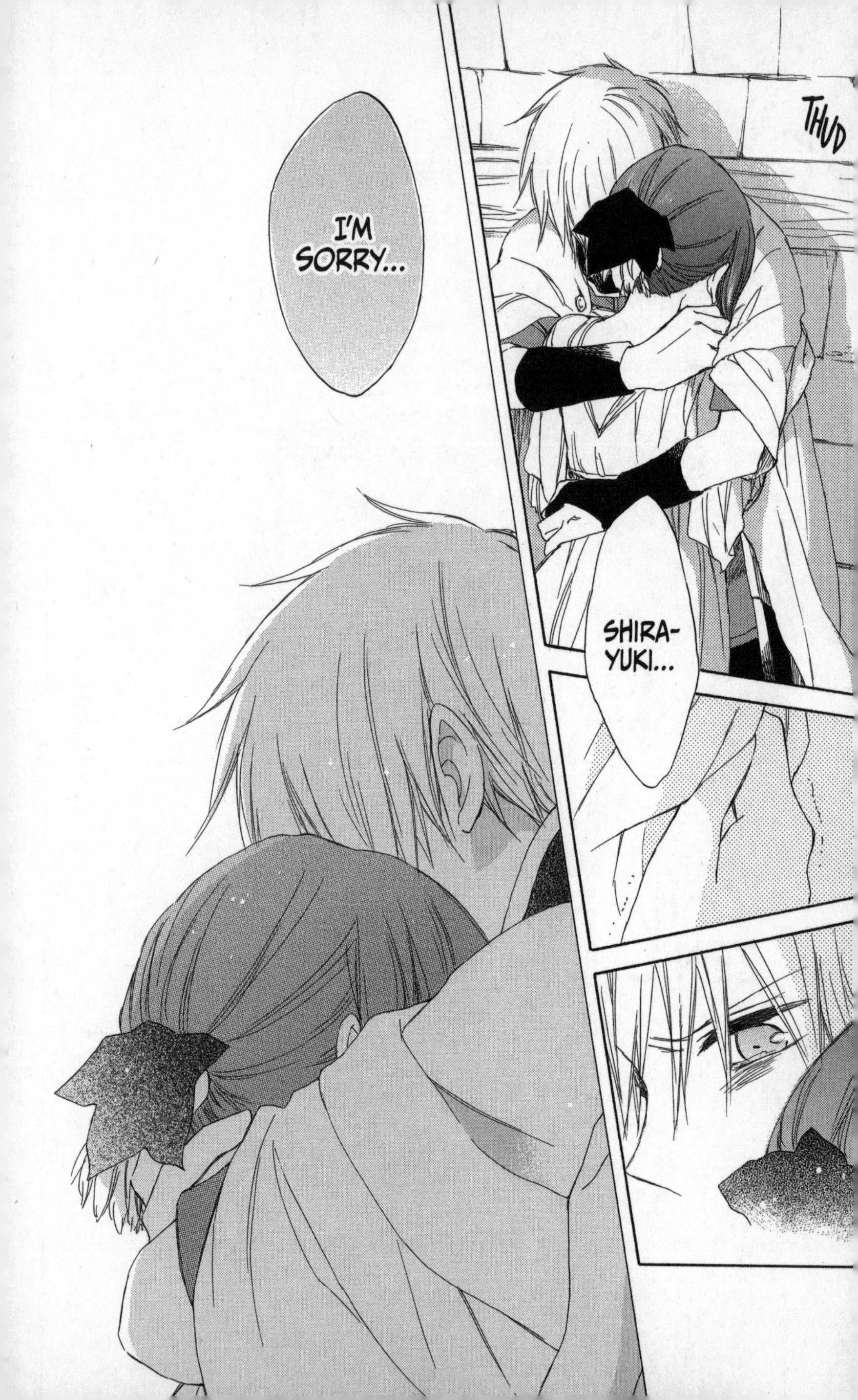
THUD
SHIRA-YUKI...
I'M SORRY...

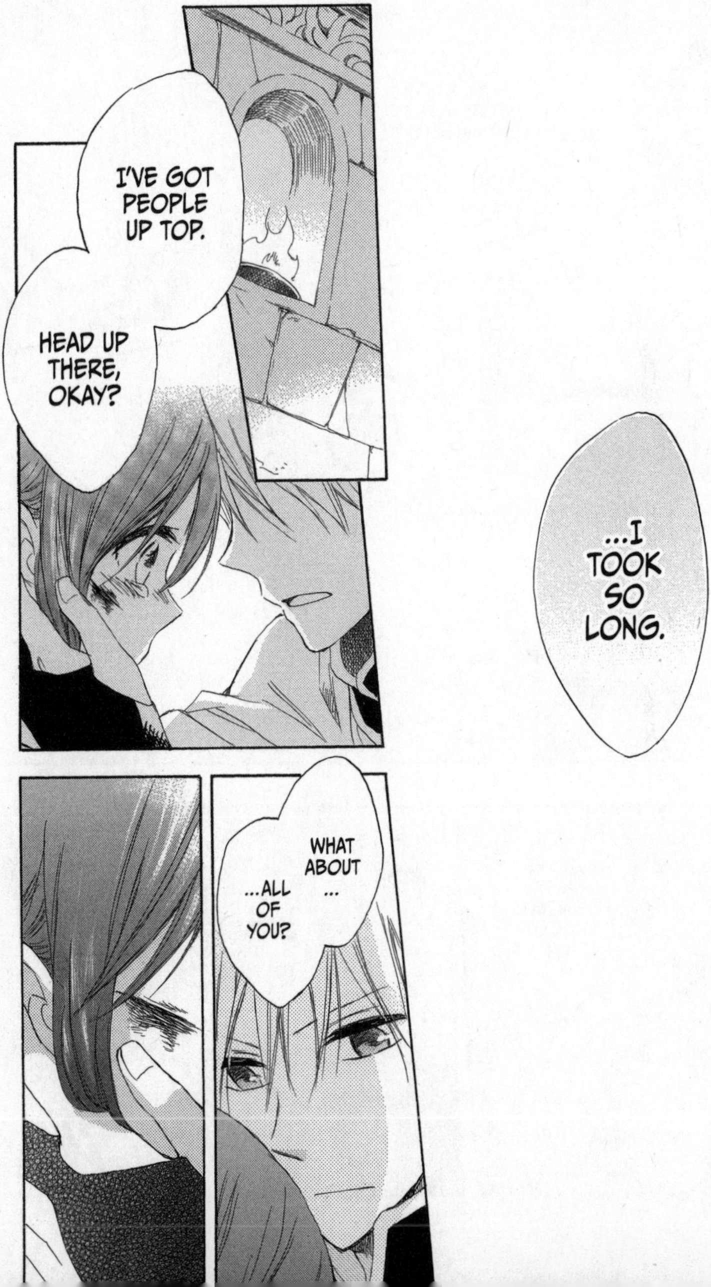
...I TOOK SO LONG.
I'VE GOT PEOPLE UP TOP.
HEAD UP THERE, OKAY?
WHAT ABOUT ...
...ALL OF YOU?

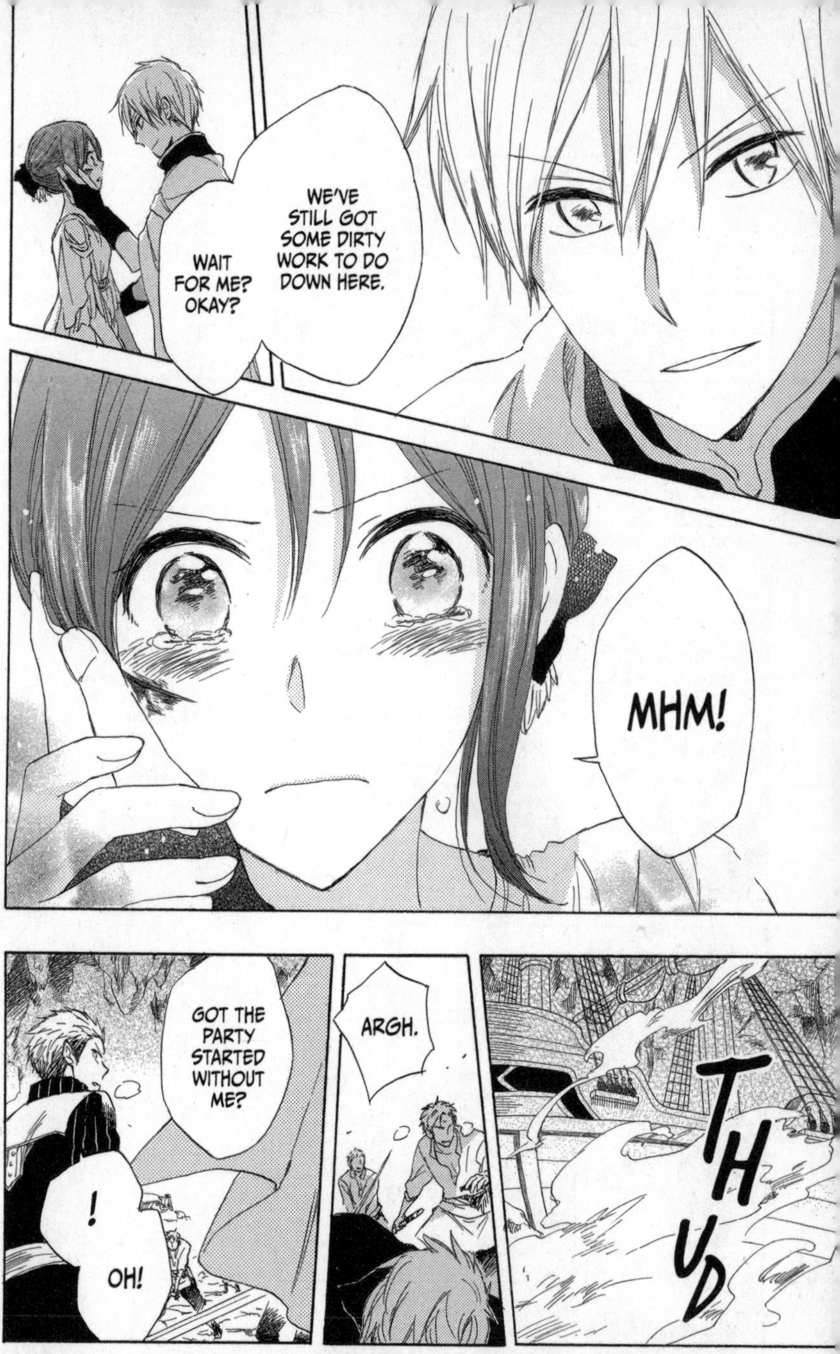
WE'VE STILL GOT SOME DIRTY WORK TO DO DOWN HERE.
WAIT FOR ME? OKAY?
MHM!
THUD
ARGH.
GOT THE PARTY STARTED WITHOUT ME?
!
OH!

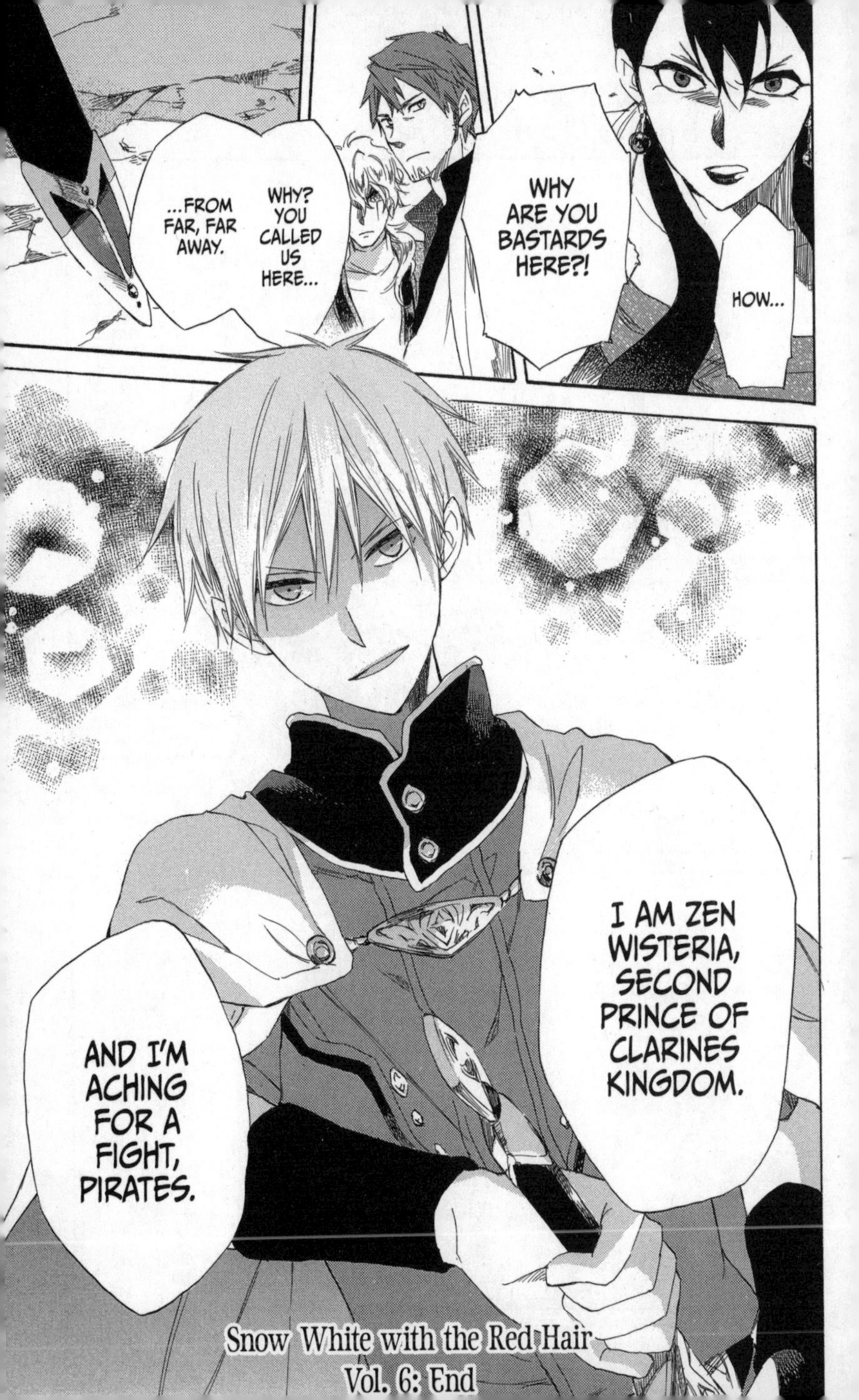
HOW...
WHY ARE YOU BASTARDS HERE?!
WHY? YOU CALLED US HERE...
...FROM FAR, FAR AWAY.
I AM ZEN WISTERIA, SECOND PRINCE OF CLARINES KINGDOM.
AND I'M ACHING FOR A FIGHT, PIRATES.

Snow White with the Red Hair
Vol. 6: End

"Couldn't Fit in the Original Chapters" Theater

Bonus Pages

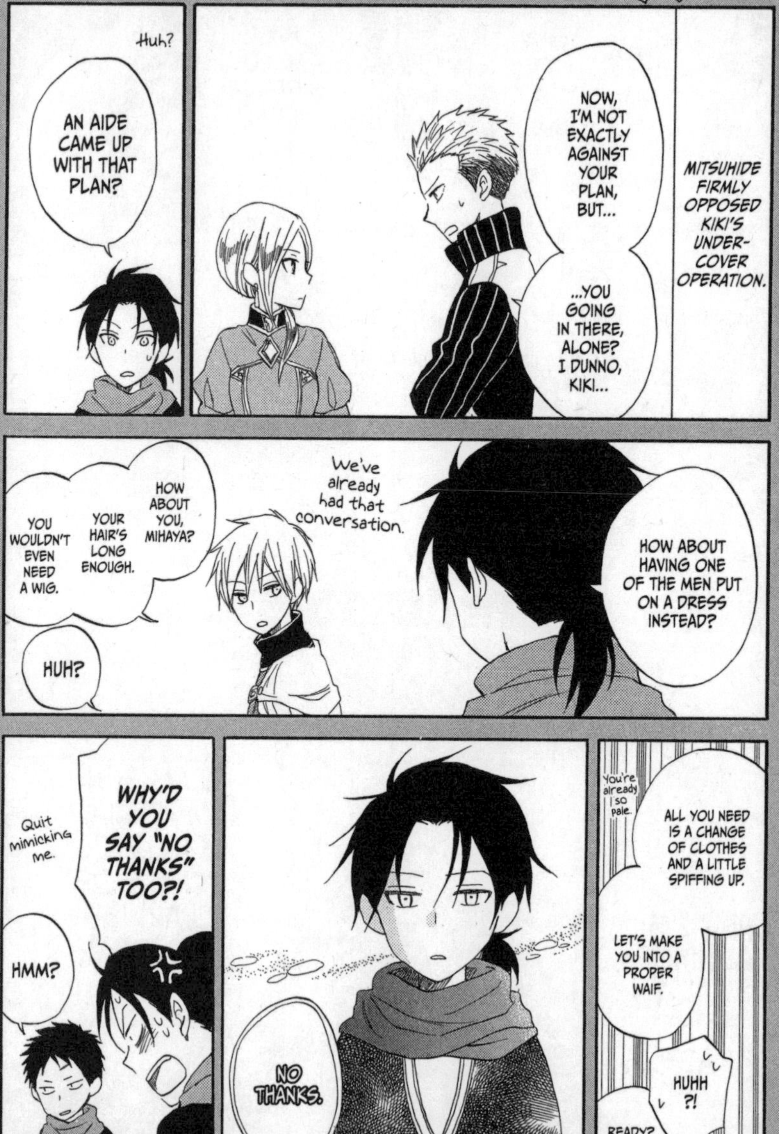
MITSUHIDE FIRMLY OPPOSED KIKI'S UNDER-COVER OPERATION.
NOW, I'M NOT EXACTLY AGAINST YOUR PLAN, BUT...
...YOU GOING IN THERE, ALONE? I DUNNO, KIKI...
Huh?
AN AIDE CAME UP WITH THAT PLAN?
HOW ABOUT HAVING ONE OF THE MEN PUT ON A DRESS INSTEAD?
We've already had that conversation.
HOW ABOUT YOU, MIHAYA? YOUR HAIR'S LONG ENOUGH. YOU WOULDN'T EVEN NEED A WIG.
HUH?
You're already so pale.
ALL YOU NEED IS A CHANGE OF CLOTHES AND A LITTLE SPIFFING UP.
LET'S MAKE YOU INTO A PROPER WAIF.
HUHH ?!
READY? LET'S DO IT!
NO THANKS.
WHY'D YOU SAY "NO THANKS" TOO?!
Quit mimicking me.
HMM?

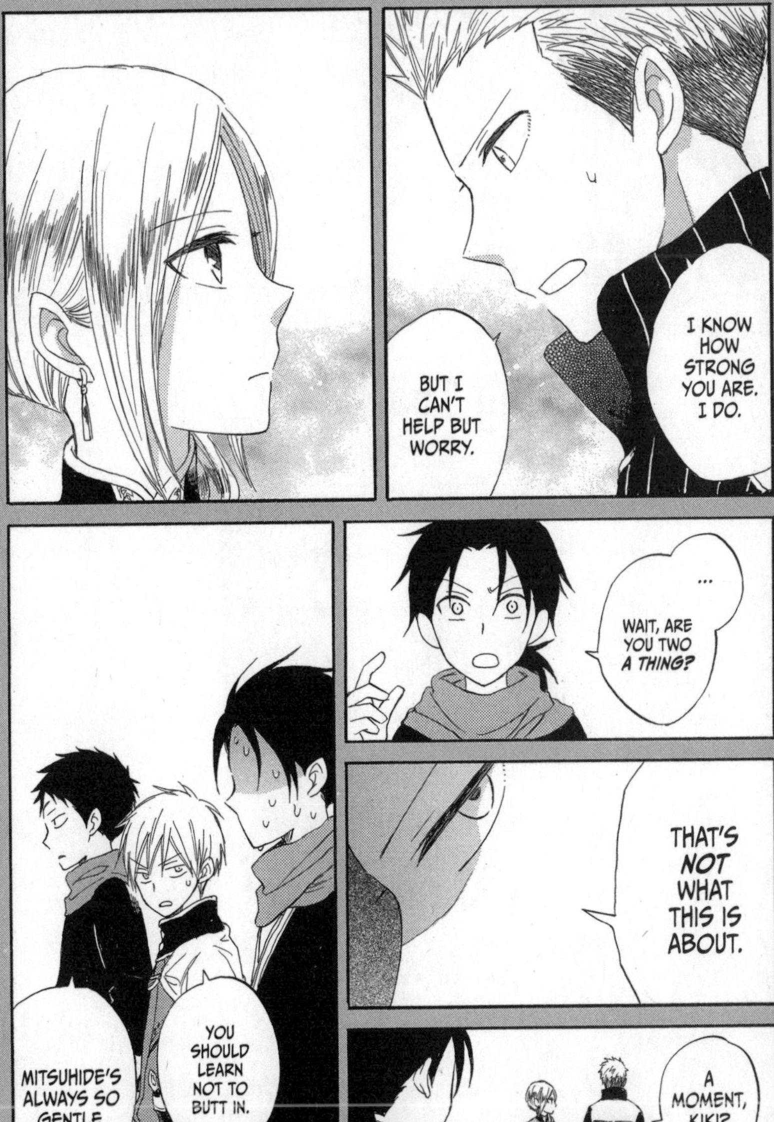
I KNOW HOW STRONG YOU ARE. I DO.
BUT I CAN'T HELP BUT WORRY.
...
WAIT, ARE YOU TWO *A THING?*
THAT'S *NOT* WHAT THIS IS ABOUT.
A MOMENT, KIKI?
YOU SHOULD LEARN NOT TO BUTT IN.
MITSUHIDE'S ALWAYS SO GENTLE.

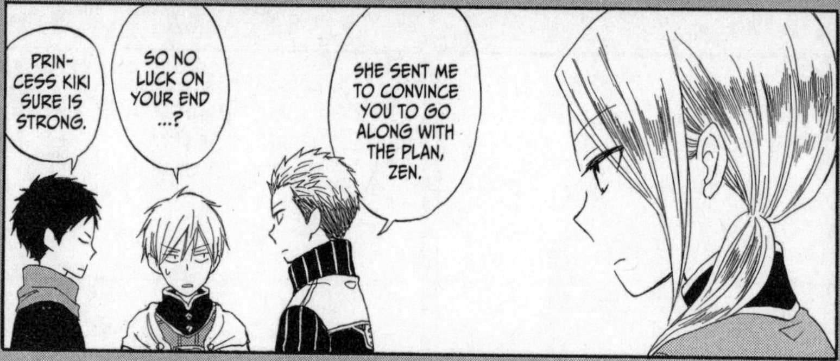
SHE SENT ME TO CONVINCE YOU TO GO ALONG WITH THE PLAN, ZEN.
SO NO LUCK ON YOUR END ...?
PRIN-CESS KIKI SURE IS STRONG.

Big Thanks To:

-My editor

-The editorial department at *LaLa*

-Yamashita-sama

-Everyone involved with publishing and sales

-My mother

-My big sister

-My father

AND YOU!

See you in the next volume!

-Sorata Akiduki
June 2011

Bonus Pages - End

Sorata Akiduki was born on March 21 and is an accomplished shojo manga author. She made her debut in January 2002 with a one-shot titled "Utopia." Her previous works include *Vahlia no Hanamuko* (Vahlia's Bridegroom), *Seishun Kouryakubon* (Youth Strategy Guide) and *Natsu Yasumi Zero Zero Nichime* (00 Days of Summer Vacation). *Snow White with the Red Hair* began serialization in August 2006 in *LaLa DX* in Japan and has since moved to *LaLa*.

Snow White
with the Red Hair

6

SHOJO BEAT EDITION

STORY AND ART BY
Sorata Akiduki

TRANSLATION **Caleb Cook**
TOUCH-UP ART & LETTERING **Brandon Bovia**
DESIGN **Alice Lewis**
EDITOR **Karla Clark**

Akagami no Shirayukihime by Sorata Akiduki
© Sorata Akiduki 2011
All rights reserved.
First published in Japan in 2011 by HAKUSENSHA, Inc., Tokyo.
English language translation rights arranged with HAKUSENSHA, Inc., Tokyo.

The stories, characters and incidents mentioned
in this publication are entirely fictional.

Printed in the U.S.A.

Published by VIZ Media, LLC
P.O. Box 77010
San Francisco, CA 94107

10 9 8 7 6 5 4 3 2 1
First printing, March 2020

VIZ MEDIA
viz.com

Shojo Beat
shojobeat.com